FORBIDDEN DESIRES

FORBIDDEN DESIRES

Deviance and Social Control

Edited by Ed Ksenych

Canadian Scholars' Press   Toronto

Forbidden Desires: Deviance and Social Control
Edited by Ed Ksenych

First published in 2003 by
Canadian Scholars' Press Inc.
180 Bloor Street West, Suite 801
Toronto, Ontario
M5S 2V6

www.cspi.org

CSPI gratefully acknowledges financial support for our publishing activities from the Government of Canada through the Book Publishing Industry Development Program (BPIDP) and the Government of Ontario through the Ontario Book Initiative.

National Library of Canada Cataloguing in Publication

　　Forbidden desires : deviance and social control / edited by Ed Ksenych.

Includes bibliographical references.
ISBN 1-55130-211-X

　　1. Deviant behavior. 2. Social control. 3. Criminal justice, Administration of. I. Ksenych, Edward, 1950-

HM811.F67 2003　　　　　　302.5'42　　　　　　C2003-904616-8

Cover art by Sandi Ksenych
Cover design by Susan Thomas/Digital Zone
Text design and layout by Brad Horning

03　04　05　06　07　08　　7　6　5　4　3　2　1

Printed and bound in Canada by AGMV Marquis Imprimeur Inc.

Canadä

COPYRIGHT ACKNOWLEDGMENTS

PART I: DEVIANCE AND SOCIETY

1. Vernon Boggs and William Kornblum, "Social Interaction in Times Square" adapted from "Symbiosis in the City," *The Sciences*, January/February 1985: 25–30. This article is reprinted with permission of *The Sciences*.
2. Linda Deutschmann, "Prescientific Approaches to Deviance" from *Deviance and Social Control*, 2nd ed., ITP Nelson Canada, 1998: 81–85, 87–88, 91–92, 98–103, 107, 115–121. Reprinted with permission of Nelson, a division of Thomson Learning: www.thomsonrights.com.
3. Robert A. Silverman, James J. Teevan, and Vincent F. Sacco, "Lay Definitions of Crime" from *Crime in Canadian Society*, 6th ed., Harcourt Brace Canada, 2000: 2–10. Reprinted with permission of Nelson, a division of Thomson Learning: www.thomsonrights.com.
4. Vincent Sacco, "Media Constructions of Deviance" from R. Silverman, J. Teevan, and V. Sacco (eds.), *Crime in Canadian Society*, 6th ed., Harcourt Brace, 2000: 11–19. Reprinted with permission of Nelson, a division of Thomson Learning: www.thomsonrights.com.
5. George Gurley, "Pleasures of the Fur" from *Vanity Fair*, March 2001: 174, 176, 181–182, 184–185, 188, 193, 196.

PART II: SOCIAL CONTROL

6. *Discipline and Punish* by Michel Foucault. (New York: Pantheon, 1977). Originally published in French as *Surveiller et Punir*. Copyright © 1975 by Editions Gallimard. Reprinted by permission of Georges Borchardt Inc., for Editions Gallimard.
7. The Commission on Systematic Racism in the Ontario Criminal Justice System, "Executive Summary" from the *Report of the Commission on Systematic Racism in the Ontario Criminal Justice System*, Queen's Printer for Ontario, 1995: i–x. Copyright © 1995 Queen's Printer for Ontario.
8. Cynthia Amsden, "The Short, Brutal Life of Terry Fitzsimmons," *Globe and Mail*, April 15, 1995.

22. Tanya Talaga, "Rethinking the Brain," *The Toronto Star*, March 24, 2000.

PART VI: YOUTH AND DEVIANCE

23. Michelle Shephard, "Teen Gangs: Fear in Our Schools," *The Toronto Star*, October 26, 1998: A1, A18, A19.
24. Julian Tanner, "Deviant Youth: The Social Construction of Youth Problems" from *Teenage Troubles: Youth and Deviance in Canada*, Nelson Canada, 1996: 1–30, 18–28, 30. Reprinted with permission of Nelson, a division of Thomson Learning: www.thomsonrights.com.
25. Stephen W. Baron, "Style and Resistance in the Punk Subculture" from L. Tepperman and J. Curtis (eds.), *Everyday Life: A Reader*, 2nd ed., McGraw-Hill Ryerson, 1995: 71–78.
26. Paul deSouza, "Youth Court Statistics, 2000/01," Canadian Centre for Justice Statistics, *Juristat,* Catalogue No. 85-002 XPE, Vol. 23, No. 3: 2–9; Dianne Hendrick, "Justice Process for Youth" from "Youth Court Statistics, 1997–98 Highlights," *Juristat*, Canadian Centre for Justice Statistics, Vol. 19, No. 2: 10–11. Statistics Canada information is used with the permission of the Minister of Industry, as Minister responsible for Statistics Canada. Information on the availability of the wide range of data from Statistics Canada can be obtained from Statistics Canada's Regional Offices, its World Wide Web site at http://www.statcan.ca, and its toll-free access number 1-800-263-1136.
27. Alan W. Leschied, D.A. Andrews, and Robert D. Hoge, "Youth at Risk: A Review of Ontario Young Offenders, Programs, and Literature That Supports Effective Intervention," Ontario Ministry of Community and Social Services, August 1992.

PART VII: STREET CRIME

28. Richard Du Wors, "The Justice Data Factfinder" from Julian Roberts (ed.), *Criminal Justice in Canada: A Reader*, Harcourt Brace Canada, 2000: 24–38. Reprinted with permission of Nelson, a division of Thomson Learning: www.thomsonrights.com; Josée Savoie, "Crime Statistics in Canada, 2001." Canada Centre for Justice Statistics, *Juristat* 22 (6):14.
29. Frederick J. Desroches, "Go Boy and Surveillance Squad" from Frederick J. Desroches (ed.), *Behind the Bars: Experiences in Crime*, Canadian Scholars' Press Inc., 1996: 203–204; 223–231. Reprinted with permission of the publisher.
30. Erin Anderson, "One on One with a Killer," *Globe and Mail*, March 25, 1999.

TABLE OF CONTENTS

PART VII: STREET CRIME

In Memory of
Jacob Ksenych, 1919–2002

This book is dedicated to my father, Jack Ksenych. It is difficult, if not impossible, to speak about all he has shared or given me over the years, so I won't try. He was a wonderful father and his influence is everywhere in the better parts of this book. And I still continue to ask, Where are you?

ACKNOWLEDGMENTS

A book such as this is not simply the result of the ideas of its author. This is a point I would like to make to highlight the collaborative, rather than individualistic, nature of academic and educational work. It is particularly true where the book is a collection of readings written by other people.

First, I'd like to thank George Brown College for providing me with the professional development time to work on this project.

Second, I want to acknowledge the contributions of John Baker and Jim Cosgrave. They have been thoughtful friends who have resisted what I have been teaching as often as they supported it in the wonderful spirit of friendship. Specifically, I want to thank them for giving their time and the benefit of their own academic training in reviewing the parts of this book I have written. I also wish to acknowledge the helpful suggestions made by my colleague Mary Gibbons regarding the issue of sentencing in the section on robbery.

Third, thanks to those who have generously agreed to be guest speakers in my course: Paddy Colfer, Kara Gillies, Adrian Goulborn, Rick Sauve, Valorie Scott, Richard Todhunter, and Lee Tustin. They have been exemplary in helping me and my students expand our understanding of deviance and social control.

Finally, I am grateful to John Ryan for giving me the tip on the "furries," as well as to production editor Rebecca Conolly and managing editor Althea Prince of Canadian Scholars' Press for their ongoing support and suggestions regarding this project.

GENERAL INTRODUCTION

> Crime is present, not only in the majority of societies of one particular species, but in all societies of all types. There is no society that is not confronted with the problem of criminality. Its form changes; the acts thus characterized are not the same everywhere; but, everywhere and always, there have been some men who have behaved in such a way as to draw upon themselves penal repression. . . . There is . . . no phenomenon that presents more indisputably all the symptoms of normality, since it appears closely connected with the conditions of all collective life. . . . To classify crime among the phenomena of normal sociology is not to say merely that it is an inevitable, although regrettable phenomenon, due to the incorrigible wickedness of men; it is to affirm that it is a factor in public health, an integral part of all healthy societies. (Durkheim, [1938] 1966:65)

Crime is normal in healthy societies. With this most unusual claim, Emile Durkheim launched a tradition of sociological inquiry into crime and deviance. It is a tradition that will require us to consider equally unusual claims about crime, and insights into deviance more generally. For example, deviance is not a property inherent in a behaviour but a socially constructed phenomenon occurring within a social context. Or the social construction of deviance within a group often involves working with very consistent but largely inaccurate depictions of the deviant that are usually accepted by the group's members even after being challenged with available evidence. Or there is a high correlation between those who are processed as deviant and criminal, and those who are also socially and economically disadvantaged and considered a threat to the more advantaged groups within a society.

But Durkheim's unusual claim also invites us to think about not only the enigma of crime and deviance but also the particular character of sociology as a form of inquiry. So in what way does this book approach the topics of deviance and social control, as well as the nature of sociological inquiry?

First of all, from a pedagogic standpoint, this book is intended to serve as a stand-alone or a supplementary reader for an introductory level, post-secondary general education course in the sociology of deviance and social control. The idea for it emerged from the task of developing a one-semester general education course on deviance for students from a wide range of college vocational programs. In developing it, I couldn't presuppose that my students had taken an introductory sociology course, or any social science course for that matter. I also couldn't assume they were aware of the social construction of reality such that they would be in the habit of questioning the validity of society's prevailing views or the events occurring within it. Finally, I couldn't assume that they had been introduced to the difference between moralistic, commonsense reactions to events, and theoretically grounded, responsibly researched inquiries into these events. At the same time, I would not offer such a course if it did not address the complex, contested human realities of crime and social control, or stand as an authentic example of sociological research and theorizing that demanded students contend with this tradition of inquiry.

The selections in this book serve as resources to respond to these challenges while offering a basic sociological inquiry into several topic areas usually taken up in introductory post-secondary courses on deviance and social control. But how does one do this? The book reflects one approach that has effectively introduced students to deviance and sociology in a manner students have repeatedly indicated is lively, interesting, and enjoyable, but rigorous and demanding at the same time.

Some articles have been chosen to present the sociological perspective as well as fundamental concepts that are presupposed in the general study of deviance. Second, this reader is attentive to the role of the media in the social construction of deviance and the legitimation of social control, and stresses the importance of being media literate. As a result, I have included not only academic articles that discuss media representations of deviance but also a sample of articles from the mass media, notably newspapers, to be assessed by students for their journalistic treatment of the topic being covered. Third, in order to provide a contrast to moralistic, commonsense reactions to wrongdoing, I have, of course, provided what I generally hope are strong examples of social scientific theorizing and research on deviance. However, I have also highlighted practices such as demonizing, the creation of moral panic, as well as the use of neutralization techniques in undertaking and responding to deviance. These practices are, of course, features of the broader social processes of deviance and social control in modern society, and they offer the opportunity for students to reflect on their own possible participation in them whether as rule-breakers, rule-makers, or rule-enforcers.

The readings vary in level of difficulty. While most are quite accessible, I have deliberately included some challenging examples of social theory and research, such as Freud's exploration of civilization and human misery, and Foucault's inquiry into the disciplinary society. Although more difficult, they make significant contributions to understanding deviance and social control, and present some of the many complexities that are involved in developing such an understanding.

In other cases, articles have been selected to illustrate key theoretic ideas or insights. For example, the almost numbing neutral report on *Youth at Risk* is included to provide a summary of the research on effective intervention for delinquent youth. But it also serves as an example of the discourse surrounding the political technology of the body, which, Foucault argues, is used in modern social control to improve the "soul." Similarly, although students may find the social scientific format of McCabe's article on neutralization techniques and cheating among college students somewhat dry and formal, it does nicely illustrate the range of practical strategies that students use to nullify the wrongdoing usually attached to cheating, and gives readers the distance to reflect on practices they may have engaged in themselves.

All in all, the introductions offer a context or rationale for the readings as well as some guiding questions or review exercises that I hope will be interesting and useful. Most are based on material I have used in discussing the articles in my college course.

Given the introductory level of this book, the overall approach taken to sociological theories of deviance and social control has been to present them in terms of the broad categories of consensus-based theories and conflict-based theories. These are categories that will be encountered in the introductory article on crime and deviance by Silverman, Teevan, and Sacco, and built upon in the commentaries on the articles. These theoretical categories are also complemented with articles that focus on very specific sociological concepts and processes that are widely acknowledged and used in the study of deviance.

For the purposes of the reader, consensus-based theories are generally those that originate out of Emile Durkheim's exploration of the normality of crime, the socially constructed nature of the pathological, and the problem of anomie (or normlessness), which arises from the social structures and social conditions that exist within a society. The category is intended to include

Merton's social strain theory, Hirshi's theory of social attachment, and other versions of structural-functionalist inquiry.

By contrast, conflict-based theories generally originate out of Karl Marx's examination of class differences and conflict, and their basis in the social organization of productive activity and ideology, as well as out of Max Weber's formulation of systems of domination and subordination within economic, socio-cultural, and political institutions. However, the category is used broadly and is intended to include the new criminology, feminist theory, Foucault's examination of the disciplinary society, as well as work arising out of Mills's conflict perspective.

There is a third set of theoretic inquiries that are sometimes described as symbolic interactionist or phenomenological. While wanting to respect the uniqueness of such theories, many of the examples offered in this book have used, or been used by, both conflict-based and consensus-based approaches. As a result, I have generally presented such work as formulating significant sociological concepts and processes. Those highlighted in this reader include subculture theory, labelling theory, and neutralization techniques.

To the teacher of a deviance course, this kind of organizing structure will probably be more or less understandable, if not agreeable. And I am aware that structuring the rich and diverse approaches to sociological theorizing in this manner oversimplifies the distinctiveness and integrity of the theoretic contributions of those mentioned. But to the student first encountering sociological inquiry, even this approach to sociological thought may be both abstract and overwhelming. Nevertheless, I have employed it mostly because I have found it to be the most effective way of orienting students to sociological inquiry in an introductory deviance course, and one that several students have commented favourably upon.

Finally, there are some basic ideas or principles that have guided me not only in the selection of the readings but also in my approach to teaching a course on deviance and social control, which may be helpful to share. First, on one level the topic is about "nuts, sluts and perverts," as Liazos coined it. However, on another level, it is about understanding the human condition and how individuals act in ways that are regarded as offensive within a group, often in conditions not of their own choosing. While both levels are important, understanding the human condition is the deeper issue. And a feature of this is that this book resists reifying the deviant or criminal as someone strange, unfamiliar, and "out there" separate from "us," all of which is a part of the conventional social construction of deviance.

Second, the book is built around the sociological notion of *deviance as a social process*, a process in which many participate and which seems to unfold according to a logic of its own. This presents a challenge to the everyday, commonsense notion of deviance where deviance is concretized into a self-evident, self-standing behaviour obviously perpetrated by a deviant. By contrast, the process involves a disturbing act that is defined as a violation of a norm or value that then becomes the basis of a societal reaction to the act so defined. As such, the book is in agreement with Durkheim's initial insight that deviance is not a property inherent to a behaviour in itself. At the same time, it repeatedly stresses the competing and often conflicting social, cultural, economic, and political groups and forces involved in the actual negotiation of this process. Moreover, this is viewed not as creating an annoying uncertainty that needs to be overcome for the sake of a clean version of what's going on, but as a part of the vitality of the puzzle of deviance and social control that social inquiry needs to recognize and sustain.

Last, I always find it helpful to remember that sociological inquiry is inherently a form of deviance. As Peter Berger pointed out many years ago, the sociological perspective debunks or challenges both commonsense and official definitions of reality, and transforms the meaning and significance of the world in which we have lived all our lives. This is not simply an enthusiastic academic sentiment intended to market a discipline. If practised properly, social inquiry really does. This is a point other sociologists such as Collins and Makowsky also make in *The Discovery of Society* when they tell us that "the facts which sociology provides are not what most people would wish them to be, and social science cannot be called in to tell them what they want to hear." But then this is all part of the particular pleasure, excitement, and danger of sociological inquiry, and of inquiry generally. It is a pleasure and an excitement that is, in some societies or sectors of a society, forbidden.

Ed Ksenych
Toronto, Canada
June 2003

INTRODUCTIONS
TO ARTICLES

1. BOGGS AND KORNBLUM

Society is invisible to us. And despite our familiarity with our society, most of us often hold illusory views about the social world in which we live. For example, Canadians generally believe that the crime rate is increasing when it's generally declining in Canada and most industrialized societies;[1] that most poor people are lazy and unemployed when the majority of poor are working poor;[2] that many Canadians are well off when they are actually on the brink of being eligible for welfare;[3] or that Canada is more ethnically diverse than the United States when indicators of assimilation of immigrants show the United States to be just as diverse as Canada.[4] Such shared perceptions and attitudes, illusory or not, are part of culture—the prevailing way of life and meaning system of a group. Culture also involves the ritual activities, customary practices, and artifacts, as well as the values, beliefs, norms, and ideas generally shared within a group or collective.

Similarly, most of us have only a vague sense of the patterns of social interactions and social relationships—that is, the social structure—within which we live out our everyday lives. Social structure also includes a group's social divisions, its social positions with their accompanying role expectations and status rights, ranking systems, and sometimes complex social institutional systems like family and education.

In this chapter, Boggs and Kornblum explore one society in terms of its social structure and cultural practices. They also bring into view sociology's key subject matter: the orderly nature of human interaction inherent in the many and often transitory encounters we have with others every day.

What are some examples of the culture and social structure of the "society" that the authors find amid the hustle and bustle of Times Square?

2. DEUTSCHMANN

In this excerpt from a larger text, Deutschmann introduces us to "prescientific approaches to deviance." Among them is the practice of demonizing those whose behaviour varies from conventional norms and values. While the author uses the example of the medieval witch craze to illustrate demonizing, this prescientific practice should not simply be relegated to an earlier era that we have progressed beyond, a point she hints at in her concluding remarks. Demonizing is a prevalent practice in how we, or those in authority, "construct" or "create" deviance in our contemporary society as well.

Based on the article and the examples used within it, what are the differences between "non-scientific" and "scientific" approaches to deviance? What might be some current examples of how we may employ demonizing in constructing "deviants" or deviance?

3. SILVERMAN, TEEVAN, AND SACCO

For most of us, the reality of deviance is represented in crime, although it is only one aspect of the broader category of deviance. Yet what precisely is crime? In this article, the authors examine everyday sociological and legal definitions of crime. They also provide an introduction to the basic terminology used in studying deviance, and highlight the human dimension involved in defining and processing crime within the judicial system.

4. SACCO

In this reading, Sacco examines how crime is constructed in the media, and the impact of exposure regarding distorted images of crime and the criminal on the public's perception of both. He tells us the public's prevailing attitude is that sensationalist media coverage inflates the public's perception and fear of crime. However, Sacco's review of the research suggests the impact is more complex and ambiguous than this simple cause-and-effect relationship.

There is a significant disparity between the public's view of the nature and incidence of crime and what is documented through official police statistics. But Saccos's research finds media representations are not as major a factor in creating this disparity as we conventionally believe. If so, then how can we account for it?

5. GURLEY

As Gurley's byline to his magazine article states: "Welcome to the world of 'furries': the thousands of Americans who've gotten in touch with their inner raccoon, or wolf, or fox. Judging from the Midwest FurFest, this is no hobby. It's sex; it's religion; it's a whole new way of life."

So, what are "furries"? And are they an example of deviance? If so, why? If not, of what are they an example?

6. FOUCAULT

Foucault offers us an analysis of the modern penal system, which is part of his overall argument that despite humanitarian ideals and the affirmation of rights and freedoms, modern society is fundamentally a "disciplinary society." In this excerpt from *Discipline and Punish*, he highlights, using the example of France, how the shift from punishment to discipline is reflected in the modern penal system.

Foucault identifies four key changes:

1. The focus of the penal system shifts from punishing the body to disciplining the "soul."
2. Punishment becomes the most hidden part of the penal process and is replaced by a detailed publicizing of the process of sentencing.
3. The public is invited to judge, not the crime, but the soul of the criminal.
4. Prison is not only a building with cells, bars, and barbed wire, but is an abstract "political technology" of the body supervised and used by technologists of the soul (e.g., educators, psychiatrists, psychologists, counsellors, etc.) to improve it.

Implicit in his analysis is the question of how the "soul" is conceived of in our modern, secularized society such that it has become the subject of such attention and efforts at improvement.

7. COMMISSION ON SYSTEMIC RACISM IN THE ONTARIO CRIMINAL JUSTICE SYSTEM

Strictly speaking, racism asserts that the conduct and characteristics of individuals are, to a significant degree, bound up biologically with the physiologically identifiable group to which they belong. The validity of the concept itself is highly debatable despite its widespread use. Many of the studies that have attempted to establish "psychological" differences based on racial differences have been challenged on a wide range of theoretical and methodological grounds. And research on race and crime that work with conventional racial categories such as Negroid, Caucasian, and Oriental have found greater variability within the racial categories than between them.[5]

Nevertheless, race continues to be a culturally important category in modern society. The following reading provides an overview of racism within the Ontario criminal justice system. It concludes by exhorting us to eliminate the systemic racism that research has found does exist in the justice system. If you agree that this is a worthy goal, then how can it actually be achieved? If you don't, then what are the reasons for your position?

8. AMSDEN

Most of us take for granted prisons and correctional institutions based on a punitive/rehabilitative model as a necessary, though possibly regrettable, part of modern society. The main problem, given public opinion polls, is finding ways of making them more punitive and/or rehabilitative.

Amsden's article raises serious questions about the basic views and assumptions with which we deal with wrongdoers: our current system manages them, but, overall, doesn't seem to really work.

What may be surprising for those who are willing to examine approaches to responding to wrongdoing is that there are alternatives to a prison-focused system, and some appear to be more effective in correcting wrongdoing and providing compensation to the sufferers of the wrongdoing than the current models.[6] One example is the restorative justice system developed from the "healing circles" of Canada's Aboriginal peoples. It is based on a communal restoration of the relationship between the perpetrator(s) of the harm and the individual(s) harmed. However, they don't enable us to experience the satisfaction of retribution. But does meting out revenge and suffering to transgressors actually benefit the well-being of our society as a whole or really meet our own moral needs?

9. BRYM

This reader organizes the diverse theoretical approaches to deviance and control in terms of consensus-based theories, conflict-based theories, and social interactionist or phenomenological contributions. But even this approach to simplifying the wide range of theories presupposes a basic understanding of the work of Durkheim, Marx, and Weber as well as the phenomenological and feminist challenges to their ideas. Brym's article provides some of the theoretical background that sociological theories of deviance and social control build upon.

10. AGNEW

Agnew's study of school crime in the United States is an example of the application of one type of consensus-based theory of deviance—namely social strain theory—to understanding juvenile crime. Consensus-based theories are based on the idea that societies have a "collective conscience" made up of widely held and commonly agreed upon societal norms, values, and ideas. Crimes represent disobeying the rules, disrespecting the values, or challenging the ideas. In doing so, crimes weaken and attack the very basis of a society by offending the collective conscience of the group.

Contemporary strain theory is based on earlier work on deviance and anomie by Robert Merton, which is discussed and illustrated in Chapter 16. Both are very effective in accounting for certain forms of deviance involving the inability of social norms to regulate human conduct in situations where individuals experience a strain between what they desire and how they are expected to fulfill those desires given the opportunities actually available to them.

11. QUINNEY

Quinney's article represents a conflict-based theory of crime. Conflict-based theories envision society as a dynamic order of interest groups competing over wealth, power, privilege, prestige, and other social rewards. But the groups have differing amounts and kinds of power, unequal access to various resources, and different ideas about how society should be organized. So society is, in many respects, a conflicted negotiation among interest groups trying to advance their ideas and improve their position using the power and resources available to them.

From this viewpoint, conflict and lack of agreement are always present in society, at times as overt conflict, but most of the time as placid, stable, institutionalized relationships of domination and subordination. One of the key institutions is law, and it becomes a means of serving dominant groups and oppressing subordinate groups while appearing to serve the interests of society as a whole. Crime is, for the most part, an expression of subordinate groups attempting to deal with their social and economic conditions or dominant groups abusing their privileged position, all from the standpoint of laws that primarily serve the interests of the dominant groups.

Quinney's article represents one example of analyzing crime using the conflict perspective. From the standpoint of sociological theory, Quinney presents a somewhat simplified version of conflict-based theory, and students interested in this approach are encouraged to pursue more complex formulations of it such as Jeffrey Reiman's *The Rich Get Richer, and the Poor Get Prison: Ideology, Class and Criminal Justice.*[7]

12. MCCABE

Is cheating on tests and assignments wrong? Most students agree. Yet many studies, including this one, find that cheating among college students is pervasive. So how is it we often violate rules and expectations, and engage in behaviours that we know are wrong?[8] One strategy is neutralization techniques.

Unlike rationalization, in which individuals justify their conduct *after* they've done it, neutralization techniques represent efforts to justify their conduct *before* performing it. By doing so they render inoperative some of the social control mechanisms that would otherwise kick in prior to engaging in a deviant act. In this study McCabe explores how college students routinely use neutralization techniques as part of cheating.

13. HALL AND LINDZEY

The focus of sociological studies is on deviance as a social phenomenon. But what moves or allows people to act in ways that are regarded as deviant? For Durkheim, Marx, Weber, and other sociologists, the critical factor is the individual's relation to social conditions and forces largely beyond their personal control. In addition, more contemporary inquiry has also examined the part played by micro-sociological processes or practices such as neutralization techniques and labelling. But for most of us, the question also involves a far more individual dimension. It is one that often arises when we encounter a particularly horrifying act and ask "How could this person do that?"

Now sociologists will be quick to point out that if the question is intended as a general question about people who break the law, then we need to recognize that on any given day 95–98 per cent of us violate the law, and if the usual sentence was given for our violations, then a third of us would be spending some time in jail or prison.[9] But while it's very important to keep such sociological realities in mind when understanding deviance, this kind of response isn't really answering the intent of the question being asked. At the risk of promoting celebrated examples of crime, how do we understand why Bernardo and Homolka did what they did? How can we make sense of serial killer McGray's violent crimes (see Chapter 30)? While such questions do have a sociological dimension, they also draw us into the field of psychology with its study of the human animal and the problem of human nature.

An overview of psychology is beyond the scope of this reader, but it is helpful to have an exposure to some psychological inquiry into the problem of human nature. While Freud's psychoanalytic theory is continuously debated regarding its validity and clinical usefulness, it does provide us with a stimulating investigation into and depiction of human nature, which centres on humans as inherently conflicted beings.

Freud theorizes that part of this conflict concerns the very nature of the human personality. In ordinary language, personality usually refers to the distinctive qualities or characteristics that consistently appear in one's behaviours and interactions with others. It's a way of describing who someone is in individual terms. But what is a personality? For Freud, it's a dynamic union of conflicting instinctual forces themselves in tension with cultural expectations, all of which are managed by our conscious, rational egos. It is in this sense that Freud proposes that humans are inherently conflicted selves.

In this article, Hall and Lindzey provide an overview of Freud's theory of personality. However, this article is also intended to offer some background for another, perhaps even more provocative aspect of humans as conflicted beings—the individual in her or his relation to other individuals, and how all of these relationships are regulated by the requirements of civilization. This second, more sociological aspect of Freud's theory is taken up in the subsequent article.

14. FREUD

The following reading is abridged from Freud's *Civilization and Its Discontents*. It was his last public work, written as the Nazi movement was emerging in Europe in the 1930s. Building on his psychoanalytic theories of personality and psychosexual development, Freud turned his attention to the broader topic of the nature and development of the human species within the context of human history. This is a context that initially may be difficult to grasp for members of a society that increasingly promotes an individualized, ahistorical consciousness focused on personal actions and achievements. In addition, Freud's formal academic writing style is dated and hard to follow at times. But despite this, the ideas in his theory may have a certain element of familiarity about them. For example, much of the symbolism of the *Star Wars* series, especially *Return of the Jedi*, reflects Freud's psychoanalytic theories and the argument he makes here regarding civilization and human unhappiness.

15. GOMME

Contrary to popular conceptions, the act of prostitution is legal in Canada. However, solicitation and other activities related to the practice of prostitution have been made illegal, creating a paradoxical situation that effectively criminalizes prostitution.

Currently, prostitution rights groups and other sectors of our society have been challenging our legal approach, social practices, and cultural attitudes toward prostitution. "It's just another job," writes Deborah Brock in her study of prostitution in Canada.[10] Or is it? Should prostitution continue to be criminalized? Should it be legalized, and hence controlled and managed by government agencies? Or should it be decriminalized and simply become subject to appropriate regulations like any other business in the open marketplace?

Another issue that emerges from the article concerns "choice," and has been stated effectively by John Lowman: "While Canadian prostitutes insist they 'choose' to prostitute and that they were not forced by anyone to become prostitutes, this choice needs to be contextualized. Certainly people choose to become prostitutes . . . but not in conditions of their own choosing."[11] Lowman's point regarding choice may be relevant to many other forms of deviance as well.

16. SCHMIDT

This newspaper article on college students engaged in prostitution offers an example of the relevance of one type of consensus-based theory usually referred to as Merton's social strain theory (See Chapter 10). Merton's theory focuses on the general social situation or social structure in which deviant activity is more likely to arise. He posits that much deviant activity is the outcome of an institutionalized gap or strain that exists when individuals internalize and pursue culturally legitimate goals, but find that they don't have adequate access to the legitimate means of achieving these goals. So they create or find other ways of achieving these goals that may be disapproved of within the wider community.

Social strain theory also works with Durkheim's concept of anomie, or normlessness. In the general social situation depicted by Merton, even though the individuals recognize the norms regarding what are considered legitimate means for achieving cultural goals they desire, these norms do not have the regulatory power to constrain the individual's conduct.

So, in this particular case, what are the legitimate cultural goals desired by the students? What is problematic about the legitimate means of achieving these goals? And how do the students discussed in the article contend with this general situation?

17. STEWART

Melissa's situation was first documented in the National Film Board's film *When Women Kill*. It was a situation of domestic abuse and, for most of us, would have been a terrifying interpersonal situation. Here she describes the experience and how Canada's judicial system responded to it. The article is taken from *The Journal of Prisoners on Prison*, a journal with contributions from inmates in Canadian and American prisons. Since the article was written, the judicial system has modified Kingston's P4W (Prison for Women), and distributed the inmates to regional penal institutions.

18. STACKHOUSE

The issue of spousal abuse is not relegated to Canada. It is prevalent within societies, whether modern or traditional, and bound up with the social institution of patriarchy. For the purposes of this book, patriarchy is a system of domination in which power and authority is vested in males. As Max Weber first noted regarding social organization generally,[12] the nature of authority involves power and legitimacy. In this case, it means males are granted "legitimate power" and the power to "legitimize." This, in turn, establishes the parameters for the particular kind of relationship between the genders and between parents and offspring.

On the one hand, it results in a social relationship of domination and subordination and, with it, differential power. At the same time, particularly within traditional societies, it also means males have the "duty," even more than the "right," of ruling the home, wife, and children, and to do otherwise would be to behave "dishonourably" or shamefully.[13]

In this article we hear about the disturbing extent of the abuse of women in families throughout the world. If you are reluctant to accept the arguments of feminist theory with its emphasis on patriarchy to account for this, then how can we explain it? And given the explanation, what can be done to ameliorate the conditions experienced by so many women?

19. SAMUELSON

This article is abridged from a much larger work by Samuelson.[14] It reflects a critical criminological analysis of the class-based nature of law, particularly of how working-class and professional-class individuals and corporations are processed differently within the criminal justice system for criminal acts.

Many media investigations and academic studies have shown that the economic and physical costs of corporate crime far exceed that of street crime. For example, as far back as 1985 a *Macleans* article estimated that white-collar crime cost Canadians $4.4 billion, including $400 million from doctors defrauding the health care system.[15] The same year, bank robberies cost Canadians about $2.8 million.

There have been several incidents in recent years, often referred to as "scandals" by the media, involving a wide range of companies that continue to indicate the large financial, as well as health and safety, costs of corporate wrongdoing contrasted with the relatively modest responses to such wrongdoing. Some notable cases being processed around the time of this book's publication include: the trading scandal at Transamerica Life Insurance Co. of Canada; the admission by tobacco companies that their product is dangerous; the scandal at the Royal Bank's pension management arm, RT Capital Management Inc., and with it the emerging evidence that stock rigging seems widespread at the Toronto Stock Exchange.[16]

We are publicly aware, yet our responses seem to be ineffective. Why? How might consensus-based and/or conflict-based theories be used to account for this?

20. HEITZEG

Mental illness is an example of ascribed rather than achieved deviance. That is, it concerns behaviours or characteristics that are defined as deviant even though the individuals are not responsible for their condition through choice.

Heitzeg's focus in this article is on DICA, or disorders usually first diagnosed in infancy, childhood, and adolescence. However, it is also about the social institution of psychiatry and social control generally. This is often the case with sociological studies of mental illness.

The point of including such an article is not to dismiss the realities of psychological distress, anguish, destructive behaviours, or frightening experiences that afflict many. Nor is it intended to trivialize the work undertaken by those who have tried to help those with such afflictions. But it does indicate that some aspects of mainstream psychiatry have been the subject of criticism and debate, and may be as sociologically puzzling in their own way as the disorders being treated.

The approach currently dominating the psychiatric profession is based on the "medical model." This refers to the professional ideology that the entire range of mental disorders have a physiological basis, either biochemical or genetic, and hence are "mental illnesses." Since mental illnesses are physiologically based, treatment of the illness usually consists of chemicals, surgical operations, electrical therapies, and behavioural modification techniques, many of which are highly interventionist.

While there is compelling evidence that there is a physiological dimension to many psychiatrically defined disorders, one major concern has been that if mental illnesses are physiologically based, then why does there seem to be such ambiguity and arbitrariness in the diagnosis and treatment of so many of them? And what would constitute a sociologically sensitive response to this issue?[17]

21. ROSENHAN

Rosenhan's classic study of schizophrenia and psychiatric hospitals challenges the commonsense belief that we can easily distinguish the normal from the abnormal, the sane from the insane. Or that if "we" can't, the "professionals" can. As he tells us, "the evidence is simply not compelling."

The article is also an excellent example of the use of labelling in the process of defining and controlling deviance. Labelling was first formulated by Becker in his study *Outsiders*.[18] Although the concept has not been without its critics,[19] it has become widespread and used in various ways. Strictly speaking it has a very specific meaning within sociology. Labelling is when a term not only describes but also explains a behaviour by locating the cause of that behaviour in some aspect of the individual's physiology or character alluded to by the term itself. In other words, the term carries within itself an explanation of the behaviour as part of the description.

For example, "criminal" is not just a description of an individual who has been found guilty of violating a public law. As a label, it is also an implicit explanation of why the individual violated the law. There's something in the individual's physiological, moral, or character makeup, such as "the criminal mind," that causes them to violate law, and this becomes a feature of how we interpret their behaviour and treat them. So how does "schizophrenic" operate as a label?

22. TALAGA

Sociologists are usually critical of reducing deviance to physiological or biological explanations at the expense of considering social, cultural, economic, and political factors. But it would also be shortsighted to ignore that humans are biological organisms and not consider the role that biological factors play in human behaviour. In the following article, Talaga reports on some rather dramatic research that indicates a physiological basis to at least some instances of severe sociopathic behaviour.

Other research indicating a physiological basis to sociopathic behaviour has been the evidence that some misbehaviour and violent conduct is linked to "fetal alcohol syndrome"; that is, brain damage in a child that results from a mother drinking alcohol during pregnancy. A child can be charming, gentle, and lovable, but simultaneously prone to rages and sudden intense violence. First diagnosed in 1973, there has been significant research into FAS. And it has been claimed that about half of young offenders in Canada have FAS.[20]

If these kinds of claims and findings are valid, then what are the implications for the assessment and control of sociopaths, such as serial killer Michael Wayne McGray (see Chapter 30), who, based on the information given in the chapter, could quite possibly be afflicted with the problem reported on by Talaga?

23. SHEPHARD

In the fall of 1998, *The Toronto Star* ran a series of articles on juvenile gangs in Toronto. This was the first article in that series.

Postscript to Shephard's article
About two weeks after the newspaper series, both the mayor of Toronto and the city's police chief played down recent media reports that 10 per cent of Toronto youth were gang members, citing 1 per cent instead. The police chief told reporters: "Listen, there's no way there are 10% of the kids that are fully

into gangs in this city. . . . I'm telling you there's not 40,000 kids in this city that are members of gangs. That's a ludicrous statement. . . . Police intelligence has identified about 20 hard core gangs across the city. . . . These gangs are not necessarily all in the schools, but some may be. . . . While a Grade 9 student may view 5 or 6 people wearing similar jackets as a gang, to us, an organized gang is a large group, I'm talking about 50 to 75 people, who are organized with guns and are bent on a bit of violence."[21] But the article did end on an interesting note. Despite the retraction, it was stated that "all at the meeting agreed the Young Offenders Act needs to be toughened."

What's happening here? Shephard's article, and the series on juvenile gangs as a whole, is an example of what Cohen first identified and John Fekete has elaborated upon as creating "moral panic."[22] Moral panic refers to the magnification of problems for political effect and arousing moral sentiment, and it often involves the misuse of statistics. Over time any statement, no matter how farfetched, becomes believable by being repeated often enough and presented using rhetorical techniques that often involve informal reasoning fallacies.

Research, even by sources actually cited in the article, tend to support the view that the article has seriously exaggerated the problem, which the newspaper claims to have presented as an act of the media's responsibility to the public.

Part of the issue has been formulated by Czerny and Swift.[23] They point out that much of the media is structured like any other commercial industry in a liberal capitalist society. It orients to news as the production of a commodity for the mass market. As a result there is pressure to turn news events into items that are:

1. intense (i.e., there is a selective focus on action and the dramatic)
2. unambiguous (i.e., news is presented in terms of clear and simple moral constructs, and complex issues and events are subjected to simplification)
3. familiar (i.e., news is presented to fit in with common notions and prevailing prejudices)
4. marketable (i.e., the content is oriented to consumer taste often at the expense of other criteria such as the actual significance of an event or issue within the community)

If we review Shephard's article, in what way do these characteristics appear or not appear in its selection and treatment of the content?

24. TANNER

This excerpt from a larger work on deviant youth examines three key topics: the concern that contemporary youth are misbehaving more than before; that youth and adolescence are fairly recent cultural constructions in industrialized societies; and the nature of youth culture. Behind all of these topics is the recognition that within modern society, youth has been generally constructed as a minor form of deviance to be subjected to a wide range of institutionalized social controls. That is, there is no other sector of society subjected to so much surveillance, intervention, and rule-based control.

The experience of "childhood" and "adolescence" are quite different in other historical ages and other contemporary societies. For example, in classical Greece "youth" described a healthy, productive person rather than a category of people no longer children, but not yet adult. Recently in Colombia, the children of that country were nominated for a Nobel Prize for actually organizing and voting in an election to end the civil war.[24] In many parts of the world, children are regularly employed in factories, similar to what occurred in Europe during the industrialization process.[25] There are millions of children involved in the sex trade industry,[26] and hundreds of thousands of boys are pressed into fighting wars.[27]

Comparative research indicates our conceptions of children appear to be more a socio-cultural construction than a natural developmental stage. What are the implications of this for growing up in our society?

25. BARON

Youth cultures began emerging shortly after the social structural and cultural changes mentioned in Tanner's article were put in place in the early twentieth century—child labour laws; the Juvenile Delinquency Act; the institution of free compulsory, universal schooling; and the acceptance of Stanley Hall's biological doctrine of adolescence, which proposed youth is a time of storm and stress in which savage biological impulses clash with civilizing forces.

Most high-profile youth subcultures have differentiated themselves from established or adult culture around language, fashion, music, and art as well as conventions regarding gender and control. And as Tanner has noted elsewhere,[28] they practise an "opposition by inversion" of selected aspects of the dominant culture that expresses and appeals to defiance. So, for example, in response to expectations regarding autocratic order and control in the 1930s and 1940s, many youth said "swing." In response to expectations about conforming to middle-class suburban life in the 1950s, many said "go bohemian." To the discipline and control of mass production, they said "rock 'n roll." To liberating the world through war in the 1960s and 1970s, they said "make love." And in response to the practice of individualistic accumulation of wealth in the 1980s and 1990s, many youth said "wear torn clothes, garbage bags, and safety pins."

In this article, Baron explores punk subculture, but finds that the subculture is a paradoxical blend of opposing and accepting particular aspects of modern society's prevailing cultural values and beliefs. What does punk subculture oppose? What does it endorse? And what are the consequences of this mix?

26. DESOUZA

The Canadian Centre for Justice Statistics is the main storehouse for justice statistics in Canada. It compiles data and distributes information based on databases such as the Uniform Crime Reporting Survey, which works with crimes reported by police across Canada; the General Social Survey, which presents crime from the victim's standpoint; as well as databases providing information on adult courts, youth courts, and correctional trends.

This article is taken from one of its publications, the *Juristat*, which is published about a dozen times a year and deals with a specific justice issue. This *Juristat* provides an overview of cases brought before youth courts in 2000/01 and how they relate to trends over the past few years.

As you read through the statistics, you might note which ones surprised you and which ones were in line with your views and expectations. This article is followed by a flowchart of the "Justice Process for Youths" under the *Young Offenders Act*.

27. LESCHIED, ANDREWS, AND HOGE

The following article represents a review of both Ontario's young offenders programs and the literature on effective intervention. It has been included for two reasons. The first is to provide readers with an overview of the research on characteristics of young offenders and effective correctional treatment, as well as to give some idea of how correctional services assess and manage youth at risk for reoffending. However, the second is to provide an example of the nature of the reviewing, proposing, and implementing of effective intervention. Quite unlike the moral outrage and flamboyant rhetoric of the public discourse over young offenders, we find a highly rational, neutral, and somewhat abstract presentation of the research intended to guide decision making about the treatment of youth. Yet despite the virtue of objectivity in assessing effectiveness of treatment, in what ways does this document participate in Foucault's characterization of social control in our modern, disciplinary society—an encounter with a political technology of the body aimed at improving the soul?

28. DU WORS

This article provides an overview of data that responds to some of the most frequently asked questions about crime and justice in Canada. It is followed by a table of federal statute offenses for Canada, 1997–2001.

29. DESROCHES

Robbery, homicide, assault, and sexual assault are perhaps the most significant in the general category of violent crimes. In this article, the author interviews Roger Caron, one of Canada's most famous bank robbers, as well as the head of the Ontario Provincial Police special unit, which arrested Roger. As Desroches points out elsewhere,[29] underlying robbery is the question of whether it is a violent crime or a property offence. After the article we will return to the question of the nature of the crime and how it is processed within our society.

Postscript to Desroches's article

A couple of years ago, Ron and Lauren Koval defrauded various financial institutions, notably the Royal Bank of Canada, of about $94 million, which far exceeds the entire amount of money stolen from Canadian banks over the past ten years. The maximum sentence for fraud is ten years. At the point of sentencing the Kovals faced a prison term of five to eight years. If five, the Kovals could have been out on day parole in nine months. If eight, they would have been eligible for day parole in fifteen months.

The Kovals' sentence turned out to be seven years, with eligibility for day parole in fourteen months.[30] For the purpose of comparison, the maximum sentence for bank robbery, not just armed robbery, is life. However, robbery involves being face to face with the victim, and hence is considered a violent crime. So, it is important to also compare fraud to other crimes such as theft over $1,000, which carries an equivalent maximum sentence of ten years. Ideally, sentencing should reflect the "principle of proportionality" where the seriousness of the crime is reflected in the incarceration rate and the average length of prison sentence imposed regardless of the maximum penalty.

If we look at statistical trends regarding sentencing for these crimes, as well as break and enter reported in a 1997 article on sentencing in Canada, we find the following.[31]

Offence and Maximum Sentence	No. of Cases (days)	Prison Sentences (days)	Incarceration Rate	Median Sentence	Longest Sentence
Robbery (life)	1,483	1,304	88%	480	3,650
Theft>$1,000 (10 yrs)	3,702	1,697	46%	90	1,740
Fraud>$1,000 (10 yrs)	3,203	1,211	38%	90	2,555
Break and enter (life)	9,363	5,693	61%	120	2,190

What are we to make of this data regarding the operation of the principle of *proportionality* in Canada's criminal justice system?

30. ANDERSON

Studies regarding the social construction of criminals frequently discuss how the "criminal" is presented by the media or by medical and judicial authorities as committing the crime for psychological reasons such as pathological greed or other disorders.[32] Social, economic, or political factors are downplayed or completely ignored. This, in turn, contributes to a public image of "them" as different kind of people from "us."

But there are several cases where some very grotesque violent crimes are committed for seemingly pathological reasons. In this article we are introduced to serial killer Michael Wayne McGray.

Postscript to Anderson's article

Although McGray's acts are horrifying, sociologically McGray is quite familiar as a criminal. That is, he fits a prevalent image of the "criminal." In fact, he provides us with an "ideal typical" example of the criminal as a remorseless, violent person—or sociopath—who terrify many of those who encounter him. And, as Anderson points out, she really does find McGray terrifying.

At the same time, in terms of those who are imprisoned for crimes, McGray is not typical. For example, about nine-tenths of offenders in Ontario's provincial prisons are sentenced for non-violent offences, and about two-thirds of offenders in Canada's federal system are there for non-violent offences. As prison activist Ruth Morris points out, "Probably no more than one to three percent of offenders, by anyone's measure, remotely fit the terror image we use to justify the incredibly inefficient, destructive, expensive prison system and punitive court system that we maintain."[33]

So what is to be done with individuals like McGray? And what do we do with a correctional system designed to treat clients as if they were like McGray when they're most often not?

NOTES

1. Canadian Centre for Justice Statistics, "Crime Statistics in Canada, 1999," *Juristat*, Vol. 20, No. 5, Catalogue 85-002-XPE.

2. National Council of Welfare, *Poverty in Canada: 1999*, Ministry of Public Works and Government Services Canada, 2000.

3. Margaret Phelp, "Nearly Half of Canadians a Few Paycheques from Welfare, Report says," *Globe and Mail*, December 13, 2002: A10.

4. R. Breton and G. Reitz, *Illusion of Difference*, University of Toronto, 1994. Also see Michael Adams, *Sex in the Snow*, Penguin, 1998 for an alternative approach to understanding diversity within Canada and the United States, and how the United States is more diverse when we examine regional variation in social values.

5. Thomas Gabor, "The Suppression of Crime Statistics on Race and Ethnicity: The Price of Political Correctness," *Canadian Journal of Criminology*, Vol. 36, No. 2: 153–163.

6. W. Gordon West and Ruth Morris, *The Case for Penal Abolition*, Canadian Scholars' Press, 2000.

7. Jeffrey Reiman, *The Rich Get Richer and the Poor Get Prison: Ideology, Class and Criminal Justice*, 5th ed., Allyn and Bacon, 1998.

8. This question actually draws us into one of the basic problems regarding the human condition: If people know what's right, why do they choose what's wrong? The formal

term for this is the problem of akrasia. For a theoretic discussion of it, which is critical of sociology's general approach, see Alan Blum, "Sociology, Wrongdoing, and Akrasia: An Attempt to Think Greek about the Problem of Theory and Practice" in Robert Scott and Jack Douglas (eds.), *Theoretical Perspectives on Deviance*, Basic Books, 1972: 342–362. Also see Dorothy Walsh, "Akrasia Reconsidered," *Ethics*, Vol. 85 (1974–1975): 151–158.

9. Laureen Snider, "The Criminal Justice System" from Dennis Forcese and Stephen Richer (eds.), *Social Issues: Sociological Views of Canada* (2nd ed.), Prentice Hall, 1988. Also see Thomas Gabor, *Everybody Does It: Crime by the Public*, University of Toronto Press, 1994.

10. Deborah Brock, *Making Work, Making Trouble: Prostitution as a Social Problem*, University of Toronto Press, 1998.

11. John Lowman, "Street Prostitution" in V. Sacco (ed.), *Deviance: Conformity and Control in Canadian Society*, 2nd ed., Prentice Hall, 1992: 61–62.

12. Max Weber, *The Theory of Social and Economic Organization*, Free Press, 1947.

13. Peter Berger, Bridgette Berger, and Hansfeld Kellner, *The Homeless Mind: Modernization and Consciousness*, Vintage Books, Random House, 1973: 83–96.

14. L. Samuelson, "Crime as a Social Problem: From Definition to Reality" from L. Samuelson and W.L. Anthony (eds.), *Power and Resistance: Thinking about Canadian Social Issues*, 2nd ed., Fernwood Press, 1998.

15. "White Collar Crime," *Macleans*, June 30, 1986.

16. "Is White-Collar Crime Giving Justice a Black Eye?", *Globe and Mail*, August 14, 2000: A1, A6; "Big Tobacco Backs Down," *Globe and Mail*, June 9, 2000: B1, B5; "RT Condones Illegal Trades: OSC," *Globe and Mail*, June 30, 2000; "Stock Rigging Appears Widespread," *Globe and Mail*, July 1, 2000: B1, B5. For a more academically researched overview of the topic, see Laureen Snider, *Bad Business: Corporate Crime in Canada*, Nelson, 1993.

17. Keith Doubt, *Towards a Sociology of Schizophrenia: Humanistic Reflections*, University of Toronto Press, 1996.

18. Howard Becker, *Outsiders: Studies in the Sociology of Deviance*, Free Press, 1963.

19. Melvin Pollner, "Sociological and Common-Sense Models of the Labelling Process" from Roy Turner (ed.), *Ethnomethodology*, Penguin, 1974: 27–40.

20. Bonnie Buxton, "Condemned to a Life of Trouble," *Globe and Mail*, May 9, 2000.

21. "Community Plan Considered for Dealing with Youth Violence," *Globe and Mail*, November 5, 1998.

22. S. Cohen, *Folk Devils and Moral Panics*, MacGibbons and Kee, 1973; and John Fekete, *Moral Panic: Biopolitics Rising*, R. Davies Publishing, 1994.

23. Michael Czerny and Jamie Swift, *Getting Started on Social Analysis in Canada*, 2nd ed., Between the Lines, 1988.

24. Juanita Darling, "Colombia's Kids Urge End to Civil War," *Globe and Mail*, October 13, 1998: A14.

25. A 1993 study by the Operations Research Group, a respected Indian organization, has pegged the number of full-time child workers at 44 million in India, with another 10 million in Pakistan, Bangladesh, Nepal, and Sri Lanka. And it is mostly girl labour; two-

thirds of child workers are female.

26. Jack Epstein, "Child-Sex Trade Fuelled by Poverty," *Globe and Mail*, August 26, 1996; Ethan Casey, "Prostitution Feeds on Prosperity," *Globe and Mail*, August 27, 1996.

27. Stephen Strauss, "The Boys of War," *Globe and Mail*, October 10, 1998.

28. Julian Tanner, "Youthful Deviance" in V. Sacco (ed.), *Deviance: Conformity and Control in Canadian Society*, 2nd ed., Prentice Hall, 1992: 203–235.

29. Frederick Desroches, "Robbery and the Law" from *Force and Fear: Robbery in Canada*, Canadian Scholars' Press, 2002: 1–23.

30. Jane Gadd, "Kovals Jailed for 7 Years in Huge Fraud," *Globe and Mail*, March 31, 2001: A18. For a fuller discussion of the Koval case, see Timothy Appleby, "A Clinical Case," *R.O.B. Magazine*, June 2001: 41–42, 45–48, 50.

31. Julian Roberts, "Sentencing Trends and Sentencing Disparity" in J. Roberts and David P. Cole, *Making Sense of Sentencing*, University of Toronto Press, 1999: 144–145.

32. One of the first studies of this was done by Craig Haney and John Manzolati, "Television Criminology: Network Illusions of Criminal Justice Realities" from Elliot Aronson (ed.), *The Social Bond*, Freeman, 1992: 120–131. Of course, the TV programs have changed since then, but their study is still worth looking at.

33. Ruth Morris, "Classism and Racism in Our Retributive Justice System," *Social Planning Council of Metropolitan Toronto*, December, 1993: 4.

Part I

DEVIANCE AND SOCIETY

Chapter 1

SOCIAL INTERACTION IN TIMES SQUARE

Vernon Boggs and William Kornblum

A WARM SUMMER NIGHT ON "THE DEUCE," WEST FORTY-SECOND STREET, THE southern boundary of Manhattan's theatre district. It is past midnight, and the Broadway audiences are long gone. Dope dealers muttering, "Smoke, smoke," stand in the glare of movie marquees touting *Dirty Radio Sex* and other films. Some alcoholic derelicts—a "bottle gang"—weave along the broad sidewalk on their way to a darker side street where they can sit and pass a pint. Men in business suits wander in and out of store-fronts whose flashing lights promise pornographic thrills. At the corner of Eighth Avenue, a prostitute begins arguing with her pimp, then tears away and heads east on Forty-second toward the intersection where Seventh Avenue crosses Broadway—the Great White Way—and forms Times Square.

To European and Asian tourists, and to many American out-of-towners as well, such sights are to be expected in any major city. But if the outsider sees Forty-second Street as a place where violent and exotic creatures tear at one another and at a victimized public in a fierce struggle to survive, those who make their homes there experience a way of life that is ordered, predictable, and controlled. There is a human ecology in Times Square that is at least as elaborate and as fascinating as the ecology of the tropical jungle to which the area has often been compared. What appears to be chaos and confusion is actually a complex interaction of social groups, each with its codes and rituals.

The literature of social science has long recognized that great urban centres create "natural areas" like Times Square where very different kinds of people come in contact. Robert Park observed in his seminal 1921 essay, "The City," that people come together in cities "not because they are alike, but because they are useful to one another. This is particularly true in great cities, where social distances are maintained in spite of geographical proximity, and where every community is likely to be composed of people who live together in relationships that can best be described as symbiotic rather than social."

Street people are all around Manhattan, but the Times Square area is among the few places where they have staked out territories. Prostitutes, drug dealers, and bottle gangs all have their "strolls," or regularly travelled routes, each with its "stations," or oases of rest. Liquor stores, dark corners, and doorways serve as stations for the alcoholic derelicts who haunt the narrower, less populous side streets. Corners where a waiting woman can pick up a trick are the stations along the prostitutes' stroll on the west side of Eighth Avenue, north of Forty-second Street. For the drug peddlers, whose stroll is the Deuce itself, the stations are recesses and courtyards where their transactions can be made out of sight.

Another type of turf is the hustling spot, set up, like a nomad's camp, only when conditions are right. People with a hustle to pull off, such as three-card montes, or the con known as the Murphy (an elaborate scheme to persuade the mark to turn over his savings), will not stage such shows along the strolls of those selling drugs or sex. Working in small teams, hustlers ply their trade with an eye always out for "the man," in both his uniformed and plainclothes guises. Periods of stepped-up police work, like times of bad weather, are viewed as natural obstacles to be overcome with cunning and luck.

Different territories in Times Square mark not only different occupations but different levels of status as well. Through the city, street people rank themselves according to a hierarchy. Alcoholics and the mentally ill occupy the bottom rungs. The young men who hustle for their living are further up. And the pimps who set up shop in bars, safe from arrest and other dangers outside, are at the top—in the street world, an admired elite. The members of each of these status groups share rituals and norms learned in prisons and on the mean streets of the city's ghetto neighbourhoods. A prostitute who has chosen a pimp knows she must "give up choosing cake"—turn over a lump sum that the pimp accepts as a kind of dowry. An older man wise in the ways of straight society will be respectfully consulted as a "wisdom brother." Even the gangs of drinkers at the bottom of the hierarchy have rituals to determine who buys a bottle and who drinks from it last. Before anyone takes a swig, a few drops are poured on the pavement in memory of those who have died or gone to jail.

By far the largest and most complex of these status groups is the hustlers. Hustling in Times Square involves running con games, selling phony jewellery, shoplifting, and a host of other activities requiring good street sense and an aptitude for calculating the risks of arrest, injury, or being taken in by somebody else's "game." Large numbers of passers-by offer a ready market for a wide variety of goods and services that the hustler can provide.

Hustling zones often overlap, and the various players sometimes try to hustle one another. But not all the relationships of hustlers are exploitative. Regulars on the street know and depend on one another. Some drug dealers are related by family ties, others are acquaintances from prison; a number live in the same buildings nearby. Though at a glance it may seem that every hustler on the stroll is fiercely competing with every other, hustlers actually belong to identifiable cliques whose members can be seen sharing drugs, loaning one another money, and calling out one another's names. They often arrive at a station on their stroll the same time every morning, as if they were going to an entirely routine job.

Though prostitutes, drug dealers, and con men are well-dispersed throughout Manhattan, their concentration in Times Square creates a permanent marketplace, the likes of which exists nowhere else in the city. Times Square is more than a home for groups of street people; it is also visited by thousands from the mainstream of society—office workers, garment-district employees, tourists, theatre-goers, retail merchants, restaurateurs, entertainers, and the middle-class and working-class people of Clinton, the residential neighbourhood to the west. Some 113,000 people use the subway stations every day, and another 100,000 arrive at and depart from the bus terminal. Most of these trips occur during the morning and late-afternoon rush hours, but in the evening, too, the area is crowded with people seeking entertainment, from Broadway plays and first-run movies to live sex shows and twenty-five-cent glimpses at silent pornographic shorts. As theatre-goers and seekers of sexual thrills head home and most of the city descends into the dark quiet of the early-morning hours, West Forty-second Street remains one of New York's liveliest streets.

Chapter 2

PRESCIENTIFIC APPROACHES TO DEVIANCE

Linda Deutschmann

IN THIS CHAPTER, WE WILL LOOK AT THE WAYS IN WHICH DEVIANCE WAS UNDERSTOOD before the great transition to rationalism and science ("the Enlightenment") in the late 1600s. Early treatment of deviance was noncausal. It used stories to illustrate the character of deviance, and to warn people about the consequences of excessive control as well as excessive deviance. The spread and penetration of monotheistic religions—especially Christianity—led to a more causal, but still supernatural, explanation according to which the "devil" caused deviance and all other ills. Deviance no longer evoked feelings of ambivalence; it was evil, as were those who failed to oppose it. This chapter devotes considerable space to explaining the nature, origins, and consequences of the witchcraft craze that shook Europe from roughly A.D. 1400 to A.D. 1700.

Witchcraft is important for the study of deviance because it provides a paradigm of the processes whereby deviants are "created" by authorities. It is relatively easy, looking back through contemporary eyes, to see that "witches," as seen by the medieval authorities, did not really exist. Once this paradigm is understood, we can look at other kinds of deviance closer to our own time, and raise the same questions. For example, how much of both the glamour and the horror of the "drug trafficker" is real, and how much is a construct made up of some truths and many inaccuracies? What is the underlying reality, and why is distortion of that reality so common?

PAST AND PRESENT REPRESENTATIONS OF DEVIANCE

Myths, Parables, and Stories

Before the Enlightenment brought us science, rationality, and an empirically bound reality, people understood life in terms of myths, parables, and stories.

These tales described their experiences and, in a nonscientific way, explained them.

Deviance has always been a powerful theme in religion, art, folklore, drama, and political life. The earliest perspectives on deviance, which persist in various forms to this day, take the shape of stories that provide examples of deviance and its consequences. While they may or may not also provide moral instruction, these stories give us an understanding of how deviance fits in the scheme of things.

The ethical message of each major religion is supported by collections of historical or mythical tales in which various kinds of offences against the powers of creation, or against social regulation, happen by accident or through carelessness. The offence is not always intended by—or even known to—the offender. The response of heaven and earth, however, is usually punitive unless mitigated by ritual reconciliation. The prodigal son, for example, may be welcomed home. For the most part, deviants are expelled from the garden, turned into pillars of salt, or condemned to perform eternal tasks. Temptation and its consequences is the theme of many stories of this kind. Eve was tempted into tasting the forbidden fruit of knowledge. Pandora's curiosity led her to open the box containing all the evils of the world. Buddha, Christ, Mohammed, and other important religious figures all had experience, at least in figurative terms, of demons or temptations.

Secular or magical stories also reinforce cultural images of deviance and control. In Heinrich Hoffman's *Der Struwwelpeter*, a classic storybook for children, a little girl plays with matches, her dress catches fire, and soon all that remains of her is a pile of ashes, two shoes, and two cats whose tears flow like a stream across the page. In another story, a boy who insists on sucking his thumbs has them cut off by a tailor with huge scissors (Hoffmann, n.d.). Many other children's stories have similar cautionary intentions. The boy who cried wolf when there was no wolf is denied help when he needs it. Little Red Riding Hood talks to a stranger in the woods and gets herself and her grandmother eaten. Cinderella's ugly stepsisters have their eyes plucked out and eaten by doves. These stories conform to the common cultural practice of warning and admonishing in order to induce polite language, table manners, caution, cooperation, and responsibility.

Trickster Legends

Despite the above examples, most of our secular tales are ambivalent about deviance in that they do not regard it as unconditionally "bad." Indeed, the deviant character is frequently more likable and sympathetic than the characters who teach and correct. This ambivalence about deviance and control is reflected in the culturally universal trickster legend (Radin, [1956] 1972:iii). In trickster stories, the smart "little guy" outwits the stupid, greedy authorities. The trickster circumvents the usual rules in disrespectful ways.

> Unburdened by scruples, tricksters dupe friends, acquaintances, and adversaries alike in the pursuit of their selfish ends and blithely reward their benefactor's generosity with sometimes deadly betrayals. In addition, they have a pronounced weakness for food but are plagued by an inveterate aversion for work, a trait that forces them to rely on trickery to obtain food both in times of want and of plenty. (Owomoyela, 1990:626)

Everything the trickster does is permeated with laughter, irony, and wit. The audience reaction is laughter tempered with awe (Radin, [1956] 1972:xxiv).

The trickster takes many forms, but is basically a smart, unethical, mischief-making character who shockingly violates many of the customary norms of honesty, mannerliness, and loyalty. In Anglo-American culture, Brer Rabbit, Roger Rabbit, and Bugs Bunny represent the amusing, human, and likable side of the trickster. Among natives, such as the Haida of the Queen Charlotte Islands, the trickster takes the form of Raven, or, in other native cultures, is sometimes Coyote (Wilkins, 1994:73). The trickster also represents darker, uncontrolled, less human forces. Batman's archenemy, the Joker, is funny in a campy way, but he is also violent, unpredictable, homicidal, and sadistic. The mean and mischievous imp Mxyzptlk in *Superman* comic books combines both comedic and demonic features. Thus, the trickster embodies the paradox of deviance—its attractiveness and dangers, and its many faces.

The trickster is found in many European picaresque tales where he/she (the form is gender-bending) represents "revolt against the rigidity of tradition" (Radin, [1956] 1972:185). Thus Goethe's *Renard the Fox*, and Thomas Mann's *The Confessions of Felix Krull, Confidence Man*, also fit within this genre.

The trickster tradition continues in the form of certain modern entertainers and political figures.

> Rock music, from Elvis Presley to Michael Jackson, regularly serves up androgynous, shaman-like figures who challenge cultural norms. In the late sixties, John Lennon consciously adopted the role of the holy fool as he and his wife Yoko Ono staged "bed-ins for peace" . . . Prince (especially in his dualistic guise as Gemini) exemplifies the gender-bending, rule-shattering rock star . . . The figures of the clown and holy fool played a large part in sixties counterculture politics as

well, specifically in the persons of Jerry Rubin and Abbie Hoffman. (Santino, 1990:662)

Cross-dressers (people who wear clothes designed for the opposite sex) sometimes fall into the trickster category. They make fun of the established order and question one of its most fundamental dichotomies, the great gender divide. Thus, the role of the fool as trickster is a contrary one that turns the accepted order of things on its head.

Contemporary Legends

Contemporary legends differ from legends of the past in that they claim to be factual rather than fantastic. These legends, it turns out, are based on hearsay rather than fact (Goode, 1992:306). An example of this is the perennial legend of the poisoned (by strangers) Halloween candy, which stirs up parental anxieties each October (Best, 1985; Brunvand, 1989). In fact, the only proven cases of Halloween poisoning show this act to have been perpetrated not by strangers but by relatives and acquaintances. The story persists, however, supported by our fear of strangers in the urban environment.

Another urban legend is the story of the man who, accompanied by his child, went to Neiman Marcus for tea and cookies. He asked for the cookie recipe, was told it cost $2.50, and agreed to buy it. Later, he was shocked to find that $250 had been charged to his credit card. Unable to get the store to delete the charge, and angry about it, he sent the recipe out on computer networks—telling users to copy and circulate it—as a way of getting back at the store. The recipe spread among friends and relatives of the computer network users, and was even reprinted in many newspapers—only to be scotched when Ann Landers revealed that Neiman Marcus does not sell any such cookie recipe. This story recently resurfaced on a women's studies e-mail list as "Cookie Recipe E-mail Empowerment 101." This time it was a mother and daughter at Neiman Marcus but the price and the request for getting back at the store was the same.

Pearson (1984) recounts a Canadian urban legend, concerning someone who came to be known as "the North York [Ontario] banana man." This man, the story went, had been hit by a car after spending the evening in a singles' bar. The nurses at the hospital discovered a banana secured to his thigh with rubber bands. Jan Harold Brunvand, University of Utah English professor and folklorist, has collected hundreds of these tales, which always betray their spuriousness by being told far too many times, and with far too many embellishments and revisions. Urban legends deal with understandings of deviance and control. They tell us that certain ways of living (deviance) are likely to lead to grief and humiliation, and in the process they express our fears (and sometimes our sense of humour).

DEVIANCE AND THE MEDIA

Deviance, especially bizarre or criminal deviance, is the bread and butter of modern journalism. This is not a new phenomenon. In the supposedly prudish Victorian era, newspapers teemed with "sensationalist" accounts of murder, suicide, child battering, and social disorder. As Boyle (1989) recounts,

> *The Times* of January 3, 1857, lay open before me. It featured an account of "The Double Murder of Children in Newington," a lead article on "Robberies and Personal Violence," an extended rendition of "A Week of Horror." Having consumed these tidbits, I decided to move on to something I assumed would be quite different. *The Miner and Workman's Advocate*—the other end of the journalistic social scale from the august *Times*—featured, on page 3 alone of the January 7, 1865, edition, "The Poisoning of Five Persons at Gresford," "Extraordinary Outrage in Ireland," "Horrible Murder at Aldershot by a Madman," "Steamer Runs Down and Four Men Drown on the Clyde," "Shocking Child Murder," and "Horrible Death by Fire." (3–4)

The contemporary mass media give even greater attention to themes of deviance, which resonate with people's anxieties about their personal safety and about threats to the social order. A brief look at the front pages of almost any city or town newspaper will confirm that deviance is a major part of the messages we receive each day. Television increasingly carries true-crime and simulated crime stories that convey a similar message. Since the early 1970s, about 30 percent of prime-time TV in the United States has been devoted to reality-based crime and law enforcement shows (Dominick, 1978:105). The figure would be much higher if dramatizations of these themes were included. As for commercial films, In Medved's words (1991):

> Indescribable gore drenches the modern screen, even in movies allegedly made for families. And the most perverted forms of sexuality—loveless, decadent, brutal and sometimes incestuous—are showing regularly at a theatre near you. (40)

Films shown on television follow the same pattern, and are even more heavily slanted toward images of the criminal and the law.

EARLY EXPLANATIONS OF DEVIANCE: THE DEMONIC PERSPECTIVE

The earliest recorded attempts to *explain* rather than describe the nature of deviance did not, as modern science does, seek causes in the empirical world. Deviance, like everything else, was deemed to be caused by forces in the supernatural realm. In theoretical terms, the independent variables were supernatural forces, often demons or devils of some kind, who acted through particular human beings to cause harm in the world. Thus, when floods came, crops failed, farm animals sickened, or women miscarried, people did not look for the causes in nature, physiology, or medicine. They did not understand that mould on the crops could produce hallucinations, miscarriages, and other problems. They looked instead to the supernatural—witches, sorcerers, demons, and the like—as an explanation for these events. In this world, there were no coincidences: if a man walked along a path and something fell on him, someone else must have willed that event to happen by invoking the powers of the supernatural.

Over time, there have been many versions of the demonic perspective, each corresponding with the different ideas about the supernatural that were typical of the particular age and culture.

Box 2.1 The Causal Model of Demonic Deviance

General Model:

Evil	→ receptive individual	→ harmful effects
Devil	→ woman, child, weak man	→ storms, illness, crop failure

Temptation:

Snake and Eve → forbidden fruit	→ alienation from God

Possession:

Witches' spell → vulnerable neighbour	→ wrongdoing

In their efforts to discredit and displace other religions, monotheistic religions have demonized the other religions' gods, made "wizards and sorcerers" of their sages, and treated their times of ritual ceremony as occasions of demonic celebration (Simpson, [1973] 1996). Witches' Sabbath, a time when witches supposedly gathered to engage in sex with the devil and his demons, was a transformation of the celebration of the Celtic Samhain, a midpoint between the autumnal equinox and the winter solstice, which marked the new year. Similarly, Baal-Zeebub, the "lord of the flies," was a fertility god worshipped by the Philistines and other Semitic groups. He was transformed by the Old Testament Israelites into Beelzebub, a powerful devil. Both the horned Celtic god Cerunnos and the Graeco-Roman Pan were remade into Judeo-Christian images of devils with horns and cloven hooves (Russell, 1984:63). Other demonized residuals of pagan times include the immoral or amoral humanlike creatures depicted as elves, fauns, trolls, satyrs, fairies, leprechauns, werewolves, dragons, ghosts, and jinn. Although now the stuff of children's storybooks, these creatures were once an accepted part of everyday life, both feared and respected. Anticipating retaliation if they failed to do so, people spoke kindly about fairies (Briggs, 1978). "Bad" children are still sometimes seen as changelings—evil replacements for "good" children stolen by goblins or trolls; the deviance of such children is in no way the fault of their parents.

The pantheistic view of the world saw deviance and suffering as phenomena more or less beyond human control. The actions of both gods and hostile spirits were neither predictable nor always preventable. In the monotheistic cosmos, however, humans bear some responsibility for evoking, or giving in to, the forces of evil. The two main paths to deviance in this view are temptation and possession. The devil tempts or possesses weaker human beings such as children or morally weak (irreligious) adults. Sometimes the deviant contributes to the process by dabbling in the occult, indulging in heretical ideas, or living a lifestyle open to corruption.

THE WITCH CRAZE OF THE EUROPEAN RENAISSANCE, 1400–1700

Historical Background

Virtually all societies have maintained some beliefs about witchcraft or sorcery. Before the witch craze, European beliefs were similar to those found on other continents. Witches and sorcerers were sometimes feared, sometimes persecuted, but they were often respected and recognized as people who served a useful role in the social order (e.g., by providing charms and amulets to protect people from harm or sickness, or by acting as oracles to decide the innocence or guilt of accused people). Magic directed against political leaders, however, was regarded as treason.

Belief in witches was "a continuing preoccupation of villagers, but not an obsession" (Cave, 1995; Garrett, 1977:462; Thomas, 1971). The penalties for unauthorized or malicious practice of witchcraft were commensurate with those enforced for other kinds of assault on individuals or their property.

In the period before A.D. 1000, Church canon law (as reflected in the *Canon Episcopi* of about A.D. 906, a compendium of popular lore on demons) tended to hold that it was both un-Christian and illegal to believe in the reality of witches (Groh, 1987:17; Trevor-Roper, 1969:13; Webster, [1982] 1996:77). The *Canon* suggested that women who believed themselves able to use love incantations or to fly at night with the pagan goddess Diana were suffering from delusions planted by the devil. The *Canon* asserted that the folklore practice associated with such beliefs would disappear as all people became Christian (Ben-Yahuda, 1985:34; Richards, 1990:77). Catastrophes were sent by God to test humankind, and witches were deluded in believing that they could affect such things. In this period, attacks on presumed witches were regarded as superstitious pagan behaviour and sometimes resulted in protests to Rome.

In the period between 1000 and 1480, witches and sorcerers (along with other manifestations of supernatural beings) were redefined. Rather than harmless and misunderstood relics of pagan life, they became agents of the devil—a vast subversive conspiracy against everything that was right, orderly, and holy. In fact, many of the accusations made against heretics and witches in this period (incest, infanticide, sex orgies, cannibalism) were the same as those that had been levelled against the early Christians by classical pagan writers (Cohn, 1976; Richards, 1990:78). The process whereby folklore, witchcraft beliefs, ritual magic, and devil worship became one overall and world-shattering conspiracy was neither smooth nor gradual: it was contested in some areas and embraced in others.

The witch craze has been described as a collective psychosis or mania (Trevor-Roper, 1969). Although it has connections with modern fears of Satanism, its scale was much broader and its impact far more devastating. The exact number of victims is difficult to ascertain, given the widespread (but nonetheless local and episodic) nature of the witch-hunt. Episodes broke out repeatedly in towns, villages, and cities throughout Europe, the British Isles, and the American colonies, sometimes receding in one area only to break out in others. Events such as plagues, wars, and famines were likely to be followed by outbreaks of witch-hunting. In all, somewhere between 100,000 and 200,000 executions probably took place (Ben-Yahuda, 1985:23), although figures as low as 60,000 (Levack, 1987) and as high as 500,000 (Harris, 1978:237), and even 9 million (Pelka, 1992:7), have been cited.

EXPLANATIONS FOR THE CRAZE

The demonic explanation for the witch craze is complete in itself and cannot be refuted by any form of natural evidence. It is an explanation built on faith, one that teaches us nothing beyond the belief we started with in the first place.

More worldly interpretations of the causes of witch-hunting can be found by examining what kinds of people were accused of witchcraft, what kinds of people profited from their persecution, and when or under what conditions the accusations were made. All of these aspects are considered in the following list, which summarized the characteristics of those selected for prosecution as witches.

Characteristics of the Accused

1. *Women.* By most accounts, at least 80 percent of those executed were women (Levack, 1992b). Male victims were frequently related to—or were trying to protect—women who had been accused. Thus, to understand the witch-hunts, it is necessary first to "confront the deeply imbedded feelings about women—among our witch-ridden ancestors" (Karlsen, 1989:xiii).

    The Malleus-Maleficarum attributed the fact that "a greater number of witches is found in the fragile feminine sex than among men" to women's moral and intellectual inferiority, their weakness, and, most especially, their sexual depravity:

    > All witchcraft comes from carnal lust, which is in women insatiable. . . .
    > Wherefore for the sake of fulfilling their lusts they consort even with devils.
    > (Kramer and Sprenger, 1971:47)

    The selection of women as targets was hardly surprising given a patriarchal Church that excluded women from all leadership roles and feared them as potential subversives (Worobec, 1995:175). Women who stepped out of their assigned roles as bearers of children and servants to men were especially vulnerable. Thus, women who were "old maids," widows without family support, sexually promiscuous, or who were lesbians were likely to be targeted (Worobec, 1995:176).

2. *Women who gave birth to deformed babies.* These infants were regarded as "Satan's spawn," the product of sexual orgies involving the mother and the devil or his demons.

3. *People seen in the dreams of others* (especially if in the form of a sexual partner).

4. *Men or women who claimed to have occult powers and played the role.* In every society, there have been people with "second sight," who have forecast the future, dispensed spells or charms, or threatened others with supernatural vengeance. In the 1692 Salem witch trials, the first accused was Tituba, a West Indian servant who entertained the local girls with voodoo and with fortune telling by palmistry. When the girls began falling into unexplained fits, Tituba's employer, the Reverend Parris, beat a confession of witchcraft out of her. People such as Tituba are tolerated in normal times, when there is no anxiety about demonic conspiracies, but are often among the first condemned when such fears are raised.

5. *People believed to be involved in treasonous conspiracies.* When the inheritance of a throne could depend on the birth of a living male baby and when poisoning was a major factor in royal succession, the practice of witchcraft for political purposes was often suspected. This form of accusation was particularly common in the early witchcraft trials (around A.D. 1400). For example, under James III of Scotland, several witches were executed on the grounds that James's brother, the Earl of Mar, had been conspiring with them against the king. The earl was mysteriously murdered, presumably on his brother's orders (Larner, 1980:53).

6. *People who did not fully accept Church dogma and practice.* Besides free thinkers and early scientists, this group consisted of people who continued to follow the customs of the earlier pagan religions. Among the evidence presented at the heresy trial of Joan of Arc was the fact that she had participated in ancient Celtic practices that were traditional in rural areas but forbidden by the Church, which saw such events as the equivalent of participating in *sabbats* with the devil. It should be noted, however, that the claim made early in this century by Margaret Murray that the "witches" were in fact members of a secret pre-Christian fertility religion is no longer supported by historians (Larner, 1980:59; Murray, 1921).

7. *Healers, herbalists, and naturopaths.* People involved in issues such as fertility, midwifery, and abortion were particularly vulnerable. Known as "cunning men" and "wise women" in England, and by equivalent names in Europe, they had "powers" that were not under the regulation of the authorities (Cassar, 1993:319). To be an expert in sexual matters in a society dominated by the clergy was dangerous. Abortion, for example, was associated with beliefs that newborn babies were being used in obscene rituals with the devil. Curing people by "magical" means was also condemned. Both "white" (good) and "black" (bad) witchcraft were considered heretical. Female midwives and herbalists were in competition

with the rising all-male, university-based medical establishment, which relied more on logic and dogma than on practical experience (Eastlea, 1980; Watts, 1984:28). Finally, people knowledgeable about drugs were also suspect because the effects of drugs such as atropine, henbane, and thornapple, which have narcotic and poisonous properties, seemed to reveal supernatural powers (Worobec, 1995:171). Vision-inducing drugs may lie at the root of beliefs about witches flying at night and being able to change shape (Harris, 1978:190). Whether these drugs were given to people by women healers, or whether they simply came to them as mould on bread (some fungi that attack grain have LSD-like properties), they could be responsible for visions.

8. *People blamed for the misfortune of others.* Many accusations of witchcraft had their root in quarrels in which one party apparently threatened another, who later became sick or experienced some misfortune. Illnesses attributed to witchcraft or sorcery included "impotence, stomach pains, barrenness, hernias, abscesses, epileptic seizures, and convulsions" (Worobec, 1995:166–167). Many cases involved beggars who seemed to be retaliating against those who had denied them assistance (Groh, 1987:19), or people who *ought* to have been seeking revenge for some previous insult or harm (Worobec, 1995:181). The most frequent cases were those in which someone repudiated a neighbour—usually an old woman seeking a favour—and then attributed personal misfortunes to her (Garrett, 1977:462–463; Macfarlane, 1970:196; Worobec, 1995:182). Situations of this kind became increasingly common as the mutual-help systems typical of rural communities were disrupted by population growth and the arrival of early capitalist forms of economy; people who had some wealth began to feel threatened by the rising numbers of beggars and indigents.

9. *Exceptional people.* Sometimes personal characteristics like an unusual appearance, or perhaps extraordinary success or talent, were seen as the result of a Faustian bargain with Satan. The story of Faust, who sells his soul to the devil in exchange for knowledge and power, goes back to at least to the ninth century. Niccolo Paganini, a composer and violin virtuoso of the 1800s, was treated as a Faustian figure, primarily because his playing was so extraordinary. Similarly, it was widely believed that Sir Francis Drake defeated the Spanish Armada with Satan's help (Russell, 1984:82). Canadian fiddler Ashley MacIsaac has similarly been accused of having made a demonic pact. Unlike Paganini, MacIsaac will not have to worry about being harmed or refused burial rites.

10. *People named by accused witches under torture or persuasion.* Almost anyone could be named, but most confessing witches did not try to implicate court officials or other powerful people; such accusations, when they occurred, were often suppressed by the court. In New England, people who denied the charges were often convicted and executed, while those who confessed and named others were set free; not surprisingly, then, a great many witches were named by the accused.

11. *People named by those suffering from illness or hardship.* In Salem in 1692, the young girls who showed signs of "possession" (screaming unaccountably, falling into grotesque convulsions, mimicking the behaviour of dogs) named everyone they had a grudge against (Erikson, 1966:142). In total, 142 persons were named, ultimately resulting in the death by hanging of 21 men and women (and one dog). A man who refused to plead either guilty or not guilty was crushed to death under heavy stones; his refusal to enter a plea was interpreted as a denial of the legitimacy of the proceedings. Only when the accusations began to include prominent people (e.g., Lady Phipps, wife of the Massachusetts colony's governor) was the process seriously questioned and, ultimately, rejected. Similarly, in Europe, the craze began to die out as it threatened more powerful people.

12. *The mentally ill.* Allowed to wander freely in normal times, those suffering from mental illness were particularly vulnerable to being caught up in the witch-hunt. Also singled out were people with psychoneurotic symptoms (manifested, for example, in a failure to react when pricked with a pin) and "hysterics," who acted out because of physical or emotional stress. As Ben-Yahuda (1985) notes,

> While Freud himself virtually ignored the European witch-craze, it contains elements to warm any analyst's heart: cruel and destructive persecutions, women, sex, and violence. These could easily by integrated into psychoanalytic interpretations, emphasizing the projection of hostility, reaction-formation, incestuous wishes, and impulses of the id. (43)

13. *People with physical disabilities or neurological disorders.* Such individuals might be seem as victims of the witchcraft of others or as suitable partners for Satan. They were likely to be accused of giving others "the evil eye." Also included in this group were the elderly and the physically unattractive.

14. *Scapegoats for the system.* These were generally people who lacked the clout to defend themselves (although few individuals were absolutely safe from accusation). As long as people believed that plagues, wars, famines, and personal troubles were caused by demons, they did not expect their

leaders to provide alternatives to scapegoating. More significantly, as long as they thought they needed their leaders to combat witches, they would not rise up against them. The control of witchcraft became a very significant reason to pay tithes to Church authorities and to obey their rules; only they knew how to diagnose and treat supernatural ills, and only they were powerful enough to oppose the devastating powers of Satan. Thus, the witch craze "divided the poor against each other in suspicion and fear" at the same time as it forced people to depend on the Church (Erikson, 1966; Harris, 1978).

The above list tells us a great deal about the conditions that informed the craze. Whether in Europe, England, or the American colonies, witch-victims represented resistance to the "sacred canopy" erected over society by their respective churches. Some of these victims were actually opposed to the system. Others served as scapegoats for the threat posed to churches by the fundamental changes that were taking place around the world. Events such as Columbus's voyage to the Americas in 1492, the opening up of trade routes to the East, and the invention of the printing press all contributed to a growth in knowledge that had the potential to undermine Church rule. Scapegoats also provided a convenient explanation for plagues and famines, which were especially acute in the period between 1400 and 1700, as was social change (Watts, 1984:7). Throughout the witch-craze period, most of the trials were held in the cultural "borderlands," where social diversity and religious conflict were the greatest, or in places where war and plague had created disorder (Coudert, 1992:89; Thomas, 1971). Even in later outbreaks, such as in pre-revolutionary Russia (late 1800s), the background of the craze was anxiety-provoking social change and economic upheaval (Worobec, 1995:168). Places that were sheltered from change did not develop the craze. For example, while the French were burning Huguenot heretics and witches, the stable French settlement in Canada was not affected; the belief in witches existed, but there was no panic associated with it (Morison, 1955:248).

Only when rational and scientific ways of thinking developed to the point that the courts became fully secular did the craze finally wither away. The courts gradually ceased to treat witchcraft as a reality other than in its associations with criminal acts, fraud, extortion, or abuse (such as ritual child abuse). Witchcraft remains part of modern law, but only in this restricted sense. The Criminal Code of Canada, for example, makes it an offence to "pretend to exercise or use any kind of witchcraft sorcery, enchantment or conjuration." In December 1988, a Toronto court found a laboratory technician guilty of practicing witchcraft because he had been treating a teenage girl's psychological problems with "herb drinks, candles and the laying on of hands," and had charged a fee for it (Kelly, 1988). Similar legislation in Australia has resulted in criminal charges against tarot card readers and other fortune tellers (Hume, 1995:148). However, when an Ontario Supreme Court judge said to murderer Peter Demeter (sentenced to five life terms in 1988) "You certainly appear to ooze evil from every pore of your body," few people in the courtroom thought that Demeter was being told he was "possessed" or in the service of Satan (Claridge, 1988).

MODERN BELIEFS ABOUT DEMONIC DEVIANCE

Despite the predominance of secular definitions of deviance, the demonic remains a theme recognized and sometimes used in our society. A 1978 Gallup poll reported that 1 out of 3 Americans believed that "the devil is a personal being who directs evil forces and influences people to do wrong," while another 1 out of 3 believed the devil as an impersonal force. A 1990 Gallup poll of 1226 adults found that 55 percent of Americans believe in the reality of the devil, and that 14 percent believe that witches are real.

The belief that there is evil in the world does not necessarily result in accusations of demonism and panic over hidden conspiracies. When it does emerge in this form, however, the modern identifying label for those suspected of conspiring is "satanist" rather than witch, and the suspects are male as often as they are female. Indeed, the emphasis on female witches has receded, and the term "witchcraft" is rarely used in this sense. A huge divide has emerged between those who use the concepts of Satanism and those who speak of witchcraft. Contemporary witches consider themselves to be practitioners of faiths such as the Mother-Goddess religion. They neither believe in nor worship Satan, and they are usually (but not always) ignored rather than feared by people with different religious convictions (Guiley, 1991; Marron, 1989).

Belief in satanic deviance is, not surprisingly, found mainly (but not exclusively) in areas with a high degree of religious consciousness, such as the Bible Belt areas of Canada and the United States. Anti-Satanism, however, goes far beyond the usual religious explanations of deviance. It shares with the various examples of witch-hunts presented earlier a tendency to label people on the basis of very insubstantial empirical evidence.

EVIL AS METAPHOR

In modern times, the demonic has become more of a metaphor than an explanation when applied to deviance. Alcoholics speak of the "devil in a bottle," and many drug addicts see their addiction as a consequence of demonic-like trickery—the drug promises euphoria but delivers death. Some people even see evil behind the apparently secular surface of everyday life:

> The iniquitous roster of evil all around us is an unending list of dark powers that are proliferating: racism, genocide, monstrous crimes, drug gang wars, merciless and random slaughter of innocent civilians, gas bombing of cities, pestilence, famine and war, governmental policies of racial cruelty, death squads, violent or insidious suppression of human rights, forms of slavery, abuse of children, bestial military action against civilians, callousness to the homeless, the AIDS victims and the poor, abuse of the elderly, sexism, rape, wanton murder, cults, terrorism, torture, the unremitting aftermath of past holy and unholy wars, the Holocaust, heinous cruelty and hatred, and the seven deadly sins: wrath, pride, envy, sloth, gluttony, lust and avarice.
>
> We go on polluting the air, the soil and the water. We think the unthinkable: atomic destruction of civilization and the earth itself. We trash outer and inner space. We literally are in danger of running amok. All the while we feed an unbridled and insatiable appetite for horror; demonic projections are made on enemies as "Evil Empire" and "The Great Satan," governments conspire with organized crime, assassinate and massacre, destroy the souls of people for power and money, arm nations and individuals, and, as a consequence human beings are now exploding in every corner of the globe. Such things as these are often nourished and cunningly abetted by the media: television, film, newspapers, and even art, literature and music. (Wilmer, 1988:2–3)

SUMMARY

Long before academics attempted to understand deviance, it was the subject of folklore and mythology, which gave it a place in the social order. While many of the early formulations were moralistic and presented the deviant as a pitiful or evil creature, the dominant kind of story emphasized the multifaceted, frightening, and humorous aspects of deviance, and did not always side with the forces of control. These forms of understanding persist in their modern descendants—children's literature (and sometimes that for adults) and the oral tradition of the "urban myth," in which terrible or embarrassing things happen to people who engage in questionable activities.

The first attempt to provide a fully causal explanation of deviance was the demonic theory, which was rooted in the idea that powers of both good and evil cause all events in the world. The demonic explained not only deviance but other kinds of troubling events, including storms, crop failure, and plagues, as well as religious doubt.

In the late Middle Ages, beginning slowly in the 1100s and becoming a veritable holocaust by the 1600s, the idea that deviance resulted from supernatural causes was transformed into a terrifying conspiracy theory. Believers felt themselves surrounded by a swelling confederacy of witches who were in league with Satan to defeat the armies of Christ.

The dominant modern interpretation of the witchcraft craze is that the "witch" was a social construct, created and maintained by religious authorities in a manner that reflected the common beliefs of the people. Witches were invented by those who feared them (Erikson, 1966) and by those who saw them as enemies of patriarchy and the extension of Church power (Daly, 1978; Hester, 1990). The witchcraft mania had its start in the challenge to Church hegemony posed by mountain regions and residual cultures that empowered women, and it reached its peak in the period in which religious wars and the rise of secular thought and science seriously threatened Church authority. It continues to emerge in places where a powerfully positioned religious worldview is challenged by alternative ideas. Thus, witchcraft beliefs were both functional for the authorities and representative of the increasing conflict between a religiously validated patriarchy and alternative views of the world.

The witch-hunt provides a paradigm that can be applied to events such as the Nazi persecution of the Jews, the McCarthyite "red scare" in North America, and the overzealous search for child molesters and Satanists. In modern times, demonology is used to explain deviance—generally in its most serious manifestations—only after all rational explanations have failed. However, the paradigm can also be applied to more mundane forms of deviance such as drug trafficking when those forms of deviance are "demonized" by political authorities.

Chapter 3

LAY DEFINITIONS OF CRIME

Robert A. Silverman, James J. Teevan, and Vincent F. Sacco

GENERALLY, THE LEGAL BUREAUCRACY AND THE AVERAGE CITIZEN AGREE ON THE acts that should be called crimes. Murder is a crime, as are shoplifting, arson, robbery, fraud, and break and enter. In some instances, however, citizens define acts as criminal when legally they are not. This is apparent in casual conversation when individuals refer to general social ills as crimes. The closing of hospitals, the decreased value of the dollar, the disrespect of youth, none of which is a *legally* defined crime, may thus be defined as crimes by some people. Even more serious examples, such as emotional neglect of children or elderly parents, are generally not criminal matters. For most people, this process of making crime roughly equal to what they consider bad in their society is not an important error (indeed, many are aware that it is wrong), and is certainly quite acceptable in an informal context. For a scientific study of crime, however, the inclusion of the bad or immoral, but not illegal, would make the boundaries of criminology vague and its content almost limitless. For these and other reasons, most criminologists reject such popular definitions of crime.

On the other hand, there are many instances in which crimes legally have occurred but the individuals involved—victim, offender, or both—do not define the act as criminal. Sometimes this is due to ignorance of the law; for instance, the general public is often unaware of the broad extent of the criminal law, and have a narrower definition of crime than is legally the case. It is a *Criminal Code* offence, for example, to give trading stamps to purchasers of goods in Canada (section 427), or even to *offer* to transport someone to a common bawdy house (section 211), but few Canadians would be aware of these crimes.

In other instances, it is more disagreement than ignorance, as when people say that what occurred is "no big deal," that no real crime occurred. Until the modern feminist movement, much spousal abuse fell into this category (cf.

Backhouse, 1991). In practice, the definition of acts as crimes or not often depends on the perceptions of the actors involved, how they define the behaviours that have occurred. For example, when one individual strikes another without consent, a criminal assault may have occurred. But suppose it was in fun, as a result of a playful struggle? Most people experience an assault in fun at some time in their lives. The pushing and shoving of children, considered to be a normal part of growing up, is just one example. Among adults as well, and not only when playing hockey and other sports, one finds the equivalents of pushing and shoving matches, little of which is defined as criminal. Even if the force used is excessive and injures one of the participants, the injury is often defined as accidental. The context is thus crucial.

Similarly, some assaults may be considered a part of daily life, and not a crime, by some segments of our society. Hitting an individual, for example, may be viewed as a legitimate way of settling a dispute in some subcultures in Canada today. If both parties agree to this solution, then neither will define the act involved as criminal and neither will call the police.

Suppose, however, that only one of the participants thinks this way or someone is hit, not by a friend or acquaintance, but by a stranger. In such cases, the "victim" may indeed define the event as a crime and call the police. In this instance, an assault as defined by the *Criminal Code of Canada* (section 265) may have been committed, not because it was *defined* differently. The attacker may even be arrested and prosecuted. Thus, the same use of force may or may not be a crime depending upon the context and upon the actors', especially the victims', perceptions of the situation.

A SOCIOLOGICAL DEFINITION

For sociologists, crimes are a part of a more general category called *deviance* (see Sacco, 1992) and involve the violation of *norms*—social rules that tell people what to do and what not to do in various situations. These rules are passed on to children in any society in a process called socialization and may vary both over time and across different societies. For example, in traditional Inuit culture, infanticide and abandoning the elderly to starve to death were not condemned, but were accepted as means to protect a limited food supply (cf. Edgerton, 1985). In the rest of Canada, strict norms would have prohibited such behaviour. While some societies do not permit the eating of pork, for others beef is not allowed; while most groups prohibit cannibalism, some societies have allowed the practice. The point of these examples is that definitions of deviance are specific to time, place, and circumstances.

Deviance also generally involves, besides the violation of a norm, the possibility of punishment. One measure of how strongly a society feels about its various norms is the punishment or sanction it applies to those who violate them. Since norms range from the important and binding (thou shalt not kill) to the less important and optional (a person should not remain seated when being introduced to another), one would expect different types of reaction to those who violate them. But breaking even the most minor norm usually results in some type of reaction, insignificant though it be in terms of punishment. For example, walking down a street has many behavioural requirements that most of us rarely think of as norms. As you approach a stranger coming toward you, you are expected to avert your eyes at a certain point. If you do not, you have violated a norm, and the reaction to the violation may be anything—from no reaction, to the other individual looking at you, to the verbal challenge, "What are you staring at?" These less severely sanctioned norms are called *folkways*; *mores* are those norms whose infractions carry more serious punishments. Violations of mores are seen as more threatening to society—most crimes are violations of mores. But while most criminal laws (for example, those prohibiting sexual assault and theft) are mores, not all mores are laws. For a large part of our society, mores include the permanence of marriage, heterosexuality, and eventually having children. Divorce, homosexuality, and childlessness are not, however, crimes in Canada.

While there have been many attempts to summarize the sociological notion of crime, one of the best is still Gillin's (1945, p. 9) classic statement that crime is

> ... an act that has been shown to be actually harmful to society, or that is *believed* to be socially harmful by a group that has the power to enforce its belief and that places such an act under the ban of positive penalties.

Gillin's definition includes the ideas that the harm involved can be a constructed (believed) harm and that power determines what will be defined as criminal. That last point is the subject of the next section.

CONFLICT VERSUS CONSENSUS DEFINITIONS

Durkheim, one of the founders of sociology, argued that a crime is a violation of a widely held norm or value, an act that attacks what he called the *collective conscience* of a society (1964, p. 79). In this view the criminal law arises out of consensus, out of commonly agreed upon norms and values. Thus, since all or most people would agree that murder, arson, and theft are serious threats to individuals, these acts are defined as crimes. Further, everyone is outraged by such crimes because they weaken and attack the very basis of society.

For conflict theorists, on the other hand, the law is a tool, part of the superstructure of institutions created by the ruling class to serve itself. The law, instead of arising from consensus and providing justice for all, is in reality a weapon of oppression. Conflict theorists disagree among themselves on the role played by the capitalist class in this process, whether it shares its power with other power groups (sometimes called *moral entrepreneurs*) or by and large controls by itself the enactment of laws (cf. Turk, 1993), but they do agree that conflict and power determine the law, not consensus (cf. Young & Matthews, 1992).

Very few sociologists take either of these two extreme positions. Underneath consensus there is always some disagreement or conflict. For example, does euthanasia, abortion, or killing in wartime constitute murder? Inside conflict there is always some consensus and negotiation, for without some co-operation there would be anarchy and lawlessness (cf. Kent, 1990). In addition, there are other more moderate positions on the sources of laws. Some sociologists, for example, have pointed to the role, not just of capitalists, but of the media, especially the publicity given to shocking crimes, and the politics of election years as having important effects on criminal legislation (McGarrell & Castellano, 1991).

This discussion is relevant to the definition of crime, since more conservative consensus and more radical conflict theorists might come to quite different definitions. Whereas conservatives would define acts that violate the *Criminal Code of Canada* as crimes, for conflict theorists, some of the building blocks of capitalism should be defined as crimes: for example, the relentless pursuit of profit, the practice of speculation, and the encouragement of overconsumption. Hence, from a conflict perspective, some of the "real" crimes have not been defined as such; they are not illegal because their victims do not control the law and thus the definition of what constitutes a crime. Thus the concept of ruling-class crimes, legal acts that "should" be illegal, provides us with another potential definition of crime.

In a less dramatic argument, conflict criminologists criticize criminology's traditional focus on the crimes of the powerless and its relative inattention to the crimes of the powerful (e.g., white-collar crime) and ask whether the media deliberately underplay their reporting of corporate crime, directing public fear to muggers rather than polluters. Comack-Antony (1980) presented a chart that compares and contrasts the ways that radical (conflict) criminology and liberal (consensus) criminology define crime (cf. Burtch, 1992). The chart, slightly modified and reproduced in Table 3.1, illustrates well how one's perspective affects definitions of crime. Before examining it, think about one final example of the point we are making, sometimes called the *social construction* of crime. Is terrorism a crime only if it is unsuccessful? In framing your answer, think about the difference between the storming of the Bastille and the reign of terror, or of the Boston Tea Party and Louis Riel.

LEGAL DEFINITION

Most classic criminology texts agree that criminal law and thus the legal definition of crime is marked by four ideals: politicality, specificity, uniformity, and penal sanction. Politicality means that only government, and in Canada this means the federal government, can make criminal laws; specificity, that the laws are quite precise in their wording, telling exactly what is forbidden (*proscribed*) or demanded (*prescribed*); uniformity, that the laws apply equally to all; and penal sanction, that violators are threatened with a penalty and punishment. A crime is then any act or omission in violation of that criminal law. Omission offences include section 129b: "Everyone who (b) omits, without reasonable excuse, to assist a public officer or peace officer in the execution of duty in arresting a person or in preserving the peace, after having reasonable notice of a requirement to do so . . . is guilty of . . ."

Legally, then, a crime is a specific act or omission forbidden to all Canadians by Parliament and punishable for all who break that law. The Law Reform Commission of Canada (1974, pp. 1–4) added the following points. (1) Not all acts against the law are crimes. Civil wrongs, called *torts* (for example, wrongful dismissal from a job), are not crimes. Criminal acts are proceeded against by *prosecution* and may result in *punishment*, while civil actions proceed by suit and may result in *compensation*. (2) Although under the *British North America Act* (now the *Constitution Act*, 1982) only the federal government can make a criminal law, the provinces can create provincial *offences* that, while technically not crimes, are treated like crimes. Examples of such legislation include traffic offences and enforced closing of stores on legal holidays. Crimes are thought of as more serious than such provincial offences because (a) they are seen to involve greater harm to individuals, (b) they are more often a violation of fundamental rules, like mores, and (c) "they are wrongs that any person *as a person* could commit. Offences are more specialized [wrongs] that people commit when playing certain special roles." For example, individuals disobey

Table 3.1 Liberal and Radical Perspectives in Defining Crime

LIBERAL CRIMINOLOGY	RADICAL CRIMINOLOGY
DEFINITION OF CRIME:	
Legalistic approach: Crime as behaviour	Legalistic approach: Crime as a definition of behaviour made by officials of the State
• leads to an examination of the characteristics and life experiences of the criminal actor; general acceptance of the State	• leads to an examination of political authority and questioning of the State
• emphasis on cultural variables as they relate to explanations of crime, e.g., how failure in school can lead to crime	• emphasis on structural variables as they relate to explanations of crime, e.g., how the whole economic system causes crime
ROLE OF CRIMINOLOGISTS:	
• criminologists as "expert advisers" to "enlightened leaders"	• commitment to Praxis, to the *application* by scientists of their results to improve society
• social research used to provide information for the smooth and efficient running of the State system	• social research used to determine the means by which desired changes can be implemented and inequalities between individuals and group diminished
IMAGE OF CRIME AND CRIMINALS:	
• crime as a universal phenomenon caused by the inadequacies of human beings; deterministic (controlled by heredity and environment) image of people	• crime as a universal phenomenon due to the conflictual nature of society; human behaviour seen as intentional and goal-oriented (more free will)
PRESCRIPTIONS FOR CHANGE:	
• adherence to the rehabilitative ideal; emphasis on changing the nature of individual offenders	• stresses political nature of crime; emphasis on changing the structural components of society
• adjustment of individuals to the needs of the system	• adjustment of the system to the needs of individuals

Source: Adapted from Cormack-Anthony, A.E. (1980). Radical Criminology. In Robert A. Silverman & James Teevan (Eds.), *Crime in Canadian Society* (2nd ed.) (pp. 246–247). Toronto: Butterworths.

speed limits as drivers; they generally commit murders or thefts as individuals (1974, p. 3).

Despite the distinctions between crimes and offences, the consequences to individuals prosecuted for committing any of the many acts prohibited by provincial and municipal legislation and named "offences" may be similar (or even worse) than the consequence for committing a crime. For violators, then, there may be only a technical difference between a federal *crime* and a provincial *offence*. Thus, for some purposes, the important components of a legal definition of crime are that it is a violation of a law made by any political body, is deemed to be a state rather than a personal matter, and involves threats of punishment rather than compensation.

In a still more technical and legal sense, for an act or omission to be considered a crime, several other conditions are necessary. First, the act must have been legally forbidden before the act was undertaken; that is, the act or omission must be in violation of an already existing law that forbids or commands the act. This means that an act or omission, no matter how ugly, mean, or distasteful, is not a crime if no law exists against it. The main rationale behind this principle is that it would be unfair to punish persons who, when they acted, did so in good faith thinking they were obeying the law. An *ex post facto* (after the fact) law thus cannot designate as criminal an act legal at the time it was committed, and the general ideal of *nullum crimen sine lege, nulla poena sine lege*, that is, no crime without law, no punishment without law, is still an important principle of Canadian jurisprudence. For example, in 1991, the Canadian Supreme Court refused to allow the extradition of two FLQ members to the United States to stand trial for the 1968 hijacking of a plane to Cuba, because in 1968 hijacking was not an offence in Canada's *Criminal Code*. That offence was created in 1972. An implication of this principle is that laws must be quite specific and not vague, again applying the logic that the public should know exactly what it legally can and cannot do. Vaguely worded laws would make attempts to obey the law problematic, as people would not be sure if their behaviour would or would not result in penal sanction.

Second, there must be an *actus reus*, or act. Merely thinking about or planning to violate the law is generally not a crime, with the exception of the crime of conspiracy (conspiracy to commit offences, *Criminal Code*, section 465). Actually there have never been many conspiracy charges laid in Canada; thus it is fairly safe to say that an *actus reus* is a requirement for a legal definition of crime.

Mens rea, or criminal intent, is a third requirement for a crime. Intentions are not the same as motives (which are the reasons why individuals commit crimes), but instead involve determination and purpose—that individuals intend the consequences of their acts. This means that they know what they are doing, for example, they are not insane, and mean to do what they are doing, for example, the acts were not accidental.

Finally, two additional requirements for the legal definition of a crime are that there should be a causal connection between the *actus reus* and any harm or outcome, and that the *mens rea* and *actus reus* must relate to the same act. These are general rules, ignored in certain circumstances, and sometimes a matter of dispute.

DEFINITIONS MADE BY POLICE, PROSECUTORS, AND JUDGES

After Parliament makes the criminal law, the agents of the Canadian criminal justice system, from the police, to Crown prosecutors, to judges, must enforce it, and all may exercise considerable discretion in deciding whether an act or omission is a crime and, if so, which specific crime it is (cf. Kennedy, 1990). For example, suppose one man attacks another and hurts him, and the victim calls the police. Under a strict and static notion of law enforcement and crime, section 267 (assault with a weapon causing bodily harm) of the *Criminal Code* would be enforced by the police: "Every one who, in committing an assault, . . . causes bodily harm to the complainant, is guilty of an indictable offence and is liable to imprisonment for a term not exceeding ten years. . . ." The Crown would then prosecute the defendant using the available evidence, the accused would be found guilty, and the convicted criminal would be given a sentence of up to ten years.

However, there are alternatives to this scenario: (1) the police arrive and the victim indicates that while he did call them, he is not willing to testify against the offender in court. His motives are private, but could include an unwillingness to see the assaulter, often a friend or a relative, sent to trial or even an unwillingness to take time off from work to appear in court as a complainant. The police in most cases will not pursue the incident because they know that they will have insufficient evidence without the testimony of the victim. According to all public records, then, no crime of assault has taken place. The legal code does not indicate that the police have such discretion, but under these conditions it is in fact normal practice. (2) The victim is abusive to the police, and in anger they decide not to record the crime. In fact, the police take many variables into consideration in deciding to write up less serious cases: how busy they are, the type of complainant, and so on. (3) The police do arrest the alleged attacker and charge him with unlawfully causing bodily harm. The Crown is ready to proceed when the defence attorney suggests a deal. If the charge is reduced to assault, punishable by a summary (less serious) conviction (*Criminal Code*, section 266b), the accused will plead guilty. Otherwise, he will plead not guilty to the original charge and insist on a trial. To speed things through the overburdened criminal justice process, the Crown agrees. (4) The police arrest the individual and the Crown proceeds with the case. The defendant pleads not guilty and is able to convince a judge that he in fact did not intend to injure the victim (recall the discussion of *mens rea*). The judge finds the defendant not guilty. Officially, then, no crime of assault causing bodily harm took place.

The combinations of events in the criminal justice system that can occur to redefine an act, compared to the behaviours that actually happened, are thus numerous. The subject is introduced here to point out that agents of social control must interpret and enforce the law, and the way in which they do so is a part of the process of defining crime (Evans & Himmelfarb, 1996).

CHANGING LAWS CHANGE DEFINITIONS

Many people think of the law as being relatively static. Lawyers know this is not so. The *Criminal Code* is frequently amended by Parliament. Minor changes are routinely made and are based on a "fine-tuning" of legislation, or on recent court interpretations. More important changes take more time and reflect broader social movements. For example, while the public and the mass media both refer to the crime of rape, or forcible sexual intercourse, "rape" is not a crime in Canada. The sections of the Criminal Code dealing with rape were repealed and replaced in a process begun in 1980, partly as a result of the modern feminist movement. These activities are now found under the general heading of assault and are specified as sexual assault (section 271); sexual assault with a weapon, threats to a third party, or causing bodily harm (section 272); or aggravated sexual assault (section 273). The sexual aspect has been downplayed—even penetration is no longer a requirement in the definition of the crime—and the physical harm emphasized. Changing the crime to assault shifted the focus away from the end sought (sexual activity) to the force used, and thus sexual assault joined a slap to the face, a punch to the stomach, or a kick to the groin as assaults to the body. So dramatic was the change in definition that in fact the term "rape" does not even appear in the index to

Carswell's latest *Pocket Criminal Code*. Thus, while many Canadians (including some journalists) call the event previously described a rape, legally, in Canada, no crime of "rape" exists.

On the other hand, in 1994, in the *R. v. Bernard*, case the Supreme Court of Canada made a change with regard to intoxication as a mitigating factor in crimes such as sexual assault. Previously, drunkenness, no matter how severe, could not be used as a defence in such cases. The Supreme Court decided that "offenders" can be acquitted of sexual assault "because they were so drunk they did not know what they were doing." But the Court also said this defence would only be used in the "rarest" of cases—where the perpetrator was so drunk he was acting like an "automaton." Thus the law reflects the priorities of different power groups, sometimes the victims and sometimes the accused.

Changes with larger implications occur even less often. The passage of the *Charter of Rights and Freedoms* (1982) led to many procedural changes (making our criminal justice system more like its U.S. counterpart) and to some substantive changes in the criminal law as well. The Charter's protection of free speech led to nullification of parts of the promotion of racial hatred sections of the *Criminal Code* and to modifications to the obscenity law. The most recent major change, however, was the 1985 introduction of the *Young Offenders Act* (YOA), which replaced the 1970 revision of the *Juvenile Delinquents Act* (originally 1908). The philosophy and effects of the YOA are well documented (cf. Carrington & Moyer, 1994; Corrado, Bala, Linden, & LeBlanc, 1992). It combined a justice model (those accused of delinquency should have the same rights as adults accused of crime, although should be treated somewhat differently) with a crime control model (society must be protected) and largely replaced the welfare model of the JDA (in which the court acted as a wise and judicious parent but often ignored legal safeguards).

Right from the beginning the changes were controversial (cf. Bala, 1997). Some felt that the welfare model philosophy of the old system was superior to the new act. With the introduction of the YOA, youths basically gained the protection of due process (legal safeguards such as right to counsel), but lost some of the informal treatment previously routinely provided under the old act. Some civil libertarians were especially concerned that the new system led to more frequent and longer custody for youths than had occurred under the old act (cf. Clark & Fleming, 1993; Doob & Meen, 1993). At the other end of the spectrum, many, especially among the public, felt that the new age limits provided by the act (12 to 17 instead of the previous lower limit of age 7) allowed younger children (up to age 11) to "get away with murder" (not to mention sexual assault, robbery, and arson). Children 11 years of age or younger were defined as incapable of having the *mens rea* necessary for crime—a view challenged when people heard of the 11-year-old who sexually assaulted a girl and then taunted the police with his underage status. Perhaps the greatest public concern surrounded the maximum sentences for those age 12 to 17 who commit serious violent crimes, such as the 1994 drive-by shooting of a British man in Ottawa. Many felt that the maximum sentences are too short for some violent crimes and that society deserves greater protection from some young offenders, including trying them in adult court.

Public pressure was successful. In February 1995, the House of Commons passed Bill C-37 (An Act to amend the *Young Offenders Act* and the *Criminal Code*), which dealt with some of the concerns of the public. While the Bill did not change the age range of young offenders, it did increase penalties, especially for the most serious crimes. When the *Young Offenders Act* was initially introduced, the maximum penalty for any crime was three years. This was later raised to five years for some crimes, and a juvenile convicted (in youth court) of first-degree murder could be sentenced to a penalty of ten years. It also visited the issue of transfer to adult court. In the case of murder, attempted murder, manslaughter, or aggravated assault by 16- or 17-year-olds, they would henceforth be dealt with by ordinary (i.e., adult) court unless they could make a successful application to have the case heard in youth court. Hence, the onus was on the teenagers to prove that they should have the privilege of being heard in youth court.

The changes did not go far enough for many, so as this is being written Parliament is considering further changes. To convince a fearful public that they are not just tinkering, a new name has been suggested, the *Youth Criminal Justice Act*. Again, those under age 12 are spared, despite strong pressure to lower the minimum age to 10, but 14- and 15-year-olds convicted of the most serious crimes like murder, aggravated sexual assault, and so on will join 16- and 17-year-olds in being vulnerable to longer sentences. In fact all repeat violent offenders aged 14 to 17 will also be punishable by longer sentences and having their names published upon conviction. These changes reflect that protecting society is the main goal of the criminal law but also that prevention and rehabilitation, including community-based sentences, are important aspects too.

CONCLUSIONS

In summary, there are several definitions of crime from which to choose: (1) acts that violate norms; (2) acts that violate *legal* norms; (3) acts that the participants define as violations of *legal* norms; (4) acts that agents of the Canadian criminal justice system interpret as violations of legal norms; (5) acts for which *mens rea* and *actus reus* have been demonstrated; and (6) acts that from a conflict perspective are the "real" crimes. Each definition may be appropriate under different circumstances. Also remember that whichever definition is chosen, the actual acts defined as criminal are not universal. They are specific to a given time and society.

Chapter 4

MEDIA CONSTRUCTIONS OF CRIME

Vincent Sacco

INTRODUCTION

Crime, like an economic recession, a lack of affordable housing, or inadequate health care, is experienced as both a private trouble and a public issue. Quite obviously, for victims, a criminal offense and the resulting loss or injury present problems of a highly personal nature. For victims and non-victims alike, however, the "plague of drugs," the "epidemic of random violence," and other aspects of the crime problems are matters for intense public discussion and political debate.

While the distinction between private troubles and public issues is an important one, these dimensions are not independent. Citizens' personal troubles with crime provide the building blocks out of which public issues are constructed. On the other hand, the warnings of danger implicit in public pronouncements about the seriousness and pervasiveness of crime problems may be a source of private trouble if they increase the fear of crime among those who have routine exposure to such pronouncements.

Central to the interplay between individuals' private troubles with crime and the social issue of crime are the mass media. The news media, in particular, provide an important forum in which private troubles are selectively gathered up, invested with a broader meaning, and made available for public consumption. The dynamic character of these processes and the consequences that they have for public understanding of crime and its solution invite close scrutiny.

FROM PRIVATE TROUBLE . . .

Numerous studies of media content have documented the fact that crime reports are a durable news commodity. While news about crime figures prominently in all types of media, important differences exist between print and electronic media, between more elite and more popular media, and among media markets. Because of this variability, estimates of the proportion of total news that is devoted to crime coverage range from 5 to 25 percent (Surette, 1992:62).

News about crime is most frequently news about the occurrence or processing of private trouble in the form of specific criminal events. Analyses of media content, however, demonstrate that the news provides a map of the world of criminal events that differs in many ways from the one provided by official crime statistics. Variations in the volume of news about crime seem to bear little relationship to variations in the actual volume of crime between places or over time (Skogan and Maxfield, 1981). Whereas crime statistics indicate that most crime is nonviolent, media reports suggest, in the aggregate, that the opposite is true (Schlesinger et al., 1991). While crime news tends to provide only sparse details about victims and offenders, what is provided is frequently at odds with the official picture. Both offenders and victims, for instances, appear less youthful in media reports than they do in statistical records (Gordon and Riger, 1989:70).

In addition, news content does not reflect, and frequently even reverses, the relationship that, according to much social scientific evidence, exists between minority group membership and criminal offending (Lotz, 1991:114), with minorities under-represented in the media compared to official data. With respect to gender, however, both crime statistics and crime news portray offending as predominantly a male activity (Bortner, 1984). Finally, news reports also distort the relationship between crime and legal control. In the news, the police appear to be more effective in apprehending offenders than police data would suggest they are (Marsh, 1991).

The images of crime, the criminal, and the victim that do appear with patterned regularity in print and broadcast news emerge quite logically from the organizational processes of news productions. For example, news stories are most useful to news organizations when they are gathered easily from credible sources; for this reason, policing agencies have become the principal suppliers of these stories (Ericson, 1989). In addition, the public view of the police as apolitical crime experts gives police-generated crime authority and objectivity. The major exception of course is corporate crime, which is covered with greater difficulty. Generally, corporate crimes are more complex and more difficult to personalize, and well-established source-reporter relationships do not exist for corporate crime as they do for personal crimes.

Ease of access to authoritative news is not the only advantage that police-generated crime stories offer, since such stories are consistent with several other professional values that structure the news production process. Much of what we call news consists of reports of specific incidents that have occurred since the publication of the previous day's newspaper or the airing of the previous night's newscast. As discrete incidents that occur at particular times and places, individual crimes conform closely to this requirement of periodicity.

Stories about individual crimes—with their characteristic portrayals of villains and victims—also have dramatic value. The dramatic potential is heightened when the victim or offender is a celebrity, when the incident is of a very serious nature, or when the circumstances of the offense are atypical. In addition, the routine crime story is a rather uncomplicated matter, and it is unnecessary for news workers to assume that readers or viewers require an extensive background in order to appreciate the story. The lack of factual complexity associated with the ordinary individual crime story generally means that it can be easily written and edited by news workers whose professional activities are consistently regulated by rigid deadlines.

The elastic character of the crime news supply offers a further advantage. On any given day, particularly in large metropolitan areas, there is an almost limitless supply of crimes that could be the object of media attention. However, from day to day, or from week to week, the demand of the news agency for crime news may vary due to other events that are seen to demand coverage. Depending on the size of the news hole, crime coverage may be expanded or contracted in compensatory fashion. A study by Sherizen (1978:221) of crime news in Chicago newspapers found, for instance, that crime reports were often located on the obituary pages so that layout difficulties resulting from the inability to plan these pages could be overcome through the use of crime news filler.

Over the last several years, a number of changes in local and national media environments have altered the nature and extent of crime coverage. The growth of cable stations, for instance, has increased the carrying capacity for news generally and for crime news specifically. More stories can be covered, and those that are judged to be particularly newsworthy can be covered in greater detail. The live television coverage of court proceedings—as in the case of the Menendez brothers, Lorena Bobbit, or O.J. Simpson—has become commonplace. The increasing sophistication of news gathering, surveillance, and home video technologies has meant that it is no longer unusual to capture thefts, robberies, or even homicides on tape. One consequence of the diffusion of these technologies has been to raise to national prominence stories that would have been a purely local affair in an earlier period. They now attract much wider attention because a videotape of the incident is available for broadcast.

The last two decades have also witnessed a redefinition of what can be considered an appropriate subject for news reporting. Changes in mores relating to public discussion of sex and violence have allowed respectable media outlets to report crimes that would have previously been seen as taboo and to do so at a level of detail that would once have been considered lurid. At the same time, the politicization of crimes such as sexual assault and domestic violence has broadened the range of crime stories that, it can be argued, legitimately require coverage (Soothill and Walby, 1991:6).

Programmatic developments in commercial broadcast media have magnified the impact of these changes. The proliferation of news magazines, daytime talk shows, docudramas, and various other forms of infotainment has ushered in a programming cycle that is heavily dependent on crime news and victim accounts. The frequent reliance of many of these programs on dramatic reenactments of real events and their mixing of factual reports with rumor and speculation blur the basic distinctions that analysts of crime content have traditionally drawn between news and entertainment media (Newman, 1990).

... *TO PUBLIC ISSUES*

Public issues grow up around private troubles when the experiences of individuals are understood as exemplifying a larger social problem, and the news media play a vital role in the construction of such problems (Best, 1989a; Gusfield, 1989; Schneider, 1985). Most notably, professional judgments of newsworthiness and the selective use of news sources allow some groups, rather than others, the opportunity to express a view about what is and what is not a problem, and how any such problem should be managed. By implication, the relationships that link the police to news agencies serve law enforcement as well as media interests. The police role as the dominant gatekeeper means that crime news is often police news and that the advancement of a police perspective on crime and its solution is facilitated (Ericson, 1989). It has been argued that this results in the adoption of an uncritical posture with respect to the police view of crime and the measures necessary to control it (Ericson, 1991). More generally, the frame of reference offered by a government bureaucracy or other recognized authority with respect to crime problems may only infrequently be called into question and, as a consequence, competing perspectives may become marginalized.

This tendency may be no less true of in-depth issue coverage than of routine news reporting. Brownstein (1991) maintains that during the 1980s, there was relatively little reporting that took issue with the official version of the drug problem constructed by government experts. In a similar way, Jenkins

(1994:212–213) has noted how experts of the Federal Bureau of Investigation were able to present themselves as the authorities on the subject of serial murder and how they made themselves available to journalists who reciprocated with favorable coverage of the agency.

It would be incorrect, however, to suggest that news media are merely the passive conveyors of the claims about problems offered up by government bureaucracies, political candidates, or other self-interested groups, since any such claims must be transformed to meet the requirements of the medium in question. In an analysis of television network news coverage of threats to children, Best argued that "inevitably, network news stories distort the problems they explore" in large part because news conventions impose severe constraints on how stories are covered (1989b:277).

Stories must be told in a few minutes, frequently by reporters who may have little more than a surface familiarity with the complexities of the problem at hand. Moreover, the topic must be viewed as serious enough and as visual enough to be chosen over competing issues. Best found, in the case of child victimization, that the stories used frightening and dramatic examples to typify the problem, and that they emphasized the existence of a consensus among knowledgeable experts regarding its scope and seriousness. In other instances, news media may more actively engage in problem construction. Investigative reporting, or the coverage of an event judged to be especially newsworthy, may contribute to the establishment of a media agenda that finds expression in the reporting of further stories or in more detailed features. A study by Protess and his colleagues (1985) revealed how one Chicago newspaper sets its own media agenda after an extensive investigative series on rape. The researchers found that, while the series did not appear to have substantial impact on the perceptions of policymakers or the general public, there were significant changes in the extent and depth of rape coverage after the series ended, even though police reports of rape were unchanged. In a related way, during the summer of 1994, the O.J. Simpson case provided an opportunity for sidebar stories relating to the prevalence and causes of domestic violence, the inadequacy of justice system responses, and pending federal and state legislation. Such coverage contextualized the original incident in a way that helped construct the social issue of violence against women at the same time that it legitimated continuing, detailed attention to the original story.

The Content of Crime Problems

Media constructions of crime problems address both the frequency and the substance of private trouble with crime. Rhetoric regarding both of these dimensions serves to impress on readers and viewers the gravity of particular crime problems and the need to confront them in particular ways.

Large numbers of problems provide convincing evidence that problems exist. This is perhaps most evident in the case of crime waves, when it is argued that crime is becoming more frequent. A study by Gorelick, for instance, of an anti-crime campaign sponsored by a New York daily newspaper found that crime in the city was frequently described as a "mushrooming cloud," a "floodtide," a "spreading cancer," or in similar terms (1989:429). Sometimes these claims about the numbers of people affected have greater specificity in that some particular segment of the population is claimed to be experiencing rapidly increasing risks of offending or victimization (Cook and Skogan, 1990).

Yet, with respect to many crime waves, it is the belief that crime is increasing, rather than crime itself, that is really on the rise (Baker et al., 1983). A recent example of a journalistic construction of rapidly rising crime is provided by Orcutt and Turner (1993). Their analysis focused on the way in which graphic artists in the national print media transformed survey data, which showed modest yearly changes in drug use, into evidence of a "coke plague." While the numbers were real, their graphical presentation in the weekly periodical under study was misleading. The dynamics of competitive journalism created a media feeding frenzy that found news workers "snatching at shocking numbers" and "smothering reports of stable or decreasing use under more ominous headlines" (1993:203).

Claims about statistical frequency are not restricted to reports about how the numbers are increasing, however. With respect to the problem of violence against women, for instance, it is argued that the numbers have always been very high but that the failure to police such incidents, the stigma associated with victimization, and an institutional unwillingness to believe the accounts of victims have resulted in statistical counts that dramatically underestimate the problem. Thus, whether or not the numbers are going up is defined as less salient than the observation that they have always been higher than we have thought.

According to Gilbert (1994), outrageous claims about the prevalence of problems sometimes make their way into news reports in part because of journalists' general inability to evaluate the data supplied to them. Too often, they lack the technical sophistication to critically assess claims about the frequency of crime or victimization in an independent fashion. Instead, they collect and validate information by talking to experts who are expected to offer informed opinions. However, in the case of emergent problems, it is often the problem advocate, interested in advancing a particular point of view, who may be among the first to collect and publicize empirical evidence. As a result, the estimates yielded by advocacy research may be the only ones available at the earliest stages of problem development. Jenkins has argued that the emergence of serial murder as a social issue in the early 1980s was spurred by "epidemic estimates" that placed the number of serial murder victims at between 20 and 25 percent of American homicides (1994:22). While such numbers continue to circulate through popular and journalistic accounts, more reasoned analysis suggests that the number of serial murder victims is closer to 2 percent of American homicides.

The emergence of crime problems is related not only to claims about the frequency of criminal events but also to claims about their character. Exactly what types of events such incidents are thought to be and who is thought to be typically involved in them matter as much as does the rate at which they are thought to occur.

Any particular social problem can be framed in many ways, and these various frames imply different causal attributions and prospective solutions (Gusfield, 1989; Schneider, 1985). Because they are able to legitimate some views and to marginalize others, the news media are an important part of this framing process. Depending on the sources accessed or the type of coverage, rape can be framed as a sex crime or as a crime of violence; the "drug problem" as a product of pushers who hook their victims or as an example of the overreach of criminal law; and violence on the part of youths as a condition necessitating either swift punishment or comprehensive community development.

In a related way, the social distributional character of victimization is frequently ignored by news coverage that stresses the random character of victimization. While the best social science literature indicates that the risks of crime, like the risks of other misfortunes, are not equally shared, media images often convey a different message. According to Brownstein (1991:95), for instance, much of the coverage of the drug issue in New York City between 1986 and 1990 emphasized the random character of drug violence even though police statistics indicated that the risks of such violence were extremely low. Themes relating to randomness serve the interests of both news workers and others who seek to frame crime problems. News stories about random crimes have great dramatic value, as the media frenzies that surround serial murders illustrate. Moreover, the advocates to whom news workers have access during the early stages of problem development often stress the random nature of a particular form of victimization, since problems must be seen as more urgent when everyone is threatened.

While much routine crime reporting can be understood as maintaining established crime problem frames, new problems are always being discovered as old problem paradigms expand or as novel elements come together with established news themes. The discovery of new problems provides a journalistic opportunity to tell a story that has not been told before, but such stories are told most effectively when they resonate with existing cultural themes. In the 1970s, the problem of crime against the elderly brought together in one package an already familiar concern about crime in the streets and victims' rights with an emerging concern about the aging population (Cook and Skogan, 1990). The problem of satanic crime, which received extensive media coverage in the 1980s, combined familiar news themes relating to religious cults, child abuse, and juvenile crime (Crouch and Damphousse, 1992; Jenkins and Maier-Katkin, 1992). Media attention to date rape and stalking extends earlier news themes relating to violence against women.

The transition from private troubles to public issues is not always a linear process, since media interest in particular crime problems can vary in intensity or decline over time. The 1987 shootings on California freeways never became a well-established problem, despite a strong start (Best, 1991). In the case of crimes against the elderly, Cook and Skogan (1990) observe that, while the issue achieved a prominent position on media and other agendas during the early 1970s, by the decade's end, it has declined precipitously. On the other hand, Fishman (1981) has argued that as long as police departments are the routine sources of crime news, the media will reinforce a climate of opinion that keeps the attention of the police focused on "crime in the streets." He concludes that, while social problems may come and go, "law-and-order news is here to stay" (1981:389).

. . . AND BACK AGAIN?

There can be little doubt that media consumers have broad and regular exposure to crime news (Garofalo, 1981). What are the consequences of this exposure? One potential consequence that has generated considerable interest relates to the deleterious effects that media attention to crime problems may have on audience members' fear of victimization. On the surface, arguments about such effects seem plausible. Public fear of crime is pervasive, and it outstrips measured levels of victimization. By implication, public anxieties would appear to be rooted in vicarious rather than direct experiences, and since messages about crime are so prevalent in the media, it seems reasonable to conclude that much public fear originates in media coverage of crime problems. At issue is whether experience with media treatments of crime as a public issue contributes to fear as a personal trouble. There is a large body of empirical evidence that bears on the relationship between audience exposure to mass media and fear of crime. In the aggregate, however, the findings are equivocal regarding the strength of such a relationship or even whether such a relationship exists (Carlson, 1985; Sacco, 1982; Sparks, 1992).

Some of the inconsistency in this respect is methodological in nature. Considerable variation exists regarding the ways in which crime news, crime news exposure, and fear of crime have been operationalized in the research literature (Sparks and Ogles, 1990). In addition, since people not only read or watch crime news but also talk about it with friends and neighbors, measured variations in media exposure are not necessarily indicative of exposure to crime news (Doob, 1982). Nor is it reasonable to assume for research purposes that people are always able to keep clear and report to researchers what is learned in which information channel (Gordon and Riger, 1989). Even when such methodological limitations are taken into account, however, the research indicates that the effects of media exposure on fear of crime are less significant than any naïve hypothesis would suggest.

Several factors explain this apparent paradox. To begin with, it would be inappropriate to assume that audience members respond passively to the warnings of danger issued by omnipotent news media. Instead, as Williams and Dickinson note, news consumers are actively involved in investing the news with meaning (1993:34). Audience members bring to the reading and viewing experience their own predispositions, which influence what crime news means for them. These predispositions may include personal experiences with crime or violence (Schlesinger et al., 1992:165), perceptions of the credibility of news media (O'Keefe, 1984), or the extent of prior concern about personal safety (Sacco, 1982). In the context of cross-sectional research, these predispositions suggest the possibility that the correlation between media usage and fear of crime may be more indicative of selective exposure than of media influence (Williams and Dickinson, 1993:51; Zillmann and Wakshlag, 1987).

While people avidly read and watch crime news, it is unclear that in so doing they extract lessons relating to their own safety. Such lessons, it appears, are more effectively learned in other contexts. The relevant research indicates that the news about crime that travels through interpersonal channels may be more likely to induce fear than is the news that travels through mass channels (Skogan and Maxfield, 1981; Tyler, 1984). To learn about crime by talking to one's neighbours is to learn about victims whose experiences cannot be easily dismissed because they are nameless or faceless or live somewhere else.

By contrast, the typical media crime story is stripped of much of its emotional character and is likely to involve victims about whom the viewer or reader has no personal knowledge. In addition, the average news story may provide readers and viewers with so little information about the victim, the setting in which the crime occurred, or other circumstances of commission that it may be irrelevant to any assessment of personal victimization risks (Gordon and Riger, 1989:75; Tyler, 1984:34). Most crime news is non-local and therefore far removed from judgments that must be made regarding the safety of the immediate environment. Not surprisingly, there is research that suggests that increased fear is, in fact, related to crime news exposure when local random violent crimes are reported in prominent fashion (Heath, 1984; Liska and Baccaglini, 1990). On the other hand, coverage of non-local violence may decrease fear by allowing the audience to feel safer by comparison. Taken together, these findings are consistent with a more general body of research that indicates that people may be less dependent on news media when they seek information about matters close to home (Palmgreen and Clarke, 1977).

Overall, it would appear that as crime news relates to matter of personal safety, consumers appear to exercise a healthy dose of skepticism (Katz, 1987:60). As Dennis Howitt observes, newspaper readers do not necessarily think that crime rates are going up just because the number of column inches devoted to crime increases (1982:125–126). They are more likely to put what is learned from the media in the context of what they learn from other sources, and they may be well aware when media are behaving in a highly sensationalist manner (Williams and Dickinson, 1993).

CONCLUSION

If the news business is concerned with the production of crime problems, then the private troubles of criminal offenders and crime victims are the raw materials. These troubles are not simply reported on, however, since they are fundamentally transformed by the news-gathering process. Screened through a law enforcement filter, contextualized by advocacy claims and culturally resonant news themes, and shaped and molded by the conventions and requirements of commercial media, these private troubles become public issues.

While news media coverage of crime may not have a powerful influence on the concern for personal safety, this should not obscure other, perhaps more significant effects.

Such effects are not narrowly attitudinal or behavioural but are broadly ideological. Some critics argue that the police perspective implicit in so much crime news reporting dramatically restricts the parameters of discussion and debate about the problem of crime. As a consequence, the causes of offending are individualized and the relationships that link crime to broader social forces are left largely unexplored (Gorelick, 1989; Humphries, 1981).

Correspondingly, traditional law-and-order responses are reaffirmed as the most efficient way to manage crime problems. A study of media coverage of attacks against women in Toronto found that explanations of the phenomenon tended to focus attention on the ways in which victims placed themselves in conditions of risk, on offender pathology, and on the need for a more coercive criminal justice response (Voumvakis and Ericson, 1984). The authors note that while these terms of reference were not unreasonable, the attention they received left little room for alternative interpretations of the problem, particularly those interpretations that link the victimization of women to structures of gender inequality.

When crime problems are successfully constructed, a consensus emerges regarding what kinds of public issues private troubles represent (Gusfield, 1989:434–436). Yet the development of such consensus—regarding what the problems are, who is responsible for them, and how they should be resolved—should not be understood in conspiratorial terms. While both news workers and their sources are interested in offering a convincing and credible construction of reality for many in the media, the construction of these problems is not a matter of activism but just another day at the office (Hilgartner and Bosk, 1988).

Chapter 5

PLEASURES OF THE FUR

George Gurley

INTRODUCTION

A moose is loitering outside a hotel in the Chicago suburb of Arlington Heights. The moose—actually a man in a full-body moose costume—is here for a convention . . . and so is the porcupine a few feet away, as well as the many foxes and wolves. Even the people in regular clothes have a little something (ferret hand puppet, rabbit ears) to set them apart from the ordinary hotel guests. One man in jeans and a button-down shirt gets up from a couch in the lobby and walks over to the elevator, revealing a fluffy tail dragging behind him. The elevator doors open. Inside, a fellow is kissing a man with antlers on his head. The other hotel guests look stunned.

"We're a group of people who like things having to do with animals and cartoons," a man in a tiger suit tells a woman. "We're furries."

"So cute," the woman says.

Welcome to the Midwest FurFest.

Here, a number of "furries"—people whose interest in animal characters goes further than an appreciation of *The Lion King*—are gathering together.

At 7:30 p.m., near the front desk, three men known as Pack Rat, Rob Fox, and Zen Wolph are scratching one another's backs—grooming one another, like macaques in a zoo. "Skritching," they call it. I am tempted to turn around and run. Instead I find myself talking with Keith Dickinson, a self-described "computer geek." Not long ago, this man, a 37-year-old from Kansas City, Kansas, was so depressed he could barely bring himself to go to the grocery store. And then it hit him. He started to believe that, somewhere deep down, he was actually . . . a polar bear.

"In normal society," Dickinson says, "two people who hardly know each other do not walk up and scratch each other's backs. But when you're one of the furs, it's one big extended family."

Next to him is his skinny, long-haired, fedora-wearing sidekick, a 23-year-old art student named Ian Johnson (nametag: R.C. RABBITSFOOT). Last year, Johnson, who has brought the ashes of his dead cat to the FurFest, persuaded Dickinson to attend another furry convention in Memphis, and that's what did it.

"It's a new way of looking at the world," Dickinson says. "It's like looking at it with baby eyes, or cub eyes."

"You regress into a child when you come to a convention," Johnson says, "because it's that kind of camaraderie, or childishness."

RIDING WITH OSTRICH

It's night. Ostrich has to run an errand. We get into his Chevrolet Metro and speed away from the Sheraton, toward the nearest mall. The headlights illuminate the road ahead.

Ostrich, whose real name is Marshall Woods, is a compact guy in a denim jacket and blue jeans. He's 39-years-old and works as a network administrator at a rubber company in Akron.

"When I was very, very young, I knew I wanted to be some type of animal," he says. "I didn't necessarily want to *be* the animal, but I wanted to have the animal shape, as far back as I can remember. It's that way for a lot of people."

He did normal things, like playing in the high-school marching band . . . but he couldn't stop thinking about cartoon animals. Throughout his teenage and college years, he hid his furriness, thinking it was a "babyish thing."

"What the hell," he says. "Now I'm old and I'm warped, everybody knows it, so I don't bother hiding anything anymore!"

It wasn't until 1994 that he came upon others who shared his interest. He was a chemist at the time, collecting dinosaur stuff on the side. One day he went to a comic-book shop and discovered *Genus*, a furry comic-book series with sexy characters. "And I looked at it and I was like, Whoa! This looks pretty much exactly what I'd like to read—I gotta have one of these," he recalls.

Now he writes a newsletter for Ohio Furs, an organization of furries with 87 members.

He got his name after taking some ballet classes and not being very good at it. "I was sincere but not impressive," he says. "I guess I was technically competent, but not very much fun to watch. And I was compared to the ostrich ballerinas in *Fantasia*. They are trying very hard, but they are not quite there."

In 1998, Ostrich put up a Web site where you can see his animal drawings, his animal-themed poems, and short stories (one of which was published in *Pawprints*, a magazine for furries), his instructions on how to build a fursuit, and pictures of himself engaged in animal-centered activities. Like the time he made a solo trip to Sea World. "There's something just inherently cheerful about ducks," reads the text next to one picture on his Web site. "They seem almost ridiculously optimistic about the world and their place in it." Next to a photo of sea lions, the caption reads: "Do they have any idea how cute they look when they beg? Who could refuse them?"

For a while, he concedes, he was a "plushie," which is the word for a person who has a strong—usually erotic—attachment to stuffed animals. He even wrote a plushie newspaper for a while, but gave it up. "It doesn't really interest me now," he says. "I just like to have the stuffed animals around. I would still say I'm a plushophile—I'm just not that interested in it that much sexually. In a casual way, but not really seriously."

He goes into a store and purchases materials for a puppet-making workshop he is scheduled to lead the next day. Back behind the wheel, Ostrich says, "I don't like the human form. I never really have. It does not please me. The body, just the flesh, the general design, I just don't like."

He says he'd prefer to be a lemur or a rabbit, and still be intelligent and keep the opposable thumbs. He thinks the technology will be available relatively soon to help him achieve this dream. Talking about all this almost causes Ostrich to miss his exit.

"I. Need. To. Drive. More. Talk. Less."

Eventually, we pull back into a parking space back at the Sheraton.

"A lot of people here are the very same way. We don't have a lot of deep real-life contact. It's superficial. I kind of skate through society. I mean, you see a lot of people—I see them at work—who have no idea what they're doing, or why, and they sit there and bang along from one hour to the next. As fucked up as I am, I at least know how I feel and what I want to do, and I have the good fortune to have a number of friends who feel the same way."

Ostrich leads me up to his suite.

It's filled with stuffed animals.

He sits on the chair and says there is a low percentage of women in the fandom, and a preponderance of gay men—or seemingly gay. "I am not really sure myself that as many of them are gay as they think they are. It's just more, you like this person because of who they are rather than for their body. And we find as the number of women increases, the number of people who thought they were gay but decided otherwise increases, too. I know a couple of people who thought they were gay until they met a furry girl."

He gets up.

"In some ways we're very closed off—sort of a subculture. I have trouble looking at it objectively, because it seems so natural. It's how I was my whole life, and all of a sudden, I'm like, Wow, here's a whole bunch of other people like this! Having not come to it from the outside, I have difficulty saying what it actually is, I'm too deeply into it."

SOME FURRY THEORY

There are many kinds of furries, but they all seem to have a few things in common. Something happened to them after a youthful encounter with Bugs Bunny or Scooby Doo or the mascot at the pep rally. They took refuge in cartoons or science fiction. After being bombarded by tigers telling them what cereal to eat, camels smoking cigarettes, cars named after animals, airplanes with eyes and smiles, shirts with alligators, they decided their fellow human beings were not nearly so interesting as those animal characters.

But it wasn't so liberating, having these intense feelings, when you thought you were the only person on earth who had them. The second big relevation for most furries came when they got on the Internet. Not only were there others like them, they learned, but they were organized! They started having conventions in the early 1990s. Now, such gatherings as the Further Confusion convention in San Jose, California, and Anthrocon in Philadelphia, attract more than 1,000 furry hobbyists apiece. (The Midwest FurFest is a smaller "con," with about 400 attending.) There are other conventions, too—even summer camps.

The furry group has its own customs and language. "Yiff" means sex, "yiffy" means horny or sexual, and "yiffing" means mating. "Fur pile" denotes a bunch of furries lying on top of one another, affectionately, while skritching. "Spooge" is semen—a possible outcome of a fur pile. A "furvert" is anyone who is sexually attracted to mascots and such.

Many furries have jobs related to science and computers. They role-play on a Web site called "FurryMUCK," a chatroom kingdom where users pretend they're red-tailed hawks, foxes, and polar bears.

A high number of furries are bearded and wear glasses. Many resemble the animal they identify with (especially wolves and foxes, the most popular "totems"). Some have googly, glazed, innocent eyes. A few are crazy-eyed.

A MOMENT WITH MIKE THE COYOTE

Down in the lobby, a coyote is sitting on a couch. His nametag reads SHAGGY, but his real name is Mike. Not all the conventioneers want people to know their full names, lest their bosses or parents find out what they're up to on the weekends. Mike the Coyote says he is a security guard in Indiana and has been going to furry conventions since 1992. The Midwest FurFest, he says, is "very mellow so far, rather surprisingly so, in fact. I hope it stays this way. We don't need the weirdies to fall out of the woodwork. For me, walking around a con with a tail hanging out my butt just seems weird. Just not my particular bag."

But Mike the Coyote has something for anyone who finds furriness strange: "Just go look at the Packers and Vikings fans at the game. You think *we're* weird? Look at the 350-pound guy that's got his body split in colors half and half, he's wearing shorts and paint and nothing else, and he's screaming, 'Vikings!' Oh my God! Anybody involved in beauty pageants? Children's beauty pageants, where they dress the little girls like they're 25-year-old prostitutes—which is just *sick*."

"THERE'S SOMETHING ABOUT RACCOONS"

One man who didn't make it to the Midwest FurFest is Ostrich's friend Fox Wolfie Galen, the King of the Plushies.

"He's O.K.," says Jack Below, a 28-year-old on-line worker at Southwestern Bell, who doubles as Spiked Punch, a wolf with a mallet. But, Below adds, Fox Wolfie Galen is "one of the people I really worry about. I really don't have anything against him: I just think if people really knew the full story on him, it would kind of set a bad image."

Two months prior to the FurFest, I visited Fox Wolfie Galen, whose real name is Kenneth, at his house in a small Pennsylvania city, where he lives with a roommate and more than a thousand stuffed animals. He was staring at his computer screen, monitoring an on-line auction. He put in a bid of $40.01 for a 40-inch skunk stuffed animal, then lay down on his mattress on the floor.

"I pretty much can't afford to pay more than a dollar an inch for plush," he said, in a voice like that of Bill Murray's gopher-chasing groundskeeper character in *Caddyshack*. "I like skunks. I mostly collect bunnies, foxes, bears, ferrets, otters, sometimes dinosaurs."

Fox Wolfie Galen, aged 39, was wearing a Mickey Mouse sweatshirt, green jeans, and thick, red-tinted glasses. (He said his eyesight is so bad that he receives $500 a month from the government: he has no job: rent is $200 a month.) Stuffed animals surrounded him and were stacked up to the ceiling against the wall by his bed. A big Meeko, the raccoon character from *Pocahontas*, in a Cub Scout uniform was looking at me with a crazed expression.

"That's what I wouldn't mind being in real life." Fox Wolfie Galen said of the Meeko, which may be the most popular stuffed animal among the plushophiles. Between this one's legs was a little opening, a tear in the seam.

Fox Wolfie Galen had never traveled much beyond his hometown until four years ago, when he went to a furry convention in California with another plushophile he had met on-line. Since then he had made it to conventions in Toronto, Chicago, and Albany, New York.

Plushophilia began for him when he was around seven years old, even though he didn't own any stuffed animals. "From the time I was born until through high school, I probably touched three or four 'plushes'," he said, using the plushophile's term for stuffed animal. "It wasn't like I couldn't get them. I was interested: I just didn't make the connection. I knew I liked them, because I'd seen them on TV, or if I visited somebody else's house and they had plush. Or if somebody came along in a furry-animal costume, like a high-school mascot, I'd always sit close to where I'd think they'd be coming out."

After pep rallies he would find himself so aroused that he would have to walk through the school's hallways with a book bag held in front of him. Growing up, he never fantasized about women. "If a mascot walked into a room surrounded by naked women, I'd be thinking about the mascot," he said.

"I'm not like a person who hasn't had a human mate before," he said. "I actually have been with four different women in my life, and I can honestly say that none of them have come close to the tactile physical pleasure. Women don't feel like that. Human skin might feel good, it's smooth and everything, but it just doesn't feel the same way."

For a long time he thought he was the only plushophile on the planet. "'Plushie' didn't exist in my vocabulary," he said. Then, in 1994, he discovered a Web site that captured his interest. There were some frequently asked questions such as "Why do you have sex with stuffed animals?" "Do you actually *go* on your stuffed animals?" and "How do you clean your stuffed animals?"

"I'm reading this and I was like, Oh my gosh, somebody else does this? I almost fell over."

He started his own Web site. There, you can see sexually explicit photos from furry conventions, doctored cartoon stills, and his short stories.

Fox Wolfie Galen said he does have intercourse with his stuffed animals but more often rubs himself externally on the fur. He doesn't believe the stuffed raccoon is alive . . . but he can dream, can't he?

"I'll look at his eyes, and I'm thinking, Oh, it's alive." he said. "There are people who do kinkier things than me with their plush. Some people put openings in all their plush. Some people even pray to their plushies. There's mutilators. That disturbs me, because they're turned on by destruction of something and I see no reason for it."

It was getting late. He was still lying on his mattress, now discussing "crush" videos—a recently outlawed form of pornography made for men who like to watch animals being crushed by women.

"I consider that immoral," he said. "You heard of Jeffrey Dahmer? He started out doing that stuff. If you could do it to an animal, you could do it to a human."

He said he wished it were possible to be part man and part beast. But if such a thing were to come about—the advent of hybrid species—he wouldn't want to be alone.

"If I was the only one, they'd find out. They'd put me in a lab and dissect me. You know, it wouldn't be fun. What I'd want is a whole new world where you had, say, Canada was all raccoons, and the United States was all foxes, and Mexico's all badgers, and every country is a different race of animals, and they're all friendly with each other and there's no war."

In an ideal world, Fox Wolfie Galen would be a ferret, a rat, a skunk, a fox, or a raccoon. "There's something about raccoons. They actually have fingers, opposable thumbs, and everything. I could imagine a raccoon being half a human and walking on two feet. It would kind of be like a living Disney cartoon."

But the government would screw it up, he figured.

"They'd probably make some hybrid human resistant to attack, something reptilian, scaly, and hard to kill. So you're probably going to have a whole bunch of alligator men or turtle-shelled men running around. They'll be intelligent, but they'll be slaves to whatever the government wants them to do, like go and kill people. I would only volunteer if we were to be considered at least remotely equal. I'd be a raccoon, most likely."

I called a taxi and went to the bathroom. When I came back to his lair, Fox Wolfie Galen was in a full-body tiger suit. He was gesturing to a rip in the costume, between his legs.

The taxi arrived.

Outside his house, Fox Wolfie Galen was waving good-bye to me—with a fox hand puppet.

CALLING DR. PERVERT

Sex researcher Katherine Gates has written about Fox Wolfie Galen, among others, in her book *Deviant Desires: Incredibly Strange Sex* (Juno Books, 2000). Now she was sitting down in the living room of her Brooklyn Heights apartment, where she lives with her husband. In the book, Fox Wolfie Galen called sex with stuffed animals a "sacramental act."

"How can you not laugh?" Gates said. "I mean, because it's absurd. Even ordinary sex is pretty damn absurd when you think about it. It's pretty silly, it's pretty awkward, and so I don't think it would be fair to point the finger entirely at these people—but, no, it's funny. And the people who do it for the most part have a great sense of humor about it. Galen is a good example."

Gates, who is 36-years-old, said some plushophiles may not be "relationship-suitable": "In some cases—and this might be cruel to say—but we may be wired for the zeta male, the lowest male, to turn to other pursuits besides the pursuit of another human being. These people need a way of having intimacy and pleasure, too."

Gates's book features chapters on fat admiration, pony play, balloon fetishists, and, on the dark side, the crush freaks. Her Web site, www.deviantdesires.com, has a forum in which different fetishists can talk to one another—the women who masturbate with bathtub toy boats can talk to the plushies, and so on.

She opened a cabinet and found a video called *Smush*, made by Jeff Vilencia, whose work is admired by crush enthusiasts.

"Jeff's quite the artiste." Gates said. "This film has actually played at a bunch of film festivals all over the world."

We watched. A pudgy woman appeared and then . . . worm after worm after worm began exploding under her footsteps. "I love to step on worms with my big feet," said the woman, actress Erika Elizondo. "I love to smush worms. I love to tease them when I press them down softly at first. I am going to step on you and *smush* you!"

Clearly, we were at the other end of the sexual spectrum from the gentle plushophiles. The men who enjoy these videos, Gates said, like to imagine themselves at the mercy of all-powerful goddesses.

"Mmmm, I am stepping on *youuuuu*!" the actress was saying.

Splat.

"They are no match for my big, beautiful feet!"

Squishhhhhh.

"That was the come shot," Gates said. "You want to see it again?"

There are probably no more than 1,500 crushers out there, Gates believes. They got some exposure last year through the ABC legal drama *The Practice*, on which Henry Winkler had a recurring role as a dentist who liked to watch women in the act of stomping on bugs. In 1999 there was a crushing death in Florida: a 28-year-old Okeechobee man named Bryan Loudermilk, deeply into the fetish, managed to have his pickup truck rolled over his body. He was killed.

Hollywood people such as Mickey Rooney and Loretta Swit have made their opposition to crush videos a cause célèbre; People for the Ethical Treatment of Animals is not a fan. Congress voted against the sale of crush videos in 1999, and President Clinton quickly signed the ban into law. Not even the American Civil Liberties Union came to the aid of Mr. Vilencia and his ilk.

"It's gross, it's disturbing, it's sort of upsetting," Gates said—but she calls the government ban "stupid." It should definitely be illegal to stomp on a cat or a dog or a monkey, she believes, but bugs and worms? "I'm not saying they're disposable, but to get up into arms about that is really a distortion," Gates said. "I have shot animals in the past as a hunter, so I can't take the sort of moral high ground. No, I don't jerk off while I'm shooting a groundhog, no, I don't derive a sense of pleasure from this torture, but in the end I don't think that the laws against these videos are appropriate."

Gates admitted she was a pervert, but only in the fantasy realm. "Little Red Riding Hood," for example: "I think that's incredibly sexy, and when I was a kid I used to masturbate to the fantasy of being eaten by a pack of wolves. And I still find that sort of thing an exciting image. I can call that into my head when necessary."

She likes furry stuff, too. "Take my word for it, I've got a really dirty mind, and my dirty mind has gone to places that are beyond the pale. I think amputee stuff is hot, I think furry stuff is hot. I think slash fiction's hot, but as far as acting stuff out . . . I mean, I've ridden pony boys and pony girls"— people dressed up with bridles and saddles, etc.—"and I found that very exciting, but I'm uninclined to ask my husband to put on a saddle. And we find the ordinary, old vanilla stuff completely satisfying and very, very perfect."

She considers the plushophiles to have a lot in common with practitioners of vanilla sex. "They may think about sex as often as we do, which is often, and they may think of stuffed animals instead of Pamela Anderson, but they're very ordinary people," she said. "Sex is not just what happens to the genitals. Everything is fetish fodder. I can't think of anything in this world that couldn't be sexualized by somebody."

Back at the convention.

THE FURRY SHOW

Now it's showtime. The Chicago Room is full of furries.

"Y'all ready for a good three, four hours of entertainment?" says Tyger Cowboy, the master of ceremonies.

Babs Bunny is the first act. Basically, it is someone in a bunny outfit hopping around while singing Cyndi Lauper's "Girls Just Want to Have Fun" in a high-pitched voice.

A group of furries in cat regalia do a few songs from *Grease*. A little boy in the front—a son of the convention chairman, Robert King—has his fingers in his ears.

The Squirrelles sing "You Can't Hurry Love." An Elmo muppet does "Tiptoe Through the Tulips." Ten seconds into the number, a wolf creeps up and rips Elmo apart. The place goes nuts.

THE FURRIES VS. THE U.S. ARMY

The next morning, at 11:50, the lobby is full of furries and . . . soldiers in camouflage gear. The 85th Army Reserve Division, headquartered in Arlington Heights, happens to be having a convention here, too—a commanders' conference, during which they're to go over what took place in 2000, and set goals for 2001. The furries in the lobby look baffled. A few military men are smirking. One square-jawed hard-ass stares at the rabbit-eared furry for a moment and, finally, says, "Yeah!" It's sarcastic. He sounds like a high-school jerk sizing up the class freak.

"Unusual," says a Sargeant Major Jennings.

"I think it's comical, myself," says one of his subordinates.

"God bless America," says the other.

Ostrich comes tearing past them, saying, "The fursuit parade's about to start!" Soon, about 40 people in mascotwear—the fursuiters—are marching quietly through the lobby. Flashbulbs pop. Furries in civilian clothes reach out to touch the fursuiters as they go by.

A big puppy.

A wolf with a huge mallet.

A bear eating a raccoon.

"Show us some tail, baby!" says a furry bystander.

"I didn't know rabbits were in season," says an army guy.

A Lieutenant Colonel Flowers is taking it all in good-naturedly. "A little unusual," he says. "Of course, they'd probably say the same thing about us."

A half-kangaroo walks by.

"Pretty good, pretty good, pretty imaginative," the lieutenant colonel says. "What are they, an advocacy group?"

Another lieutenant colonel, named Farrar, is unfazed. "Well, when you see people wearing dog collars and chains . . . you know, I went to college," he says. "It doesn't take much imagination to figure out what these people might be doing behind closed doors. The clean aspect, O.K., these guys are cartoon figures, I can see that. But if you go a little *left* of that, then suddenly you're adding a new dimension to it. It doesn't make me very comfortable. Certainly nothing I agree with. Tantric sex comes to mind. People that have problems." He thinks some more. "But we're all getting along!" Without hesitation, he poses for a picture with a brown bear.

Another man in uniform, Lieutenant Patrick George, is chatting with a young raccoon. "This is something nice to bring kids to," Lieutenant George says.

The raccoon suggests there might be no more war if everyone adopted the furry attitude toward life. Lieutenant George smiles. "There will always be wars as long as there's people on this earth," he says. "Not if they all pretend to be animals," the raccoon says, then rejoins the parade.

Lieutenant George has been watching some of the furries. "Touchy-feely, with each other," he says. "I noticed that last night. They're scratching each other and laying in the lap. You don't have to be too smart to figure it out. It's easy." He stops his friendly chuckling, however, when he learns he has been chatting with a guy who might *really* want to be a raccoon.

"That's different," he says. "But different people have different beliefs in this world. We can't be the same, we're all individuals. So to each his own."

FOX TALK

It's Saturday evening, and a discussion group, "Foxes in the Fandom," is in progress. It is moderated by a pudgy, bearded man who goes by the name Craig Fox. About two dozen males are present: half look like foxes. Like Randy Foxx and Phallon. And Rowdy Fox, smiling naughtily as his fox hand puppet nibbles on his free hand.

"Do you think movies and books portray foxes evil more, or good more?" Mr. Fox the moderator asks.

"If the main character was a mouse or a rabbit, then the fox would be the evil villain," says Denver, a long-haired guy in an ELTONJOHN.COM T-shirt. "It also depends if the main character is, for example, a lion. I've run into a couple where the fox is a bumbling sidekick. It depends on basically the line of the food chain with who's the star."

"Right," says Mr. Fox. "Um, another thing about foxes, in general, is that—how can I say this?—the fandom looks upon them as extremely yiffy. Why do you think that is?"

There is some giggling.

"If you want to go yiffy," Mr. Fox continues, "let's look at the rabbits! Whereas foxes actually mate for life, as a general rule."

Now it's time for tales of real-life fox encounters.

"Has anyone been around an actual fox?" the moderator asks, before telling of how he once went to a petting zoo, where red foxes sat on his head and licked his face.

Denver says he has had 12 encounters with foxes, all in the wild. "There is one fox that lives in Gloucester, Massachusetts, that apparently likes me, because he has been staring in my window *all* night."

Everyone laughs hard.

After everyone agrees that it would be wrong to have a fox as a pet, there is a pause.

"What would people like to see the image of the fox be in the new millennium?" Mr. Fox asks. "What would you like to see, foxwise?"

"I got a question," says a woman in the back. She is half bat, half cat. "What's everyone's passion for foxes? Because I don't know anything about it."

THE GRIFFIN IN THE BAR

Matt Davis, a slender 30-year-old dude with black close-cropped hair, is in the hotel bar. His T-shirt reads MY SEXUAL PREFERENCE IS NOT YOU. Davis drove up to the Midwest FurFest with a few other furs from Arkansas. He's a security guard and furry artist who fantasizes about being a griffin, which would make him half eagle, half lion.

"I'd be a security-guard griffin," he says, "I could fly and patrol the area." He would have a griffin mate who would look like him but "a little bit thinner-boned" and "adorable."

"I've had fantasies that I've spent a long hunt through the forest catching my prey and bringing home to my nest moose and deer, something like that. Something large. Carrying it home to my nest, where my mate is waiting for me, and after eating, we engage in ferocious sex and fall asleep cuddling together in the nest."

With him is a rotund fellow with long blond hair. He says he is the March Hare (real name: O. Holcomb). "Being human, first of all, we're not all that cute," he says, "In fact, we're bare-ass ugly. Second of all, intelligence, while it is a wonderful thing, is not that wonderful. Having what we think is understanding and then realizing it's *not* is more painful than being hunted down and killed by your predator." Being furry, on the other hand, is a solution to life. "It gives me thunder." Says the March Hare, "I can walk into any situation and go, 'I am the dude!' It's like having a switch, a psychological switch you can tap into and turn something on." It helps even when he's flipping burgers, "You have 30 orders up there," he says, "If I wasn't the hare, I wouldn't be fast enough to get those 30 orders out—and in under three minutes—and be the dude."

THE FURRY HATERS

Later on at the bar, at two a.m., a dozen 30-ish patrons, part of a wedding party, are making noise. I hear the word "faggots."

"They're freaks," says a blonde, who gives her name as Sylvia.

"No," says Johnny, "*Star Trek* people that have lost *Star Trek*. Now they run around with mouse costumes on. Very disturbing."

"A bunch of *freaks* running around!" Sylvia insists, "What is the purpose of the fur costume?"

"Pretty much guys that can't deal with society," Johnny says. "There's more to it than the costumes—they're blatant homosexuals."

"Bestiality!" Sylvia says.

"It's a shame, because there's a lot of people here who are getting the wrong impression of Chicago," says Johnny. "Like, a bunch of queers running around in a mouse costume. It, uh, it just makes me sick. Whitey!"

Whitey comes over. He is wearing a Phish shirt and a red University of Wisconsin cap. "Oh, these fucking clowns running around?" says Whitey, who is drinking whiskey, smoking a Dunhill, and swaying a bit. "I'd love to take my 10/22 and take a couple of plink shots at them!"

Today is the opening day of deer season, and Whitey missed it because of his "dumb-ass" friend's wedding.

"Freaks," Sylvia says, cracking up.

Still, Whitey says he is not one to "fucking cast judgment on anybody. And if that's their bag of tricks, that's cool, but it's just kind of like, I just think I could come up with a better hobby." For example? "Killing real animals," he says. "Snowmobiling."

FURRY COMEDOWN

Sunday is the comedown day. At noon, furries are catching vans to the airport. Uncle Kage, the biomedical researcher and auctioneer, is in the lobby, still wearing his white lab coat. "They put little bears with sweaters in our cribs," he is saying. "We have cartoons where rabbits make us laugh. Shirts with little alligators on them. Anthropomorphic animals are part of our culture."

R.C. Rabbitsfoot comes over with his dead cat's ashes in a soup can and hands it to Uncle Kage, who looks puzzled.

About 40 furries are in the lobby now. They're hugging and skritching one another good-bye.

"I'm going to cry when I leave here," says the March Hare. "Probably everyone's going to. That's my closing statement."

TOWARD A FURRY FUTURE

A month after the Midwest FurFest, I call Ostrich at his apartment in Ohio. He has been sitting around drawing a picture of a fox and playing with his cat. The FurFest was a success, he says. "I've heard nothing but good about it." Ostrich says, "I've heard two complaints about it, and they're both from known malcontents." He confirms there was a fair amount of wild sex at the convention: "Oh yeah, I know there was for a fact. I probably would have been involved in it if I hadn't been so busy."

Was he still hopeful about the possibility of genetic engineering?

"Oh yeah. That's pretty much the future of the world—there's no way around it. If I can live another 30 or 40 years, I might live several hundred more. Obviously, I'd like to rework my body to make my physical body conform more to my body image. I'd want a tail, I'd want some fur, and, basically, some cute cartoon eyes and stuff. The technology for that's coming. I don't think it's as far off as most people think."

Part II

SOCIAL CONTROL

Chapter 6

THE BODY OF
THE CONDEMNED

Michel Foucault

On 2 March 1757, Damiens the regicide was condemned "to make the *amende honorable* before the main door of the Church of Paris" where he was to be "taken and conveyed in a cart, wearing nothing but a shirt, holding a torch of burning wax weighing two pounds"; then, "in the said cart, to the Place de Grève, where, on a scaffold that will be erected there, the flesh will be torn from his breasts, arms, thighs and calves with red-hot pincers, his right hand, holding the knife with which he committed the said parricide, burnt with sulphur, and, on those places where the flesh will be torn away, poured molten lead, boiling oil, burning resin, wax and sulphur melted together and then his body drawn and quartered by four horses and his limbs and body consumed by fire, reduced to ashes and his ashes thrown to the winds" (*Pièces originales* ..., 1757:372–374).

Bouton, an officer of the watch, left us his account: "The sulphur was lit, but the flame was so poor that only the top skin of the hand was burnt, and that only slightly. Then the executioner, his sleeves rolled up, took the steel pincers, which had been especially made for the occasion, and which were about a foot and a half long, and pulled first at the calf of the right leg, then at the thigh, and from there at the two fleshy parts of the right arm; then at the breasts. Though a strong, sturdy fellow, this executioner found it so difficult to tear away the pieces of flesh that he sets about the same spot two or three times, twisting the pincers as he did so, and what he took away formed at each part a wound about the size of a six-pound crown piece.

"After these tearings with the pincers, Damiens, who cried out profusely, though without swearing, raised his head and looked at himself; the same executioner dipped an iron spoon in the pot containing the boiling potion, which he poured liberally over each wound. Then the ropes that were to be harnessed to the horses were attached with cords to the patient's body; the horses were then harnessed and placed alongside the arms and legs, one at each limb."

Eighty years later, Léon Faucher drew up his rules "for the House of young prisoners in Paris":

Art. 17. The prisoners' day will begin at six in the morning in winter and at five in summer. They will work for nine hours a day throughout the year. Two hours a day will be devoted to instruction. Work and the day will end at nine o'clock in winter and at eight in summer.

Art. 18. *Rising*. At the first drum-roll, the prisoners must rise and dress in silence, as the supervisor opens the cell doors. At the second drum-roll, they must be dressed and make their beds. At the third, they must line up and proceed to the chapel for morning prayer. There is a five-minute interval between each drum-roll.

Art. 19. The prayers are conducted by the chaplain and followed by a moral or religious reading. This exercise must not last more than half an hour.

Art. 20. *Work*. At a quarter to six in the summer, a quarter to seven in winter, the prisoners go down into the courtyard where they must wash their hands and faces, and receive their first ration of bread. Immediately afterwards, they form into work-teams and go off to work, which must begin at six in summer and seven in winter.

Art. 21. *Meal*. At ten o'clock the prisoners leave their work and go to the refectory; they wash their hands in their courtyards and assemble in divisions. After the dinner, there is recreation until twenty minutes to eleven.

Art. 22. *School*. At twenty minutes to eleven, at the drum-roll, the prisoners form into ranks, and proceed in divisions to the school. The class lasts two hours and consists alternately of reading, writing, drawing and arithmetic.

Art. 23. At twenty minutes to one, the prisoners leave the school, in divisions, and return to their courtyards for recreation. At five minutes to one, at the drum-roll, they form into work-teams.

Art. 24. At one o'clock they must be back in the workshops: they work until four o'clock.

Art. 25. At four o'clock the prisoners leave their workshops and go into the courtyards where they wash their hands and form into divisions for the refectory.

Art. 26. Supper and recreation that follows it last until five o'clock: the prisoners then return to the workshops.

Art. 27. At seven o'clock in the summer, at eight in winter, workshops; bread is distributed for the last time in the workshops. For a quarter of an hour one of the prisoners or supervisors reads a passage from some instructive or uplifting work. This is followed by evening prayer.

> Art. 28. At half-past seven in summer, half-past eight in winter, the prisoners
> must be back in their cells after the washing of hands and the inspection of clothes
> in the courtyard; at the first drum-roll, they must undress, and at the second get
> into bed. The cell doors are closed and the supervisors go the rounds in the
> corridors, to ensure order and silence. (Faucher, 1838:274–282)

We have, then, a public execution and a time-table. They do not punish the same crimes or the same type of delinquent. But they each define a certain penal style. Less than a century separates them. It was a time when, in Europe and in the United States, the entire economy of punishment was redistributed. It was a time of great "scandals" for traditional justice, a time of innumerable projects for reform. It saw a new theory of law and crime, a new moral or political justification of the right to punish; old laws were abolished, old customs died out.

Among so many changes, I shall consider one: the disappearance of torture as a public spectacle. Today we are rather inclined to ignore it; perhaps, in its time, it gave rise to too much inflated rhetoric; perhaps it has been attributed too readily and too emphatically to a process of "humanization," thus dispensing with the need for further analysis.

Punishment, then, will tend to become the most hidden part of the penal process. This has several consequences: it leaves the domain of more or less everyday perception and enters that of abstract consciousness; its effectiveness is seen as resulting from its inevitability, not from its visible intensity; it is the certainty of being punished and not the horrifying spectacle of public punishment that must discourage crime; the exemplary mechanics of punishment changes its mechanisms. As a result, justice no longer takes public responsibility for the violence that is bound up with its practice.

The disappearance of public executions marks therefore the decline of the spectacle; but it also marks a slackening of the hold on the body.

Generally speaking, punitive practices had become more reticent. One no longer touched the body, or at least as little as possible, and then only to reach something other than the body itself. It might be objected that imprisonment, confinement, forced labour, penal servitude, prohibition from entering certain areas, deportation—which have occupied so important a place in modern penal systems—are "physical" penalties: unlike fines, for example, they directly affect the body. But the punishment—body relation is not the same as it was in the torture during public executions. The body now serves as an instrument or intermediary: if one intervenes upon it to imprison it, or to make it work, it is in order to deprive the individual of a liberty that is regarded both as a right and as property. The body, according to this penality, is caught up in a system of constraints and privations, obligations and prohibitions. Physical pain, the pain of the body itself, is no longer the constituent element of the penalty. From being an art of unbearable sensations punishment has become an economy of suspended rights. If it is still necessary for the law to reach and manipulate the body of the convict, it will be at a distance, in the proper way, according to strict rules, and with a much "higher" aim. As a result of this new restraint, a whole army of technicians took over from the executioner, the immediate anatomist of pain: warders, doctors, chaplains, psychiatrists, psychologists, educationalists; by their very presence near the prisoner, they sing the praises that the law needs: they reassure it that the body and pain are not the ultimate objects of its punitive action. Today a doctor must watch over those condemned to death, right up to the last moment—thus juxtaposing himself as the agent of welfare, as the alleviator of pain, with the official whose task it is to end life.

The modern rituals of execution to this double process: the disappearance of the spectacle and the elimination of pain. The same movement has affected the various European legal systems, each at its own rate: the same death for all—the execution no longer bears the specific mark of the crime or the social status of the criminal; a death that lasts only a moment—no torture must be added to it in advance, no further actions performed upon the corpse; an execution that affects life rather than the body.

Punishment had no doubt ceased to be centred on torture as a technique of pain; it assumed as its principal object loss of wealth or rights. But a punishment like forced labour or even imprisonment—mere loss of liberty— has never functioned without a certain additional element of punishment that certainly concerns the body itself: rationing of food, sexual deprivation, corporal punishment, solitary confinement. Are these the unintentional, but inevitable, consequence of imprisonment? In fact, in its most explicit practices, imprisonment has always involved a certain degree of physical pain. The criticism that was often levelled at the penitentiary system in the early nineteenth century (imprisonment is not a sufficient punishment: prisoners are less hungry, less cold, less deprived in general—that was never explicitly denied: it is just that a condemned man should suffer physically more than other men. It is difficult to dissociate punishment from additional physical pain. What would a non-corporal punishment be?

There remains, therefore, a trace of "torture" in the modern mechanisms of criminal justice—a trace that has not been entirely overcome, but which is enveloped, increasingly, by the non-corporal nature of the penal system.

If the penality in its most severe forms no longer addresses itself to the body, on what does it lay hold? The answer of the theoreticians—those who, about 1760, opened up a new period that is not yet at an end—is simple, almost obvious. It seems to be contained in the question itself: since it is no longer the body, it must be the soul. The expiation that once rained down upon the body must be replaced by a punishment that acts in depth on the heart, the thoughts, the will, the inclinations. Mably formulated the principle once and for all: "Punishment, if I may so put it, should strike the soul rather than the body" (Mably, 1789:326).

During the 150 or 200 years that Europe has been setting up its new penal systems, the judges have gradually, by means of a process that goes back very far indeed, taken to judging something other than crimes, namely, the "soul" of the criminal.

It would be wrong to say that the soul is an illusion, or an ideological effect. On the contrary, it exists, it has a reality, it is produced permanently around, on, within the body by the functioning of a power that is exercised on those punished—and, in a more general way, on those one supervises, trains, and corrects, over madmen, children at home and at school, the colonized, over those who are stuck at a machine and supervised for the rest of their lives. This is the historical reality of this soul, which, unlike the soul represented by Christian theology, is not born in sin and subject to punishment, but is born rather out of methods of punishment, supervision, and constraint. This real, non-corporal soul is not a substance; it is the element in which are articulated the effects of a certain type of power and the reference of a certain type of knowledge, the machinery by which the power relations give rise to a possible corpus of knowledge, and knowledge extends and reinforces the effects of this power. On this reality reference, various concepts have been constructed and domains of analysis carved out: psyche, subjectivity, personality, consciousness, etc.; on it have been built scientific techniques and discourses, and the moral claims of humanism. But let there be no misunderstanding: it is not that a real man, the object of knowledge, philosophical reflection or technical intervention, has been substituted for the soul, the illusion of the theologians. The man described for us, whom we are invited to free, is already in himself the effect of a subjection much more profound than himself. A "soul" inhabits him and brings him to existence, which is itself a factor in the mastery that power exercises over the body. The soul is the effect and instrument of a political anatomy; the soul is the prison of the body.

That punishment in general and the prison in particular belong to a political technology of the body is a lesson that I have learnt not so much from history as from the present. In recent years, prison revolts have occurred throughout the world. There was certainly something paradoxical about their aims, their slogans, and the way they took place. They were revolts against an entire state of physical misery that is over a century old: against cold, suffocation, and overcrowding, against decrepit walls, hunger, physical maltreatment. But they were also revolts against model prison, tranquillizers, isolation, and the medical or educational services. Were they revolts whose aims were merely material? Or contradictory revolts: against the obsolete, but also against comfort; against the warders, but also against the psychiatrists? In fact, all these movements—and the innumerable discourses that the prison has given rise to since the early nineteenth century—have been about the body and material things. What has sustained these discourses, these memories, and invectives are indeed those minute material details. One may, if one is so disposed, see them as no more than blind demands or suspect the existence behind them of alien strategies. In fact, they were revolts, at the level of the body, against the very body of the prison. What was at issue was not whether the prison environment was too harsh or too aseptic, too primitive or too efficient, but its very materiality as an instrument and vector of power; it is this whole technology of power over the body that the technology of the "soul"—that of the educationalists, psychologists, and psychiatrists—fails either to conceal or to compensate, for the simple reason that it is one of its tools.

Chapter 7

EXECUTIVE SUMMARY

The Commission on Systemic Racism in the Ontario Criminal Justice System

THE COMMISSION WAS ESTABLISHED IN 1992 TO INQUIRE INTO AND MAKE recommendations about the extent to which criminal justice practices, procedures, and policies in Ontario reflect systemic racism. As directed by our Terms of Reference, "anti-black racism" was a focal point of the Commission's inquiry, and the experiences and vulnerabilities of all racial minority communities were also recognized.

The inquiry examined practices, procedures, and policies in the three major components of the criminal justice system: the police, courts, and correctional institutions. Professionals involved in the administration of justice and members of the public were consulted extensively by such means as interviews, public meetings, focus group sessions, written and oral submissions, and public hearings across the province. The Commission also conducted empirical studies of perceptions, experiences with and outcomes of the criminal justice process.

RACISM IN JUSTICE: PERCEPTIONS

Many Ontarians believe that racial minority people are treated worse than white people in the criminal justice system. A major survey conducted in Metropolitan Toronto found that more than five in ten (58%) black residents, three in ten (31%) Chinese residents, and more than three in ten (36%) white residents believe judges do not treat black people the same as white people. More than eight in ten of those who perceive differential treatment believe judges treat black people worse than white people.

Perceptions that judges discriminate against Chinese people were less common but still significant. Four in ten (40%) black residents, close to three in ten (27%) Chinese residents, and about two in ten (18%) white residents believe judges do not treat Chinese people the same as white people. Eight in ten of those who perceive differential treatment believe judges treat Chinese people worse than white people.

Surveys of judges and lawyers indicate substantial variation in views about racial discrimination in the criminal justice system. While many judges and lawyers reject—some flatly—even the possibility that systemic racism might be a genuine problem in Ontario's criminal courts, others acknowledge differential treatment within the system based on race as well as class or poverty. Four in ten (40%) defence counsel and three in ten (33%) provincial division judges appointed since 1989 perceive differential treatment of white and racial minority people in the criminal justice system. About one in ten crown attorneys (13%), general division judges (10%), and provincial division judges appointed before 1989 (10%) also perceive unequal treatment by race.

RACISM IN JUSTICE:
UNDERSTANDING SYSTEMIC RACISM

Racism has a long history in Canada. It was fundamental to relationships between Canada's First Nations and the European colonizers. Racism has shaped immigration to this country and settlement within it. It has led to denials of basic civil and political rights to Canadian citizens, excluded adults from jobs and children from schools, limited opportunities to acquire property, and barred people from hotels, bars, theatres, and other recreational facilities. In these ways racism has restricted the opportunities and deformed the lives of some Canadian residents, while directly benefiting others.

Though many Canadians throughout history have accepted racism, others have campaigned and protested against the fundamental denial of humanity that it represents. These efforts have had significant results. While the law once permitted or promoted unequal treatment because of race, today it generally prohibits such discrimination. Equality is now a fundamental right.

Despite these formal changes, racism continues in practices that affect the lives and opportunities of people in Ontario. The current challenge is to grapple with this systemic dimension of racism.

Systemic racism means the social processes that produce racial inequality in decisions about people and in the treatment they receive. It is revealed by specific consequences, incidents, and acts that indicate differential decisions or unequal treatment, but it is the underlying processes that make such events "systemic." One key process is racialization, the other is the social system.

Racialization in Canada consists of classifications of people into racial groups by reference to signs of origin—such as skin colour, hair texture, and place of birth—and judgments based on these signs about their character, skills, talents, and capacity to belong in this country. These social constructions of races as different and unequal have historically justified economic exploitation of other societies by European imperial powers. Imperial elites organized societies they colonized using racialized classifications and judgments, which they incorporated into the religious, educational, cultural, and political practices of their own societies.

Once accepted by a society, judgments about races being different and unequal may be adopted, established, and perpetuated by social systems. Social systems are ways of organizing action in order to accomplish tasks. They are made up of personnel and policies, decision-making procedures, and operating norms for managing their work. Racialization is introduced into social systems through the decisions and actions of system personnel. However, it is often impossible to identify those responsible for introducing or perpetuating racialization because its transmission and acceptance are often cumulative and diffuse. Racialization within a system has an adverse impact upon racialized persons, but may pass unrecognized by those who do not experience its effects.

Racialization may be tolerated by the policies, procedures, and norms of a system. It may be transmitted within particular systems or among different systems. These processes of introducing, perpetuating, tolerating, and transmitting racialization within social systems constitute systemic racism.

PRISON

Isolating people from society and confining them in prisons is the harshest action that the Canadian criminal justice system can take. The principle that everyone is equally protected against unfair or unjust imprisonment and the principle of restraint are fundamental to the state's authority to take this action. But practices do not always live up to principles when officials are granted broad discretion.

A major study of admissions to Ontario prisons indicates that for the period studied, the majority of prisoners are white, but that black men, women, and male youths are massively over-represented. Aboriginal men, women, and youths are also over-represented in provincial prisons, but not to the same extent as black people. Members of other racialized groups are generally not over-represented.

The over-representation of black people reflects a dramatic increase in their admissions to prison between 1986/87 and 1992/93. By the end of these six years, black adults were admitted to prison at over five times the rate of white adults, proportionate to their representation in Ontario's population.

Although many more black men than black women are in jail, black women are more over-represented among prison admissions than black men. Whereas black men were admitted to prison at a rate just over five times that of white men in 1992/93, the admission rate for black women was almost seven times that of white women.

The over-representation of black adults is much worse among those imprisoned before trial than among sentenced admissions. While white people were imprisoned before trial at about the same rate as after sentence (approximately 329 per 100,000 persons in the population before trial, and 334 after sentence), the pre-trial admission rate of black people was twice their sentenced admission rate (approximately 2,136 per 100,000 before trial, and 1,051 after sentence).

The most dramatic differences in admission rates of white and black adults involve pre-trial imprisonment for highly discretionary charges. In 1992/93 the black pre-trial admission rate for drug trafficking/importing charges was 27 times higher than the white rate; for drug possession charges, the black pre-trial admission rate was 15 times higher; and for obstructing justice charges, the black pre-trial admission rate was 13 times higher.

These data cannot be rationalized by racial or cultural propensities to commit offences. Nor can they be explained as a product of a criminal justice system composed of overtly or covertly racist officials.

However, racialization in Canadian society is a recognized fact both inside and outside the criminal justice system. Wherever broad discretion exists, racialization can influence decisions and produce racial inequality in outcomes. Such discretion is evident at several stages of the process that results in imprisonment before trial or after conviction.

IMPRISONMENT BEFORE TRIAL

The discretionary powers of officials who deal with accused persons before trial provide considerable scope for racialization to influence detention decisions. Racialization may influence police decisions about whether to release accused persons, and may affect the bail process through information the police supply to crown attorneys. Racialized decisions may also be promoted by criteria used to predict whether an accused will fail to appear at trial or is "substantially likely" to commit a criminal offence before trial.

A major study of detention decisions about black and white accused charged with the same offences indicates that white accused were more likely to be released by the police and less likely to be detained after a bail hearing. White accused were treated more favourably even though they were more likely than black accused to have a criminal record and to have a more serious record.

Detailed analysis of these data revealed no evidence of differential treatment for some types of charges laid against white and black accused, but substantial differences for other charges. Differential treatment was most pronounced for accused charged with drug offences. Within this sub-sample, white accused (60%) were twice as likely as black accused (30%) to be released by the police. Black accused (31%) were three times more likely than white accused (10%) to be refused bail and ordered detained.

Further analysis of the drug charge sample indicates separate patterns of discrimination at the police and court stages of pre-trial detention. Across the sample as a whole, the results of differential treatment evident at the police stage were subsequently transmitted into the court process. Police decisions to detain black accused at a higher rate than white accused meant that the bail courts saw a significantly higher proportion of black accused. Thus, even similar rates of denying bail at court resulted in larger proportions of black accused being jailed before trial.

Employment status (as described by the police) accounted for some of the racial inequality in imprisonment before trial, both for the sample as a whole and for the drug charge sample. But it does not fully explain the findings. Other ties to the community considered at bail court, such as fixed address and single status, also fail to account for the differential outcomes.

The data disclose distinct and legally unjustifiable differences in detention decisions about black and white accused across the sample as a whole and for some specific offences. The conclusion is inescapable: some black accused who were imprisoned before trial would not have been jailed if they had been white, and some white accused who were freed before trial would have been detained had they been black.

In light of these findings, the Commission makes 13 major recommendations to address differential treatment in the bail process. The Commission recommends training programs and operating guidelines based on the principle of restraint in exercising powers to detain. The police should be required to explain their decisions to detain people, and should receive explicit direction about preparing reports on accused persons for bail hearings. *The Crown Policy Manual* should be amended to help crown attorneys address the problem, and education for judges should emphasize avoidance of discriminatory assumptions and practices. Persons in police custody should be assisted in preparing for bail hearings to ensure that they are not detained because the bail court lacks crucial information about them.

CHARGE MANAGEMENT

Charge management is the complex administrative system for processing criminal charges outside trial courts. It includes decisions about laying and reviewing charges, diversion of cases away from court proceedings, plea negotiations and other resolutions before charges are tried, and criminal justice services for accused persons and victims. Discretion is the essence of charge management. Access to high-quality services is necessary to ensure that people do not experience the charge management system as discriminatory.

During the early stages of criminal proceedings, police, crown attorneys, and defence counsel often made rapid decisions, based on limited information and hidden from public scrutiny. Racialized assumptions and stereotypes may influence these decisions in various ways, some quite subtle. Decision-makers engaged in their daily routines may not recognize any such bias unless they are constantly alert to the risk.

Commission research disclosed widespread perceptions and many experiences of racial discrimination in police charging. A Commission study comparing outcomes of crown attorney decisions to proceed summarily or by indictment indicates small but statistically significant differences favouring white accused.

Inadequate access and low participation rates of racialized people in diversion programs are serious concerns. Some defence and duty counsel say these problems reflect arbitrary guidelines and unwillingness by crown attorneys to divert charges. Others blame the police for failing to tell eligible accused persons from racialized communities how to apply for diversion programs.

Racialized Ontarians have serious concerns about access to legal aid services. Services need to be expanded and publicized so that all Ontarians know about the legal aid system and understand their rights to apply for assistance.

Deep distrust of plea negotiations was among the most recurrent themes of the Commission's public consultations. Three aspects of this system are of particular concern. First, many unrepresented accused who may be offered a resolution in return for a guilty plea have little understanding of the case against them or how the evidence may affect the resolution proposal. Second, represented accused persons are generally excluded from discussions about resolving the charges without a contested trial, which creates suspicion about the agreements that lawyers present to their clients. Third, even after apparently accepting an agreement, many accused persons from racialized communities do not understand its implications.

The dominant issue of systemic racism raised by victims concerned mandatory charging policies in family violence cases. These policies are intended to reduce or eliminate police discretion to handle family violence informally and crown attorney discretion to withdraw charges or otherwise abandon prosecutions. They require charges to be laid and prosecutions to proceed even against the wishes of the victim.

There are two conflicting views about whether these policies protect women from racialized communities. One is that mandatory charging may be driving family abuse underground. Women who require protection but are unwilling to pursue criminal prosecution may not call for police protection from violence. The second is that directives to charge and prosecute are still not treated as mandatory by the police and crown attorneys when the victim is from a racialized community.

The Commission makes 17 major recommendations to structure the exercise of discretion and improve the charge management process. They include alternatives to police charging, expanding the scope of diversion programs, reforms to legal aid services, greater openness in resolution discussions, more flexibility in the prosecution of violent offences within families, and expansion of services for victim/witnesses.

COURT DYNAMICS

Many Ontarians perceive courts as unfairly biased against black or other racialized people. Toleration of practices that may contribute to such perceptions is a significant problem because Ontario legal tradition has long held that public confidence is fundamental to an effective criminal justice system. Nowhere is this confidence more important than in the courts, where the system's commitment to equality is most visible.

Commission studies indicate that some judges, justices of the peace, and lawyers frequently refer in open court to the foreign origins or ethnic backgrounds of the accused, and sometimes also of victims or other witnesses. Some references were obviously intended to be benign, and in a few instances were linked to a legally relevant issue. More often, it was hard to discern any legitimate purpose; occasionally, foreignness was explicitly mentioned as a reason for a harsh decision about an accused person. The tendency for some judicial officers and lawyers to act as if a person's origin matters to the criminal justice system results in a sense of exclusion among members of racialized communities and lack of confidence that the system treats everyone equally.

Communication barriers also cause black and other racialized participants in court proceedings to feel excluded. Under-representation of black and other racialized persons among jurors, judges, and lawyers creates a sense of exclusion by conveying an image of the criminal justice system as a white institution.

The Commission makes 12 major recommendations to modify courtroom practices and dynamics that contribute to the appearance of racial injustice. These include procedures to restrict references to race, foreign origins, or immigration status; reforms to complaints mechanisms; improvements to in-court interpretation services; and measures to ensure more representative juries.

IMPRISONMENT AFTER CONVICTION

Sentencing is highly discretionary, with considerable scope for disparate outcomes. Differences in how the facts of a case come before judges, how judges view those facts, the goals and principles of sentencing, and the role of courts in passing sentence may all contribute to disparities.

Racialized judgments and assumptions may also contribute to differential sentencing. They may directly influence the decisions of sentencing judges, or may be transmitted from decisions made at earlier stages of the criminal justice process.

A major study of imprisonment decisions for the same offences indicates that white persons found guilty were less likely than black persons to be sentenced to prison. White people were sentenced more leniently than black people found guilty, even though they were more likely to have a criminal record and to have a more serious record. The differential was most pronounced among those convicted of a drug offence. Within this sub-sample, 55% of black but only 36% of white convicted persons were sentenced to prison.

Detailed analysis revealed no significant differences in the incidents that led to the charges. Employment status and differences in criminal justice variables such as imprisonment before trial accounted for some of the racial inequality in incarceration rates. But a significant (though small) differential in incarceration rates remains, which is not due to gravity of charge, record, plea, crown election, pre-trial detention, unemployment, or other social factor. The most likely explanation for this differential is racial discrimination at sentencing.

The average prison term of black prisoners in this study were significantly shorter than those of white prisoners. This is consistent with differential incarceration rates producing imprisonment of convicted black persons whose offences and records would not have led to imprisonment had they been white.

Another reason may be that because black accused are more likely to have been imprisoned before their trials, they are more likely than white accused to receive discretionary "credit" for their pre-trial detention.

The Commission makes six major recommendations to address differential outcomes in sentencing. These include a call for restraint in the use of prison sentences, education for judges on the practical implications of imprisonment, providing more information on programs for serving sentence in the community, and reforms giving crown attorneys more guidance on sentence submissions.

RACISM BEHIND BARS REVISITED

The treatment of black and other racialized prisoners was the subject of the Commission's Interim Report, *Racism behind Bars*. This report showed that racism may operate as an indirect means of controlling prisoners and made 10 major recommendations to reduce overt and systemic racism in Ontario prisons.

Racialized judgments and assumptions may also influence direct mechanisms of control in prisons, such as the discretion of authorities to impose punishments, and to limit access to benefits, such as discretionary release programs.

An exploratory Commission study indicates racial differences exist in the application of institutional discipline. The data suggest trends indicating over-representation of black men, women, and male youths among prisoners charged with misconducts. They also indicate that black prisoners were more likely than white prisoners to be charged with the types of misconducts over which correctional officers exercise greater subjective judgment. Black prisoners were less likely than white prisoners to be disciplined when the discretionary powers of correctional officers are limited by the need to show objective proof.

Discretionary release programs, such as temporary absence and parole, allow convicted prisoners to begin supervised reintegration into the wider community while serving sentence. Exploratory studies indicate that prisoners from racialized and linguistic minority communities are more likely to obtain equal access to these programs if institutions adopt a proactive "case management" model rather than a reactive, ad hoc approach.

The Commission makes seven major recommendations to supplement those in the Interim Report. These include measures to enhance openness and public accountability of prison practices, review of the discipline process to foster greater restraint and consistency in their application, and establishment of a case management system to advise and counsel every prisoner about available prison services and programs.

COMMUNITY POLICING

Community policing is based on a philosophy of partnership between the police and the community, emphasizing peacekeeping, problem-solving, and crime prevention. Many Ontario police services have recently adopted policies that reflect this philosophy. However, members of black and other racialized communities, particularly women and youths, feel excluded from co-operative partnerships with the police and fear that racial equality is not on the community policing agenda.

Perceptions that the police discriminate against black and other racialized people are widespread. A Commission survey shows that 74% of black, 54% of Chinese, and 47% of white Metropolitan Toronto residents believe that the police do not treat black people the same as white people. About nine in ten of those who perceive differential treatment believe the police treat black people worse than white people, and more than seven in ten think it occurs about half the time or more.

Perceptions of discrimination against Chinese people are less common but still significant. In Metropolitan Toronto, 48% of black, 42% of Chinese, and 24% of white residents think the police do not treat Chinese people the same as white people. Eight in ten of those who perceive differential treatment believe the police treat Chinese people worse than white people, and more than half think such differential treatment occurs about half the time or more.

How the police exercise their discretion to stop and question people contributes significantly to lack of confidence in equal treatment. Black Metro residents (28%) are much more likely than white (18%) or Chinese residents (15%) to report having been stopped by the police in the previous two years. Black residents (17%) are also more likely than white (8%) or Chinese (5%) residents to report multiple stops in the previous two years.

Black men are particularly vulnerable to being stopped by the police. About 43% of black male residents, but only 25% of white and 19% of Chinese male residents report being stopped by the police in the previous two years. Significantly more black men (29%) than white (12%) or Chinese (7%) report two or more police stops in the previous two years.

The Commission makes nine major recommendations designed to improve the governance and delivery of community policing in Ontario. These include local community committees to establish policing objectives that reflect community needs, action plans to secure equality in policing, guidelines for the exercise of police discretion to stop and question people, and enhancing the complaints system to promote systemic monitoring of police practices.

SYSTEMIC RESPONSES TO POLICE SHOOTINGS

Since 1978, 16 black civilians have been shot—10 fatally—by on-duty police officers in Ontario. The number of shootings and their circumstances have convinced many black Ontarians that they are disproportionately vulnerable to police violence. These concerns have spurred strong opinions about how the criminal justice system should respond to police shootings of black and other racialized people. One key demand is that any death or serious injury caused by the police be closely scrutinized by an open and fair process designed to determine if the use of force was justified. A crucial element of such a process is that it should explicitly examine the contribution, if any, of systemic racism to the death or injury.

The criminal trial process deals only with strictly circumscribed issues in a strictly circumscribed manner. Thus expectations that the criminal trials will provide a forum for examination of systemic racism are unrealistic. Nevertheless, criminal prosecutions should continue to be invoked to enhance accountability for improper use of force.

Unlike a criminal trial, a coroner's inquest has a broader capacity to canvass the role of systemic racism in police killings of black civilians. The Commission recommends that legally trained persons serve as coroners for cases involving police shootings and that these coroners rely exclusively on independent investigators and special crown attorneys. The Commission also recommends that the Ontario Civilian Commission on Police Services be provided with adequate resources to investigate systemic racism in police shooting cases.

AN EQUALITY STRATEGY FOR JUSTICE

Specific reforms need the support of a framework for securing racial equality in the administration of justice. This framework has four key elements: anti-racism training of justice personnel; employment of racialized persons in the administration of justice; participation of racialized persons in the development of justice policies; and monitoring of practices for evidence of racial inequality. The Commission makes five broad recommendations to achieve these goals.

LOOKING FORWARD

The elimination of systemic racism from Ontario's criminal justice system requires collective action from all its members. Above all an aggressive commitment is needed to secure racial equality. This will require integrating principles of inclusion, responsiveness, and accountability into all aspects of the criminal justice system, together with an overriding commitment to restraint when invoking judicial sanctions. Only by working in partnership with the community can an accountable system reduce the risk of inadvertent acceptance of racial inequality.

Chapter 8

THE SHORT, BRUTAL LIFE OF TERRY FITZSIMMONS

Cynthia Amsden

In 1984, TERRY FITZSIMMONS, A CONFUSED 18-YEAR-OLD, BEGAN HIS CRIMINAL career as a convenience store thief. In July, 1993, he ended it by injecting himself with the HIV-infected blood of his fourth murder victim and turning himself in to the police. For 577 days he waited to die of AIDS. Finally, he got tired of waiting. Two weeks ago, he hanged himself in his cell at Kingston Penitentiary.

Mr. Fitzsimmons did what every murder victim's family and every capital-punishment advocate wants. In a manner the courts and prison could not, he instituted his own brand of capital punishment, at least in part because he understood that Canada's corrections system has nothing to do with correcting the crime problem—that, in fact, it manufactures the very people society fears.

And Terry Fitzsimmons was a star example of what the system can produce. Sadly, the mould that formed him wasn't broken with his death. The lethal combination of repressive high-security facilities and inadequate counselling and rehabilitation mean more convicts like him will mutate in our prisons.

I first met Mr. Fitzsimmons in February, as part of my research for a book about John Hill, a prison-rights lawyer, and about his law clerk, Howard Massicotta, a former armed robber. Over the weeks leading up to his death, we spent about seven hours together on the telephone. The initial hype and braggadocio about deliberately infecting himself with the HIV virus soon gave way to something more interesting: a dark tour of penitentiary logic.

In our last conversation, five days before his death on March 29, he said that though there was nothing he could do about his own situation, he would like the world to know just what a creature of the system he had become. "I got nothing to gain by it, like I could sit back in my cell and die, but I want them to know that, hey, I came on this planet one thing and I'm leaving this planet a totally different thing, and how the hell did I go from one extreme to the other. Not that anybody's at fault, but let's see where maybe we could have prevented it."

In contrast to his media billing as a deranged monster, there was an engaging vitality about him. He was a pitiless realist who confronted the facts head on. In short, I found him to be a lucid voice from the other side of the law, unresistant to questions, honest in his answers—and only occasionally truly frightening.

A Criminal Curriculum Vitae

1981: Obstructing a police officer.

1982: Carrying a concealed weapon.

1984: Four robbery charges, including one involving a weapon.

1986: Murder of Mark Shannon.

1993: Murder of Toronto dentist Norman Rasky, Montreal cab driver Fernand Talbot, partner-in-crime Don Hebert, an HIV-positive Toronto travel agent.

Terrence Fitzsimmons was born into an upper-middle-class family in London, Ont., the third of four brothers. His childhood ended at age nine, by which time he had developed a drug-abuse problem. His education ended at age 15 when he graduated to the streets of Toronto. He held a series of restaurant jobs, though he never kept a job for longer than six months.

A 1981 conviction for obstructing a peace officer begat a 1982 conviction for carrying a concealed weapon, followed by four robbery charges and a three-year sentence in 1984. In 1988, he killed a fellow inmate. He was sentenced to nine years and served six. He was released in December, 1992, but wasn't on the street for long. At the end of July, he murdered three people over the course of four days.

Between his first conviction at age 18 and his death at age 31, he was out of jail for just eight months.

Was he a natural-born killer? Probably not. In describing his initiation to life at the medium-security Joyceville Penitentiary in Kingston, he told me: "When I first came in I was around 5-feet-5. I was 18, 96 pounds, blond hair, green eyes. Just a little cutie at a party which I hadn't been invited to." He was raped during his first week.

Slowly, he learned the ropes: "You get to learn about all the different aspects of crime and all the attitudes of violence that pertain to prison subcultures and life. If you have an altercation, you have to use what you learned—killing someone else, having a fight, taking hostages, attempting escapes from prison. You use the knowledge you've learned. And you lose the humanity of just being a nice person."

One day, he witnessed the fatal stabbing of a close friend by another inmate. Because the Crown wished to call him as a witness, he was transferred for his protection to Kingston Penitentiary, a maximum-security facility.

Shortly after he arrived there at the age of 22, he found himself in the path of rapist-murderer Mark Shannon, who made him a sexual do-or-die offer. "The threats started about 6 p.m. the night before," recalled Mr. Fitzsimmons. By morning, he decided he had "no choice." By 10 a.m., Mr. Shannon was dead.

Mr. Fitzsimmons spent a year in solitary, waiting to be tried for manslaughter—for which he got nine years added to his tab. He was then transferred to the Saskatchewan Penitentiary in Prince Albert, an ultra-maximum security prison with one of Canada's two Special Handling Units (SHU).

This was the crucible for the final stage of Mr. Fitzsimmons's development. Howard Massicotte calls SHUs "the Siberia of prisons." It is designed to maximize sensory deprivation—a completely automated unit, two by three metres, lined with steel. The windows of each cell are covered with steel slats; the solid steel doors have a small peephole about five centimeters square.

Prisoners are locked up 23 hours a day; outside the cell, the prisoner is handcuffed to waist restraints and hobble-chained ankle-to-ankle. Only one prisoner is allowed out at a time. Television, radio, and reading material are privileges for good behaviour.

Mr. Fitzsimmons told me, "I was forgotten for three years when they left me in the SHU. I didn't realize it was doing any damage, to be perfectly honest. You come to enjoy the isolation. I was numb, confused. I became used to screaming into the speaker in the SHU. When you're talking to an inanimate object, you don't give it too much respect."

Dr. Stuart Grassian, of the Harvard School of Medicine and author of *Psychopathological Effects of Solitary Confinement*, consulted on the Fitzsimmons case: "These kinds of units (SHUs) are like factories, and the product they create is rage. Many people who've been in solitary become more rageful, more irritable, more explosive. The kind of thing Terry described is certainly consistent with what I've seen."

Mr. Fitzsimmons was 26 when he emerged, and soon after was returned to the general prison population at Kingston. On one occasion, he became disruptive after being refused shower privileges for four days. On his way to solitary confinement, he smashed his fist into a steel wall, shattering his hand.

"On the way to the hole, I started freaking out like within myself, not physically. I said 'You're going to lock me up for breaking my hand? Obviously you just want a piece of me,' so I ended up biting a chunk out of my arm. It took 14 stitches inside and 12 stitches outside 'cause I started pulling at it as well, ripping it with my teeth."

The new personality had emerged.

The authorities felt his behaviour warranted extended time in Kingston's solitary and Prince Albert's SHU, with the result that Mr. Fitzsimmons spent fewer than two years in the general population before two-thirds of his sentence was completed and he was eligible for release.

And so it was that in January, 1993, without a structured and gradual reintroduction to life beyond the penitentiary, he was discharged directly to the street to serve the final one-third on statutory release, which means he had to report regularly to his parole officer.

"They didn't 'gate' (refuse parole to) me because I did a lot of groups (in anger control, problem solving, life skills) and they couldn't justify it. I wasn't a repeat offender. The first anybody mentioned 'cascading' (gradual introduction into society) was after a parole breach. I turned myself back in and the parole people in Millhaven (Penitentiary) thought I had been on a prerelease program, that I had seen the street prior to getting out."

Lawyer John Hill, a long-time adversary of solitary confinement, says Correction Services was at fault. "They should have realized he was a danger to himself and to society." Mr. Massicotte adds that, "if a policy change has to come into effect, it should be that every person who has spent time in an SHU who is close to statutory release should be flagged automatically for (continued) detention. That might seem a negative thing coming from a defence lawyer, but (prisoners) need it."

Regardless of policy or responsibility, Mr. Fitzsimmons was now on the streets of Kingston. Six months before his release, he had married Tammy Lynn McGuire, the sister of an inmate. The union lasted 10 days into his freedom. He then moved in with beauty-salon owner Sheryl Blackadder, a relationship that lasted until July, when he stole $10,000 of her jewelry and disappeared into Toronto's gay community.

He soon met up with Don Hebert, an HIV-positive travel agent who was infatuated with him. The two found they had a common interest in cocaine. To get money for drugs, Mr. Fitzsimmons robbed a midtown Canada Trust; a few days later, this time accompanied by Mr. Hebert (who fancied them as "the first gay Bonnie and Clyde"), he held up the branch again.

Back at their apartment, they were joined by a retired Toronto dentist named Norman Rasky, who had a crack problem and moved in with them the day before. Dr. Rasky, 62, figured out that they had robbed a bank to buy cocaine and threatened to call the police. Mr. Fitzsimmons, high on drugs, bludgeoned and repeatedly stabbed him while Mr. Hebert looked on. He says it was then that Mr. Hebert asked him to kill him so he could escape the torments of a death by AIDS. Mr. Fitzsimmons agreed, and said he wished to die, too. It was likely then that he injected himself with some of Mr. Hebert's blood.

Mr. Hebert and Mr. Fitzsimmons fled to Montreal by train, leaving behind the beaten and stabbed body of Mr. Rasky in the basement of their apartment building. On Aug. 1, their money gone, they robbed and killed cab driver Fernand Talbot.

The next day, they went to Ottawa. They decided that this was the day Mr. Hebert would die. In a secluded spot in a Red Barn restaurant, Mr. Fitzsimmons choked Mr. Hebert into semi-consciousness, then plunged a knife into his chest.

He went to an Ottawa police station and turned himself in: "It's got to stop," he told them. "I'm tired of killing people."

When I first met him, Mr. Fitzsimmons had had time to reflect on the four murders and his decision to end his life by giving himself AIDS. "I wish none of the murders had happened, but wishing isn't going to change it. They're very deep experiences, very violent experiences, and I don't think one's easier than the other to live with. I have different emotions for each person. Hatred for Mark Shannon. Rasky? Pity. The cab driver? I wished it never happened. Don, the best friend I ever had? I miss him but I'm happy for him because he's where he wanted to be.

"I believed in our friendship. I believed that if he was willing to die by my hands then I should be willing to die by his blood. I'm giving society exactly what they want. I'm going to give them capital punishment. Instead of it being a five-minute thing, they'll see it for five or 10 years and watch it eat away at a person.

"I believe strongly that I'm more a product of the system than of my own family upbringing. Maybe they should start looking at trying to correct their mistakes before more of me get out."

Mr. Fitzsimmons died by his own hand on Tuesday, March 29. A memorial service was held for him this week at Kingston Penitentiary.

Part III

SOCIOLOGICAL CONCEPTS AND APPROACHES

Chapter 9

FOUNDATIONS OF
SOCIOLOGICAL THEORY

Robert J. Brym

INTRODUCTION

Sociology will inevitably appear a confusing enterprise to students just beginning to study it. Sociologists occupy themselves with problems that also concern political scientists, economists, psychologists, social workers, urban planners, psychiatrists, and lawyers. In what sense, then, is sociology distinct from these other disciplines?

The answer has more to do with the unique *approach* of sociologists to their subject matter than with the nature of the subject matter itself. While many kinds of scholars are interested in, say, crime, economic development, elections, and mental disorders, sociologists ask relatively distinct questions about these and other social issues.

I will examine three of the main questions that have animated sociology since its origins in the nineteenth century: (1) What is the relationship between the individual and society? (2) Are the most important determinants of social behaviour cultural or economic? (3) What are the bases of social inequality?

The debates surrounding these questions are recurrent. It is the tenacity and longevity of these disputes that allows me to characterize them as key issues in sociology. But the enduring character of these disputes may also be a source of frustration to the introductory student. It may appear that nothing ever gets resolved in sociology. However, careful study of the discipline demonstrates that sociological knowledge is, to a degree, cumulative. In other words, although sociologists ask much the same questions today as they did a century ago, their answers are now much more precise, complex, and enlightening than they were then; the classic questions of sociology continue to engage lively minds in a debate that gets more and more sophisticated over time.

Let us begin by examining Emile Durkheim's *Suicide*, which, a century ago, set out a highly controversial idea about the individual's relationship to society.

INDIVIDUAL AND SOCIETY

Durkheim on "Social Facts" and Suicide

Usually we assume that any act—a suicide, a marriage, a revolution, extraordinary economic success—is the outcome of an individual's (or many individuals') motives. Features of society are, in turn, usually viewed as the result of many individual passions and decisions. Durkheim, however, turned this conventional wisdom on its head. He argued that individual passions and decisions are the result of certain features of society, that the social whole is greater than the sum of its individual parts. And, according to Durkheim, the study of how social forces influence individual behaviour is what sociology is all about (Durkheim, [1895] 1966).

Consider, for example, the act of suicide. For two reasons, no act appears to be more personal than the taking of one's own life. First, common sense suggests that suicide is the outcome of some profound problem in the mind of the *individual*. Second, suicide seems the most *anti-social* act imaginable: it negates—indeed, destroys—society, at least for one person.

Yet, in 1897, Durkheim proposed the controversial idea that the causes of suicide are not just personal. If suicide rates are high in one group of people and low in another, that is due, said Durkheim, to the operation of *social facts*, impersonal social forces that lie outside an individual's mind and compel him or her to act in certain ways.

In order to make his case Durkheim first disposed of psychological and other common explanations of suicide.[1] For example, Durkheim examined the association between rates of suicide (the number of suicides among 100,000 people) and rates of psychological disorder (the number of cases of psychological disorder among 100,000 people) in various groups. The notion that psychological disorder causes suicide is supported, Durkheim reasoned, only if suicide rates tend to be high where rates of psychological disorder are high, and if suicide rates tend to be low where rates of psychological disorder are low.

Durkheim's analysis of European government statistics, hospital records, and other sources revealed nothing of the kind. For example, he discovered that: (1) There were slightly more women than men in European insane asylums. But there were four male suicides for every female suicide. (2) Jews had the highest rate of psychological disorder among the major religious groups in France. But they had the lowest suicide rate. (3) Psychological disorders occurred most frequently when a person reached maturity. But suicide rates increased steadily with age.

Clearly, suicide rates and rates of psychological disorder did not vary directly; in fact, they often appeared to vary inversely. Why, then, did men commit suicide more frequently than women, the aged more than the young, Jews less than Catholics, and Catholics less than Protestants? Durkheim saw these regularities as results of variations in the degree of *social solidarity* in different categories of the population. Accordingly, he expected groups whose members interact more frequently and intensely to exhibit lower suicide rates. For instance, Durkheim found that married adults were half as likely as unmarried adults to commit suicide. He explained this difference as a result of the fact that marriage creates social ties that bind the individual to society. Likewise, large families provide their members with more social ties than do small families, that is why, wrote Durkheim, the suicide rate is lower in large families. In general, he wrote, "suicide varies with the degree of integration of the social groups of which the individual forms a part. . . . The more weakened the groups to which he[2] belongs, the less he depends on them, the more he consequently depends only on himself and recognizes no other rules of conduct than what are founded on his private interests," the greater the chance that an individual will take his or her own life (Durkheim, [1897] 1951:209). Of course, this generalization tells us nothing about why any particular individual may take his or her life. It does, however, say something uniquely sociological about why the suicide rate varies from group to group.

The Phenomenological Response
Many contemporary sociologists continue to argue that the proper focus of the discipline is the study of social pressures that constrain or influence individuals. Today, researchers can use statistical techniques to measure the independent and combined effects of many social variables on many types of behaviour. The choice of a marriage partner may, for example, seem to be a question exclusively of love. But even love is constrained by social facts: research reveals that a very large proportion of marriages join partners from the same ethnic groups and classes.

However, not all marriages take place within ethnic groups and class groupings. This, opponents of the Durkheimian position argue, points to an important flaw in his theory. They argue that Durkheim paints an altogether too mechanical and deterministic view of the individual in society, making it seem as if people behave like billiard balls, knocked about on predetermined trajectories, unable to choose to alter their destinations. But, Durkheim's critics continue, we know from our everyday experience that this is not the case. People *do* make choices—often difficult ones—about what career to follow, what country to live in, whether and in what form they will adopt an established religion, whether to engage in heterosexual or homosexual relationships (or both), and so forth. Two people with similar social characteristics may react quite differently to similar social circumstances because, according to Durkheim's detractors, they may *interpret* these circumstances differently. In the opinion of such *phenomenological* sociologists, an adequate explanation of social phenomena requires that we understand the *subjective meanings* that people attach to social facts and the ways in which they actively *create* these social facts.

In order to better understand the phenomenological school of thought, let us return to the problem of suicide. If a police officer discovers a dead person at the wheel of a car that has run into a tree, it may be very difficult to establish with any certainty whether the death was accidental or suicidal. Interviewing friends and relatives in order to find out the dead person's state of mind immediately before the crash may help to rule out the possibility of suicide. But, as this example illustrates, understanding the intention or motive of the actor is critical to explaining or labelling a social action. Suicide, then, is not just an objective social fact, but an inferred, and therefore subjective, social fact. A state of mind must be interpreted—usually by a coroner—before the dead body becomes a suicide statistic (Douglas, 1967).

Because social stigma is attached to suicide, coroners are inclined to classify deaths as accidental whenever such an interpretation is at all plausible. Experts believe that, for this reason, official suicide rates are about one-third lower than actual suicide rates. The phenomenological study of social life reveals many such inconsistencies between objective and subjective reality. For instance, if increased crime rates among aboriginal Canadians are reported in the newspapers, this may reflect more crimes being committed by aboriginal Canadians. But the phenomenological sociologist is unlikely to accept such reports at face value. The higher crime rate may result from a politically motivated change in the official definition of what constitutes a crime, or increased police surveillance in areas where aboriginal Canadians reside. Here, inquiry into the subjective underside of the official picture may deepen our understanding of how society works.

Some phenomenological sociologists tend to ignore the impact of objective, outside social forces on the lives of men and women, reducing the study of society to an analysis of subjective interactions in small settings: how person A perceives person B's actions, how person A responds to these actions, and so forth (Goffman, 1959). Just as one-sidedly, strict Durkheimians ignore the subjective side of social life, and draw attention only to objective, outside forces. But many modern sociologists endorse neither extreme. They think it makes more sense to combine the Durkheimian and phenomenological approaches and analyze how men and women interpret, create, and change their social existence—but within the limits imposed on them by powerful social constraints. This synthetic approach is found in the work of Karl Marx and, to an even greater degree, Max Weber, who, along with Durkheim, established the groundwork of modern sociology. Let us now turn to a brief examination of their work.

STRUCTURE VERSUS CULTURE

Marx's Legacy

Both Marx and Weber stressed the importance of analyzing subjective and social actions *and* objective social constraints (Gerth and Mills, 1946:57–58; Marx, [1932] 1972:118; Weber, [1922] 1947:103). They also had compatible (though different) ideas about the *nature* of these constraints.

Marx, like Weber, recognized that the external determinants of behaviour consist of economic, political, and cultural forces. Marx tended to assign overwhelming causal priority to the economic realm. Weber did not deny the primacy of economic arrangements, but he rounded out Marx's analysis by showing how the political and cultural facts of life can act as important, independent causes of many social phenomena.

In the middle of the nineteenth century Marx proposed a sweeping theory of the development of human societies. In this theory the locus of change is economic organization—more precisely, society's class structure and its technological base. In 1859 Marx succinctly put his argument as follows:

> At a certain stage of their development, the material forces of production in society come into conflict with the existing relations of production, or—what is but a legal expression of the same thing—with the property relations within which they had been at work before. From forms of development of the forces of production those relations turn into fetters. Then occurs a period of social revolution. With the change of the economic foundation the entire immense super-structure is more or less rapidly transformed. (Marx, [1859] 1904:11–12)

How does Marx's theory apply to the rise of capitalism? In European feudal society peasants tilled small plots of land that were owned not by the peasants themselves but by landlords. Peasants were legally bound to the land, obliged to give landlords a set proportion of their harvest and to continue working for them under any circumstances. In turn, landlords were expected to protect peasants against poor economic conditions and marauders.

By the late fifteenth century, certain processes had been set in motion that eventually transformed feudal society into a modern capitalist system. Most important was the growth of exploration and trade, which increased the demand for many goods and services in commerce, navigation, and industry. By the seventeenth and eighteenth centuries some urban dwellers—successful artisans and merchants—had accumulated sufficient capital to expand their production significantly. In order to maximize their profits, these capitalists required an abundant supply of workers who could be hired in periods of high demand and fired without obligation during slack times. It was therefore necessary to induce and coerce indentured peasants to leave the soil and transform them into legally free workers who would work for wages (Marx and Engels, [1848] 1972:336 ff).

In Marx's view, the relations between wage labourers and capitalists at first facilitated rapid technological innovation and economic growth. Capitalists were keen to adopt new tools, machines, and production techniques. These changes allowed capitalists to produce more efficiently, earn higher profits, and drive their competitors out of business. Efficiency also required that workers be concentrated in larger and larger industrial establishments, that wages be kept as low as possible, and that as little as possible be invested in improving working conditions. Thus, according to Marx, workers and capitalists would stand face-to-face in factory and mine: a large and growing class of relatively impoverished workers opposing a small and shrinking class of increasingly wealthy owners.

Marx argued that in due course all workers would become aware of belonging to the same exploited class. This sense of *class consciousness* would, he felt, encourage the growth of working-class organizations, such as trade unions and political parties. These organizations would be bent on overthrowing the capitalist system and establishing a classless society. According to Marx, this revolutionary change was bound to occur during one of the recurrent and worsening crises of overproduction characteristic of the capitalist era. The productive capacity of the system would, Marx said, come to far outstrip the ability of the relatively impoverished workers to purchase goods and services. Thus, in order to sell goods and services, capitalists would be forced to lower their prices. Profits would then fall, the less efficient capitalists would go bankrupt, and massive unemployment of workers would result—thus deepening the economic crisis still further. The capitalist class system had originally encouraged economic growth. Eventually the crises of overproduction it generated would hinder such growth. At that time the capitalist class system would be destroyed and replaced by socialism, Marx argued.

As this thumbnail sketch shows, beliefs, symbols, and values—in short, culture—play a quite minor independent causal role in Marx's theory. Marx analyzed how, under most circumstances, ruling-class ideology forms a legitimizing cement in society and how, under rare circumstances, subordinate class consciousness can become an important force for change. But in his work it is always the material circumstances of existence that ultimately determine the role ideas play.

Weber on Capitalism and the World Religions

Weber, like Marx, was interested in explaining the rise of modern capitalism. And, like Marx, he was prepared to recognize the "fundamental importance of the economic factor" in his explanation (Weber, [1904–1905] 1958:26). But Weber was also bent on demonstrating the one-sidedness of any *exclusively* economic interpretation. After all, the economic conditions that Marx said were necessary for capitalist development existed in Catholic France during the reign of Louis XIV; yet the wealth generated in France by international trade and commerce tended to be consumed by war and the luxurious lifestyle of the aristocracy rather than invested in the growth of capitalist enterprise. For Weber, what prompted vigorous capitalist development in non-Catholic Europe and North America was a combination of (1) favourable economic conditions such as those discussed by Marx and (2) the spread of certain moral values by the Protestant reformers of the sixteenth century and their followers in the seventeenth century.

For specifically *religious* reasons, followers of the Protestant theologian John Calvin stressed the need to engage in intense worldly activity, to demonstrate industry, punctuality, and frugality in one's everyday life. In the view of men like John Wesley and Benjamin Franklin, religious doubts could be reduced, and a state of grace assured, if one worked diligently and lived ascetically. This idea was taken up by Puritanism, Methodism, and other Protestant denominations; Weber called it the *Protestant work ethic* (Weber, [1904–1905] 1958:183).

According to Weber, this ethic had wholly unexpected economic consequences where it took root, and where economic conditions were favourable, early capitalist enterprise grew robustly. In other words, two independent developments—the Protestant work ethic (which derived from purely religious considerations) and the material conditions favouring capitalist growth (which derived from specifically economic circumstances)—interacted to invigorate capitalism. Weber made his case even more persuasive by comparing Protestant Western Europe and North America with India and China. He concluded that the latter cases differed from the former in one decisive (but certainly not exclusive) respect: Indian and Chinese religion inhibited capitalist economic action. In contrast to ancient Judaism and Christianity, Asiatic religions had strong other-worldly, magical, and anti-rational components that hindered worldly success in competition and accumulation. As a result, capitalism developed very slowly in India and China (Zeitlin, [1968] 1987:135–150).

Subsequent research has demonstrated that the association between the Protestant ethic and the strength of capitalist development is weaker than Weber thought (Brym, 1986:24–27; Samuelsson, [1957] 1961). In some places, Catholicism has co-existed with vigorous capitalist growth and Protestantism with relative stagnation. Nonetheless, even if Weber was wrong about this particular case, his *general* view—that religious developments cannot be reduced to economic developments, and that religious ideas have economic consequences—is still widely regarded as a brilliant and valid insight.

Just as some Marxist sociologists have adopted a strict economic determinism, some Weberians have misinterpreted Weber's ideas in a way that supports a sort of cultural determinism. But the plain fact is that Weber assigned nearly the same relative weight to economic and cultural forces as did Marx; and there is nothing in Marx's work that is incompatible with Weber's insights into the relative autonomy of religious developments. Disputes between orthodox Marxists and orthodox Weberians over the relative weight of economic versus cultural causes of change may thus be as specious as the disagreement between rigid Durkheimians and equally rigid phenomenologists.

THE BASES OF SOCIAL INEQUALITY

Marx Versus Weber

Thus far I have singled out areas of similarity or compatibility in the thought of Marx and Weber. In Weber's "long and intense debate with the ghost of Karl Marx" (Albert Salomon, quoted in Zeitlin, [1968] 1987:xi), there also emerged some ideas that are incompatible with those of Marx. This is especially obvious in Weber's work on social inequality.

Marx regarded ownership or non-ownership of property as the fundamental basis of inequality in capitalist society. In his view, there are two main classes under capitalism. Members of the capitalist class, or *bourgeoisie*, own means of production (tools, factories, etc.) but they do not work them. Members of the working class, or *proletariat*, work but do not own means of production. In addition, Marx discussed some minor classes that are vestiges of pre-capitalist times. Most important, members of the *petite bourgeoisie* (e.g., farmers, owners of small family businesses) own and work means of production. Marx also analyzed various divisions within the major classes. These class segments were distinguished from one another by their sources of income (e.g., financial versus industrial capitalists) or skill level (e.g., skilled versus unskilled manual workers).

In defining classes in this way, Marx was not trying to account for gradations of rank in society. Instead, he sought to explain the massive historical change that results from the materially grounded opposition of interests between classes. In his view, the major classes were potentially self-conscious groups engaged in conflict that would eventually result in societal transformation.

Weber agreed that "'property' and 'lack of property' are . . . the basic categories of all class situations" (Weber, [1922] 1946:182). But his analysis of inequality differed from Marx's in three main ways. First, he was profoundly skeptical about Marx's interpretation of historical development. As a result, he stressed that members of classes do not necessarily become class-conscious and act in concert. Second, Weber argued that property relations are just one aspect of a more general "market situation" that determines class position. For example, expertise acquired through formal education is a scarce commodity on the labour market. Such expertise increases one's advantages or "life-chances" and is therefore an important factor structuring the class system. On this basis, and in addition to the capitalist and manual working classes, Weber distinguished large and growing classes of technical/managerial personnel and white-collar workers who perform routine tasks.

Third, Weber was less concerned than Marx with the sources of conflict between discrete classes and more concerned with the structure of complex social hierarchies. For this reason he showed that the bases of social inequality are not exclusively economic. One non-economic source of inequality is the way honour (or esteem or prestige) is distributed in society. Weber referred to groups distinguished from one another in terms of prestige as *status groups*. For example, line of descent (including ethnic origin) may account for the level of esteem in which a status group is held, and esteem affects the life-chances of status-group members. A second non-economic source of inequality is the political party. A party, in Weber's definition, is an association that seeks to gain control over an organization—ranging all the way from, say, a sports club to a state—for purposes of implementing specific policies. Parties may recruit members from specific classes or status groups, or both. As such, and to the degree that they achieve organizational control, parties bestow more advantages on their supporters than on non-supporters.

If parties and status groups are independent bases of social inequality, then, according to Weber, they are not wholly independent, especially in capitalist societies. There is an association between status-group and party membership, on the one hand, and class position on the other. The structure of class inequality helps to shape status-group and party membership; in fact, "today the class situation is by far the predominant factor" (Weber, [1922] 1946:190).[3]

Much of modern sociology has been devoted to exploring the ramifications of Weber's refinement of Marx's stratification model. What are the economic determinants of class that do not derive from ownership versus non-ownership of property? How does the concentration of ethnic and other status groups in particular class locations reinforce status-group cohesion? How do ethnic and other forms of status-group identification serve to reinforce patterns of inequality? To what degree do classes serve as recruitment bases for political parties? To what degree do different types of political parties enact policies that redistribute income? These are among the most popular questions asked by modern sociologists, and they are all indebted to Weber's elaboration of the Marxian schema.

Gender Inequality

Recent years have also witnessed an important addition to the stratification model sketched above. It is now generally acknowledged that gender is a basis of social inequality quite on a par with status groups, parties, and classes (see Figure 9.1). Thus, in Canada and elsewhere, gender is an important a determinant of annual income as class (Ornstein, 1983) because women in the paid labour force tend to be segregated in low-pay, low-prestige jobs (Fox and Fox, 1986). One study conducted in the early 1980s found that even if one matches a group of Canadian men and a group of Canadian women in terms of education, occupation, amount of time worked each year, and years of job experience, one discovers that the women earn only 63 per cent of what the men earn (Goyder, 1981:328). Meanwhile, the great bulk of household labour continues to be performed by women, even if both spouses work; one study conducted in Vancouver found that when their wives entered the paid labour force, husbands did on average only one hour more of housework per week (Meissner et al., 1975).

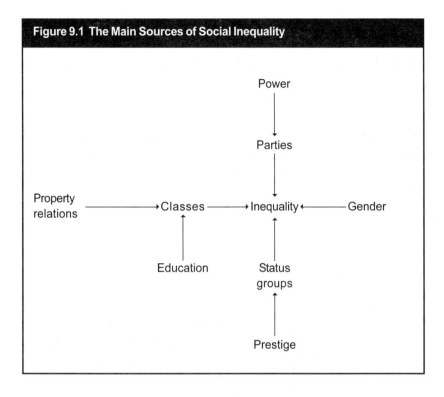

Figure 9.1 The Main Sources of Social Inequality

Classical theories teach us little about the causes of such gender inequality. That is, while Marx and Weber offered important insights into the reasons for the expansion and contraction of particular locations in the stratification system, they "give no clues about why *women* are subordinate to *men* inside and outside the family and why it is not the other way around" (Hartmann, [1978] 1984:174).

Over the past 25 years, biological, cultural, and social-structural theories of gender inequality have been proposed. Accumulated research suggests that while biological factors—especially women's child-bearing function—may have encouraged some division of labour between the sexes in primitive societies, there is no biological reason why male and female jobs should have been rewarded differently, let alone why they continue to be rewarded differently today. Cultural theories, which locate the causes of gender inequality in the way people learn established practices, cannot account either for the origins of gender inequality or for the sources of variation in such inequality. Explanations that root gender inequality in social structure appear more promising. While the subordination of women is evident in virtually every known society, it takes on different forms and degrees in different times and places. Unravelling the relationship between social structure, on the one hand, and the form and degree of gender inequality, on the other, is a complex task that lies at the cutting edge of contemporary research on social inequality.

CONCLUSION

In this brief essay I have set out three questions that lie at the foundation of classical sociology. I have emphasized that the significance of these questions derives from their proven ability to continue provoking the sociological imagination.

NOTES

I would like to thank Jim Curtis, Jim Richardson, and Lorne Tepperman for helpful comments on a draft of this article.

1.   Durkheim actually analyzed several types of suicide and disposed of several types of explanations. However, strict space limitations preclude a full discussion of these.
2.   For the most part, classical sociology (as well as history, political science, economics, and so forth) virtually ignored the existence of women in society. This was reflected not only in the use of sexist language, but in major oversights and imbalances in sociological theorizing, as will be illustrated later in this essay.
3.   Unfortunately, many modern sociologists, particularly in the United States, have trivialized Weber—and rendered him much more "anti-Marxist" than he in fact was— by exaggerating the independence of the various bases of inequality, unnecessarily multiplying the number of bases, regarding inequality as a continuous ranking of statistical categories, and highlighting the subjective evaluation of prestige as the major basis of inequality. For a critique of these tendencies, see (Parkin, [1971] 1972: esp. pp. 13–47).

Chapter 10

STRAIN THEORY
AND SCHOOL CRIME

Robert Agnew

THERE ALREADY WAS MUCH CONCERN ABOUT SCHOOL CRIME WHEN TWO STUDENTS at Columbine High School in Littleton, Colorado, shot 13 others to death and then killed themselves in April 1999. This incident prompted massive concern about school crime, with people across the country, including politicians and criminologists, asking the following questions:

1. How common is crime and violence in our schools? The incident at Columbine was preceded by several other well-publicized school incidents involving multiple deaths. Such incidents have led many to seriously question the safety of our schools.
2. How can we explain the crime in our schools? That is, why do some students kill, injure, and steal at school? Related to this, why do some schools have higher crime rates than do other schools?
3. What can we do to make our schools safer?

This chapter addresses each of these questions.

I begin by briefly reviewing the evidence on the extent of crime, including violence, in our nation's schools. Some of this evidence will surprise you. I then use strain theory to explain why some *students* are more likely to engage in school crime than are other students and why some *schools* have higher rates of crime than do other schools. In particular, I focus on the ways in which *school-related factors* can contribute to school crime. Whereas strain theory is just one of several theories capable of explaining school crime, I believe that it has some important and unique insights to offer. Finally, I draw on strain theory to suggest strategies for reducing school crime.

HOW COMMON IS SCHOOL CRIME?

Perhaps the best way in which to estimate the extent of school crime is with data from the National Crime Victimization Survey (NCVS). This survey involves interviews with people in 55,000 representative households throughout the United States. Each person age 12 years or over in these households is asked whether he or she has been the victim of various violent and property crimes, and each person is asked a number of questions about each victimization including the location of the victimization. Because we are dealing with a representative sample of people, we can use their responses to estimate the extent of crime, including school crime, in the United States as a whole. The NCVS provides a more accurate estimate of the extent of crime than do police reports because most crimes are not reported to the police. The NCVS includes both crimes that are and are not reported to the police, although it probably still underestimates the true extent of crime (Wells and Rankin, 1995). Data from the 1996 NCVS indicate the following about the extent of school crime (Kaufman et al., 1998; also see Anderson, 1998; Elliott, Hamburg, and Williams, 1998).

There were about 1.3 million violent crimes committed against students ages 12 through 18 years at school, or on the way to or from school. That works out to about five incidents of violence per 100 students. The large share of these crimes were minor in nature; that is, they involved fistfights or other minor altercations in which no one was physically hurt or there were only minor injuries. About 255,000 of these crimes were serious in nature—rapes/ sexual assaults, robberies, or serious assaults. That works out to about one incident of serious violence per 100 students. There were about 2.1 million thefts at school. That works out to about eight thefts per 100 students.

Is school more or less safe than the environment outside of school? It depends on the type of crime we are discussing. Students are about as likely to experience a violent crime away from school as they are at school. But they are about three times as likely to experience a *serious* violent crime away from school as they are at school. So, students are much more vulnerable to serious violence outside of school (violence peaks during the few hours after the school day ends). Students, however, are somewhat more likely to experience thefts at school than away from school.

What about the chances of being killed at school? A total of 76 students were murdered or committed suicide at school during the combined 1992– 1993 and 1993–1994 school years. Another 29 individuals, including teachers and staff, also suffered violent deaths at school during this period. During the 1992 and 1993 calendar years, 7,294 juveniles ages five to 19 years were murdered and 4,353 committed suicide away from school. So, students are much more likely to be killed or commit suicide away from school than at school. Only about 1 percent of all violent deaths to school-age children occur at school. For school-age children, the chance of being the victim of a violent death at school is about one in 1 million.

How about trends in school crime? Are schools becoming less safe? Data from several sources suggest that the answer is no. Generally, rates of violence and theft at school have been stable or declining during recent years. This also is true of violent *deaths* at school. I should note, however, that there has been a very recent increase in the number of "multiple-death" incidents at schools. There was an average of one multiple-death incident per year at schools from August 1992 to July 1995, but that increased to an average of five incidents per year from August 1995 to June 1998 (this increase in multiple-death incidents occurred even though the *overall* rate of violent deaths at school decreased). These incidents receive a great deal of publicity, and they partly account for the widespread impression that schools are unsafe and school violence is increasing.

Overall, the data indicate that serious violence is not as common at school as many people might believe, that it is not increasing, and that it is much more common away from school. At the same time, a large number of serious violent incidents do occur at school, and less serious crime is common at schools. Furthermore, certain schools, particularly schools in poor urban areas, suffer from high rates of both minor crime and serious violence. For example, some data indicate that poor schools in urban areas have rates of serious violence up to 15 times higher on average than less poor schools in suburban, small town, and rural areas (Kaufman et al., 1998:61).

It is, of course, important to understand why some students are more likely than others to engage in school crime and why some schools have much higher rates of crime than do others. Such crime not only has a devastating effect on many of its victims, but it interferes with the fundamental mission of schools. It is difficult for learning to occur when one's safety is in doubt.

HOW CAN WE EXPLAIN SCHOOL CRIME?

Politicians and others have blamed school crime on several factors including the effects of mass media violence, an increase in gangs, the absence of school prayer, the availability of guns, lax security in the schools, the "breakdown" of the family, and a failure to impose severe punishments on juvenile offenders. Many of these explanations reflect the two dominant theories of crime:

differential association/social learning theory, and control theory. Differential association/social learning theory says that we learn to engage in crime from others including family, friends, gang members, and the media. These others might model criminal behaviour (which we then imitate), reinforce or reward our criminal behaviour, and teach us beliefs conducive to crime (e.g., we should respond with violence if someone treats us with disrespect). Control theories argue that we are more likely to engage in crime when we are low in social control. Social control can be external or internal. When external control is low, we have little fear of sanction from others including family, friends, teachers, and police. We feel that these others will not catch us committing crimes or that, if they do catch us, we have little fear of the punishments they will impose. When internal social control is low, we can engage in crime with little guilt because we do not believe that crime is wrong.

I do not deny the relevance of these and other theories.

My focus, however, is on strain theory. Strain theory makes a rather simple argument: when other people treat us badly, we might get upset and respond with crime. I elaborate on this simple idea and then apply it to the explanation of school crime.

A BRIEF OVERVIEW OF STRAIN THEORY

Strain theory first describes the two major ways in which people can treat us badly, that is, treat us in ways we do not like.

First, people can prevent us from achieving our goals. Strain theory argues that juveniles can pursue a variety of goals. These goals include money and the things that money can buy such as nice clothes and a good car. They include status and respect; most people want to be positively regarded and treated in a respectful manner by others. They include autonomy, as many juveniles have a strong desire for autonomy from adults; they do not like to be told what to do and instead want the freedom to make their own decisions. Juveniles, however, often are prevented from achieving these goals through legitimate channels. For example, their parents do not give them the money to buy the clothes they want or finance their social activities. Certain people do not treat them with the respect they feel they deserve, and their parents and teachers try to control things such as how they dress, how late they stay out, and with whom they associate.

Second, people can take things that we value or present us with negative or noxious stimuli. For example, people can take our possessions, or our romantic partners can break up with us. So, we lose something that we value. Or, people can verbally insult us or physically attack us.

Strain theory then argues that this bad treatment makes us *feel* bad; that is, it makes us feel angry, frustrated, depressed, anxious, and the like. These bad feelings create pressure for corrective action; we want to do something so that we will not feel so bad. This is especially true if we are angry or frustrated. These emotions energize us for action, create a desire for revenge, and lower our inhibitions. There are several possible ways in which to respond to the strain and negative emotions we feel, certain of which involve crime. We might engage in crime to end the bad treatment we are experiencing. For example, we might steal to get the money we want, or we might attack people to stop them from harassing us. We might engage in crime to seek revenge against the people who are mistreating us, and we might engage in a crime such as illicit drug use to make us feel better.

Whether we engage in crime is said to depend on a number of factors. Individuals are more likely to respond to strain with crime if they have poor problem-solving skills. For example, individuals who lack the verbal skills to negotiate with others are more likely to respond to harassment with crime. Individuals are more likely to respond to strain with crime if they have few conventional social supports. For example, individuals who cannot turn to their parents for assistance when they face problems are more likely to resort to crime. Individuals are more likely to respond with crime when they are in situations where the costs of crime are low and the rewards are high. For example, individuals are more likely to steal when there are no police or teachers around and valuable objects are within easy reach. Individuals also are more likely to respond with crime when they have dispositions for crime. For example, some individuals have traits that are conducive to crime such as impulsivity and irritability. Some individuals are low in social control; they do not fear sanctions from others, and they do not believe that crime is wrong. Furthermore, some individuals have been taught to engage in crime in certain situations (For fuller descriptions of strain theory, see Agnew, 1992, 1997, forthcoming.)

USING STRAIN THEORY TO EXPLAIN WHY SOME INDIVIDUALS ARE MORE LIKELY TO ENGAGE IN SCHOOL CRIME

At the most basic level, some individuals are more likely to engage in crime, both within school and outside of school, because they experience more strain and are more likely to respond to strain with crime. Studies suggest that individuals are more likely to engage in crime when they experience the following types of strain: dissatisfaction with the amount of money they have, child abuse or neglect, criminal victimization, physical punishment by parents, negative relations with parents, negative relations with peers, neighbourhood problems, homelessness, and a wide range of stressful life events such as the divorce/separation of parents, parental unemployment, and changing schools (Agnew, 1997, forthcoming). There has been less research on those factors that influence whether one responds to strain with crime, and the few studies in this area have produced mixed results (Agnew, forthcoming). Nevertheless, strain theory would predict that crime is especially likely among strained individuals who are low in problem-solving skills and conventional social support, are in situations where the costs of crime are low and the rewards are high, and have dispositions for crime.

Much of the strain that individuals experience originates outside of school. The family, for example, is a major source of strain. But a good deal of strain occurs at school, and such strain is the focus of this chapter. We might classify school strain into four categories: negative peer relations, negative teacher relations, low grades, and a general dissatisfaction with school. Data suggest that individuals who experience these types of strain are more likely to engage in crime including school crime (Agnew, 1985, 1997, forthcoming; Agnew and Brezina, 1997; Cernkovich and Giordano, 1992; Hawkins and Lishner, 1987; Jenkins, 1997; Maguin and Loeber, 1996; Welsh, Greene, and Jenkins, 1999).

Negative Peer Relations

Schools, in particular middle schools and high schools, usually bring together large numbers of students. These students did not choose to associate with one another, they have different interests and personalities, and they do not have much experience coping with different situations. Nevertheless, they are concentrated in the same small space for several hours a day, and they often are placed in situations where they compete against one another for things such as good grades and status in the adolescent world. It is not surprising that many of them get into conflicts with one another. In particular, they sometimes treat one another in disliked ways. One common problem in schools, for example, is "bullying," which occurs when a person "is exposed, repeatedly and over time, to negative actions on the part of one or more other persons" (Olweus, 1991:413). Negative actions are defined as those intentional actions that inflict or attempt to inflict injury or discomfort on another person.

Negative peer relations such as bullying are a major type of strain. In fact, when students are asked about the things that upset or anger them, they frequently talk about interpersonal problems with peers. Surprisingly, criminologists have not devoted much attention to the impact of such problems on crime. But the few studies that have been done in this area suggest that such problems increase the likelihood of crime (Agnew and Brezina, 1997). In this connection, I should note that many of the students who have committed mass murder at school were in part motivated by the fact that they had been bullied by others or had experienced other interpersonal problems with peers. The large majority of students, of course, do not react to peer problems in such an extreme manner. Nowadays, it is difficult to explain, and especially difficult to predict, why a few students go to such extremes. Nevertheless, negative peer relations is one source of school crime.

Lockwood (1997) has done some fascinating research on the connection between peer problems and crime including school crime. He interviewed 110 middle and high school students from schools with high rates of violence. These students discussed 250 violent incidents in which they had been involved. About half of these incidents occurred at school, followed by public areas and homes. Most of these incidents (58 percent) involved acquaintances, followed by friends (16 percent) and family members (15 percent). Only 11 percent involved strangers. So, the most common setting for a violent crime was an encounter with an "acquaintance" at school. These violent incidents almost always began when one of the students did something that the other student did not like. One of the most common things was "unprovoked offensive touching" such as pushing, grabbing, hitting, or throwing something at someone. Other disliked behaviours included interfering with someone else's possessions, refusing to do something when requested, saying something bad about someone else, verbally teasing someone, and deliberately insulting someone. These actions threaten one's status and autonomy, involve the loss of valued things, and/or involve the presence of negative stimuli. They usually lead to an argument, the argument sometimes escalates with insults being exchanged, and violence sometimes is the result. The violence is performed to end the disliked behaviour, seek revenge, and/or save face.

Negative Teacher Relations and Poor Grades
Data also suggest that poor relations with teachers increases the likelihood crime. Teachers might present students with negative stimuli. One study, for example, found that crime was more likely among students who reported that their teachers often lost their tempers, made negative comments, and talked down to students (Agnew, 1985). Related to this, students might become upset when they receive poor grades from teachers. Not all students care

about their grades, but some do, and limited data suggest that the receipt of poor grades is an important source of strain and crime in certain cases.

School Dissatisfaction

Finally, many students experience a more general type of strain at school. They find school boring and a "waste of time," partly because they have trouble understanding what is going on in class and keeping up with schoolwork. They do not feel that school is relevant to their future lives. They have little involvement in school activities, and they would rather be elsewhere. In short, they dislike school. Data suggest that such students also are more likely to engage in crime.

I should note that the association between crime and factors such as poor grades and dissatisfaction with school does not prove that strain theory is correct. These factors might be related to crime for reasons that have to do with social control theory or other theories. Individuals who have poor grades and dislike school, for example, are lower in social control. They have less to lose by engaging in crime and so are less deterred by the threat of punishment. Nevertheless, some data suggest that these factors affect crime at least partly by increasing the anger of students (Agnew, 1985).

USING STRAIN THEORY TO EXPLAIN WHY SOME SCHOOLS HAVE HIGHER CRIME RATES

Some schools have much higher crime rates than do other schools. A few researchers have tried to determine why this is the case. They usually find that school differences in crime are largely a function of differences between the students who attend the schools and the communities in which the schools are located. School crime usually is higher in schools that have higher percentages of students who are less able, poor, male, and members of minority groups. School crime usually is higher in schools that are located in urban communities with high rates of crime, poverty, unemployment, and female-headed households. To a large extent, then, school crime is a function of forces that are external to the school. However, when we take account of student and community characteristics, we find that school characteristics do have a small to modest association with rates of school crime (Catalano and Hawkins, 1996; Elliott et al., 1998; Gottfredson and Gottfredson, 1985; Hawkins and Lishner, 1987; Hellman and Beaton, 1986; Lawrence, 1998; Weishew and Peng, 1993; Welsh et al., 1999).

Although not all studies agree with one another, the evidence suggests that school crime tends to be lower in the following types of schools:

- Small schools with good resources.
- Schools with good discipline where there are clear rules for behaviour and these rules are consistently enforced in a fair manner (there is some evidence, however, that overly punitive discipline contributes to higher rates of school crime; certain studies, for example, suggest that delinquency rates are higher in schools that use physical punishment and that make frequent use of punishment).
- Schools that provide opportunities for students to succeed, including students who do not plan to attend college, and that praise student accomplishments.
- Schools that have high expectations for students and that make rigorous but not unrealistic work demands on them.
- Schools where teachers have positive attitudes towards students, show concern for students, and create pleasant physical space for students to work.
- Schools with good cooperation between the administration and teachers with the administration keeping teachers informed of disciplinary problems and supporting/assisting teachers in their disciplinary efforts.

The association between these factors and school crime can be partly explained in terms of strain theory. Schools with the preceding characteristics create less strain among students. On the one hand, schools with these characteristics are firm; rules are clearly stated and consistently enforced. One likely consequence of this firmness is that students are less likely to mistreat one another; such mistreatment is not tolerated. So, a major source of school strain is reduced. At the same time, these schools show much concern for students. Whereas there are firm rules for behaviour, such rules are not overly strict or punitive, and they are fairly enforced. This also reduces strain because students resent punishments that are overly harsh or unfairly applied. These schools provide more opportunities for student success and involvement, which reduces poor grades and dissatisfaction with school. Teachers in these schools try to create good relationships with students and positive working relationships with them. For example, they frequently praise student accomplishments as they attempt to assist students in need. Not only does this reduce strain, but teachers are more likely to help students cope with the strain they do experience.

SUMMARY

So, students who are high in strain are more likely to engage in crime including school crime. I focused on four types of strain: negative peer relations, negative teacher relations, low grades, and dissatisfaction with school. Also, it might be the case that strained students are more likely to engage in crime when they have low problem-solving skills and low social support, encounter situations in which the costs of crime are low and the rewards are high, and have dispositions for crime. Again, there are other reasons why students engage in school crime, but these are the primary reasons derived from strain theory. Schools are more likely to have high rates of crimes when they do not possess the characteristics listed in the previous subsection. Whereas these characteristics likely are related to school crime for a variety of reasons, their association with school crime can be partly explained in terms of strain theory.

CONCLUSION

Much data suggest that one of the major causes of school crime is the strain that students experience including the strain experienced at school. Strain theory focuses on several important sources of school crime that have not received much attention in the media, and it highlights the importance of several strategies for controlling school crime that have been neglected in the media and by many politicians.

Chapter 11

THE SOCIAL REALITY
OF CRIME

Richard Quinney

A THEORY THAT HELPS US BEGIN TO EXAMINE THE LEGAL ORDER CRITICALLY IS THE one I call the *social reality of crime*. Applying this theory, we think of crime as it is affected by the dynamics that mold the society's social, economic, and political structure. First, we recognize how criminal law fits into capitalist society. The legal order gives reality to the crime problem in the United States. Everything that makes up crime's social reality, including the application of criminal law, the behaviour patterns of those who are defined as criminal, and the construction of an ideology of crime, is related to the established legal order.

The social reality of crime is formulated as follows.

THE OFFICIAL DEFINITION OF CRIME

Crime as a legal definition of human conduct is created by agents of the dominant class in a politically organized society.

The essential starting point is a definition of crime that itself is based on the legal definition. Crime, as *officially* determined, is a *definition* of behaviour that is conferred on some people by those in power. Agents of the law (such as legislators, police, prosecutors, and judges) are responsible for formulating and administering criminal law. Upon *formulation* and *application* of these definitions of crime, persons and behaviours become criminal.

Crime, according to this first proposition, is not inherent in behaviour, but is a judgment made by some about the actions and characteristics of others. This proposition allows us to focus on the formulation and administration of the criminal law as it applies to the behaviours that become defined as criminal.

Crime is seen as a result of the class-dynamic process that culminates in defining persons and behaviours as criminal. It follows, then, that the greater the number of definitions of crime that are formulated and applied, the greater the amount of crime.

FORMULATING DEFINITIONS OF CRIME

Definitions of crime are composed of behaviours that conflict with the interests of the dominant class.

Definitions of crime are formulated according to the interests of those who have the power to translate their interests into public policy. Those definitions are ultimately incorporated into the criminal law. Furthermore, definitions of crime in a society change as the interests of the dominant class change. In other words, those who are able to have their interests represented in public policy regulate the formulation of definitions of crime.

The powerful interests are reflected not only in the definitions of crime and the kinds of penal sanctions attached to them, but also in the legal policies on handling those defined as criminals. Procedural rules are created for enforcing and administering the criminal law. Policies are also established on programs for treating and punishing the criminally defined and programs for controlling and preventing crime. From the initial definitions of crime to the subsequent procedures, correctional and penal programs, and policies for controlling and preventing crime, those who have the power regulate the behaviour of those without power.

APPLYING DEFINITIONS OF CRIME

Definitions of crime are applied by the class that has the power to shape the enforcement and administration of criminal law.

The dominant interests intervene in all the stages at which definitions of crime are created. Because class interests cannot be effectively protected merely by formulating criminal law, the law must be enforced and administered. The interests of the powerful, therefore, also operate where the definitions of crime reach the application stage. As Vold has argued, crime is "political behaviour and the criminal becomes in fact a member of a 'minority group' without sufficient public support to dominate the control of the police power of the state." Those whose interests conflict with the ones represented in the law must either change their behaviour or possibly find it defined as criminal.

The probability that definitions of crime will be applied varies according to how much the behaviours of the powerless conflict with the interests of those in power. Law enforcement efforts and judicial activity are likely to increase when the interests of the dominant class are threatened. Fluctuations and variations in applying definitions of crime reflect shifts in class relations.

Obviously, the criminal law is not applied directly by those in power; its enforcement and administration are delegated to authorized *legal agents*. Because the groups responsible for creating the definitions of crime are physically separated from the groups that have the authority to enforce and administer law, local conditions determine how the definitions will be applied. In particular, communities vary in their expectations of law enforcement and the administration of justice. The application of definitions is also influenced by the visibility of offenses in a community and by the public's norms about reporting possible violations. And especially important in enforcing and administering the criminal law are the legal agents' occupational organization and ideology.

The probability that these definitions will be applied depends on the actions of the legal agents who have the authority to enforce and administer the law. A definition of crime is applied depending on their evaluations. Turk has argued that during "criminalization," a criminal label may be affixed to people because of real or fancied attributes: "Indeed, a person is evaluated, either favorably or unfavorably, not because he *does* something, or even because he *is* something, but because others react to their perceptions of him as offensive or inoffensive." Evaluation by the definers is affected by the way in which the suspect handles the situation, but ultimately the legal agents' evaluations and subsequent decisions are the crucial factors in determining the criminality of human acts. As legal agents evaluate more behaviours and persons as worthy of being defined as crimes, the probability that definitions of crime will be applied grows.

HOW BEHAVIOUR PATTERNS DEVELOP IN RELATION TO DEFINITIONS OF CRIME

Behaviour patterns are structured in relation to definitions of crime, and within this context people engage in actions that have relative probabilities of being defined as criminal.

Although behaviour varies, all behaviours are similar in that they represent patterns within society. All persons—whether they create definitions of crime or are the objects of these definitions—act in reference to *normative systems* learned in relative social and cultural settings. Because it is not the quality of the behaviour but the action taken against the behaviour that gives it the character of criminality, that which is defined as criminal is relative to the behaviour patterns of the class that formulates and applies definitions. Consequently, people whose behaviour patterns are not represented when the definitions of crime are formulated and applied are more likely to act in ways that will be defined as criminal than those who formulate and apply definitions.

Once behaviour patterns become established with some regularity within the segments of society, individuals have a framework for creating *personal action patterns*. These continually develop for each person as he moves from one experience to another. Specific action patterns give behaviour an individual substance in relation to the definitions of crime.

People construct their own patterns of action in participating with others. It follows, then, that the probability that persons will develop action patterns with a high potential for being defined as criminal depends on (1) structured opportunities, (2) learning experiences, (3) interpersonal associations and opportunities, and (4) self-conceptions. Throughout the experiences, each person creates a conception of self as a human social being. Thus prepared, he behaves according to the anticipated consequences of his actions.

In the experiences shared by the definers of crime and the criminally defined, personal-action patterns develop among the latter because they are so defined. After they have had continued experience in being defined as criminal, they learn to manipulate the application of criminal definitions.

Furthermore, those who have been defined as criminal begin to conceive of themselves as criminal. As they adjust to others' reactions, therefore, people may develop personal-action patterns that increase the likelihood of their being defined as criminal in the future. That is, increased experience with definitions of crime increases the probability of their developing actions that may be subsequently defined as criminal.

Thus, both the definers of crime and the criminally defined are involved in reciprocal action patterns. The personal-action patterns of both the definers and the defined are shaped by their common, continued, and related experiences. The fate of each is bound to that of the other.

CONSTRUCTING AN IDEOLOGY OF CRIME

An ideology of crime is constructed and diffused by the dominant class to secure its hegemony.

This ideology is created in the kinds of ideas people are exposed to, the manner in which they select information to fit the world they are shaping, and their way of interpreting this information. People behave in reference to the *social meanings* they attach to their experiences.

Among the conceptions that develop in a society are those relating to what people regard as crime. The concept of crime must of course be accompanied by ideas about the nature of crime. Images develop about the relevance of crime, the offender's characteristics, the appropriate reaction to crime, and the relation of crime to the social order. These conceptions are constructed by communication, and, in fact, an ideology of crime depends on the portrayal of crime in all personal and mass communication. This ideology is thus diffused throughout the society.

One of the most concrete ways by which an ideology of crime is formed and transmitted is the official investigation of crime. The President's Commission on Law Enforcement and Administration of Justice is the best contemporary example of the state's role in shaping an ideology of crime. Not only are we as citizens more aware of crime today because of the President's Commission, but official policy on crime has been established in a crime bill, the *Omnibus Crime Control and Safe Streets Act* of 1968. The crime bill, itself a reaction to the growing fears of class conflict in American society, creates an image of a severe crime problem and, in so doing, threatens to negate some of our basic constitutional guarantees in the name of controlling crime.

Consequently, the conceptions that are most critical in actually formulating and applying the definitions of crime are those held by the dominant class. These conceptions are certain to be incorporated into the social reality of crime. The more government acts in reference to crime, the more probable it is that definitions of crime will be created and that behaviour patterns will develop in opposition to those definitions. The formulation of definitions of crime, their application, and the development of behaviour patterns in relation to the definitions, are thus joined in full circle by the construction of an ideological hegemony toward crime.

CONSTRUCTING THE SOCIAL REALITY OF CRIME

The social reality of crime is constructed by the formulation and application of
definitions of crime, the development of behaviour patterns in relation to these
definitions, and the construction of an ideology of crime.

The first five propositions are collected here into a final composition proposition.
The theory of the social reality of crime, accordingly, postulates creating a
series of phenomena that increase the probability of crime. The result,
holistically, is the social reality of crime.

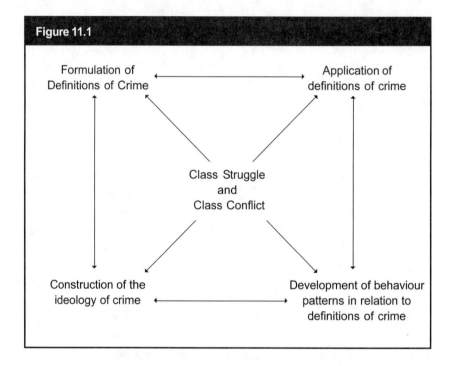

Figure 11.1

Formulation of Definitions of Crime ⟶ Application of definitions of crime

Class Struggle and Class Conflict

Construction of the ideology of crime ⟷ Development of behaviour patterns in relation to definitions of crime

Because the first proposition of the theory is a definition and the sixth is a
composite, the body of the theory consists of the four middle propositions.
These form a model of crime's social reality. The model, as diagrammed,
relates the proposition units into a theoretical system (see figure above). Each
unit is related to the others. The theory is thus a system of interacting
developmental propositions. The phenomena denoted in the propositions and
their relationships culminate in what is regarded as the amount and character
of crime at any time—that is, in the social reality of crime.

The theory of the social reality of crime as I have formulated it is inspired by a change that is occurring in our view of the world. This change, pervading all levels of society, pertains to the world that we all construct and from which, at the same time, we pretend to separate ourselves in our human experiences. For the study of crime, a revision in thought has directed attention to the criminal process: All relevant phenomena contribute to creating definitions of crime, development of behaviours by those involved in criminal-defining situations, and constructing an ideology of crime. The result is the social reality of crime that is constantly being constructed in society.

Chapter 12

THE INFLUENCE OF SITUATIONAL ETHICS ON CHEATING AMONG COLLEGE STUDENTS

Donald L. McCabe

Numerous studies have demonstrated the pervasive nature of cheating among college students (Baird, 1980; Davis et al., 1992; Haines, Diekhoff, LaBeff, and Clark, 1986; Michaels and Miethe, 1989).

Although the factors examined in these studies (for example, personal work ethic, gender, self-esteem, rational choice, social learning, deterrence) are clearly important, the work of LaBeff, Clark, Haines, and Diekhoff (1990) suggests that the concept of situational ethics may be particularly helpful in understanding student rationalizations for cheating.

LaBeff et al. believe a utilitarian calculus of "the end justifies the means" underlies this reasoning process and "what is wrong in most situations might be considered right or acceptable if the end is defined as appropriate" (1990, p. 191). As argued by Edwards (1967), the situation determines what is right or wrong in this decision-making calculus and also dictates the appropriate principles to be used in guiding and judging behaviour.

Sykes and Matza (1957) hypothesize that such rationalizations, that is, "justifications for deviance that are seen as valid by the delinquent but not by the legal system or society at large" (p. 666), are common. However, they challenge conventional wisdom that such rationalizations typically follow deviant behaviour as a means of protecting "the individual from self-blame and the blame of others after the act" (p. 666). They develop convincing arguments that these rationalizations may logically precede the deviant behaviour and "[d]isapproval from internalized norms and conforming others in the social environment is neutralized, turned back, or deflated in advance. Social controls that serve to check or inhibit deviant motivational patterns are rendered inoperative, and the individual is freed to engage in delinquency without serious damage to his self-image" (pp. 666–667).

Using a sample of 380 undergraduate students at a small southwestern university, LaBeff et al. (1990) attempted to classify techniques employed by students in the neutralization of cheating behaviour into the five categories of neutralization proposed by Sykes and Matza (1957): (1) denial of responsibility, (2) condemnation of condemners, (3) appeal to higher loyalties, (4) denial of victim, and (5) denial of injury. Although student responses could easily be classified into three of these techniques, denial of responsibility, appeal to higher loyalties, and condemnation of condemners, LaBeff et al. conclude that "[i]t is unlikely that students will either deny injury or deny the victim since there are no real targets in cheating" (1990, p. 196).

METHODOLOGY

The data discussed here were gathered as part of a study of college cheating conducted during the 1990–1991 academic year. A seventy-two-item questionnaire concerning cheating behaviour was administered to students at thirty-one highly selective colleges across the country. Surveys were mailed to a minimum of 500 students at each school and a total of 6,096 completed surveys were returned (38.3 percent response rate). Eighty-eight percent of the respondents were seniors, 9 percent were juniors, and the remaining 3 percent could not be classified. Survey administration emphasized voluntary participation and assurances of anonymity to help combat issues of non-response bias and the need to accept responses without the chance to question or contest them.

RESULTS

Of the 6,096 students participating in this research, over two-thirds (67.4 percent) indicated that they had cheated on a test or major assignment at least once while an undergraduate. This cheating took a variety of different forms, but among the most popular (listed in decreasing order of mention) were: (1) a failure to footnote sources in written work, (2) collaboration on assignments when the instructor specifically asked for individual work, (3) copying from other students on tests and examinations, (4) fabrication of bibliographies, (5) helping someone else cheat on a test, and (6) using unfair methods to learn the content of a test ahead of time. Almost one in five students (19.1 percent) could be classified as active cheaters (five or more self-reported incidents of cheating). This is double the rate reported by LaBeff et al. (1990), but they asked students to report only cheating incidents that had taken place in the last six months. Students in this research were asked to report all cheating in which they had engaged while an undergraduate—a period of three years for most respondents at the time of this survey.

Students admitting to any cheating activity were asked to rate the importance of several specific factors that might have influenced their decisions to cheat. These data establish the importance of denial of responsibility and condemnation of condemners as neutralization techniques. For example, 52.4 percent of the respondents who admitted to cheating rated the pressure to get good grades as an important influence in their decision to cheat, with parental pressures and competition to gain admission into professional schools singled out as the primary grade pressures. Forty-six percent of those who had engaged in cheating cited excessive workloads and an inability to keep up with assignments as important factors in their decisions to cheat.

In addition to rating the importance of such preselected factors, 426 respondents (11.0 percent of the admitted cheaters) offered their own justifications for cheating in response to an open-ended question on motivations for cheating.

As shown in Table 12.1, denial of responsibility was the technique most frequently cited (216 responses, 61.0 percent of the total) in the 354 responses classified into one of Sykes and Matza's five categories of neutralization. The most common responses in this category were mind block, no understanding of the material, a fear of failing, and unclear explanations of assignments. (Although it is possible that some instances of mind block and a fear of failing included in this summary would be more accurately classified as rationalization, the wording of all responses included here suggests that rationalization preceded the cheating incident. Responses that seem to involve post hoc rationalizations were excluded from this summary.) Condemnation of condemners was the second most popular neutralization technique observed (99 responses, 28.0 percent) and included such explanations as pointless assignments, lack of respect for individual professors, unfair tests, parents' expectations, and unfair professors. Twenty-four respondents (6.8 percent) appealed to higher loyalties to explain their behaviour. In particular, helping a friend and responding to peer pressures were influences some students could not ignore. Finally 15 students (4.2 percent) provided responses that clearly fit into the category of denial of injury. These students dismissed their cheating as harmless since it did not hurt anyone or they felt cheating did not matter in some cases (for example, where an assignment counted for a small percentage of the total course grade).

Detailed examination of selected student responses provides additional insight into the neutralization strategies they employ.

Table 12.1 Neutralization Strategies: Self-Admitted Cheaters		
Strategy	**Number**	**Percent**
Denial of responsibility	216	61.0
Mind block	90	25.4
No understanding of material	31	8.8
Other	95	26.8
Condemnation of condemners	99	28.0
Pointless assignment	35	9.9
No respect for professor	28	7.9
Other	36	10.2
Appeal to higher loyalties	24	6.8
Help a friend	10	2.8
Peer pressure	9	2.5
Other	5	1.5
Denial of injury	15	4.2
Cheating is harmless	9	2.5
Does not matter	6	1.7

DENIAL OF RESPONSIBILITY

Denial of responsibility invokes the claim that the act was "due to forces outside of the individual and beyond his control such as unloving parents" (Sykes and Matza, 1957, p. 667). For example, many students cite an unreasonable workload and the difficulty of keeping up as ample justification for cheating:

> Here at . . ., you must cheat to stay alive. There's so much work and the quality of materials from which to learn, books, professors, is so bad that there's no other choice.

> It's the only way to keep up.

> I couldn't do the work myself.

The following description of student cheating confirm fear of failure is also an important form of denial of responsibility:

> . . . a take-home exam in a class I was failing.

> . . . was near failing.

Some justified their cheating by citing the behaviour of peers:

> Everyone has test files in fraternities, etc. If you don't, you're at a great disadvantage.

> When most of the class is cheating on a difficult exam and they will ruin the curve, it influences you to cheat so your grade won't be affected.

All of these responses contain the essence of denial of responsibility: the cheater has deflected blame to others or to a specific situational context.

DENIAL OF INJURY

As noted in the table above, denial of injury was identified as a neutralization technique employed by some respondents. A key element in denial of injury is whether one feels "anyone has clearly been hurt by [the] deviance." In invoking this defense, a cheater would argue "that his behaviour does not really cause any great harm despite the fact that it runs counter to the law" (Sykes and Matza, 1957, pp. 667–668). For example, a number of students argued that the assignment or test on which they cheated was so trivial that no one was really hurt by their cheating.

> These grades aren't worth much therefore my copying doesn't mean very much. I am ashamed, but I'd probably do it the same way again.

> If I extend the time on a take-home it is because I feel everyone does and the teacher kind of expects it. No one gets hurt.

As suggested earlier, these responses suggest the conclusion of LaBeff et al. that "[I]t is unlikely that students will . . . deny injury" (1990, p. 196) must be re-evaluated.

THE DENIAL OF THE VICTIM

LaBeff et al. (1990) failed to find any evidence of denial of the victim in their student accounts. Although the student motivations for cheating summarized in Table 12.1 support this conclusion, at least four students (0.1% of the self-admitted cheaters in this study) provided comments elsewhere on the survey instrument which involved denial of the victim. The common element in these responses was a victim deserving of the consequences of the cheating behaviour and cheating was viewed as "a form of rightful retaliation or punishment" (Sykes and Matza, 1957, p. 668).

This feeling was extreme in one case, as suggested by the following student who felt her cheating was justified by the:

> . . . realization that this school is a manifestation of the bureaucratic capitalist system that systematically keeps the lower classes down, and that adhering to their rules was simply perpetuating the institution.

This "we" versus "they" mentality was raised by many students, but typically in comments about the policing of academic honesty rather than as justification for one's own cheating behaviour. When used to justify cheating, the target was almost always an individual teacher rather than the institution and could be more accurately classified as a strategy of condemnation of condemners rather than denial of the victim.

THE CONDEMNATION OF CONDEMNERS

Sykes and Matza describe the condemnation of condemners as an attempt to shift "the focus of attention from [one's] own deviant acts to the motives and behaviour of those who disapprove of [the] violations. [B]y attacking others, the wrongfulness of [one's] own behaviour is more easily repressed or lost to view" (1957, p. 668). The logic of this strategy for student cheaters focused on issues of favoritism and fairness. Students invoking this rationale describe "uncaring, unprofessional instructors with negative attitudes who were negligent in their behaviour" (LaBeff et al., 1990, p. 195). For example:

> In one instance, nothing was done by a professor because the student was a hockey player.

> The TA's who graded essays were unduly harsh.

> It is known by students that certain professors are more lenient to certain types, e.g., blondes or hockey players.

> I would guess that 90% of the students here have seen athletes and/or fraternity members cheating on an exam or papers. If you turn in one of these culprits, and I have, the penalty is a five-minute lecture from a coach and/or administrator. All

these add up to a "Who cares, they'll never do anything to you anyway" attitude here about cheating.

Concerns about the larger society were an important issue for some students:

When community frowns upon dishonesty, then people will change.

If our leaders can commit heinous acts and then lie before Senate committees about their total ignorance and innocence, *then why can't I cheat a little?*

In today's world you do anything to be above the competition.

In general, students found ready targets on which to blame their behaviour and condemnation of the condemners was a popular neutralization strategy.

THE APPEAL TO HIGHER LOYALTIES

The appeal to higher loyalties involves neutralizing "internal and external controls . . . by sacrificing the demands of the larger society for the demands of the smaller social groups to which the [offender] belongs. [D]eviation from certain norms may occur not because the norms are rejected but because other norms, held to be more pressing or involving a higher loyalty, are accorded precedence" (Sykes and Matza, 1957, p. 669). For example, a difficult conflict for some students is balancing the desire to help a friend against the institution's rules on cheating. The student may not challenge the rules, but rather views the need to help a friend, fellow fraternity/sorority member, or roommate to be a greater obligation which justifies the cheating behaviour.

Fraternities and sororities were singled out as a network where such behaviour occurs with some frequency. For example, a female student at a small university in New England observed:

There's a lot of cheating within the Greek system. Of all the cheating I've seen, it's often been men and women in fraternities and sororities who exchange information or cheat.

The appeal to higher loyalties was particularly evident in student reactions concerning the reporting of cheating violations. Although fourteen of the thirty-one schools participating in this research had explicit honour codes that generally require students to report cheating violations they observe, less than one-third (32.3 percent) indicated that they were likely to do so. When asked if they would report a friend, only 4 percent said they would and most students felt that they should not be expected to do so. Typical student comments included:

> Students should not be sitting in judgment of their own peers.
>
> The university is not a police state.

For some this decision was very practical:

> A lot of students, 50 percent, wouldn't because they know they will probably cheat at some time themselves.

For others, the decision would depend on the severity of the violation they observed and many would not report what they consider to be minor violations, even those explicitly covered by the school's honour code or policies on academic honesty. Explicit examination or test cheating was one of the few violations where students exhibited any consensus concerning the need to report violations. Yet even in this case many students felt other factors must be considered. For example, a senior at a woman's college in the Northeast commented:

> It would depend on the circumstances. If someone was hurt, *very likely*. If there was no single victim in the case, if the victim was [the] institution . . . then *very unlikely*.

Additional evidence of the strength of the appeal to higher loyalties as a neutralization technique is found in the fact that almost one in five respondents (17.8 percent) reported that they had helped someone cheat on an examination or major test. The percentage who have helped others cheat on papers and other assignments is likely much higher. Twenty-six percent of those students who helped someone else cheat on a test reported that they had never cheated on a test themselves, adding support to the argument that peer pressure to help friends is quite strong.

CONCLUSIONS

From this research it is clear that college students use a variety of neutralization techniques to rationalize their cheating behaviour, deflecting blame to others and/or the situational context, and the framework of Sykes and Matza (1957) seems well supported when student explanations of cheating behaviour are analyzed. Unlike prior research (LaBeff et al., 1990), however, the present findings suggest that students employ all of the techniques described by Sykes and Matza, including denial of injury and denial of victim. Although there was very limited evidence of the use of denial of victim, denial of injury was not uncommon. Many students felt that some forms of cheating were victimless crimes, particularly on assignments that accounted for a small percentage of the total course grade. The present research does affirm LaBeff et al.'s finding that denial of responsibility and condemnation of condemners are the neutralization techniques most frequently utilized by college students. Appeal to higher loyalties is particularly evident in neutralizing institutional expectations that students report cheating violations they observe.

Chapter 13

FREUD'S PSYCHOANALYTIC THEORY OF PERSONALITY

Calvin S. Hall and Gardner Lindzey

THE STRUCTURE OF PERSONALITY

The personality is made up of three major systems, the *id*, the *ego*, and the *superego*. Although each of these provinces of the total personality has its own functions, properties, components, operating principles, dynamisms, and mechanisms, they interact so closely with one another that it is difficult if not impossible to disentangle their effects and weigh their relative contribution to man's behaviour. Behaviour is nearly always the product of an interaction among these three systems; rarely does one system operate to the exclusion of the other two.

The Id

The id is the original system of the personality; it is the matrix within which the ego and the superego become differentiated. The id consists of everything psychological that is inherited and that is present at birth, including the instincts. It is the reservoir of psychic energy and furnishes all the power for the operation of the other two systems. It is in close touch with the bodily processes from which it derives its energy. Freud called the id the "true psychic reality" because it represents the inner world of subjective experience and has no knowledge of objective reality.

The id cannot tolerate increases of energy, which are experienced as uncomfortable states of tension. Consequently, when the tension level of the organism is raised, either as a result of external stimulation or of internally produced excitation, the id functions in such a manner as to discharge the tension immediately and return the organism to a comfortably constant and low energy level. This principle of tension reduction by which the id operates is called the *pleasure principle*.

In order to accomplish its aim of avoiding pain and obtaining pleasure, the id has at its command two processes. These are *reflex action* and the *primary process*. Reflex actions are inborn and automatic reactions like sneezing and blinking; they usually reduce tension immediately. The organism is equipped with a number of such reflexes for dealing with relatively simple forms of excitation. The primary process involves a somewhat more complicated psychological reaction. It attempts to discharge tension by forming an image of an object that will remove the tension. For example, the primary process provides the hungry person with a mental picture of food. This hallucinatory experience in which the desired object is present in the form of a memory image is called *wish-fulfillment*. The best example of the primary process in normal people is the nocturnal dream, which Freud believed always represents the fulfillment or attempted fulfillment of a wish. The hallucinations and visions of psychotic patients are also examples of the primary process. Autistic or wishful thinking is highly coloured by the action of the primary process. These wish-fulfilling mental images are the only reality that the id knows.

Obviously the primary process by itself is not capable of reducing tension. The hungry person cannot eat images of food. Consequently, a new or secondary psychological process develops, and when this occurs the structure of the second system of the personality, the ego, begins to take form.

The Ego

The ego comes into existence because the needs of the organism require appropriate transactions with the objective world of reality. The hungry person has to seek, find, and eat food before the tension of hunger can be eliminated. This means that he has to learn to differentiate between a memory image of food and an actual perception of food as it exists in the outer world. Having made this crucial differentiation it is then necessary for him to convert the image into a perception, which is accomplished by locating food in the environment. In other words, the person matches his memory image of food with the sight or smell of food as they come to him through his senses. The basic distinction between the id and the ego is that the former knows only the subjective reality of the mind whereas the latter distinguishes between things in the mind and things in the external world.

The ego is said to obey the *reality principle* and to operate by means of the *secondary process*. The aim of the reality principle is to prevent the discharge of tension until an object which is appropriate for the satisfaction of the need has been discovered. The reality principle suspends the pleasure principle temporarily because the pleasure principle is eventually served when the needed object is found and the tension is thereby reduced. The reality principle asks in effect whether an experience is true or false, that is, whether it has external existence or not, while the pleasure principle is only interested in whether the experience is painful or pleasurable.

The secondary process is realistic thinking. By means of the secondary process the ego formulates a plan for the satisfaction of the need and then tests this plan, usually by some kind of action, in order to see whether or not it will work. The hungry person thinks where he may find food and then proceeds to look in that place. This is called *reality testing*. In order to perform its role efficiently the ego has control over all of the cognitive and intellectual functions; these higher mental processes are placed at the service of the secondary process.

The ego is said to be the executive of the personality because it controls the gateways to action, selects the features of the environment to which it will respond, and decides what instincts will be satisfied and in what manner. In performing these highly important executive functions, the ego has to try to integrate the often conflicting demands of the id, the superego, and the external world. This is not an easy task and often places a great strain upon the ego.

It should be kept in mind, however, that the ego is the organized portion of the id, that it comes into existence in order to forward the aims of the id and not to frustrate them, and that all of its power is derived from the id. It has no existence apart from the id, and it never becomes completely independent of the id. Its principal role is to mediate between the instinctual requirements of the organism and the conditions of the surrounding environment; its superordinate objectives are to maintain the life of the individual and to see that the species is reproduced.

The Superego

The third and last system of personality to be developed is the superego. It is the internal representative of the traditional values and ideals of society as interpreted to the child by his parents, and enforced by means of a system of rewards and punishments imposed upon the child. The superego is the moral arm of personality; it represents the ideal rather than the real and it strives for perfection rather than pleasure. Its main concern is to decide whether something is right or wrong so that it can act in accordance with the moral standards authorized by the agents of society.

The superego as the internalized moral arbiter of conduct develops in response to the rewards and punishments meted out by the parents. To obtain the rewards and avoid the punishments, the child learns to guide his behaviour along the lines laid down by the parents. Whatever they say is improper and punish him for doing tends to become incorporated into his *conscience*, which is one of the two subsystems of the superego. Whatever they approve of and reward him for doing tends to become incorporated into his *ego-ideal*, which is the other subsystem of the superego. The mechanism by which this incorporation takes place is called *introjection*. The conscience punishes the person by making him feel guilty; the ego-ideal rewards the person by making him feel proud of himself. With the formulation of the superego, self-control is substituted for parental control.

The main functions of the superego are (1) to inhibit the impulses of the id, particularly those of a sexual or aggressive nature, since these are the impulses whose expression is most highly condemned by society, (2) to persuade the ego to substitute moralistic goals for realistic ones, and (3) to strive for perfection. That is, the superego is inclined to oppose both the id and the ego, and to make the world over into its own image. However, it is like the id in being non-rational and like the ego in attempting to exercise control over instincts. Unlike the ego, the superego does not merely postpone instinctual gratification; it tries to block it permanently.

In concluding this brief description of the three systems of the personality, it should be pointed out that the id, ego, and superego are not to be thought of as manikins which operate the personality. They are merely names for various psychological processes which obey different system principles. Under ordinary circumstances these different principles do not collide with one another nor do they work at cross purposes. On the contrary, they work together as a team under the administrative leadership of the ego. The personality normally functions as a whole rather than as three separate segments. In a very general way, the id may be thought of as the biological component of personality, the ego as the psychological component, and the superego as the social component.

THE DYNAMICS OF PERSONALITY

Freud was brought up under the influence of the strongly deterministic and positivistic philosophy of nineteenth-century science and regarded the human organism as a complex energy system, which derives its energy from the food it consumes and expends it for such various purposes as circulation, respiration, muscular exercise, perceiving, thinking, and remembering. Freud saw no reason to assume that the energy which furnishes the power for breathing or digesting is any different, save in form, from the energy which furnishes the power for thinking and remembering. After all, as nineteenth-century physicists were firmly insisting, energy has to be defined in terms of the work it performs. If the work consists of a psychological activity such as thinking, then it is perfectly legitimate, Freud believed, to call this form of energy *psychic energy*. According to the doctrine of the conservation of energy, energy may be transformed from one state into another state but can never be lost from the total cosmic system; it follows from this that psychic energy may be transformed into physiological energy and vice versa. The point of contact or bridge between the energy of the body and that of the personality is the id and its instincts.

Instinct

An instinct is defined as an inborn psychological representation of an inner somatic source of excitation. The psychological representation is called a *wish*, and the bodily excitation from which it stems is called a *need*. Thus, the state of hunger may be described in physiological terms as a condition of nutritional deficit in the tissues of the body whereas psychologically it is represented as a wish for food. The wish acts as a motive for behaviour. The hungry person seeks food. Instincts are considered therefore to be the propelling factors of personality. Not only do they drive behaviour but they also determine the direction that the behaviour will take. In other words, an instinct exercises selective control over conduct by increasing one's sensitivity for particular kinds of stimulation. The hungry person is more sensitive to food stimuli; the sexually aroused person is more likely to respond to erotic stimuli.

An instinct has four characteristic features: a *source*, an *aim*, an *object*, and an *impetus*. The source has already been defined as a bodily condition or a need. The aim is the removal of the bodily excitation. The aim of the hunger instinct, for example, is to abolish the nutritional deficiency, which is accomplished, of course, by eating food. All of the activity which intervenes between the appearance of the wish and its fulfillment is subsumed under the heading of *object*. That is, object refers not only to the particular thing or condition which will satisfy the need but it also includes all of the behaviour which takes place in securing the necessary thing or condition. For instance, when a person is hungry he usually has to perform a number of actions before he can reach the final consummatory goal of eating.

The impetus of an instinct is its force or strength, which is determined by the intensity of the underlying need. As the nutritional deficiency becomes greater, up to the point where physical weakness sets in, the force of the instinct becomes correspondingly greater.

According to Freud's theory of instinct, the source and aim of an instinct remain constant throughout life, unless the source is changed or eliminated by physical maturation. New instincts may appear as new bodily needs develop. In contrast to this constancy of source and aim, the object or means by which the person attempts to satisfy the need can and does vary considerably during the lifetime of the person. This variation in object choice is possible because psychic energy is *displaceable*; it can be expended in various ways. Consequently, if one object is not available either by virtue of its absence or by virtue of barriers within the personality, energy can be invested in another object. If that object proves also to be inaccessible another displacement can occur, and so forth, until an available object is found. In other words, objects can be substituted for one another, which is definitely not the case with either the source or the aim of an instinct.

Number and Kinds of Instincts

Freud did not attempt to draw up a list of instincts because he felt that not enough was known about the bodily states upon which the instincts depend. The identification of these organic needs is a job for the physiologist, not the psychologist. Although Freud did not pretend to know how many instincts there are, he did assume that they could all be classified under two general headings, the *life* instincts and the *death* instincts.

The life instincts serve the purpose of individual survival and racial propagation. Hunger, thirst, and sex fall in this category. The form of energy by which the life instincts perform their work is called *libido*.

The life instinct to which Freud paid the greatest attention is that of sex, and in the early years of psychoanalysis almost everything the person did was attributed to this ubiquitous drive (Freud, 1905). Actually, the sex instinct is not one instinct but many. That is, there are a number of separate bodily needs which give rise to erotic wishes. Each of these wishes has its source in a different bodily region, which are referred to collectively as *erogenous zones*. An erogenous zone is a part of the skin or mucous membrane, which is extremely sensitive to irritation and which when manipulated in a certain way removes the irritation and produces pleasurable feelings. The lips and oral cavity constitute one such erogenous zone, the anal region another, and the sex organs a third. Sucking produces oral pleasure, elimination anal pleasure, and massaging or rubbing genital pleasure. In childhood, the sexual instincts are relatively independent of one another but when the person reaches puberty they tend to fuse together and to serve jointly the aim of reproduction.

The death instincts, or, as Freud sometimes called them, the destructive instincts, perform their work much less conspicuously than the life instincts, and for this reason little is known about them, other than that they inevitably accomplish their mission. Every person does eventually die, a fact which caused Freud to formulate the famous dictum, "the goal of all life is death" (1920a:38). Freud assumed specifically that the person has a wish, usually of course unconscious, to die. He did not attempt to identify the somatic sources of the death instincts although one may wish to speculate that they reside in the catabolic or breaking-down processes of the body. Nor did he assign a name to the energy by which the death instincts carry on their work.

An important derivative of the death instincts is the *aggressive drive*. Aggressiveness is self-destruction turned outward against substitute objects. A person fights with other people and is destructive because his death wish is blocked by the forces of the life instincts and by other obstacles in his personality which counteract the death instincts. It took the Great War of 1914–1918 to convince Freud that aggression was as sovereign a motive as sex.

The life and death instincts and their derivatives may fuse together, neutralize each other, or replace one another. Eating, for example, represents a fusion of hunger and destructiveness which is satisfied by biting, chewing, and swallowing food. Love, a derivative of the sex instinct, can neutralize hate, a derivation of the death instinct. Or love can replace hate, and hate love.

Since the instincts contain all the energy by which the three systems of the personality perform their work, let us turn now to consider the ways in which the id, ego, and superego gain control over and utilize psychic energy.

THE DISTRIBUTION AND UTILIZATION OF PSYCHIC ENERGY

The dynamics of personality consists of the way in which psychic energy is distributed and used by the id, ego, and superego. Since the amount of energy is a limited quantity there is competition among the three systems for the energy that is available. One system gains control over the available energy at the expense of the other two systems. As one system becomes stronger the other two necessarily become weaker, unless new energy is added to the total system.

Originally the id possesses all of the energy and uses it for reflex action and wish-fulfillment by means of the primary process. Both of these activities are in the direct service of the pleasure principle by which the id operates. The investment of energy in an action or image which will gratify an instinct is called an instinctual *object-choice* or *object-cathexis*.

Since the ego has no source of power of its own it has to borrow it from the id. The diversion of energy from the id into the processes that make up the ego is accomplished by a mechanism known as *identification*. This is one of the most important concepts in Freud's psychology, and one of the most difficult to comprehend. It will be recalled from a previous discussion that the id does not distinguish between subjective imagery and objective reality. When it cathects an image of an object it is the same as cathecting the object itself. However, since a mental image cannot satisfy a need, the person is forced to differentiate between the world of the mind and the outer world. He has to learn the difference between a memory or idea of an object which is not present and a sensory impression or perception of an object which is present. Then, in order to satisfy a need, he must learn to match what is in his mind with its counterpart in the external world by means of the secondary process. This matching of a mental representation with physical reality, of something that is in the mind with something that is in the outer world, is what is meant by identification.

Finally, the ego as the executive of the personality organization uses energy to effect an integration among the three systems. The purpose of this integrative function of the ego is to produce an inner harmony within the personality so that the ego's transactions with the environment may be made smoothly and effectively.

The work performed by the superego is often, although not always, in direct opposition to the impulses of the id. This is the case because the moral code represents society's attempt to control and even to inhibit the expression of the primitive drives, especially those of sex and aggression. Being good usually means being obedient and not saying or doing "dirty" things. Being bad means being disobedient, rebellious, and lustful. The virtuous person inhibits his impulses, the sinful person indulges them. However, the superego can sometimes be corrupted by the id. This happens, for example, when a person in a fit of moralistic fervour takes aggressive measures against those whom he considers to be wicked and sinful. The expression of aggression in such instances is cloaked by the mantle of righteous indignation.

Once the energy furnished by the instincts has been channelled into the ego and the superego by the mechanism of identification, a complicated interplay of driving and restraining forces becomes possible. The id, it will be recalled, possesses only driving forces or cathexes whereas the energy of the ego and the superego is used both to forward and to frustrate the aims of the instincts. The ego has to check both the id and the superego if it is to govern the personality wisely, yet it must have enough energy left over to engage in necessary intercourse with the external world. If the id retains control over a large share over the energy, the behaviour of the person will tend to be impulsive and primitive in character. On the one hand, if the superego gains control of an undue amount of energy, the functioning of the personality will be dominated by moralistic considerations rather than by realistic ones.

In the final analysis, the dynamics of personality consist of the interplay of the driving forces, cathexes, and the restraining forces, anticathexes. All of the conflicts within the personality may be reduced to the opposition of these two sets of forces. All prolonged tension is due to the counteraction of a driving force by a restraining force. Whether it be an anticathexis of the ego opposed to a cathexis of the id or an anticathexis of the superego opposed to a cathexis of the ego, the result in terms of tension is the same. As Freud was fond of saying, psychoanalysis is "a dynamic conception which reduces mental life to the interplay of reciprocally urging and checking forces" (1910b:107).

Anxiety

The dynamics of personality is to a large extent governed by the necessity for gratifying one's needs by means of transactions with objects in the external world. The surrounding environment provides the hungry organism with food, the thirsty one with water. In addition to its role as the source of supplies, the external world plays another part in shaping the destiny of personality. The environment contains regions of danger and insecurity; it can threaten as well as satisfy. The environment has the power to produce pain and increase tension as well as to bring pleasure and reduce tension. It disturbs as well as comforts.

The individual's customary reaction to external threats of pain and destruction with which it is not prepared to cope is to become afraid. The threatened person is ordinarily a fearful person. Overwhelmed by excessive stimulation which the ego is unable to bring under control, the ego becomes flooded with anxiety.

Freud recognized three types of anxiety: *reality* anxiety, *neurotic* anxiety, and *moral* anxiety or feelings of guilt (1926). The basic type is reality anxiety or fear of real dangers in the external world; from it are derived the other two types. Neurotic anxiety is the fear that the instincts will get out of control and cause the person to do something for which he will be punished. Neurotic anxiety is not so much a fear of the instincts themselves as it is a fear of the punishment that is likely to ensue from instinctual gratification. Neurotic anxiety has a basis in reality, because the world as represented by the parents and other authorities does punish the child for impulsive actions. Moral anxiety is fear of the conscience. The person with a well-developed superego tends to feel guilty when he does something or even thinks of doing something that is contrary to the moral code by which he has been raised. He is said to feel conscience-stricken. Moral anxiety also has a realistic basis; the person has been punished in the past for violating the moral code and may be punished again.

The function of anxiety is to warn the person of impending danger; it is a signal to the ego that unless appropriate measures are taken the danger may increase until the ego is overthrown. Anxiety is a state of tension; it is a drive like hunger or sex but instead of arising from internal tissue conditions it is produced originally by external causes. When anxiety is aroused it motivates the person to do something. He may flee from the threatening region, inhibit the dangerous impulse, or obey the voice of conscience. When the ego cannot cope with anxiety by rational methods it has to fall back upon unrealistic ones. These are the so-called *defense mechanisms* of the ego, which will be discussed in the following section.

THE DEVELOPMENT OF PERSONALITY

Freud was probably the first psychological theorist to emphasize the developmental aspects of personality and in particular to stress the decisive role of the early years of infancy and childhood by laying down the basic character structure of the person. Indeed, Freud felt that personality was pretty well formed by the end of the fifth year, and that subsequent growth consisted for the most part of elaborating this basic structure. He arrived at this conclusion on the basis of his experiences with patients undergoing psychoanalysis. Inevitably, their mental explorations led them back to early childhood experiences, which appeared to be decisive for the development of a neurosis later in life.

Personality develops in response to four major sources of tension: (1) physiological growth processes, (2) frustrations, (3) conflicts, and (4) threats. As a direct consequence of increases in tension emanating from these sources, the person is forced to learn new methods of reducing tension. This learning is what is meant by personality development.

Identification and *displacement* are two methods by which the individual learns to resolve his frustrations, conflicts, and anxieties.

Identification

This concept was introduced in an earlier section to help account for the formation of the ego and superego. In the present context, identification may be defined as the method by which a person takes over the features of another person and makes them a corporate part of his own personality. He learns to reduce tension by modelling his behaviour after that of someone else. Freud preferred the term *identification* to the more familiar one *imitation* because he felt that imitation denotes a kind of superficial and transient copying behaviour whereas he wanted a word that would convey the idea of a more or less permanent acquisition to personality. Features which he believes will help him achieve a desired goal. There is a good deal of trial and error in the identification process because one is usually not quite sure what it is about another person that accounts for his success. The ultimate test is whether the identification helps to reduce tension; if it does the quality is taken over, if it does not it is discarded. One may identify with animals, imaginary characters, institutions, abstract ideas, and inanimate objects as well as with other human beings.

Identification is also a method by which one may regain an object that has been lost. By identifying with a loved person who has died or from whom one has been separated, the lost person becomes reincarnated as an incorporated feature of one's personality. Children who have been rejected by their parents tend to form strong identifications with them in the hope of regaining their love. One may also identify with a person out of fear. The child identifies with the prohibitions of the parents in order to avoid punishment. This kind of identification is the basis for the formation of the superego.

The final personality structure represents an accumulation of numerous identifications made at various periods of the person's life, although the mother and father are probably the most important identification figures in anyone's life.

Displacement

When an original object-choice of an instinct is rendered inaccessible by external or internal barriers (anti-cathexes), a new cathexis is formed unless a strong repression occurs. If this new cathexis is also blocked, another displacement takes place, and so on, until an object is found which yields some relief for the pent-up tension.

A substitute object is rarely if ever as satisfying or tension-reducing as the original object, and the less tension is reduced the more remote the displacement is from the original object. As a consequence of numerous displacements, a pool of undischarged tension accumulates which acts as a permanent motivating force for behaviour. The person is constantly seeking new and better ways of reducing tension.

Freud pointed out that the development of civilization was made possible by the inhibition of primitive object-choices and the diversion of instinctual energy into socially acceptable and culturally creative channels (1930). A displacement which produces a higher cultural achievement is called a *sublimation*. Freud observed in this connection that Leonardo da Vinci's interest in painting Madonnas was a sublimated expression of a longing for intimacy with his mother from whom he had been separated at a tender age (1910a). Since sublimation does not result in complete satisfaction, any more than any displacement does, there is always some residual tension. This tension may discharge itself in the form of nervousness or restlessness, conditions which Freud pointed out were the price that man paid for his civilized status (1908).

The Defense Mechanisms of the Ego
Under the pressure of excessive anxiety, the ego is sometimes forced to take extreme measures to relieve the pressure. These measures are called defense mechanisms. The principal defenses are repression, projection, reaction formation, fixation, and regression (Anna Freud, 1946). All defense mechanisms have two characteristics in common: (1) they deny, falsify, or distort reality, and (2) they operate unconsciously so that the person is not aware of what is taking place.

Repression
This is one of the earliest concepts of psychoanalysis. Before Freud arrived at his final formulation of personality theory in terms of the id, ego, and superego, he divided the mind into three regions, consciousness, preconsciousness, and unconsciousness. The preconscious consisted of psychological material that could become conscious when the need arose. Material in the unconscious, however, was regarded by Freud as being relatively inaccessible to conscious awareness; it was said to be in a state of repression.

When Freud revised his theory of personality, the concept of repression was retained as one of the defense mechanisms of the ego. Repression is said to occur when an object-choice that arouses undue alarm is forced out of consciousness by an anti-cathexis. For example, a disturbing memory may be prevented from becoming conscious or a person may not see something that is in plain sight because the perception of it is repressed.

Repressions once formed are difficult to abolish. The person must reassure himself that the danger no longer exists, but he cannot get such reassurance until the repression is lifted so that he can test reality. It is a vicious circle.

Projection
Reality anxiety is usually easier for the ego to deal with than is either neurotic or moral anxiety. Consequently, if the source of the anxiety can be attributed

to the external world rather than to the individual's own primitive impulses or to the threats of his conscience, he is likely to achieve greater relief for his anxious condition. This mechanism by which neurotic or moral anxiety is converted into an objective fear is called projection. This conversion is easily made because the original source of both neurotic and moral anxiety is fear of punishment from an external agent. In projection, one simply says "He hates me" instead of "I hate him," or "He is persecuting me" instead of "My conscience is bothering me." Projection often serves a dual purpose. It reduces anxiety by substituting a lesser danger for a greater one, and it enables the projecting person to express his impulses under the guise of defending himself against his enemies.

Reaction formation
This defensive measure involves the replacement in consciousness of an anxiety-producing impulse or feeling by its opposite. For example, hate is replaced by love. The original impulse still exists but it is glossed over or masked by one that does not cause anxiety.

The question often arises as to how a reaction formation may be distinguished from a genuine expression of an impulse or feeling. For instance, how can reactive love be differentiated from true love? Usually, a reaction formation is marked by extravagant showiness—the person protests too much—and by compulsiveness. Extreme forms of behaviour of any kind usually denote a reaction formation.

Fixation and Regression
In the course of normal development, as we shall see in the next section, the personality passes through a series of rather well-defined stages until it reaches maturity. Each new step that is taken, however, entails a certain amount of frustration and anxiety and if these become too great, normal growth may be temporarily or permanently halted. In other words, the person may become fixated on one of the early stages of development because taking the next step is fraught with anxiety. The overly dependent child exemplifies defense by fixation; anxiety prevents him from learning how to become independent.

A closely related type of defense is that of regression. In this case, a person who encounters traumatic experiences retreats to an earlier stage of development. For example, a child who is frightened by his first day at school may indulge in infantile behaviour, such as weeping, sucking his thumb, hanging on to the teacher, or hiding in a corner.

Fixation and regression are ordinarily relative conditions; a person rarely fixates or regresses completely. Rather his personality tends to include infantilisms, that is, immature forms of behaviour, and predispositions to display childish conduct when thwarted. Fixations and regressions are responsible for the unevenness in personality development.

Chapter 14

WHY IS IT SO DIFFICULT FOR PEOPLE TO BE HAPPY?

Sigmund Freud

OUR ENQUIRY CONCERNING HAPPINESS HAS NOT SO FAR TAUGHT US MUCH THAT IS not already common knowledge. And even if we proceed from it to the problem of why it is so hard for men to be happy, there seems no greater prospect of learning anything new. We have given the answer already by pointing to the three sources from which our suffering comes: the superior power of nature, the feebleness of our own bodies, and the inadequacy of the regulations which adjust the mutual relationships of human beings in the family, the state, and society. In regard to the first two sources, our judgment cannot hesitate long. It forces us to acknowledge those sources of suffering and to submit to the inevitable. We shall never completely master nature; and our bodily organism, itself a part of that nature, will always remain a transient structure with a limited capacity for adaptation and achievement. This recognition does not have a paralyzing effect. On the contrary, it points the direction for our activity. If we cannot remove all suffering, we can remove some, and we can mitigate some: the experience of many thousands of years has convinced us of that. As regards the third source, the social source of suffering, our attitude is a different one. We do not admit it at all; we cannot see why the regulations made by ourselves should not, on the contrary, be a protection and a benefit for every one of us. And yet, when we consider how unsuccessful we have been in precisely this field of prevention of suffering, a suspicion dawns on us that here, too, a piece of unconquerable nature may lie behind—this time a piece of our own psychical constitution.

When we start considering this possibility, we come upon a contention which is so astonishing that we must dwell upon it. This contention holds that what we call our civilization is largely responsible for our misery, and that we should be much happier if we gave it up and returned to primitive conditions.

I call this contention astonishing because, in whatever way we may define the concept of civilization, it is a certain fact that all the things with which we seek to protect ourselves against the threats that emanate from the sources of suffering are part of that very civilization.

It is time for us to turn our attention to the nature of this civilization on whose value as a means to happiness doubts have been thrown. We shall not look for a formula in which to express that nature in a few words, until we have learned something by examining it. We shall therefore content ourselves with saying once more that the word "civilization"[1] describes the whole sum of the achievements and the regulations which distinguish our lives from those of our animal ancestors and which serve two purposes—namely to protect men against nature and to adjust their mutual relations.[2] In order to learn more, we will bring together the various features of civilization individually, as they are exhibited in human communities.

The first stage is easy. We recognize as cultural all activities and resources which are useful to men for making the earth serviceable to them, for protecting them against violence of the forces of nature, and so on. As regards this side of civilization, there can be scarcely any doubt. If we go back far enough, we find that the first acts of civilization were the use of tools, the gaining of control over fire, and the construction of dwellings.

We recognize, then, that countries have attained a high level of civilization if we find that in them everything which can assist in the exploitation of the earth by man and in his protection against the forces of nature—everything, in short, which is of use to him—is attended to and effectively carried out.

But we demand other things from civilization besides these, and it is a noticeable fact that we hope to find them realized in these same countries.

Beauty and cleanliness and order obviously occupy a special position among the requirements of civilization. No one will maintain that they are as important for life as control over the forces of nature or as some other factors with which we shall become acquainted. And yet no one would care to put them in the background as trivialities. That civilization is not exclusively taken up with what is useful is already shown by the example of beauty, which we decline to omit from among the interests of civilization. The usefulness of order is quite evident. With regard to cleanliness, we must bear in mind that it is demanded of us by hygiene as well, and we may suspect that even before the days of scientific prophylaxis the connection between the two was not altogether strange to man. Yet utility does not entirely explain these efforts; something else must be at work besides.

No feature, however, seems better to characterize civilization than its esteem and encouragement of man's higher mental activities—his intellectual, scientific, and artistic achievements—and the leading role that it assigns to ideas in human life. Foremost among those ideas are the religious systems, on whose complicated structure I have endeavoured to throw light elsewhere.[3] Next come the speculations of philosophy; and finally what might be called man's "ideals"—his ideas of a possible perfection of individuals, or of peoples, or of the whole of humanity, and the demands he sets up on the basis of such ideas.

The last, but certainly not the least important, of the characteristic features of civilization remains to be assessed: the manner in which the relationships are regulated—relationships which affect a person as a neighbour, as a source of help, as another person's sexual object, as a member of a family and of a State. Here it is especially difficult to keep clear of particular ideal demands and to see what is civilized in general. Perhaps we may begin by explaining that the element of civilization enters on the scene with the first attempt to regulate these social relationships. If the attempt were not made, the relationships would be subject to the arbitrary will of the individual: that is to say, the physically stronger man would decide them in the sense of his own interests and instinctual impulses. Nothing would be changed in this if this stronger man should in his turn meet someone even stronger than he. Human life in common is only made possible when a majority comes together which is stronger than any separate individuals. The power of this community is then set up as "right" in opposition to the power of the individual, which is condemned as "brute force." This replacement of the power of the individual by the power of the community constitutes the decisive step of civilization. The essence of it lies in the fact that the members of the community restrict themselves in their possibilities of satisfaction, whereas the individual knew no such restrictions. The first requisite of civilization, therefore, is that of justice—that is, the assurance that a law once made will not be broken in favour of an individual. This implies nothing as to the ethical value of such a law. The further course of cultural development seems to tend towards making the law no longer an expression of the will of a small community—a caste or a stratum of the population or a racial group—which, in its turn, behaves like a violent individual towards other, and perhaps more numerous, collections of people. The final outcome should be a rule of law to which all—except those who are not capable of entering a community—have contributed by a sacrifice of their instincts, and which leaves no one—again with the same exception—at the mercy of brute force.

The liberty of the individual is no gift to civilization. It was greatest before there was any civilization, though then, it is true, it had for the most part no value, since the individual was scarcely in a position to defend it. The development of civilization imposes restrictions on it, and justice demands that no one shall escape those restrictions. What makes itself felt in a human community as a desire for freedom may be their revolt against some existing injustice, and so may prove favourable to a further development of civilization; it may remain compatible with civilization. But it may also spring from the remains of their original personality, which is still untamed by civilization and may thus become the basis in them of hostility to civilization. The urge for freedom, therefore, is directed against particular forms and demands of civilization or against civilization altogether. It does not seem as though any influence could induce a man to change his nature into a termite's. No doubt he will always defend his claim to individual liberty against the will of the group. A good part of the struggles of mankind centre round the single task of finding an expedient accommodation—one, that is, that will bring happiness—between this claim of the individual and the cultural claims of the group; and one of the problems that touches the fate of humanity is whether such an accommodation can be reached by means of some particular form of civilization or whether this conflict is irreconcilable.

At this point we cannot fail to be struck by the similarity between the process of civilization and the libidinal development of the individual.

In most cases this process coincides with that of the *sublimation* (of instinctual aims) with which we are familiar, but in some it can be differentiated from it. Sublimation of instinct is an especially conspicuous feature of cultural development; it is what makes it possible for higher psychical activities, scientific, artistic, or ideological, to play such an important part in civilized life.

Finally, and this seems the most important of all, it is impossible to overlook the extent to which civilization is built up upon a renunciation of instinct, how much it presupposes precisely the non-satisfaction (by suppression, repression, or some other means?) of powerful instincts. This "cultural frustration" dominates the large field of social relationships between human beings. As we already know, it is the cause of the hostility against which all civilizations have to struggle. It will also make severe demands on our scientific work, and we shall have much to explain here. It is not easy to understand how it can become possible to deprive an instinct of satisfaction. Nor is doing so without danger. If the loss is not compensated for economically, one can be certain that serious disorders will ensue.

But if we want to know what value can be attributed to our view that the development of civilization is a special process, comparable to the normal maturation of the individual, we must clearly attack another problem. We must ask ourselves to what influences the development of civilization owes its origin, how it arose, and by what its course has been determined.[4]

The communal life of human beings has a two-fold foundation: the compulsion to work, which was created by external necessity, and the power of love, which made the man unwilling to be deprived of his sexual object—the woman—and made the woman unwilling to be deprived of the part of herself which had been separated off from her—her child. Eros and Ananke [Love and Necessity] have become the parents of human civilization, too. The first result of civilization was that even a fairly large number of people were now able to live together in a community. And since these two great powers were co-operating in this, one might expect that the further development of civilization would proceed smoothly towards an even better control over the external world and towards a further extension of the number of people included in the community. Nor is it easy to understand how this civilization could act upon its participants otherwise than to make them happy.

Before we go on to enquire from what quarter an interference might arise, this recognition of love as one of the foundations of civilizations may serve as an excuse for a digression which will enable us to fill in a gap which we left in an earlier discussion.

We said there that man's discovery that sexual (genital) love afforded him the strongest experiences of satisfaction, and in fact provided him with the prototype of all happiness, must have suggested to him that he should continue to seek the satisfaction of happiness in his life along the path of sexual relations and that he should make genital erotism the central point of his life. We went on to say that in doing so he made himself dependent in a most dangerous way on a portion of the external world, namely, his chosen love-object, and exposed himself to extreme suffering if he should be rejected by that object or should lose it through unfaithfulness or death.

A small minority are enabled by their constitution to find happiness, in spite of everything, along the path of love. But far-reaching mental changes in the function of love are necessary before this can happen. These people make themselves independent of their object's acquiescence by displacing what they mainly value from being loved on to loving; they protect themselves against the loss of the object by directing their love, not to single objects but to all men alike; and they avoid the uncertainties and disappointments of genital love by turning away from it sexual aims and transforming the instinct into an impulse with an inhibited aim. What they bring about in themselves in this way is a state of evenly suspended, steadfast, affectionate feeling, which has little external resemblance any more to the stormy agitations of genital love, from which it is nevertheless derived.

The love which founded the family continues to operate in civilization both in its original form, in which it does not renounce direct sexual satisfaction, and in its modified form as aim-inhibited affection. In each, it continues to carry on its function of binding together considerable numbers of people, and it does so in a more intensive fashion than can be effected through the interest of work in common. The careless way in which language uses the word "love" has its genetic justification. People give the name "love" to the relation between a man and a woman whose genital needs have led them to found a family; but they also give the name "love" to the positive feelings between parents and children, and between the brothers and sisters of a family, although *we* are obliged to describe this as "aim-inhibited love" or "affection." Love with an inhibited aim was in fact originally fully sensual love, and it is so still in man's unconscious. Both—fully sensual love and aim-inhibited love—extend outside the family and create new bonds with people who before were strangers. Genital love leads to the formation of new families, and aim-inhibited love to "friendships" which become valuable from a cultural standpoint because they escape some of the limitations of genital love, as, for instance, its exclusiveness. But in the course of development the relation of love to civilization loses it unambiguity. On the one hand love comes into opposition to the interests of civilization; on the other, civilization threatens love with substantial restrictions.

But civilization demands other sacrifices besides that of sexual satisfaction.

So far, we can quite well imagine a cultural community consisting of double individuals like this, who, libidinally satisfied themselves, are connected with one another through the bonds of common work and common interests. If this were so civilization would not have to withdraw any energy from sexuality. But this desirable state of things does not, and never did, exist. Reality shows us that civilization is not content with the ties we have so far allowed it. It aims at binding the members of the community together in a libidinal way as well and employs every means to that end. It favours every path by which strong identifications can be established between the members of the community, and it summons up aim-inhibited libido on the largest scale so as to strengthen the communal bond by relations of friendship. In order for these aims to be fulfilled, a restriction upon sexual life is unavoidable. But we are unable to understand what the necessity is which forces civilization along this path and which causes its antagonism to sexuality. There must be some disturbing factor which we have not yet discovered.

The clue may be supplied by one of the ideal demands, as we have called them,[5] of civilized society. It runs: "Thou shalt love thy neighbour as thy self." It is known throughout the world and is undoubtedly older than Christianity, which puts it forward as its proudest claim.

Let us adopt a naïve attitude towards it, as though we were hearing it for the first time; we shall be unable then to suppress a feeling of surprise and bewilderment. Why should we do it? What good will it do us? But, above all, how shall we achieve it? How can it be possible? My love is something valuable to me which I ought not to throw away without reflection. It imposes duties on me for whose fulfillment I must be ready to make sacrifices. If I love someone, he must deserve it in some way.

On closer inspection, I find still further difficulties. Not merely is this stranger in general unworthy of my love; I must honestly confess that he has more claims to my hostility and even my hatred. He seems not to have the least trace of love for me and shows me not the slightest consideration. If it will do him any good he has no hesitation in injuring me, nor does he ask himself whether the amount of advantage he gains bears any proportion to the extent of the harm he does to me.

The element of truth behind all this, which people are so ready to disavow, is that men are not gentle creatures who want to be loved, and who at the most can defend themselves if they are attacked; they are, on the contrary, creatures among whose instinctual endowments is to be reckoned a powerful share of aggressiveness. As a result, their neighbour is for them not only a potential helper or sexual object, but also someone who tempts them to satisfy their aggressiveness on him, to exploit his capacity for work without compensation, to use him sexually without his consent, to seize his possessions, to humiliate him, to cause him pain, to torture, and to kill him. *Homo homini lupus.*[6] Who, in the face of all his experience of life and of history, will have the courage to dispute this assertion?

The existence of this inclination to aggression, which we can detect in ourselves and justly assume to be present in others, is the factor which disturbs our relations with our neighbour and which forces civilization into such a high expenditure [of energy]. In consequence of this primary mutual hostility of human beings, civilized society is perpetually threatened with human beings, civilized society is perpetually threatened with disintegration. The interest of work in common would not hold it together; instinctual passions are stronger than reasonable interests. Civilization has to use its utmost efforts in order to set limits to man's aggressive instincts and to hold the manifestations of them in check by psychical reaction-formations. Hence, therefore, the use of methods intended to incite people into identifications and aim-inhibited relationships of love, hence the restriction upon sexual life, and hence too the ideal's commandment to love one's neighbour as oneself—a commandment which is really justified by the fact that nothing else runs so strongly counter to the original nature of man. In spite of every effort, these endeavours of civilization have not so far achieved very much. It hopes to prevent the crudest excesses of brutal violence by itself assuming the right to use violence against criminals, but the law is not able to lay hold of the more cautious and refined manifestations of human aggressiveness. The time comes when each one of us has to give up as illusions the expectations which, in his youth, he pinned upon his fellowmen, and when he may learn how much difficulty and pain has been added to his life by their ill-will.

If civilization imposes such great sacrifices not only on man's sexuality but on his aggressivity, we can understand better why it is hard for him to be happy in that civilization. In fact, primitive man was better off in knowing no restrictions of instinct. To counterbalance this, his prospects of enjoying this happiness for any length of time were very slender. Civilized man had exchanged a portion of his possibilities of happiness for a portion of security. We must not forget, however, that in the primal family only the head of it enjoyed this instinctual freedom; the rest lived in slavish suppression. In that primal period of civilization, the contrast between a minority who enjoyed the advantages of civilization and a majority who were robbed of those advantages was, therefore, carried to extremes.

In none of my previous writings have I had so strong a feeling as now that what I am describing is common knowledge.

For that reason I should be glad to seize the point if it were to appear that the recognition of a special, independent aggressive instinct means an alteration of the psycho-analytic theory of the instincts.

We shall see, however, that this is not so and that it is merely a matter of bringing into sharper focus a turn of thought arrived at long ago and of following out its consequences. Of all the slowly developed parts of analytic theory, the theory of the instincts is the one that has felt its way the most painfully forward.[7]

Starting from speculations on the beginning of life and from biological parallels, I drew the conclusion that, besides the instinct to preserve living substance and to join it into ever larger units,[8] there must exist another, contrary instinct seeking to dissolve those units and to bring them back to their primaeval, inorganic state. That is to say, as well as Eros, there was an instinct of death. The phenomena of life could be explained from the concurrent or mutually opposing action of these two instincts. It was not easy, however, to demonstrate the activities of this supposed death instinct. The manifestations of Eros were conspicuous and noisy enough. It might be assumed that the death instinct operated silently within the organism towards its dissolution, but that, of course, was no proof. A more fruitful idea was that a portion of the instinct is diverted towards the external world and comes to light as an instinct of aggressiveness and destructiveness. In this way the instinct itself could be pressed into the service of Eros, in that the organism was destroying some other thing, whether animate or inanimate, instead of destroying its own self. Conversely, any restriction of this aggressiveness directed outwards would be bound to increase the self-destruction, which is in any case proceeding.

The name "libido" can once more be used to denote the manifestations of the power of Eros in order to distinguish them from the energy of the death instinct.[9] It must be confessed that we have much greater difficulty in grasping that instinct; we can only suspect it, as it were, as something in the background behind Eros, and it escapes detection unless its presence is betrayed by its being allowed with Eros. It is in sadism, where the death instinct twists the erotic aim in its own sense and yet at the same time fully satisfies the erotic urge, that we succeed in obtaining the clearest insight into its nature and its relation to Eros. But even where it emerges without any sexual purpose, in the blindest fury of destructiveness, we cannot fail to recognize that the satisfaction of the instinct is accompanied by an extraordinarily high degree of narcissistic enjoyment, owing to its presenting the ego with a fulfillment of the latter's old wishes for omnipotence. The instinct of destruction, moderated and tamed, and, as it were, inhibited in its aim, must, when it is directed towards objects, provide the ego with the satisfaction of its vital needs and with control over nature.

In all that follows I adopt the standpoint, therefore, that the inclination to aggression is an original, self-subsisting instinctual disposition in man, and I return to my view that it constitutes the greatest impediment to civilization. At one point in the course of this enquiry was led to the idea that civilization was a special process which mankind undergoes, and I am still under the influence of that idea. I may now add that civilization is a process in the service of Eros, whose purpose is to combine single human individuals, and after that families, then races, peoples, and nations, into one great unity, the unity of mankind. Why this has to happen, we do not know; the work of Eros is precisely this.[10] These collections of men are to be libidinally bound to one another. Necessity alone, the advantages of work in common, will not hold them together. But man's natural aggressive instinct, the hostility of each against all and of all against each, opposes this programme of civilization. This aggressive instinct is the derivative and the main representative of the death instinct which we have found alongside of Eros, and which shares world-dominion with it. And now, I think, the meaning of the evolution of civilization is no longer obscure to us. It must present the struggle between Eros and Death, between the instinct of life and the instinct of destruction, as it works itself out in the human species. This struggle is what all life essentially consists of, and the evolution of civilization may therefore be simply described as the struggle for life of the human species.[11]

The fateful question for the human species seems to me to be whether and to what extent their cultural development will succeed in mastering the disturbance of their communal life by the human instinct of aggression and self-destruction. It may be that in this respect precisely the present time deserves a special interest. Men have gained control over the forces of nature to such an extent that with their help they would have no difficulty in exterminating one another to the last man. They know this, and hence comes a large part of the current unrest, their unhappiness, and their mood of anxiety. And now it is to be expected that the other of the two "Heavenly Powers," eternal Eros, will make an effort to assert himself in the struggle with his equally immortal adversary. But who can foresee with what success and with what result?[12]

NOTES

1. *"Kultur."* For the translation of this word, see the Editor's Note to *The Future of an Illusion* (1927) translated in S. Freud, Standard Edition (24 volumes), London and New York, from 1953.
2. See *The Future of an Illusion* (1927).
3. [Cf. *The Future of an Illusion* (1927).]
4. [Freud returns to the subject of civilizations as a "process" . . . in his open letter to Einstein, *Why War?* (1933) in S. Freud, Collected Papers (5 volumes), London, 1924–1950.]
5. ["'Civilized' Sexual Morality" (1908), *Standard Ed.*, 9, 199.]
6. ["Man is a wolf to man." Derived from Plautus, *Asinaria* II, iv, 88.]
7. [Some account of the history of Freud's theory of the instincts will be found in the Editor's Note to his paper "Instincts and Their Vicissitudes" (1915), *Standard Ed.*, 14, 113 ff.]
8. The opposition which thus emerges between the ceaseless trend by Eros towards extension and the general conservative nature of the instincts is striking, and it may become the starting-point for the study of further problems.
9. Our present point of view can be roughly expressed in the statement that libido has a share in every instinctual manifestation, but that not everything in that manifestation is libido.
10. [See *Beyond the Pleasure Principle* (1920), translated in S. Freud, Standard Edition, 18, 3.]
11. And we may probably add more precisely, a struggle for life in the shape it was bound to assume after a certain event which still remains to be discovered.
12. [The final sentence was added in 1931—when the menace of Hitler was already beginning to be apparent.]

Part IV

SEXUAL, DOMESTIC, AND COMMERCIAL DEVIANCE

Chapter 15

PROSTITUTION

Ian Gomme

INTRODUCTION

While it is unlikely that prostitution is Canada's oldest profession, it has been in evidence for a considerable length of time. Prostitution in Canada dates back at least to the time when Europeans began to settle here and, depending on one's definition of the practice, to even earlier periods, when the Native people were the country's sole inhabitants. After colonization began, houses of ill-repute became common near military establishments, fishing and trading ports, and other commercial centres (SCPP, 1985).

Sex solely for the sake of pleasure flies in the face of traditional moral values and religious beliefs. The free expression of sexuality and the immediate gratification of sensual desires are often regarded as sins of the flesh. Because prostitution is a commercialized form of sex practiced solely for the enjoyment of recipients and the profit of providers, Canadians historically have disapproved of it and rebuked its participants. Rough traders, working girls, and children of the night have met with disapproval from citizens and legal sanctions from the criminal justice system. Despite the condemnation, there has been and always will be a commercial demand for illicit sex.

Contrary to popular conception, prostitution has never been illegal in Canada, although it is illegal in parts of the United States (Sansfacon, 1985). Rather than make prostitution itself illegal, the *Criminal Code of Canada* in 1972 prohibited *solicitation* for the purposes of prostitution. In 1985, the solicitation law was changed, and *communication* for the purpose of prostitution became illegal. The Code also bans a number of other related activities, such as operating a common bawdy house, living off the avails of prostitution, and procuring. Similarly some U.S. states do not prohibit prostitution per se but rather forbid the solicitation of clients for sexual purposes.

Legal bans on prostitution and solicitation are by no means universal. Prostitution is legal in the Netherlands and Germany. A few counties in the state of Nevada are the only areas in the United States where prostitution and many of its adjunct activities are lawful. Under a system of legalized prostitution, governments control and regulate the enterprise through licensing and inspection. State regulations give prostitutes and their clients legal protection, require prostitutes to undergo regular medical checkups for sexually transmitted diseases, and impose taxes on sales of sexual services (Sansfacon, 1985).

The word "hooker" conjures familiar images that fascinate and intrigue—painted ladies, dimly lit street corners, seedy hotels, and rundown bars. These well-worn images provide people with their common-sense understandings of this illicit profession. However, like many deviant vocations, prostitution is romanticized, misunderstood, and stereotyped.

DEFINING PROSTITUTION

Little empirical research has been done on prostitution in Canada until the 1980s, when two federally mandated committees' investigations generated considerable data. The Committee on Sexual Offences Against Children and Youth (CSOACY), headed by Robin Badgley, investigated prostitution among children and youth, while the Special Committee on Pornography and Prostitution (SCPP), headed by Paul Fraser, examined the illegal sex trade among adults.

Prostitution is not easily defined. Most Canadians (90 percent) conceive of it as a simple exchange of sexual services for money (SCPP, 1985). According to this perspective, people who have sex and accept money in return are prostituting themselves. But what about people who accept as remuneration for sex other material goods or benefits in lieu of cash? Are these people also prostitutes? Over half of Canadians (57 percent) would agree. Does this mean that those who, on occasion, engage in sexual relations in return for a night on the town, a "line of coke," a place to "crash," or a week in Jamaica are prostitutes? What about people who engage in relationships or marry for financial security? To what extent are they prostituting themselves? Where does one draw the line?

For most Canadians, the exchange of sex solely for material gain fails to meet their moral standards—62 percent feel that exchanging sex for money is indecent, improper, and worthy of disapproval. Fewer (53 percent) believe that sex in return for material goods other than money is also wrong (SCPP, 1985). Clearly, Canadians disagree both on what constitutes prostitution and on how objectionable the practice is.

Although a consensus on a definition of prostitution is probably impossible, most sociologists of deviance agree on several points. First, it is sexual in nature, and the reward for performing the sexual act is either money or other material goods exchanged at or near the time of the act. Second, the relationship between the provider and the recipient of sexual services involves neither love nor affection. Finally, because there is an exchange of material reward for a service, prostitution is a full- or part-time vocation (Benjamin and Masters, 1964). Furthermore, prostitutes are not necessarily female (Visano, 1987) and not necessarily adults (Weisberg, 1985). Male and female prostitutes of various ages provide sexual services for both the opposite and the same sex.

MISCONCEPTIONS ABOUT PROSTITUTION

Prostitution has always been a subject of both curiosity and controversy. Inaccurate depictions in both the news and the entertainment media encourage popular misconceptions about the sex trade. Many people believe that pimps force large numbers of women into prostitution through a combination of threats, violence, and drugs. Canadian research, however, suggests that this is relatively rare; about half of all prostitutes enter "the life" without any outside encouragement, let alone coercion (SCPP, 1985).

Force seems to play a role in the recruitment of teenage runaways. Still, while more young persons than adults may be coerced into prostitution, this means of entry is uncommon even for them. The rarity of forced teenage participation in prostitution is underscored by the Badgley Committee's report (1984), which stated that 50 percent of young prostitutes interviewed could not identify a key person who got them into the trade. Moreover, of those who could name such a person, only 1 percent of males and 10 percent of females identified the person as a pimp. Since not all pimps are violent, physical coercion into prostitution in Canada appears uncommon.

Sixty percent of the Canadians surveyed by the Fraser Committee in its national opinion poll believed that most prostitutes work for pimps. However, many prostitutes report that they are self-employed. Again, 60 percent of Canadians believe that organized crime controls much of Canada's sex trade. Empirical research also disputes this, finding few links between prostitution and Canadian organized crime.

The widespread belief that many people take up prostitution to support their addiction to drugs is another misconception. Canadian prostitutes do make use of drugs, but the extent of their addictions and drug trafficking does not appear to be great. Although most prostitutes do have criminal records, the offences for which they have been convicted tend to be relatively minor crimes, such as petty theft and shoplifting. Not surprisingly, many prostitutes also have previous convictions for soliciting and other crimes directly related to prostitution (Sansfacon, 1985).

Many Canadians (69 percent) believe that prostitution is prominent in the spread of sexually transmitted diseases (SCPP, 1985). Common-sense notions of how prostitutes perform sexual acts and of how people spread sexually transmitted diseases are at the root of these beliefs.

The extent to which prostitution contributes to the spread of sexually transmitted diseases seems to be exaggerated. Prostitutes in Canada and the United States likely transmit sexual diseases no more, and perhaps less, than other sexually active people who have many partners. Since the introduction of the birth control pill in the early 1960s, the number of people engaging in sexual activity with more than one partner has increased dramatically. More important than the popularity of promiscuous sexual activity, however, is the fact that most female prostitutes insist on using a condom when performing vaginal, anal, and oral sex acts. Recent Canadian research shows that over 90 percent of adult female prostitutes use condoms extensively; the same is true for 30 to 40 percent of male hustlers (SCPP, 1985). The recent publicity regarding HIV transmission among homosexual males and the public campaign for safer sexual practices makes it likely that condom use among male prostitutes will increase.

Many people think that prostitution is extremely distasteful and unpleasant work and that prostitutes are miserable, guilt ridden, and dislike their clients. Because of the severely limited number of legitimate jobs available to many of those who enter the trade, prostitution presents itself as a relatively forthright way to earn a living. Little formal education, inadequate vocational training, and a lack of experience in the labour force routinely translate into extremely low-status, part-time, low-paying menial work, if not unemployment. This situation is particularly common for many young women during economic recessions.

The emotional and psychological costs of prostitution are not as great as many commonly assume. Like others who provide services to customers, prostitutes find some customers likable, some objectionable, and most nondescript. The image of female prostitutes as man-haters or lesbians is incorrect. Most male and female prostitutes are heterosexual and many have enjoyable sex lives with those whom they love (Carman and Moody, 1985).

THE EXTENT OF PROSTITUTION

Determining the extent of prostitution in Canada is difficult. Using official crime data to count the number of prostitutes is virtually impossible, for a variety of reasons. A prostitute may be arrested once, occasionally, or frequently; thus the number of charges for communicating for the purposes of prostitution (or, before 1985, soliciting charges) does not indicate the number of prostitutes. Moreover, prostitutes may be arrested for offences other than communicating or soliciting, such as vagrancy and public indecency. In these cases, officials underestimate both the incidence of prostitution and the number of prostitutes. Also, because higher-class prostitutes do not work the street and hence are far less likely to be arrested, their numbers remain largely unknown. Since prostitution is an illicit activity without an angry victim, it is less likely to be reported to or recorded by the police. Finally, prostitution routinely generates police crackdowns, which result in many charges being laid in short periods of time. While these brief escalations in charging appear to show an increase in the number of prostitutes, the growth in numbers is artificial. It is more a reflection of police activity than of an influx of prostitutes (Clinard and Meier, 1989).

Only somewhat more accurate than official records are the estimates of the numbers of prostitutes made by the police. In several Canadian cities, as part of the research for the Fraser Committee's report, police officers were asked to estimate the numbers of working prostitutes in their cities. Many factors, particularly transience, contaminate estimates of this type. While some researchers argue that these data are among the best available, the counts they produce are highly speculative. These estimates are the educated guesses of police officers, and it is not surprising that the appraisals of police officers in the same cities vary considerably.

According to police, Eastern Canada has relatively few prostitutes. Twenty-five women and 10 men work the streets in St. John's. The comparable figures for Halifax are 50 women and 25 men. Saint John and Moncton police report little prostitution, while in smaller eastern cities, such as Gander, Dartmouth, Charlottetown, and Summerside, commercial sex seems virtually nonexistent (Crook, 1984). Police in Quebec City report about 400 prostitutes, 64 percent of them female and 32 percent male. Street prostitution in Quebec City is practically nonexistent; most prostitutes work either out of clubs (35 percent) and agencies (28 percent), or from advertisements (25 percent) (Gemme et al., 1984).

Montreal and Toronto police reckon that between 500 and 600 more or less full-time prostitutes operate in their cities. If police include temporary and occasional prostitutes, the numbers increase from two to six times. In Montreal, police estimate that about half of prostitutes are female, about a third are male, and the rest transsexual or transvestite. According to law-enforcement estimates, about 60 percent of Montreal prostitutes work the street. Of the remainder, 11 percent work for escort services, 11 percent operate out of bars, and 11 percent advertise their services in the classified sections of local newspapers. Five percent of prostitutes, mostly male, operate from bath houses, while a further 2 percent, mostly female, work in body-rub parlours (Gemme et al., 1984).

Police estimates of numbers of prostitutes working in Ontario cities range from about 20 in Windsor and St. Catharine's to 600 in Toronto. London reportedly has between 150 and 200 prostitutes, while Ottawa has between 75 and 125. Niagara Falls prostitutes reportedly number around 100; that number increases dramatically when reinforcements roll in for the summer months (Fleischman, 1984). In prairie cities, police estimates range from 10–55 prostitutes in Saskatoon to 100–200 in Calgary to 120–450 in Winnipeg (Lautt, 1984). City police estimate that about 600 prostitutes work in Vancouver (Lowman, 1984).

TYPES OF PROSTITUTES

Like any other occupation, prostitution is diversified and each of its several types has different status characteristics and modes of operation. Ranging from low to high on the status continuum are prostitutes who ply their trade in the streets, in bars, in brothels and massage parlours, and in the employ of escort services. At the very top of the status hierarchy are call girls and call boys. Upward mobility through these ranks is extremely unlikely; street prostitutes, for example, rarely become call persons (Sansfacon, 1985).

The prostitute's position in this status hierarchy is reflected in the amount of money made, the means of operation, the type of clientele, and the degree of safety on the job.

Lower-status prostitutes make less money, hand over a larger proportion of it to pimps, and exercise less choice regarding whom they service. They must process more customers more quickly to earn an acceptable income. Lower-class prostitutes must solicit clients in public places and as a consequence are more subject to public haranguing and police harassment. They are also more likely to be the victims of violence, drug abuse, and exploitation by pimps and procurers. Finally, streetwalkers are more likely than call persons to have criminal records, although they usually involve minor crime.

PROFILE OF CANADIAN PROSTITUTES

Canadian prostitutes surveyed by the Badgley (1984) and Fraser (1985) committees range in age from 14 to 56 years. Most are between the ages of 22 and 25, although the majority began their careers while they were still in their teens. Since the prostitute's earning power is directly related to physical attractiveness, most careers last less than 10 years. On average, Canadian prostitutes enter the occupation around age 16 and retire around age 26. Prostitutes working off the street tend to be older than those working on the street, partly because laws restrict access to bars and lounges on the basis of age. For similar reasons, the young are ineligible for employment by escort agencies. Consequently, off-the-street prostitution is the exclusive domain of adults.

For males, the prostitution career is shorter than for females because they tend to lose their youthful appearance earlier. Most males exit the ranks around the age of 21, while many females remain in the trade until the age of 30. As women age, they lose their competitive edge and become downwardly mobile. Prostitutes visibly beyond their physical prime are forced to work in less desirable locations, both on the street and in bars. They also find that they must increasingly offer their services for lower prices.

Survey data collected for the two committees suggest that the ratio of female to male prostitutes is about 4 to 1. Most, especially males, are single, but 20 percent of females are married. A minority of prostitutes support and care for dependent children. In terms of family backgrounds, Badgley (1984) reports that 49 percent of child and teenage prostitutes come from broken homes. Similarly, 43 percent of the adult prostitutes surveyed by Crook (1984) in selected cities in Atlantic Canada and 56 percent of the Vancouver prostitutes surveyed by Lowman (1984) came from disrupted families.

Both the Fraser and the Badgley reports indicate that the socioeconomic backgrounds of Canadian prostitutes vary widely. Most come from lower-middle or middle-class backgrounds, while a few come from more affluent families. Most prostitutes, particularly those working the street, are poorly educated. In Vancouver, 70 percent had not completed high school. For the Prairies, Quebec, and the Maritimes, the comparable figures were 77 percent, 68 percent, and 84 percent, respectively. In the Ontario report on prostitution, Fleischman (1984) attempted to ascertain the education levels of prostitutes according to the type of prostitution in which they were engaged. Fleischman reports, for street prostitution, that females tend to have completed only the early years of high school, while males are most likely either to have completed higher grades or to have graduated. Not surprisingly, call girls report higher levels of education; most had at least a postsecondary education of some sort.

Another background trait commonly reported by prostitutes is childhood abuse at the hands of a male. Twenty-five percent of boys and 33 percent of girls interviewed for the Badgley Committee had suffered physical assault. Seven percent of boys and 21 percent of the girls reported being victims of some form of sexual assault. Among Vancouver prostitutes, Lowman found that 67 percent were physically assaulted and 33 percent were sexually assaulted in the family context. Seventy-two percent had been attacked in settings outside the family. Similarly, Crook reports that 40 percent and 28 percent of her sample of prostitutes in Atlantic Canada had suffered physical and sexual assault, respectively. In Quebec, 44 percent of prostitutes questioned had been sexually assaulted by some member of the family and 33 percent had been raped (Gemme et al., 1984).

The backgrounds of many Canadian prostitutes appear to be a combination of humble origins and physical and sexual abuse. Although these findings are generally consistent with those of investigations of prostitution in other countries, one must be cautious in assuming that these traits are precipitators of prostitution. The studies from which these findings were taken necessarily focussed on the lower echelons of prostitution. Streetwalkers do tend to have lower-class backgrounds, but so do automobile assembly line workers and secretaries. Alternatively, call girls, like female teachers and bank managers, tend to come from middle-class backgrounds.

To establish a link between abuse and entry into prostitution, it would have to be demonstrated that far more streetwalkers were physically and sexually attacked during childhood than were other persons who are not prostitutes but who have the same social and economic backgrounds. Thus, although many street prostitutes report being physically and sexually abused during childhood, information is scant on how many lower-class children in general suffer such abuse. Furthermore, prostitutes may exaggerate the extent of their victimization to portray themselves as innocent victims not entirely responsible for their vocation. In reference to the impact of prior abuse, Badgley goes so far as to conclude that children and youth who become prostitutes are no more likely to have been abused than those children and youth who do not (CSOACY, 1984). Lowman (1995) argues, however, that closer examination of the committee's data suggests that juvenile prostitutes are twice as likely as non-prostitutes to have been the victims of sexual assault involving threats or actual force.

ENTRY INTO PROSTITUTION

In her investigation of prostitution in the prairie provinces, Lautt (1984) documents three entry processes: exploitation, recruitment by the big-sister figure, and the independent pragmatic decision. Exploitation appears most frequently in the recruitment of girls aged 12 to 16. In search of young female candidates, street pimps patrol bus depots, train stations, airports, and other points of entry to the city. When they spot suitable prospects, the pimps follow them until dusk. At nightfall, pimps approach the young girls and engage them in conversation. Afterwards, they buy the young girls refreshments and offer them places to stay. After a short time, when financial and emotional dependencies have been created, pimps ask their newfound friends to engage in commercial sex. If the girls resist manipulation, pimps occasionally use more coercive tactics, including threats and assaults.

According to Lautt, the influence of a "big sister" is a very important means of occupational recruitment. In this process, older, experienced female prostitutes influence novices aged 15 to 19 to take up prostitution. Davis (1978) details this process in her American research. First, sexually active girls are attracted to companions with similar values and predispositions. The promiscuous girls offer each other support in their search for adventure and excitement. The second step, receiving occasional remuneration for partying is a short one. What begins as sex for fun becomes sex for profit. Those in the group already accepting money for sex convince novices to redefine the meaning of their sexual activity. Davis suggests that the transformation to professional prostitute is complete when girls begin to view the selection of their sexual partners predominantly in monetary terms.

The third entry process observed by Lautt involves the more mature individuals aged 18 to 24. These young women usually base their independent pragmatic decision to enter the occupation on economic necessity. Usually having little formal education, these women simply decide that they can make more money through prostitution than by pursuing the limited alternatives available to them in legitimate careers. The words of several prostitutes illustrate this rational decision-making:

> The same night, after I lost my job, I thought about the advantages and the disadvantages of it and to me it seemed very rational in my mind . . . Like most of the books I have read, the prostitute is a sweet innocent little girl at first and she knows nothing about nothing and she gets talked into or tricked into it by the pimp, that is sort of the common stereotype. You know, the girl comes to the big

city and she doesn't know what all is happening. Whereas with me, I sort of looked at it and said, "Well, I am not sweet and innocent. I know about the whole thing." I knew there was good money in it and I knew it was easy work, so to me it made sense at the time. (Prus and Irini, 1988: 54–55)

I got to Canada and couldn't find a job. I needed money to live, so I became a prostitute. (SCPP, 1985:376)

I was in a locked setting for youths. Some of the girls there were involved in prostitution. They told me about it, so I went out and did it. I was on the run and needed the money to eat. (SCPP, 1985:376)

Some people take up prostitution because they are emotionally attached to someone, a friend or a lover, who encourages them to enter the trade. Fraser (SCPP, 1985) reports that 50 to 60 percent of prostitutes in Canada indicate that another person played some role in their recruitment. Similarly, Badgley (CSOACY, 1984) found that about half of young prostitutes were enlisted by others. These entry factors, according to Canadian research, are much the same for males and females.

Once entered, a career in prostitution is difficult to leave behind. After several years in prostitution, individuals have acquired no legitimate marketable skills. Moreover, they cannot claim experience on their work records. Offering a prospective employer a satisfactory explanation for several years of inexperience and a complete lack of references is no easy matter. As one prostitute explains,

Most of the girls I know are 26 or 28 and have been in the business for 10 years and they don't see an end to it. They say they'd all like to get out, that they're going to leave, but if they've been doing that since they were 16, what else are they going to do? Like, I've worked in an office and I know I couldn't go back to that. I could if I had to, but I wouldn't want to. And most of them haven't even had that experience. So what are they going to do, go out with no experience? So they just stick with it. It's the only way they know how to make money. They know what they're doing and their friends are there. (Prus and Irini, 1988:48)

LEARNING THE SUBCULTURE OF PROSTITUTION

An apprenticeship period normally follows the decision to enter "the life." While training varies by the type of prostitution, certain aspects are common. Novice prostitutes learn the trade from trainers—pimps, madams, or, more often, experienced prostitutes. Trainers may or may not receive a fee; some experienced prostitutes instruct without charge novices who are friends. Pimps and madams who teach neophytes the tricks of the trade are often recompensed later, when the trainees go to work for them. Aspiring call girls are usually taught by their more experienced colleagues, who receive a fee for their instructional services. For each trick turned by the novice call girl during training, the instructor receives 40 to 50 percent of the fee charged to the client.

The training period for most prostitutes other than call girls is quite short—usually only a few days. The major reason for the call girl's lengthier training period is that it involves not only the acquisition of skills and occupational values, it also involves the development of a client list for later use. Customers recruited at this stage return again and again after the apprenticeship. Moreover, clients acquired in this way usually refer new customers to the beginner. Training ends when apprentices feel that they have a long enough list of clients to keep them busy (Bryan, 1965). The importance of the "good book" is evident in the words of one prostitute interviewed by Prus and Irini (1988:70):

> If a call girl has a good book and clients that have money, then she has a good set up. But if she has a little book, like thirty or forty names in it, then she is probably not going to make that much money. Some girls try to work off a book that is very small but it is just not possible. You have to have a big number of customers, you have to have that volume, just to keep you going . . . Some girls don't keep that much information on their clients so that it isn't much help to them when they are working on the phone calling the clients. Even things like favorite drinks and what the guys like, it really helps.

The skills associated with prostitution involve locating and initiating contact with clients, negotiating the type of service and the fee, shielding oneself from disease, and protecting oneself from the hazards presented by customers, pimps, irate citizens, and the police. Streetwalkers determine the best locations in which to display their wares. They learn quickly that areas on the street are distributed on the basis of seniority and power. Encroaching on other prostitutes' territories may well result in retaliation from those threatened prostitutes or from their pimps.

Mastering solicitation is particularly important. To avoid interference from citizens and police, streetwalkers learn to advertise their services without being unduly pressing. In their opening lines, prostitutes mention neither sex nor money (Sansfacon, 1985). Rather, they use phrases such as "show you a good time" or "have some fun." Higher-status prostitutes frequently "confess" to their customers that they need the "date" money for rent or doctor's bills. Last but not least, trainers instruct their higher-status protégés in the proper use of the telephone. Novices learn how to introduce themselves, what to say, what tone of voice to use, and the importance of personalizing calls by mentioning things particular to the client (Bryan, 1965).

Street and bar prostitutes make the least money per client and must therefore work to increase their number of clients. Being able to induce orgasms in customers quickly is a useful talent. Having learned that they must be paid before the service is rendered, prostitutes refine tactics that induce customers to "come" early, during the inspection and washing of their genitals. One prostitute interviewed by Prus and Irini (1988:46) explains:

> So you not only check him for VD, but what you are up there for is to get him to come, and if he comes while you're checking him, great, you can leave! Sometimes they get really mad in that situation, but that was the deal, until they come. That is something you learn over time, and you find the less you get the guy inside of you, the less likely you are to have any problems or get sore, or whatever. So you try to do as much as you can by hand. Then if he has a hard on and gets on top of you, he comes very shortly, to where he is not doing very much to you. And that is good too.

Prepayment discourages customers from withholding the fee, and rapid service enables prostitutes to search for more clients. The time spent with a customer from the very beginning of a transaction until the return to the street or the bar is usually less than half an hour. Most prostitutes feel that processing three or four customers represents a good day. One or no customers is a bad day, while anything over half a dozen is exceptional for most (SCPP, 1985).

Prostitutes' fee structures in given locations are remarkable consistent, and the perils of charging bargain prices are considerable. Undercutting brings potentially violent retaliation from competitors, as a bar prostitute points out:

> The standard minimum fees at Central are $40. You try to get as much as you can. You don't go for less than that. Any girl who does will get into trouble with the other girls if she undercuts their fees. (Prus and Irini, 1988:42)

Of great importance to prostitutes' livelihoods is avoiding customers who have sexually transmitted diseases. Should an individual or an area become associated with the transmission of "social diseases," business can suffer dramatically. These concerns lead prostitutes to demand that customers wear condoms during most sexual activity. To gain compliance from customers, prostitutes learn to warn them about infecting girlfriends or wives if they "pick up something." In the words of a street prostitute:

> All of my dates have to wear safes. Also, I do not let them kiss me or go down on me. If a safe breaks, I don't do anything with anyone until I know I'm all right. Some of the girls out there aren't that careful, though . . . I go for regular check ups with my own doctor, but if I just want to check for something specific I will go to the clinic. They are really polite there and don't make any comments about what I do. If a date doesn't want to use a safe I just explain to him what could happen—taking home something to his wife. (SCPP, 1985:384)

The person who poses the greatest threat to most prostitutes is the customer. Danger is particularly acute for streetwalkers whose work frequently isolates them from assistance. To protect themselves from abuse or injury by clients, prostitutes employ several techniques. Streetwalkers avoid customers who are known to be violent, who behave suspiciously, or who appear to be carrying weapons. Many prostitutes carry a weapon, usually a knife, for protection. Occasionally, they work together as a safety measure. One streetwalker will record the customer's licence number, while the other goes off to service the trick. The "watch" informs police if the colleague is overdue in returning. Other precautions include not providing services in the isolation of a customer's van, not performing alone for more than one client at a time, and not engaging in transactions at a client's residence (Sansfacon, 1985).

Prostitutes do not, as a rule, use alcohol or drugs on the job. They reserve these substances for use after a hard evening's work, to cope with the stresses and strains of the job. Prostitutes know that being drunk or high in the company of potentially dangerous strangers can be fatal. Those engaging in coitus learn to keep one arm across their chests as a means of leverage should they suddenly need to ward off blows. When prostitutes do agree to work under hazardous conditions, they usually demand a higher fee (SCPP, 1985).

Acquiring job skills is only part of successful performance in the role of prostitutes. Prostitutes must also master the proper social values and occupational ideologies. As in other fields of work, their values perform vital functions. They affect self-concept and guide relations with others in or near the occupation. Prostitutes learn not to undercut one another and not to leak information about the identities and activities of pimps and colleagues. They also learn that clients are to be "tricked" and exploited and that authorities cannot be trusted.

Prostitutes are highly devalued in our society. Learning to cope with stigma and to justify disreputable activities is an important part of becoming a member of this deviant enterprise. Many prostitutes maintain that they perform vital functions for society. They meet people's needs for a variety of sexual experiences that many spouses, girlfriends, or boyfriends find distasteful. Moreover, they claim that much of their work consists of "counselling" clients about personal and family problems.

Prostitutes often present themselves as ministering to the sexual needs of a variety of social outcasts, including the unattractive, the deformed, the physically disabled, and those with psychological or emotional deficiencies. Given their rendering of unique sexual services and psychological counselling, prostitutes argue that they contribute to the maintenance of family accord. After all, their services spare their clients' spouses undue pressures to perform acts or discuss sensitive topics that they might prefer to avoid. The same line of reasoning is used to argue that the availability of their services reduces both sexual assaults and other sexually oriented crimes. In either case, prostitutes see themselves as safety valves through which the sexually frustrated can let off steam (Bryan, 1965).

In order to view themselves in a favourable moral light, many prostitutes believe that they are little different from men and women who, to attain material security, marry or become involved in long-term relationships. Thus, prostitutes claim that they are more honest and more straightforward about the real motivations underlying sexual relationships. Along similar lines, prostitutes contrast their honesty to their customers' hypocrisy. They point to the irony of clients' using their services while decrying the existence of commercial sex.

Although rationalizations of functional contribution and moral superiority form the core of prostitution's occupational ideology, the extent to which prostitutes actually embrace this philosophy is not entirely clear. Just as many members of legitimate occupational and professional groups demonstrate various degrees of commitment to their occupation's ideological framework, many prostitutes appear uncommitted to the value system associated with their deviant profession.

Most prostitutes perform a limited range of sexual acts for which they receive virtually no training. Most frequent activities for both male and female prostitutes are manual and oral sex, known in the trade as "locals" and "blow jobs," respectively. About 60 percent of all requests by clients of Canadian prostitutes are for oral sex. For female prostitutes, the next most frequently requested act is coitus, which on the street is termed a "straight lay." Some customers ask male prostitutes to engage in anal intercourse (Fleischman, 1984; Gemme et al., 1984). Research does not substantiate the notion that prostitutes will perform any act with anyone, providing that the price is met. More exotic specialty services such as spatting (being defecated upon), golden showers (being urinated upon), and various forms of sadomasochism are rare. As one prostitute explained to Prus and Irini (1988:24):

> Another problem with the tricks is that some of them think that all the girls are the same, that all the girls will do everything, and that they are all into Greek or S & M. And it's just not the case, but they all have their own ideas, and so when they get a girl in the room, they figure that she should go along with whatever it is that they want. Now if they would explain things to you at the table, it would be different, because you could tell them who is into this or that, but they often don't do that. They just expect that when they get there, they will get whatever they want.

Estimates of prostitutes' incomes vary widely. Crook (1984) estimates that female street prostitutes in Eastern Canada earn without any deductions for expenses, about $28,000 working alone and $8,000 working for a pimp. Researchers estimate that males make more than females; gross incomes for males average approximately $31,000. For Montreal street prostitutes, Gemme et al. (1984) suggest that incomes of $1,000 for a 5- or 6-day working week are the norm. Badgley (1984) reports that male and female juvenile prostitutes earn about $140 and $215, respectively, per day. Lowman (1984), deducting projected overhead costs, believes that the incomes of Vancouver prostitutes range from nothing to around $22,000. At the other end of the scale, income levels for escort-service prostitutes and call girls appear to be as high as $144,000 (Crook, 1984). While the accuracy of the various estimates is difficult to assess, some trends are clearly discernible. On the whole, males earn more than females and, in particular, more than females managed by pimps. Street prostitutes earn less than those working off the street, and juveniles earn less than adults.

TWO THEORIES OF PROSTITUTION

Functionalism

Prostitution is something of a social institution. It has endured despite ridicule, strong opposition, and concerted attempts to eradicate it. Cognizant of prostitution's longevity and stability, functionalist Kingsley Davis (1937) developed a sociological theory of prostitution to explain how such a devalued social practice could contribute to order, stability, and the maintenance of society. Davis began by noting the existence of a value system that condemns sex outside of the family for purposes other than the expression of love or the procreation of children. Moral values extol the virtues both of premarital chastity and of marital fidelity.

While society condemns promiscuity and adultery, males experience a powerful sex drive, more intense than that of females. They must either sublimate their sex drives or seek release. When sublimation of the sex drive is not possible, males are forced to look beyond the legitimate outlets for their passions—their wives—to women who are unmarried, or, worse, married to someone else. Since promiscuous and adulterous activities cause social conflict, prostitution enables the powerful sex drives of many men to be dissipated by a relatively small number of women. Prostitution is a safety valve because men can satisfy their need for sex without creating social disruption. Men who are serviced by prostitutes can avoid extramarital romantic entanglements that might undermine the security of their family and work lives.

Davis's theory also explains why customers of prostitutes are seldom criminalized. Being male, they are integrated into the labour force and their services are needed by society's economic institutions. Jailing workers would disrupt economic productivity. But society can express its denigration of prostitution by locking up its female practitioners. They, after all, are less integral to the economy. Finally, from the functionalist perspective, prostitution contributes to social solidarity through the general societal condemnation of exchanging sex for money. Those whose sexual practices conform to society's moral standards can feel virtuous while heaping ridicule on their tainted targets, prostitutes.

Feminism

Feminists have rejected the functionalist theory of prostitution on two fundamental counts. First, they argue that Davis roots his perspectives in a faulty biological premise, the overwhelming sex drives of males. Second, the functionalist approach overlooks the role of sexual inequality in creating and perpetuating prostitution. Feminists point out that money, prestige, and power are stratified on the basis of sex. In patriarchal societies, males command higher incomes, are accorded more prestige, and wield more power than women do. In stratified societies, those with power dominate while those without it serve. In a sexually stratified society, males are dominant and females are devalued, oppressed, sexually objectified, and exploited. As sex objects, women and girls become commodities to be purchased and sold at the will of men.

Women can be either exclusive or common property. Females are the exclusive property of males within the framework of the family. Marriage contracts dictate that husbands will provide economic security while wives provide domestic and sexual services. Failure of wives to do so has traditional justified discipline or dissolution of the arrangement. Daughters also are exclusive property insofar as they are under the control of their fathers until they marry.

Women can also be common property. Promiscuous females meet this definition, and women whose promiscuity generates income are at the extreme end of an exploitive sexual stratification system (Heyl, 1979). Thus, prostitution represents the ultimate commodification and exploitation of females as sex objects because prostitutes are the most dominated of a dominated social segment, women. First, prostitutes must minister to the desires of their male clients. Second, they must satisfy the dictates of their male pimps. Third, they must endure harassment and arrest by male police officers while these officers largely ignore the illegal conduct of male clientele. Customers, feminist theory points out, avoid legal sanction not because of their functional necessity to the economy but rather because of their position of power and privilege as males in a sexually stratified society. Fourth, prostitutes must suffer the consequences of their chosen vocation as male judges find them and lock them up. Finally, prostitutes are subjected to the scorn and derision that society heaps upon its "scarlet women."

Feminists advocate two responses to prostitution. First, prostitution needs to be decriminalized to reduce or eliminate the victimization of its female practitioners by the criminal justice system. Second, and more difficult to achieve, feminists call for the eradication of the system of gender stratification that promotes the sexual objectification and commodification of women and largely creates the demand for illicit commercial sex.

THE CONTROL OF PROSTITUTION

There are three basic approaches to the control of prostitution: prohibition, regulation, and abolition (Sansfacon, 1985: SCPP, 1985). Under the prohibition model, criminal law strictly prohibits any exchange of sexual services for remuneration. The prohibition approach to the control of prostitution is prevalent in 38 of the U.S. states and in most eastern European nations.

Regulation involves the state administering prostitution as a legal, although perhaps restricted, enterprise. In jurisdictions such as Mexico, Panama, Germany, and the state of Nevada, governments ensure that the provision of prostitution services meets legal requirements in terms of customer relations, hours of operation, disease control, and the reporting of income for taxation purposes.

Abolition does not make prostitution itself an offence but rather designates as illegal a number of closely related activities, including communicating for the purposes of prostitution, soliciting, keeping a common bawdy house, procuring, and living off the avails of prostitution. Canada, the United Kingdom, and a minority of the U.S. states have adopted the abolition strategy. The United Nations also officially endorses this approach.

From 1892, when Canada enacted its first Criminal Code, until 1972, the government controlled prostitution largely by enforcing vagrancy laws. As a result of difficulties associated with gathering evidence and gaining convictions and because the existing legislation discriminated against women, Parliament repealed the relevant sections of the Criminal Code in 1972 and replaced them with laws designed to suppress soliciting in public places (SCPP, 1985).

Not long after the enactment of this new anti-solicitation law, however, the question arose in the courts as to whether or not certain actions by prostitutes actually constituted soliciting. In a controversial decision in 1978, a Canadian judge ruled that the propositioning of potential customers had to be both pressing and persistent for a soliciting charge to hold up in court (SCPP, 1985). The main impact of what became known as the "Hutt decision" was to make the anti-solicitation law toothless. Since customers usually play a large part in initiating transactions with prostitutes, police found it almost impossible to prove that the solicitation in question was both pressing and persistent. As a result, public officials in many Canadian communities, and the police themselves were not pleased with the ruling.

The intensity of police efforts to enforce laws intended to curb prostitution vary considerably across the country (SCPP, 1985). The extent of enforcement depends upon the resources available to the police, the visibility of the prostitutes and their actions, the ardour of local public opinion, and the general political climate. Also significant are police officers' predications of court decisions in prostitution cases. Police are most likely to step up law enforcement when the sex trade is obvious enough to produce negative public opinion and mobilize citizens. Moreover, when police think that a conviction is at least possible, they have been more prone to lay charges. Alternatively, where the likelihood of a conviction for soliciting is faint, they have tended to lay charges on morality offences instead. Regardless of all other factors, however, police vigorously enforce anti-prostitution laws when the prostitutes are children or teenagers.

Prostitution is less likely to become a salient issue as long as it remains hidden from the view of potentially disapproving citizens. It confronts few concerned citizens in the established red-light districts of Canadian cities. Sometimes, operators of commercial establishments actually welcome the revenue generated by the use of their facilities (e.g., restaurants, hotel rooms, bars) by prostitutes and their customers. The expansion of the sex trade into residential areas, however, increases the likelihood of public outcry. Residents complain about the provocative attire of prostitutes, the exposure of children to unsavoury individuals, and the increases in traffic congestion. Another problem is the harassment of residents with sales pitches from prostitutes and with misguided overtures from prospective customers. Many citizens also believe that prostitution results in significant increases in drug dealing, robbery, and assault (Sansfacon, 1985).

When prostitution encroaches into neighbourhoods, people frequently mobilize in opposition. For example, the practice of soliciting along sections of Toronto's Queen Street West, Montreal's St. Louis Square, and Halifax's Barrington Street led property owners and renters in these areas to lobby city councillors and police for a cleanup of the streets. Residents of Vancouver's West End launched a widely publicized reaction. They traded abuse, insults, and projectiles with local streetwalkers. In addition, they formed an organization to combat prostitution and began a controversial "shame the johns" campaign.

Despite widespread and sometimes vociferous public outcries, police action against prostitution has usually been ineffective. The legal precedent set by the Hutt decision in 1978 made it virtually impossible for the police to gain convictions on charges of solicitation because prostitutes generally do not persist when prospective clients demonstrate little interest. Given the constraints imposed by the Hutt decision, police either ignored prostitution or resorted to other means of control. One tactic involved charging both prostitutes and their customers with other violations, such as disrupting the flow of traffic, jaywalking, littering, loitering, or conducting sales without a city permit. The fact that police enforced such laws selectively against those whom they felt were members of a class of undesirables was not without its problems.

Sometimes police bent on deterring customers have adopted informal strategies of dubious legality (SCPP, 1985). One police initiative involved stopping clients, asking for identification, and threatening to inform the customers' family members and employers. Police also forewarned customers that they would receive additional surveillance if they approached a prostitute in that location again. Law-enforcement officers explain their tactics as follows:

> We don't as often search the girls. Sometimes we take them in and search them. It takes them (the women) off the street and interrupts their business flow. If we see a guy talking to a prostitute, we'll stop and converse with them. They usually get

nervous and drive away when we pull up. If we see them in a parking lot with a guy, we may approach and talk to them. Run the client's name for warrants. Maybe give them a parking violation. A lot of them know we can't do much, but the average person gets embarrassed and leaves. If they get offensive, we try to embarrass them and dissuade them from returning. We make it clear to some people that we don't want them back. We tell them they'll get in trouble from prostitutes or us. We say, "Who knows what will happen in a dark alley," and let them draw their inferences from that. If they do come back, nothing happens. Sometimes it works. Sometimes it doesn't. (SCPP, 1985:391)

We spot check clients. We ask for two things, a driver's licence and hospitalization card. That way we can tell if he has a wife and kids. If he does, we tell him if we see him down there one more time, his wife will be getting an anonymous phone call telling her where her husband is. We do this if we see the guy enough. These guys backtrack like you wouldn't believe, even don't take the girl back to where they pick her up, to miss us. The department [police] would rake us over the coals if they ever found out we did this. (SCPP, 1985:391)

The basic intention of these formal and informal control strategies is to reduce prostitutes' turnover of customers and thereby to reduce income.

In the early 1980s, since none of these approaches had proved particularly effective, several municipalities, including Montreal, Vancouver, and Niagara Falls, introduced municipal by-laws prohibiting solicitation for the purpose of prostitution. Not surprisingly, prostitutes fought the charges and appealed their convictions. The courts ruled that municipal by-laws prohibiting prostitution were unconstitutional because neither municipal not provincial governments have jurisdiction to create criminal law.

In response, Vancouver officials issued injunctions against individual prostitutes that barred them from certain parts of the city. Other Canadian municipalities quickly followed suit. The principal outcome of this tactic was to initiate a cycle of "displacement"—barred from pursuing their vocation in one area of a city, prostitutes simply moved to a new area and set up business as usual. As a result of mounting public complaint and increased police frustration, changes were made to the Criminal Code that made it unnecessary to prove that solicitation was both pressing and persistent. In December 1985, "communicating" for the purpose of engaging in prostitution or of obtaining the services of a prostitute was outlawed. The new legislation specifically targets both the providers and the consumers of illicit sex.

Principal among the goals of the communicating legislation were to lower the numbers of prostitutes and to reduce their visibility, to target the consumers as well as the providers of illicit sex, and to make it easier for police and the courts to lay charges and obtain convictions (Moyer and Carrington, 1989). It is ironic that Parliament introduced this law at the same time that the Fraser Committee released its recommendations favouring some combination of decriminalization and legalization as the official response to prostitution (Boritch, 1997). Among its recommendations, for example, were changing bawdy-house laws to allow one or two prostitutes to work out of a private residence, empowering provincial governments to license small-scale prostitution establishments, and revising the "living on the avails" laws to apply only to coercive behaviour (Lowman, 1991).

The communicating law increased substantially the charges laid in an effort to control prostitution. In 1985, police laid only 129 charges for soliciting. The next year, after the communicating law was introduced, they laid 5,868 charges (Boritch, 1997). By 1995, that number had grown modestly, to 6,710. Over half (55 percent) of those charged with communicating for the purposes of prostitution were female. Since December 1985, there has been a shift toward charging more males. Males accounted for 36 percent of soliciting charges between 1977 and 1985; by comparison, 47 percent of those charged with communicating between 1986 and 1995 were male (Duchesne, 1997).

Although more men are being charged under the communicating law, a number of researchers point out that men remain under-represented among the ranks of those officially processed. First, female prostitutes outnumber males in the trade by about four to one. Second, the clients of both male and female prostitutes are overwhelmingly male. Third, females service twice as many male clients as male sex workers do. From this perspective, simple math suggests that only about 4 percent of those involved in the selling and purchasing of sexual services are female (Shaver, 1993). Research in several Canadian cities provides evidence that police charge more prostitutes (predominantly female) than clients (predominantly male) and fewer male than female prostitutes. An investigation of charging practices involving prostitutes and clients in ten Canadian cities in 1986–1987 showed that police lay the lion's share of charges, 70 percent on average, against the sellers as opposed to the purchasers of sex. Percentages of charges against prostitutes as opposed to customers ranged from a low of 55 percent in Calgary to a high of 83 percent in Toronto. Compared to customers, prostitutes were more likely to be detained overnight, found guilty, and confined (Lowman, 1990; Shaver, 1993.

In another piece of research, head-counts in Calgary, Toronto, and Halifax estimated the percentages of prostitutes who are male at 18 percent, 25 percent, and 33 percent, respectively. Corresponding percentages for charges laid were 12 percent, 5 percent, and 11 percent. Montreal was an exception, with male prostitutes representing 20 percent of the total but 27 percent of charges laid (Shaver, 1993). Despite the increases in charging and the tendency to charge more men than was the case under the previous legislation, the focus of criminal justice initiatives remains firmly fixed on female sex workers and on street prostitution. Moreover, while arrests have increased sharply under the new law, it does not appear that the prevalence of street prostitution has been reduced but rather that it has simply been displaced to other locations (Boritch, 1997).

Police have found it equally troublesome to control the activities of those involved in roles related to prostitution. Pimping is not against the law in Canada, although procuring is. Part-time procurers who also work in legitimate jobs are difficult to catch in the act of receiving kickbacks from prostitutes. Police have also found it arduous to convict full-time procurers, such as those operating in the context of escort services. Not only is the procuring law ambiguous, but the individuals and the organizations charged often have considerable resources with which to fight their cases in court. Legal proceedings have been time consuming, costly, and of uncertain outcome. For example, Lowman (1984) cites a Vancouver case where the costs of closing two establishments against which charges of procuring had been laid reached $1 million. In one of the cases, the appeal court overturned the conviction of the accused, and in the other, the establishment, a nightclub, burned to the ground before the police could complete their investigation.

Chapter 16

COLLEGE GIRL
TO CALL GIRL

Sarah Schmidt

Sᴛᴀᴄʏ ɪꜱ ᴅᴇᴀʟɪɴɢ ᴡɪᴛʜ ᴀʟʟ ᴛʜᴇ ᴛʏᴘɪᴄᴀʟ ᴇɴᴅ-ᴏꜰ-ᴛᴇʀᴍ ᴘʀᴇꜱꜱᴜʀᴇꜱ ᴏꜰ ᴜɴɪᴠᴇʀꜱɪᴛʏ term paper angst, exam anxiety, career stress. And by day, she is indeed a typical, perhaps model student, working at her co-op job placement and visiting the library at York University in Toronto to prepare for a career in advertising.

But at around eight, most evenings, Stacy heads out to pay the bills.

And this 25-year-old, from an upper-middle-class Oakville, Ontario, home, doesn't serve up coffee at Starbucks. Though she grew up much like any suburban child of a chartered accountant and a homemaker—bedtime stories, piano lessons, cottage weekends, trips to Disneyland—Stacy now goes out on "calls," as many as six times a night, condoms in hand, to pleasure clients as a prostitute.

Most men expect intercourse. A few are satisfied with oral sex. The odd one—either "really drunk or really lonely," she says—just wants to talk. But she doesn't wear high heels, fishnet stockings, or short skirts. As a student "escort," Stacy dresses like any college girl going out to the movies or a bar. That's the way men like it.

For a growing number of middle-class youths graduating this spring, prostitution isn't seen as a shameful trap, but as a means of making it through the lean student years on the way to a respectable career. Escorts like Stacy are dispatched by agencies to upscale hotel rooms, private homes, and even offices. She may turn tricks, but in her own mind she is far away from the streets and alleys and whores desperate for $20 for a fix. She serves most professionals, who can afford the house call.

"You're looking at a very different kind of situation in the year 2000. Most people don't know what prostitution looks like. People have no clue," says sex-trade researcher John Lowman, a professor of criminology at Simon Fraser

University in Vancouver. "What we have is a class-based system of prostitution. Just like you have a hierarchy of food services, you have a hierarchy of sex services."

Over the last nine years, tuition fees in Canada have risen on average by 126 per cent, far more rapidly than inflation and the minimum wage. About half of the student population graduates with an average debt load of $25,000, up from $8,000 in 1990.

Off-street prostitution has experienced a similar explosion, and many Canadian cities have cashed in by charging annual licensing fees to "massage parlours," "escort agencies," and "encounter counsellors." Researchers estimate that off-street prostitution now comprises approximately 80 per cent of Canada's sex trade. And student work is every part of it, from phone sex and stripping up to turning tricks. Ads in weekly newspapers promote "College Cuties," "Adorable Students," "University Girls," and "Hot College Hard Bodies."

Fifteen years ago, such ads were unheard of. This year alone, escort ads in the *Montreal Mirror*, for example, have increased by 50 per cent. Since 1995, they've increased five-fold in Victoria's *Monday Magazine*. Even NBC's new megahit, "The West Wing," has featured a sub-plot about a Washington, D.C. law student who doubles as a high-priced call girl.

For her part, Stacy stumbled into the business three years ago. She knew someone else who was doing it. She was ineligible for student loans because she had defaulted on a previous one, and her stepfather did not want to pitch in. "There's no way a $7-an-hour job is going to pay my rent and tuition. It's not possible."

Escort work is far more lucrative. Stacy scores $170 for a one-hour call, $130 for a half-hour (the agency keeps $80 and $70 in each case). On the other hand, it's also a lot more demanding than steaming up latte while wearing a funny hat.

"I remember the first time, I felt sick," recalls Stacy. And it has not gotten much easier with time. "It's not something I want to be doing. I hate it."

"People think, 'Students? Not students!'" says sociologist Cecilia Benoit. "They think of sex workers as marginal women, women who are down and out. It ain't like that."

The University of Victoria professor, in partnership with the Prostitution Empowerment and Education Society of Victoria, is undertaking a study on the health conditions of the city's off-street sex-trade workers. Findings so far show that some come from troubled backgrounds, but many don't, and their control over working conditions also varies. The danger of assault or murder is certainly lower than it is for street prostitutes.

Stacy's boyfriend knows how she pays her bills. "He doesn't like it, but he doesn't make me feel bad about it." Otherwise she doesn't discuss it with family or friends.

Still, Detective Bert O'Hara of the Sexual Exploitation Squad of the Toronto Police Services observes that off-street sex work has "become more socially acceptable." In the past, it occurred in cheap motels; now, it's in private homes and commercial establishments. When Det. O'Hara and his colleagues take a peek inside, they find a range of participants: housewives earning extra cash, students covering their bills, single moms making grocery money.

Police continue to focus on the more visible, and cheaper, blue-collar street prostitution, Lowman says, while "men with money can buy sex with impunity." And at this end of the sex trade, both sides get to pretend they're just having a normal social interaction, at least to a degree.

Louis, manager of a Montreal escort service, knows students sell well to a particular class of men. His Baby Boomers' Playground serves up "young female students for your utmost fantasy," according to the ad. It's a perfect match: the clients, middle-aged professionals, prefer to mix sex with intelligent talk, not just idle chatter, Louis says.

Harvard grad Bennett Singer came to the same conclusion when he investigated the sex industry to research a novel he co-authored about his alma mater. *The Student Body*, to be released in paperback next month, is based on a real-life prostitution scandal that rocked the prestigious Brown College in 1986. "They enjoy an intelligent conversation with a young, refined person with an active mind," says Singer, executive editor of *Time* magazine's education program.

Anna, the daughter of a businesswoman and an academic, was recruited a few years ago to pursue graduate work at one of Canada's leading research institutions, but a financial and personal crisis led her to work as a "high-end call girl." Her clients' education matched her own.

And you can see why they would fall for Anna's quick wit, wholesome face, welcoming eyes, and warm smile. As an escort, she dressed business casual, "so we could get past the front desk." Her first client, "a virgin who didn't want to be a virgin anymore," made it easier for her to break into the business.

"I still felt cold, though," she says, and she never got over that feeling. She just put on a happy face even on the night she had seven calls. "I was in total shock. That night was a bit stunning."

Still, she says she actually met one man, a broker whom under different circumstances she would have dated. "My God, you're like a girlfriend," Anna remembers him saying. Unlike most, he "needed a full connection. He was so nice."

University of Toronto student and former escort Alicia Maund has heard similar coping strategies from Toronto's sex-trade workers. "They say, 'He's a banker. It's at the King Eddie [a high-class hotel], so it's okay.'"

Stacy is a case in point. "To me, there's a difference," she says. "It's not prostitution. I realize in essence everybody's doing the same thing, but I portray myself with a level of respect." That doesn't mean she's all that fond of her regulars, though. "They like to think we have something. I just fake it. I don't want these people to know me. I don't want to be friends with them."

Carolyn Bennett shakes her head at Stacy's rationalizations. "Whatever way you look at it, it's prostitution. You still get paid for sex," says the outreach worker for the Halifax-based Stepping Stone Association, a drop-in centre for street prostitutes.

John, a general-studies college student and former sex worker in Vancouver, agrees completely. "It's a cop-out," he says. "I don't mind being called a hustler." Before he started hustling, minimum-wage work was "killing my spirit," he says, and his parents, a nurse and labourer, couldn't really help out. He was saddled with a growing student loan when his girlfriend, also a student, introduced him to the idea of escort work.

"It really freaked me out initially. It was unimaginable for me. It seemed horrible, but I was totally desperate for money."

John has floated in and out of the massage business since 1996. There, the rules were clear: the rub-down always included a hand job, but nothing else. But he had more flexibility as an independent. On outcalls, "I charged what I could get away with," he says, which sometimes exceeded $150 an hour.

Though he was raised with "traditional values" in the suburbs, John, like many young, educated sex workers, is also a bit of an adventurist. "To have someone project a fantasy onto you, for the purposes of the hour, to see you as the fantasy, that's powerful. I think there's something that draws me in."

Nonetheless, at first he didn't tell anyone. "I didn't want to deal with them trying to comfort me, or seeing me differently." Today, most of his friends know, but not his parents. "It would kill my mom. It would kill them both." They're still wrestling with his bisexuality, he says, though he feels like his father should understand. "He's done the worst jobs."

John is facing a more immediate decision, though. He's been out of the business for awhile, but a friend at the University of British Columbia has a regular client that would like to add John to the equation. "I have to figure that out for myself and my partner. But I could sure use the money."

His caution makes sense. For many students, it seems, the real stigma in sex work is tied to how long you do it. Anna only lasted six weeks—her parents intervened when they found out, and gave her "total freedom, total choice, and support." She still sounded a bit stunned by the experience. "It was a very healthy choice in a bizarre situation. Had I stayed longer, it would have hurt me," says Anna, now a high-tech professional.

Another reason to get out quickly is to minimize the risk of running into former clients in later life. Anna says she would pretend not to recognize them. "People don't deal with the issue well." But she also wishes people would "get over their hang-ups." She says, "It's just a job."

Maybe so, but Stacy would rather land that advertising job after graduation and put this kind of work behind her for good. "I don't want to be doing this," she says. "I want to do something for myself. I know I'm an intelligent person."

Chapter 17

PRISON FOR WOMEN'S INVISIBLE MINORITY

Melissa Stewart

I WOULD LIKE TO BEGIN BY TELLING YOU ABOUT HOW I CAME TO BE A PRISONER AT the P4W. Here is how my life unfolded, from being sane, joyful, community spirited, and relatively calm, to living a nightmare.

I remember the very first time I met Gordon. He was immaculately dressed, his hair neatly combed. He was wearing a suit, with a perfectly knotted tie. Everything was in place. He was big and powerful and moved purposefully. I thought he was the most handsome, suave, debonair man I had ever met. He was very polite and seemed totally taken with me. I was settling real estate at the time. He told me he wanted to buy a small piece of land near the ocean, on which to build a cottage. He kept telephoning me with excuses to have dinner with me, and the like.

Two weeks later we were living together common-law. What started off as a honeymoon became the worst nightmare of my life. Gordon was a violent alcoholic, as were his father and brother. I never really knew his family very well, except the one time Gordon and his father landed in detox centres at the same time. His younger brother committed suicide about three years before Gordon died.

My whole life was centred around keeping this man "happy." During those years of knowing him and living with him, I felt certain I could "save" him. He criticized me constantly, and I developed feelings of inadequacy and insecurity. I did not feel that I was capable of doing anything right. During this time I was living in limbo, trying to fight off depression.

The physical beatings started right after we were legally married. I wore heavy make-up to cover the contusions and bruises inflicted at various times. He would play one cruel game in which he would put a plastic bag over my head while we were having sexual intercourse and strangle me, saying he wanted me to have a stronger orgasm. He would strangle me to the point where I would almost pass out.

Prior to the physical assaults on me, Gordon would always tell me I was "cruising for a bruising." I wish I could go back and undo the pain of the past. I lived in constant fear. I believe he was a psychopath who liked to inflict pain. He put welts all over my back by beating me with a leather strap. On other occasions he kicked me and cracked my ribs and collarbone. My kidneys were bruised from his beatings.

Gordon began threatening both my daughter and me, stating that he would kill her. About this time he began making sexual advances towards her. He was drinking a lot and taking cocaine and valium. I was at rock bottom.

On another occasion he held a loaded handgun to my head and pulled the trigger. The firing pin jammed in the gun, saving my life. I called the police. He was charged with the careless discharge of a firearm. They seized his guns and when he went to court he was prohibited from having any firearms for five years.

On the day that Gordon died, he had just been released from jail where he had served two months for assaulting me. This was his second charge of assault against me. On the day that he died, he came after me with a knife. I was asleep in bed when suddenly he was standing over me and holding the knife to my throat. He abducted me at knifepoint after ordering me to get dressed. We left the apartment and drove around in the car. That day, I told him I was never going to live with him again as man and wife. And that day, he raped me. He performed oral sex on me. He put his penis on my face, then in my mouth. I choked and gagged. I was so frightened. He started striking me on the head. There was no safe place. I could not get away. I was trapped.

After the years of battering, verbal abuse, sexual abuse, alcohol and drug abuse, I finally recognized that my life was on the line. Everything was unmanageable. My relationship with my children had deteriorated. I had been mentally and emotionally denying the torture I had lived through.

I did not mean to kill Gordon. I only wanted to get away from him. When he was standing behind the car urinating, I sensed that it was my only chance to get away. I slid over under the driver's wheel, turned on the ignition very quickly, and put the car in gear. But I put it in the wrong gear; I put it in reverse instead of forward. I backed the car over him, and I left the area at a very high speed. I just wanted to get out of there. We were on a logging road in the woods. I very much regret what happened on that day. I believe my survival can only be credited to luck.

The R.C.M.P.'s Lower Sackville department charged me with first-degree murder. At my preliminary hearing, the judge threw the charge out, saying there was not enough evidence to support a first-degree murder charge. He had me stand trial on second-degree murder instead.

The trial only focused on that one day in our lives. No mention was made of any battering or sexual abuse in our relationship. My defence lawyer should have brought that up. Only the rape was discussed. There was courtroom testimony about my pubic hair and Gordon's seminal fluid analysis. I felt nauseated with shame.

I pled "not guilty" all through the trial. When I was found guilty of manslaughter by the jury, the judge said his reason for sending me to the federal prison was "deterrence to the public."

After sentencing, I was taken to the Halifax County Correctional Centre. After spending three months there, I was taken from my cell in that dirty rat- and bug-infested hole at 4:00 a.m., with no prior warning, in shackles and handcuffs. I arrived by van at Springhill Institution around 6:30 a.m. There I was fingerprinted, had my mug shot taken and was listed as a number, before being taken to Moncton N.B. to fly in an R.C.M.P. airplane along with some male prisoners to Kingston, Ontario. All prisoners were designated to different prisons in the Kingston area.

The ride in the airplane was turbulent, but worst of all I was seated next to a very large, odorous, garrulous man, who continually leered against me. His flesh sprawled onto my chair and seat and he kept leaning against me. It was my first close encounter with a man since my husband died. I found this very uncomfortable and completely unnerving, and I thought it was insensitive on the part of the R.C.M.P. to seat a battered woman next to such an aggressive man. We arrived in Kingston and were taken in different vans to local area prisons. I was taken to the Prison for Women (P4W).

My first impression of the P4W was its dungeon-like appearance. There was a stench of urine and cigarette smoke in the air. I was admitted into the basement area of the prison, along with two other female prisoners. By this time it was around 8:00 p.m.

The walls inside the P4W were gray and ugly, with paint peeling off the bars. Everything was steel and concrete. I was asked routine questions on admittance such as whether I had any enemies amongst the other prisoners. This would influence the decision on where to put me. Most prisoners are placed on the "A" Range for the first three months, for assessment, unless they are in need of protective custody or are mentally ill.

After the questions, a nurse was called and a body cavity search was performed on me and the other women. It was a terrifying and humiliating experience.

"A" Range in the P4W resembled a zoo. There are 50 cells, six by nine feet each in size, in two tiers, with a small sink, toilet, single cot, and a steel dresser in each. I was put in the upper cell level. By this time I was totally exhausted from the 16-hour trip. The noise level was incredible, with clanging, banging, screaming, and cursing. Some curious prisoners were peering at me inside the cell, wondering who the new "fish" was and whether I would fit into the prison sub-culture. Paired uniform guards patrol "A" Range every hour.

My first months in the P4W caused me severe emotional deprivation, fear, pain, and panic as I began to come to terms with where I was and how I would survive. I suffered multiple crises: being away from my family, the loss of relationships, social isolation, social stigmatization, economic losses, the loss of home and goods, and feelings of unworthiness. My self-hate grew into thoughts of suicide. I entered into an agonizing, dark aloneness. I felt emotionally shredded. I was completely numb and my mind was blank. I had no sense of time passing. It helped me to block the pain. I was like this for three months.

LIFE AT P4W

Upon entering prison, each prisoner is assigned a case management officer who collects all information pertaining to the prisoner from the police, court and sentencing reports, and the judge's recommendations. When this information is correlated, the case management officer classifies the prisoner. In the fourth month after my classification I was moved to the wing area of the prison. Usually the more quiet prisoners reside there, along with some protective custody cases. Fifty women are caged on the two wings. Lately, with the increase in women prisoners, double-bunking has occurred.

Women prisoners in the P4W do not receive natural light and fresh air. They are housed in dismal surroundings, with a lack of privacy. It is a maximum-security prison, caging three security levels of prisoners. Intrusive security measures are in force daily. Prisoners have little access to adequate health, education, and professional services. There is also a lack of women-centred and culturally sensitive programs.

The contraband system is very common in the P4W, commodities such as drugs, alcohol, contraband appliances, clothing, institutional privileges, contraband food, and canteen items. Sometimes, suicide seems like the only alternative for a prisoner if she owes money to one of the range's leaders. The prisoners' code keeps women from talking too much.

A typical day in prison begins when you are awakened at 6:00 a.m. In one hour, each woman is to shower, dress, make her bed, tidy up her cell, and be ready to go to the common dining room to eat breakfast by 7:00 a.m. Breakfast consists of "juice," cereal or toast, coffee or tea, sometimes a piece of fruit. On Sundays, prisoners are served bacon and eggs and pancakes for breakfast.

During the day, some women are assigned work duties within the prison and go to work at 8:00 a.m. Some attend a program to upgrade their education to the Grade 10 level. Others might play cards if they have purchased their own deck, or do nothing. The work day finishes at 3:00 p.m. The gym is also open one hour per day for those who wish to exercise.

Lunchtime is from 12:00 noon to 1:00 p.m. It consists of soup, a sandwich, a dessert, and tea, coffee, or "juice." Meals are adequate. Dinner takes place between 5:00 p.m. and 6:00 p.m. Each section of the prison eats separately. The wing area, which houses 50 women, eats first, then "B" Range. Women in segregation are served meals in their cells. In the punitive area of segregation women are served what looks like a large overcooked hamburger, made of questionable ingredients. Liquids are controlled and are given at the discretion of the guards.

Most prison programs focus on counteracting aggressiveness, anger, and volatility. As such, the programs treat women as offenders rather than as victims. The prison system is not interested in fostering assertiveness. An assertive prisoner is a potential nuisance to prison authorities, who are mostly concerned with keeping "the good order of the institution," rather than viewing prisoners as future citizens.

The answer to the suicides of Native women in the P4W (as well as the suicides of two Anglo-Saxon women) by administrative staff was to ban some Native programs and suspect [*sic*] some Native social workers from entering the P4W. The other measure they took was to increase the ratio of guards/prisoners to 78/96.

These degrading conditions and the lack of constructive activity can lead to suicidal thoughts and attempted suicides. Suicide is a mechanism to escape the brutal conditions. Rather than receive appropriate treatment/counselling, the suicidal prisoner will be placed in the new secure segregation units.

In response to the April 1994 riot, brought to public attention by the CBC television program *The Fifth Estate*, this new higher security segregation was ready in April 1995 at a cost of $475,000 to the taxpayers. Prison officials thought this would be the answer to "those unruly women." It consists of 10 cells located across from the kitchen area, in the basement of the prison. The cells have steel doors in place of bars. Each cell is monitored 24 hours a day by individual TV cameras. The beds are welded to the walls. This new segregation unit has a smaller closed outdoor pen for exercise. One of the cells can even accommodate a handicapped person. Why would someone in a wheelchair need to be put in segregation? A reason given by acting prison warden Maureen Blackler was, "There are a few women that are violent and are dangerous to others; they pose a risk to both staff and inmates."

BATTERED WOMEN AND PEER COUNSELLING AT THE P4W

I soon realized that there were a number of women who were in prison for an act committed in self-defense. These were battered women. These women numbered 25 to 30 (a group which included me), were of all different ages, and came from very different educational, cultural, and ethnic backgrounds. Despite these differences, almost all of them had been victims of physical, psychological, or sexual abuse both as children, and then later from their spouses. Eventually, this abuse led to the crimes that brought them their federal sentences: often the killing of the abusers. These desperate acts stood in stark contrast to the women's usually meek, self-effacing personalities.

Many of the P4W's repeat offenders, who are familiar with the prison culture, have developed skills to cope with its harsh environment. Battered women prisoners are horrified by their first encounter with incarceration. The stress of their abuse and their subsequent removal from mainstream society are compounded by their sense of shame and alienation within the prison population.

Within the overburdened federal prison system, these shy and reclusive individuals can become invisible. They sometimes go months between meetings with their case management officers and often find their most basic rights neglected. Women of faith miss out on passes to attend church, and in the most extreme cases, prisoners do not receive their allocations of clothing or even feminine hygiene products.

As a result, the combined emotional and practical needs of battered women prisoners are urgent. However, until I became a member of the prison's Peer Support Team in 1992 and first became aware that we made up a distinctive category of prisoner, there were no programs through which these women could take recourse.

The first P4W Peer Support Team was formed in May 1990, after two years of suicides in which time four Native women hanged themselves. There were eight suicides in total from 1988 to 1996 in the P4W, when again on

February 21, 1996, another young woman, Brenda D., was found hanged in her cell.

Prison psychologist Julie Darke and social worker Jan Heney began the first P4W Peer Support Team. Heney had done a study on self-injurious behaviour at the P4W and discovered there existed amongst the women prisoners an informal network of counselling and support. She recommended that a team be formed and formal training started. The first class of five prisoner/ counsellors graduated in May 1992. These women could be available to help other women in crises; thus began a team of women prisoners ready and willing to help others. It gave me the opportunity to help other women; something positive which came out of something so overwhelmingly negative.

Peer Support Team members have many of the same experiences as the people who use their services. However, peer support counsellors' own access to many resources are limited. As well, confidentiality is difficult since service users and counsellors live in the same close quarters among the very same people. While correctional staff still have more resources at their disposal than peer counsellors, many prisoners are more comfortable dealing with peer counsellors as they often feel they are in an adversarial relationship with correctional staff.

In the absence of programs specifically designed for battered women, many relied heavily on peer-support counselling to help them cope. Sometimes a woman would call three or tour times a week. Realizing that the peer-support program could not effectively meet this sort of demand, I approached the administration and suggested that a battered women's support group be formed. Nothing happened. Then Dr. Heather McLean of the psychology department wrote a letter in praise of the proposal, and permission was granted. Under the supervision of chaplain John Hess, we held our first meeting in April 1993.

Together, members formulated the criteria for admission to the group. They decided that each member must be the survivor of abuse, that she must support the group's vision of itself, which is founded on a "hope to heal in a non-healing environment," that she must respect fellow members' rights to confidentiality, and she must be in prison for a crime committed in self-defense.

We also established group guidelines, drawing heavily from the Quaker-sponsored Alternatives to Violence Project, which has offered workshops in the prison since 1992. These guidelines include looking for and affirming one another's good points, volunteering oneself only, committing oneself to non-violence, and being willing to take risks and possibly to suffer, if necessary, in order to maintain that non-violent stance. We recognized that non-violence is not passivity, submissiveness, or martyrdom. Members also have the right not to participate in an activity. The aim of these guidelines is to establish a "principled space" in which members can encounter the most positive aspects of themselves and each other.

Soon the Battered Women's Support Group (BWSG) grew into a positive force in the P4W. Membership in the group was voluntary, as was attendance. Members were permitted to drop out at any time if they needed to, then return as their circumstances permitted. Instead of being referred to the group by staff, prisoners learned of the group by word of mouth and attended entirely of their own volition.

Meetings were informal. Members sat in a circle for presentations, which were then followed by question and answer sessions. However, some evenings were reserved for taking things out and struggling with the emotions stirred by the talk. Vital to the group's success was the commitment of volunteers from outside the prison. These volunteers visited from as far as Toronto and came from a mixed bag of backgrounds. As founder of the BWSG in the P4W, I was invited by the previous warden to attend group meetings as a community volunteer when I left the prison on day parole in July 1994. This was something close to my heart, so attendance at meetings was something I enjoyed. The group had always functioned as a collective and made its decisions accordingly. Over the three years we had been meeting the group had evolved into a cohesive entity. I marvelled at the level of trust that had developed, and at the feeling of camaraderie we had built up.

The dedicated community volunteers attending the battered women's support group included Jo-Ann Connolly, a Kingston lawyer and currently chairperson of the Canadian Association of Elizabeth Fry Societies Battered Women's Defense Committee. We also worked with Queen's University law professor, Sheila Noona, who originally did the ground work for a legal process which would permit women incarcerated for defending themselves against abusive partners to have an "en bloc" review of their cases. Sheila has offered insights into how the battered women's syndrome could affect reintegration into a small community because of the nature of the offense and the complex relationship between victim and offender in small, often isolated communities. The communities themselves are often unwilling to accept prisoners back after release from prison. Today, Sheila continues to be a support to many group members.

Toronto broadcaster Sian Cansfield commuted weekly to show her solidarity with the women and gave them a voice on her radio program. She did a one-hour show just before Christmas 1994, and discussed issues surrounding abuse survivors and how the group members were dealing with their pain and separation from family members during the festive season. The broadcast resulted in Christmas gifts being donated to group members.

Sandra Dean, a local interior designer, has offered constructive suggestions on dressing and speaking in ways that increase women's chances of being treated with dignity and consideration. She did a presentation on colours and the right choices of wardrobe, as well as proper etiquette.

Addictions counsellor Carol Bielby brought in three of the Boston Terrier pups she breeds. She talked about the love and devotion a dog can offer, and the respect and affection they deserve in return. The direct emotional connection between the women and those six-week-old pups was intensely moving. Some group members had lost touch with their feelings, and the puppies provided a way to emotionally connect again. In prison, women are not encouraged to express their feelings. And all of the feelings associated with addictions, along with the unique and serious emotional experiences these women have endured, can be so overwhelming. Only a pet could bring these feelings to the fore.

Healer Bonita Currier helped some of the women release residual feelings from childhood sexual abuse, and Salvation Army Major Carol Barkhouse brought in entertaining and instructive videos. Some of these topics dealt with same-sex relationships, addictions, group dynamics, family violence, as well as comedies.

Supplementing the steady contributions from our six stalwart volunteers were presentations from various guest speakers, including:

- Dr. Mary Pearson, on diet, exercise, and wellness
- Shiatsu therapist Beth Morris, teaching massage techniques
- Criminal lawyer Josh Zambrowsky, on the impact of Bill C45 on women prisoners
- George Best (who counsels battering men), on the connections between early childhood conditioning, gender roles, and male violence
- Four University of Ottawa criminologists: Sylvie Frigon and Christa Armitage, on the legal use of the battered women's syndrome; and Ashley Turner and Irene Sernowski, on the value of keeping a journal (along with gifts of a notebook and pen for each group member)
- Kingston Interval House staffers Terri Fleming and Pamela Needham, on power and control issues in relation to domestic violence and the importance of equality in partnerships
- Drama workshop facilitator Susan Raponi, of the Salvation Armies in Toronto, leading illuminating role plays

Two gatherings were particularly outstanding. One was the Christmas party—with "imported" home-made foods, portable piano keyboard to accompany carols, and, best of all, carefully selected gifts for each member of the group. As much as the gifts themselves, the women appreciated the fact that they had been specially purchased by people from the outside who just wanted to express their support and affection. The gifts came at a time when, for the first time in years, parcels from home were not being permitted into the institution because of concerns about contraband.

The other important gathering was the National Day of Awareness, held in the gymnasium on August 30, 1994, and attended by representatives from North American Native societies, local community and church groups, and the various levels of government. Group members told their personal stories. Film producer Barbara Doran then showed her film, *When Women Kill*, which kicked off a panel discussion. Journalist June Callwood spoke, as did federal justice committee chairman Warren Allmand. Also in attendance was Member of Parliament, Peter Milliken. This gathering was attended by over 110 guests. Substantial donations of money were sent by retired Supreme Court Justice Bertha Wilson and the Kenora Sexual Assault Centre. Despite the resounding success of this event, prison authorities ruled out the possibility of such gatherings in the future. As a concession, they let us use the gymnasium for a bingo on March 22, 1995, to which no outsiders were invited.

Later, in response to the fall-out from the Commission of Inquiry into Certain Events at the Prison for Women (1995), chaired by Madame Justice Arbour, corrections department officials took over the operation of the Battered Women's Support Group and began to regulate it as a prison program. Prisoners must now attend the group for six weeks, at the end of which time they receive certificates of completion. All meetings are chaired by a guard instead of having a member facilitate. Instead of sharing their feelings when they are ready, participants are told when to express themselves. These conditions violate the original goal of the group, which was to provide a "safe space" in which abuse survivors could share their experiences and work to heal themselves. The presence of the guard can be intimidating for many members, while the six-week certificate of completion trivializes the emotional pain with which survivors of long-term abuse must wrestle.

The good news is that as of September 3, 1996, after I relayed these concerns to corrections officials, I have been assured the group can go back to its original mandate, without the presence of the guard. Once more I will attend the group to help members draw up a new constitution, as well as arrange to have a different group member volunteer to facilitate the next meeting.

This will give members a chance to hone their organizational skills and to feel more comfortable in the limelight. This is especially crucial now, as the Correctional Service of Canada is gearing up to relocate the P4W's population to five new regional facilities across the country. Prisoners have no choice about where they will go and, in many cases, the move will separate women from their partners of long-standing. The turmoil and pain this process poses for prisoners is exacerbated by a lack of information about the relocation process. There seems to be a little information about the move available to many Corrections employees, and what information exists is not filtering down to the prisoners. This has created an atmosphere of fear, suspicion, and tension. Prisoners will need ongoing support as they adjust to their new environments.

After the fall-out from the P4W inquiry, access to the prison by outside groups in 1996 has been increasingly restricted. Currently, only three community volunteers are allowed to attend the Battered Women's Support Group: Sandra Dean, Jo-Ann Connolly, and me.

A news release from the Department of Justice in Ottawa, October 4, 1995, stated:

> The Solicitor General of Canada, Herb Gray, and the Minister of Justice and Attorney General of Canada, Allan Rock, today announced the appointment of the Honourable Lynn Ratushny, a judge of the Ontario Court of Justice (Provincial Division), to lead a review of cases involving women convicted of killing their abusive partners, spouses, or guardians.

When I spoke with Judge Ratushny on August 13, 1996, she told me there were 98 cases submitted for review. The "in custody" applications total 63; 35 cases are not in custody. She states that she has dealt thoroughly and fairly with 45 cases, and has contacted the women involved. Some of these files have been looked at, because she is dealing with the women in custody first. There are still 15 women in custody, whose cases need to be reviewed.

Upon leaving the P4W in July 1994, I began developing my vision of having an agency run by and for prisoners, enlarging upon the peer support team model I had learned in the P4W. With the help of important community leaders and since its incorporation in April of 1995, Project Another Chance Inc. has, with the support of the Trillium Foundation, made great strides towards establishing a conduit to the community for women in prison and female parolees. We now have 75 committed volunteers, many of whom have received intensive crisis response and suicide intervention training, as well as orientation on Native women's issues. The "Right-On Line," a crisis phone line for women prisoners and parolees, has been in official operation since December 1995. I have been taking calls on restricted hours since May 1995, and already the response from service users is very positive. After a great deal of organization and training, we are beginning to see the results of the very necessary service we provide. We have made a specific mandate to seek the cooperation of prison administrators across the country in order to allow prisoners, who have increasingly restricted telephone access to the outside, to use our services.

Operated by a tiny staff and over 40 professionally trained volunteers (including several ex-prisoners), the Right-On Line offers quiet, non-judgmental support, suicide intervention, referrals to prison and community resources, and strives to establish a community link for women in conflict with the law. Parolees who call the Right-On Line can tap into practical information on resume-writing, conquering addictions, and finding affordable products and services, as well as building a supportive network of friends and advisors.

The P4W has always been and continues to be a living nightmare, designed and operated as a maximum-security prison. This in inappropriate and harmful to federally sentenced women. They struggle with geographical and cultural dislocation, and have little or no contact with their children, families, and communities.

When leaving prison, you are usually told a day or so ahead of time that you will be released. This gives the prisoner time to pack up her belongings, clean up her cell, say her farewells, and prepare herself for the outside. It is quite disorienting and overwhelming when you know you will be released. Some women panic at this stage and are unsure if they can "make it" outside.

The dehumanizing aspects of incarceration cause prisoners to become more angry and bitter. They lose faith in the "system," and while imprisoned they are essentially schooled in the commission of crime. Those released are less able to function as responsible, caring citizens.

Prisons represent a temporary warehouse where goods will eventually come out. But what if these goods are then more spoiled? We have prisons because we have come to believe in them, even though they do represent only a small proportion of the criminalized. Prisons represent that end of the system where we put the most readily detected, the most readily prosecuted, and the most readily forgotten about.

Chapter 18

VIOLENCE STALKS WORLD'S WOMEN

John Stackhouse

In a cramped suburban flat in New Delhi, Subhadra Butalia watches a group of physically abused housewives stitch clothes, and wonders what all the global talk about women will do for them.

For 16 years, Mrs. Butalia has helped battered women build a sense of independence through small enterprises such as stitching.

"Income security is a very powerful asset," she said, "because even in the face of domestic violence, many women can't leave home."

But increasingly, Mrs. Butalia said she finds it difficult to raise funds from international donors, who prefer high-profile advocacy campaigns.

Away from the rhetoric of the Fourth World Conference on Women, which opened yesterday in Beijing, women almost everywhere have struggled against what many say is the greatest silent crisis of the twentieth century: domestic violence. From the United States, where an average of 240 women a day are raped, to Papua, New Guinea, where two-thirds of women report physical abuse at home, violence against women has continued apparently unabated into the 1990s.

"Domestic violence is one of the leading causes of female injuries in almost every country in the world," a news report on women's rights by the Washington-based group Human Rights Watch says.

Although the issue of violence against women has been placed high on the agenda at Beijing, there are few signs of it slowing and even fewer signs of an international effort to stop it.

"Few mainstream development organizations, even among those devoted to health issues, have focused on violence," said the World Bank in a report last year entitled *Violence against Women: The Hidden Health Burden.*

In India, despite a nationwide increase in income and female education levels, police reported a 170 per cent increase during the past decade of women being killed by husbands who felt their wives did not provide a sufficient dowry—including 6,200 last year. In the country's most populous state, Uttar Pradesh, the number of rape cases doubled over five years to 2,700 in 1994.

Since the previous international women's conference in 1985, the same disturbing pattern has been documented on every continent.

- 25 per cent of Canadian women surveyed reported being physically assaulted by a current or former male partner since the age of 16.
- One-half of suicide attempts by black American women are preceded by abuse.
- 20 per cent of women surveyed in Colombia said they had been abused physically; 10 per cent said they had been raped by their husbands.
- Of 2,000 cases recorded in 1987 at an all-women's police station in the Brazilian city of Sao Paulo, more than 70 per cent involved domestic violence.
- 42 per cent of women surveyed in Kenya said they were beaten regularly. In 1991, when schoolboys raided a girls' dormitory, raping 71 girls and killing 19, the school's principal was quoted as saying, "The boys never meant any harm to the girls. They just wanted to rape."
- Nearly 60 per cent of women surveyed in Japan reported sexual abuse.

In recent years, domestic violence has been identified as a major public-health issue.

The World Bank calculated that domestic violence and rape cost women physically and economically as much as HIV and tuberculosis, and about four times as much as war. In Papua, New Guinea, one survey found that 18 per cent of urban married women had been sent to hospital because of domestic abuse, adding enormously to public health costs.

Several new studies also show how violence against women may be a major barrier to community development. In Ethiopia, one group of women said they cook fewer meals because they were not willing to walk far for firewood for fear of rape. In rural Bangladesh, women health workers have stayed home because of a new threat of acid-throwing attacks by Islamic fundamentalists.

"But violence is not inevitable," the World Bank says, "Cross-cultural research shows that, although violence against women is an integral part of virtually all cultures, there are societies in which gender-based abuse does not exist."

THE THREAT
Domestic violence is so widespread that it is called the silent crisis of the 20th century

THE RESPONSE
Some governments have made efforts to punish offenders and to set up services for victims. Others have enacted legislation that effectively reduces women's protection.

THE OPPORTUNITY
Women's organizations, including some of those attending the United Nations' Fourth World Conference on Women, are raising the profile of domestic violence and seeking to force governments to respond to the problem.

THE QUESTION
Will governments attending the UN conference in Beijing be able to agree on and follow through with action to reduce domestic assault?

The Platform for Action under debate at Beijing aims to condemn violence against women, regardless of cultural or religious considerations; to increase funding for shelters and relief support for victims of violence; and to ratify and enforce international treaties on trafficking and slavery.

The conference also aims to establish the equality of women and men internationally. Human Right Watch identified Iran, India, Guatemala, and Egypt as countries that assign special legal status to women that can be used to discriminate against them.

"These governments promote the concept that women have a 'special' role in society and the family as an excuse to deny women their equality, civil liberties, and the right to be free from violence," it said.

Many women's groups point to the need for legal reform in countries like Pakistan, where the Islamic sharia law requires a woman to produce at least two male witnesses to substantiate a rape charge.

Two-thirds of all women in Pakistan's jails have been charged with adultery under sharia law, a crime which carries a seven-year jail term for women, but none for men.

The World Bank study found that domestic violence tends to decrease as women gain economic and social power outside the home. Community intervention and sanctuary for women victims can also be important, the study said.

After previous international women's conferences, governments established all-women police stations to encourage women to seek outside help.

Other governments have tried to cut to what they believe are the roots of domestic violence such as alcohol. In southern India, a party promising prohibition was swept to power earlier this year, largely on the votes of rural women.

Chapter 19

THE CANADIAN CRIMINAL JUSTICE SYSTEM: INEQUALITIES OF CLASS

Leslie Samuelson

IN THIS CHAPTER WE PROVIDE A CRITICAL CRIMINOLOGICAL ANALYSIS OF THE Canadian criminal justice system [which concerns class]. . . . We first outline the core of a critical criminological analysis of law and society, as well as some important developments within it.

The critical, or conflict, perspective in criminology emerged largely in the 1970s, and challenged conservative neoclassical and liberal pluralist conceptions of law and society (cf. Taylor, Walton, and Young, 1973). The central focus for the emerging critical criminology was on how class-based inequality was enforced and legitimated by legal codes and state agencies of control. As Ratner and McMullan (1987, 10) note, conservative and liberal criminologists more or less tacitly accepted the bourgeois legal ideology that had evolved over the past 200 years.

Here law is treated as relatively unproblematic. Citizens are expected to obey the law on the assumption that the legal system and the state are neutral institutions seeking to advance the common good (the conservative point of view) or the interests of successful competitors (the pluralist position) by rational and efficient means (Ratner and McMullan, 1987, 10). As these and other critical criminologists point out, however, this ideology perpetuates an uncritical acceptance of the legal system and of the political-economic order that is both supportive of, and supported by, the legal system.

Early critical analysis of law, crime, and the state were, however, criticized on several fronts. First, it was noted, they ignored gender. A range of analyses are emerging that focus on how criminal and civil law, and the treatment of women in the justice system, reinforce not only capitalist society with its inequalities, but also the patriarchal subjugation of women (Chesney-Lind and Bloom, 1997).

Early critical criminology can also be criticized for its analysis of "race." In most early critical criminological research, such as that by Quinney (1970), and Chambliss and Seidman (1971), race is largely ignored as an issue in its own right; it appears mainly as a proxy indicator of social class status—the central concern of critical criminology (cf. Hawkins, 1987).

Finally, Ratner and McMullan (1987) note that current conflict analyses of society must attempt to integrate substantive investigations into a general political economy of state control of social relations through law. As they point out, none of the conservative, liberal pluralist, or early orthodox Marxist analyses of society offered any cohesive statement of the role of the state in the functioning of law and social control in capitalist society. The perspective advocated by Ratner and McMullan is particularly appropriate when analyzing state-sponsored legal reforms, such as victim-offender mediation programs and sentencing reforms.

There are two basic dimensions in the critical criminological analyses of the class-biased nature of law. One is what gets defined in legislation as crime and what is controlled through regulatory law. The second is the differential processing of working-class and professional-class individuals and corporations in the criminal justice system for "criminal acts."

Critical criminologists, who follow a *political economy* approach to the analysis of crime, hold that a relatively small group of individuals control a very large proportion of the wealth and political power in our society. While not necessarily acting in unison, this elite is able to influence the political-legal process so that the social, economic, and physical harms they inflict upon society in the process of capital accumulation are not treated seriously under either criminal or regulatory law. By contrast, the crimes committed by working-class people, which are frequently a result of their marginalized life circumstances, are prosecuted more severely under the law, with incarceration frequently being the result. As Engels (1892, 95) had long ago noted:

> When one individual inflicts bodily injury upon another, such injury that death results, we call the deed manslaughter; when the assailant knew in advance that the injury would be fatal, we call his deed murder. But when society places hundreds of proletarians in such a position that they inevitably meet a too early and an unnatural death, one which is quite as much a death by violence as that by the sword or bullet; when it deprives thousands of the necessaries of life, places them under conditions in which they *cannot* live—forces them, through the strong arm of the law, to remain in such conditions until that death ensues which is the inevitable consequence—knows that these thousands of victims must perish, and

yet permits these conditions to remain, its deed is murder just as surely as the deed of the single individual.

The pioneering Canadian research in this area (Goff and Reasons, 1978) has established the state's failure to define as *corporate crime* behaviours whose economic and physical costs, both to individuals and the environment, far exceed those of street crime (Gordon and Coneybeer, 1995; Snider, 1994). Corporate crime, or "suit crime," is defined as "crime" committed by a corporate official in the pursuit of organizational goals, usually profit. These acts are illegal under either criminal or regulatory law—or would be if we applied the criterion of economic and physical harm to society, which is ostensibly the core criterion of prohibitions and punishments in the Canadian Criminal Code.

Critical criminologists essentially agree that the cost to society of corporate crime far exceeds that of street crime. Exact Canadian data are hard to come by. However, Snider (1994, 276) puts the issue into focus with U.S. data: "Corporate crime costs far more than street crime—all the street crime in the U.S. in a given year is estimated to cost around $4 billion, much less than 5 percent of the average take from corporate crime." U.S. junk bond king Michael Milken alone, she notes, was indicted on 98 racketeering and securities fraud charges and assorted offences. This theft was given an initial very conservative estimate of $325 billion. His company, Drexel Burnham, pleaded guilty to some charges and was fined a small fraction of the losses. The massive Bre-X swindle in Canada constitutes another notable recent similar case of fraud. Or consider the crime of homicide: virtually no one disputes the fact that killing someone is a serious criminal act, and there are continuing flurries and at times much debate over whether or not we should have the death penalty for first-degree murder. In Canada there is one homicide roughly every twelve hours, but even conservative estimates indicate that a worker dies from a preventable employment condition almost every six hours. From 1985 through 1987, actual on-the-job fatalities averaged approximately 907 per year in Canada (Reasons, Ross, and Patterson, 1991). In comparison, there were 335 first-degree murder cases in Canada in 1987 (Statistics Canada, 1988). Not so long ago, as Reasons, Ross, and Patterson (1991) show, occupational hazards were the third leading cause of death in Canada, preceded only by heart disease and cancer.

In considering "assault," Desmond Ellis (1986, 94–95) states: "If official statistics on work-related injuries are compared with statistics on criminal code assaults in Canada, then the corporate assault rates are conservatively estimated to be 25 times greater than the conventional street assault rate." Unfortunately, this statistic is much less publicized.

In the 1991 update to their article, Charles Reasons, Lois Ross, and Craig Patterson note, using U.S. data, that only about one-third of all deaths and job injuries can be related to worker carelessness. About 40 percent of job injuries are due to illegal working conditions, while legal but unsafe working conditions account for about another 25 percent of injuries on the job. Snider (1994, 276) notes that the United States has the highest rate of homicide for the developed world, with 20,000 murders in an average year. By contrast, there are 14,000 deaths per annum from industrial accidents, frequently due to safety code violations, and 30,000 deaths from unsafe and usually illegal consumer products.

This issue can be vividly, and sadly, illustrated by recent multiple death industrial events in Canada. To classify these industrial deaths as "accidents," as they generally are, completely obscures the context within which they occur. McMullan and Smith's analysis of the 1982 Ocean Ranger oil rig tragedy, in which 84 lives were lost, puts the case more clearly. According to the conclusions of the official investigation itself, "intervention could have offset design flaws and overcome lax shipping classifications, inadequate seaworthy standards, and poor marine training of staff and prevented the disaster" (cited in McMullan and Smith, 1997, 62). I grew up in St. John's, the supply depot for this rig. Local people working on the rig had nicknamed the rig the "Ocean Danger" because of its poor safety standards and operation. But jobs are in short supply on the East Coast; for some of these local people whom I knew, it was their last job. More recently, in 1992 the (Nova Scotia) Westray mine explosion claimed 26 lives and also was no accident. "Initial investigations suggest the existence of careless management, unsafe working conditions that included explosively high levels of methane and coal dust, outdated equipment, and a remarkably lax and inept regulations and enforcement system" (McMullan and Smith, 1997, 62). They then add, "Sadly, further evidence shows that both federal and provincial governments overruled their own officials who had warned them against opening the mine for health and safety reasons, and then covered up their roles in the disaster."

Governmental complicity of this type is not unique. The Dalkon intrauterine device had severe problems reported by women right from the start of its marketing in North America in 1971. These problems were largely ignored, and by 1974 the Dalkon shield had killed 17 women and infected and injured another 200,000 (McMullan, 1992, 15). But the shield was not removed from the so-called marketplace. Instead, corporate executives of A.H. Robins dumped several million unsterilized units in bulk packages onto foreign Third World markets—distributed by the U.S. Agency for International Development's Office of Population. Costing only 25 cents to produce (Sherrill, 1987, 51), these several million IUDs were sold for $4.35, a good profit still for A.H. Robins, with the justification "that any contraceptive device was better than none, especially since birth rates were so high in Third World countries" (McMullan, 1992, 15). An example of a rationally calculated and even budgeted corporate crime is the Ford Motor Company's Pinto design-flaw consumer deaths. McMullan (1992, 10) notes that "crash test prior to marketing had shown the gas tank would rupture if hit from behind, even by cars moving at 21 miles per hour." To further quote McMullan (1992, 10):

> Corporate executives had full knowledge of these [Pinto] faults but deliberately decided not to correct them. They had calculated that they would save more than $85 million by delaying lifesaving correctives but would lose no more than $200,000 per death in legal suits. As a result, they chose to put profits before people. Here is how a company memorandum put it:

> **Benefits**
> | | |
> |---|---|
> | Savings: | 180 burn deaths, 180 burn injuries, 2,100 burned vehicles |
> | Unit Cost: | $200,000 per death, $67,000 per injury, $700 per vehicle |
> | Total Benefit: | $(180 \times \$200,000) + (180 \times \$67,000) + (2,100 \times \$700) = \$49.5$ million |

> **Costs**
> | | |
> |---|---|
> | Sales: | 11 million cars, 1.5 million light trucks |
> | Unit Cost: | $11 per car, $11 per truck |
> | Total Cost: | $(11 \text{ million} \times \$11) + (1.5 \text{ million} \times \$11) = \$137$ million |

> This cold calculus suggested that delaying action on car improvement and safety was cost-effective and therefore desirable, even if such safety standards and correctives would result in fewer auto fires and fewer burn death and injuries.

Corporate disregard for the health and safety of workers and consumer—coupled with extremely lax governmental control and sanctioning of corporate lawlessness—has been well documented as the basic cause of these injuries and deaths (Brannigan, 1984; Hagan, 1985; McMullan, 1992; Reasons, Ross, and Patterson, 1991; Snider, 1988). While there has since been a move to harsher penalties, even when charges are forthcoming, most corporate officials and corporations generally experience few economic, social, or legal penalties. Why is this so? Many analysts see the answer in the class bias of criminal law.

In the first place, the corporate lawlessness documented above is often not even defined as criminal. Most often these costly and harmful behaviours are illegal, but within regulatory law rather than in the Criminal Code where most street crime is placed. This distinction is often made on the basis of legal notions of culpability that were established to prosecute individual offenders for street crime, but not corporations or corporate officials for industry-related killings. In Canada, prior to 1941, corporations were immune from any criminal liability because they were deemed to have no mind of their own (McMullan, 1992, 80). There was little progress in this area until the late 1970s and early 1980s. Cases heard before the Supreme Court of Canada, such as *Sault St. Marie* (1978), *The Canadian Dredge and Dock Co. Ltd* (1985), and *Southam Inc. v. Hunter* (1983), have made some progress toward fitting corporate offenders into an individualist model of liability, evidence, procedure, and sanction (McMullan, 1992).

But McMullan (1992) also notes the dispute and confusion existing over whether the *Canadian Charter of Rights and Freedoms* under section 7 and section 1(d) is meant to enforce relatively rigid *mens rea* (guilty mind) requirements for the prosecution of corporate offenders. Decisions at the provincial appeal court level have generally muted the penalty in corporate prosecutions by eliminating incarceration.

McMullan (1992) also states that in the *Irwin Toy Ltd.* case, the Supreme Court of Canada ruled that a corporation's economic rights were not protected by section 7 of the charter, as are the "life, liberty, or security of the person." While the matter is still up in the air, Canadian judicial history suggests that Canadian courts have not been inclined to extend the scope of corporate criminal proceedings to include the illegal acts or omissions of a corporation's agents or employees. In addition to the problem of *mens rea*, corporations have almost exclusively been prosecuted only for regulatory violations—such as those governing health and safety—and not for the consequences of those violations (McMullan, 1992; Reasons, Ross, and Patterson, 1986).

For example, a company would be fined for not installing safety bolts in a construction crane, but not prosecuted for the death of several workers who were below the crane when it collapsed (as in a recent case in Western Canada). Corporations have frequent and vociferous input into the regulations governing them, generally under the guise of being enlisted to co-operate in creating "workable laws." The result is a lax system of regulation.

One of the most notable examples of this co-optation of law by corporations is the matter of workers' compensation schemes. While the programs have improved the lot of workers in some ways, injured workers lost all rights of prosecution of or compensation from corporations covered by the schemes. The only sources of redress and appeal are the compensation boards (Reasons, Ross, and Patterson, 1991, 124).

Two further dimensions of legal regulation—or more specifically the lack thereof—are responsible for the high cost to society of corporate crime. First, corporations are often able to avoid prosecution for illegal activity. Second, even when they are prosecuted, the penalty is usually an inconsequential fine levied against the corporation, while individual corporate decision-makers are usually not singled out, legally or publicly. Even when individual corporate offenders are named, the penalties, both legal and social, are usually only nominal.

In the early 1970s, the Ford Motor Company was fined a total of $7 million. The next year the salaries of all the chief executives—to whom apparently no very great amount of opprobrium was attached—were increased. Moreover, Clinard and Yeager (1980) found that if corporate executives do resign or get fired, they frequently get rehired very shortly afterwards, often as "consultants." Finally, it appears that corporations as a whole also do not suffer greatly from opprobrium. An international study failed to find evidence that a company's "stock prices, reputations, sales, or anything else suffered more than temporary embarrassment as result of involvement in corporate crime" (cited in Snider, 1988, 261).

Snider (1993) documents the extremely low rate of prosecution and nominal penalties under the *Canadian Combines Investigation Act*, which was instituted in 1889 and replaced by the *Competition Act* in 1986. The act has been one of four major forms of regulatory law ostensibly governing corporations. Over a recent 22-year period there were 89 prosecutions under the act, with 57 offences deemed founded. The fines levied in these cases were small, averaging from $7,000 to $8,000 per company. Snider also notes that the infrequent recommendations for prosecution coming from the conservative Restricted Trade Practices Commission could still be turned down by the Department of Justice, and were in over 10 percent of the cases. It appears that in the period Snider was studying the legal-political system had little interest in prosecuting corporate crime, and things since then have not improved. The *Competition Act* focuses on the provision of a stable and predictable climate for business, and meaningful punishment for offenders has been virtually removed (Snider, 1993, 110).

These examples indicate a significant class bias in the application of criminal, regulatory, and social justice. It should not be hard to understand why Edwin Sutherland (1977) found, in his pioneering work on corporate crime, that 90 percent of the 70 largest corporations in the United States were habitual offenders, with an average of fourteen convictions per corporation (see also Clinard and Yeager, 1980). John Hagan (1992, 465) reports that more than half of Canada's largest corporations have been recidivists (convicted more than once), with an average of 3.2 decisions against them.

Perhaps we need punitive corporate "three strikes and you're out" legislation. Canada has seen fit to get tough on street crime in the past decade, with amendments to the Criminal Code and sentencing practices. As a result, federal inmates, most notably, will likely increase by 100 percent (8,938 to 18,000) between 1982 and 2000 (*The Globe and Mail*, 1995, A6). At least the lenient attitude toward corporate crime and white-collar criminals is hardening, socially and judicially, as power confronts resistance. First, opinion polls reveal that popular thinking and sentiment are in favour of much tougher laws, regulations, and sanctions regarding corporate misconduct than the state has been delivering. Second, in some instances judicial decisions have emphasized corporate responsibility for harmful acts. For example, the Alberta Court of Appeal recently held that a bankrupt oil company had to spend money to clean up hazardous well sites before creditors received money (McMullan, 1992, 116). Finally, there have been proposals to break down the individual and organizational inducements to corporate crime, and traditional defences for it, through the creation of a culture that does not tolerate corporate crime. The proposed solutions include "shaming and positive repentance, new legal tools and controls, corporate accountability and restructuring, new forms of penalty and criminal sanctioning, and the application of countervailing force against corporate crime" (McMullan, 1992, 118).

In Canada, one of the strongest indicators of this hardening is the 1987 replacement of the *Environment Contaminants Act* with new legislation providing for fines of up to $41 million per day and up to five years' imprisonment for guilty executives. Consistent with the global concern over the environment, legislation is apparently beginning to get tougher in Canada, both provincially and federally. For example, the federal environment department prosecuted 22 corporate polluters in 1991, compared with only one in 1987. As well, in the early 1990s, the former president of Varnicolor Chemical Lt. was sentenced to eight months in jail for contaminating soil and ground water on company property in a southwestern Ontario town—perhaps the longest sentence ever for an environmental offence in Canada (*Calgary Herald*, 1992, B14).

A final, but very important dimension of class bias in the criminal justice system is the differential conviction and sentencing for street crime involving poor and working-class offenders as compared with middle-class or wealthier offenders. Griffiths and Verdun-Jones (1994, 290) review the literature on this concern. They note that the question is somewhat complex, depending on the charge, previous record, whether individuals are found guilty on all or some charges, and the sentence given. However, a couple of things stand out fairly clearly. Research found that privately represented defendants were found guilty in 54 percent of their trials, while the equivalent figure for poor defendants with legal aid lawyers was 72 percent. As Michael Mandel's (1983) study of the relatively lenient sentencing practices for middle-class and upper-class offenders showed, even when found guilty the judicial myth that the "social opprobrium of trial" punishes upper-class offenders sufficiently was pervasive.

There is some hope, Snider (1994) notes, that at least in some respects the rich won't always get richer, often at great physical and economic cost to society, while the poor get prison. Snider states, "pro-regulatory pressure groups (for example, environmental activities, 'green' politicians trying to eliminate chemicals from farmers' fields, unionists working to secure stronger health and safety laws in the workplace, and feminists working to control the pharmaceutical industry) are absolutely central to the regulatory process" (1994, 278). It is the pressure they exert, she adds, that provides the crucial leverage that forces the state to direct at least some attention to the area of corporate crime.

Part V

MENTAL ILLNESS

MEDICAL DEVIANCE AND DICA: DISORDERS USUALLY FIRST DIAGNOSED IN INFANCY, CHILDHOOD, OR ADOLESCENCE

Nancy Heitzeg

I T IS FITTING THAT THE DISORDERS USUALLY FIRST DIAGNOSED IN INFANCY, Childhood, or Adolescence (DICA) is the first and largest diagnostic category in the DSMIV. Its placement and inclusivity clearly illustrate the discretion inherent in the medical model, as well as the pervasive overlap with other models of social control. All the diagnostic categories included in DICA are simultaneously subject to the informal social control of family, school, or media, as well as the formal social control of the juvenile justice system. Further, it is an indicator of the nature and extent to which juveniles are subject to an ever-widening net of norms and sanctions.

The disorders included in this diagnostic category fall into several general subclassifications: mental retardation; learning disorders; motor skills disorder; communications disorders; pervasive developmental disorders; attention-deficit and disruptive behaviour disorders; feeding and eating disorders of infancy or early childhood; tic disorders; elimination disorders; and other disorders of infancy, childhood, or adolescence.[1] In earlier editions of *Diagnostic and Statistical Manual of Mental Disorders*, eating disorders (i.e., anorexia nervosa and bulimia nervosa) and gender identity disorders were also included in DICA. The justification was the earlier age of onset for these disorders. Although these two disorders are now primarily in adult diagnoses, they still are believed to be rooted in childhood or adolescent experiences. Further, many adults receive diagnoses which are listed in DICA; this is especially true for the attention-deficit disorders. Juveniles may additionally be diagnosed with any other disorder listed in DSMIV. Frequently they are diagnosed with substance use or manic-depressive disorders. This DSMIV classification, then, is not limited to juveniles; its title is based on the assumption that these disorders are usually first diagnosed in infancy, childhood, or adolescence.

The DICA category encompasses an incredible range of problematic conditions. Everything from severe retardation to slight difficulties with math is included here. Discretion and the scope of medical model control is further maximized by the fact that what constitutes many of these disorders might actually be indicative of typical childhood or adolescent behaviours. For example, we might expect most children to exhibit anxiety over separation from their loved one, or many adolescents to undergo distress over identity, popularity, and career goals. It is difficult to imagine how one might clearly distinguish the "normal" developmental process from mental illness.

This diagnostic category is further complicated by the almost perfect overlap that exists between these disorders and the informal and formal models of social control. Much of what is included here, especially those disorders involving disruptive behaviour or development, is fundamentally related to informal relations with family or at school. Still others have as their primary symptomology evidence of legal violations and disregard for formal rules. Trouble at home, school, or with the law becomes the diagnostic criteria for a mental illness. This is overlap in the most complete sense.

The discretion and overlap that characterize DICA is yet another example of the rule-laden status of juveniles. The young have more rules—informal, medical, formal—than any other social group. They are subject to the informal social control of family and school, the organizational co-optation, stereotyping and censorship of media, the all-encompassing diagnostic categories of DSMIV, and the complete array of administrative, civil, and criminal law. The multitude of norms governing youth in each model merges and overlaps to create a seamless web of social control. This is evidenced by the juvenile justice system, which draws from all three models to expand the rules that further limit the rights of juveniles. Whether such extensive social control is warranted is beside the point. It will soon be clear that the combined approach of informal, medical, and formal control mechanisms results in the near total subjugation of juveniles to the rules. It is to these youth-oriented rules—first medical, then the overlapping informal and formal—that we now turn.

SOCIETAL REACTION TO DICA

The conditions and associated behaviours enumerated in the DICA category may be defined and controlled as deviant medically, informally, or formally. While many were once controlled exclusively by informal mechanisms, and later by law, the medical model presently has simultaneous jurisdiction over all these problems of youth. Each of these models of social control, and the norms and sanctions they apply to juveniles, will be examined in detail.

Medical Definition and Control of DICA

DSMIV's definition of the Disorders Usually First Diagnosed in Infancy, Childhood, and Adolescence includes a broad range of conditions. These disorders may vary in their severity and longevity. Some represent rather minimal problems; others, pervasive and severely debilitating disorders. Some of these disorders are short-lived, while others are persistent conditions that never result in full recovery.

As already noted, the DICA classification includes several subcategories of disorders, which will be discussed in the following pages.

Disorders Related to Development: Mental Retardation, Learning Disorders, Motor Skills Disorders, Communication Disorders, Pervasive Developmental Disorders

The developmental disorders involve some disturbance in the "acquisition of cognitive language, motor, or social skills." The developmental delay may be general, involving an overall lack of normal progress, or it may be limited to a specific area of skill acquisition. All these disorders have their onset before age eighteen, although many may appear in very early childhood. The developmental disorders include several specific conditions. Included are mental retardation, learning disorders, communication disorders, motor skills disorders, and the pervasive developmental disorders.

The essential features of mental retardation are "significantly subaverage general intellectual functioning" with impairments in social skills, communication, and daily living skills. Onset must be before the age of eighteen, and may be further evidenced by lack of personal independence and social responsibility. Degree of severity is measured by standard IQ levels, and may be mild (IQ 50–55 to 70), moderate (IQ 35–40 to 50–55), severe (IQ 20–25 to 35–40), or profound (IQ below 20 or 25).

Other developmental disorders are less pervasive and severe. This subset of disorders refers to developmental delays in specific areas: learning, motor skills, and communication. The difficulties detailed here are much less pervasive and problematic than with other developmental disorders. The learning disorders involve arithmetic, expressive writing, or reading "skills, as measured by a standardized, individually administered test, markedly below the expected level." The communication disorders are similarly diagnosed by standardized measures, and include delays in articulation, as well as expressive and receptive language. And, finally, the motor skills disorder is defined as marked impairment in the development of motor coordination.

These disorders represent very specific intellectual and physical conditions that may affect at least 10 percent of school-age children. It is important to remember that diagnostic criteria are based on standardized measures that may be flawed. In addition, these developmental delays, however problematic, often seem to run their course without psychiatric intervention. Viewing them as "mental illnesses" must be questioned. Being behind in one's reading skills, for example, certainly seems very different from hearing strange voices who instruct you to kill. Earlier editions of DSM even acknowledged this point: "The inclusion of these categories in a classification of 'mental disorders' is controversial, since many children with these disorders have no other signs of psychopathology. Further, the detection and treatment of many of these disorders usually take place within schools rather than the mental health system.

The pervasive development disorders are characterized by significant social and physical underdevelopment. The essential feature of these disorders is the qualitative impairment of reciprocal social interaction, in the development of verbal and nonverbal communication skills, and in imaginative activity. Onset usually occurs before age three, and may also be associated with abnormalities in cognitive skills, posture and motor behaviour, odd responses to sensory input, self-injurious behaviour, and abnormalities in eating, drinking, sleeping, and mood. Included are autism (i.e., markedly abnormal development in social interaction and communication with a restricted repertoire of activity); Rett's disorder (i.e., abnormal physical, motor, and social development); childhood disintegrative disorder (i.e., regression in physical, communicative, and social development after two years of normal progress); Aspergers's disorder (i.e., severe and sustained impairment in social interaction, and the development of restricted, repetitive patterns of behaviour, interests, and activities), and unspecified pervasive developmental disorders.

Attention-Deficit and Disruptive Behaviour Disorders

These disorders are "characterized by behaviour that is socially disruptive and is often more distressing to others than to the people with the disorders." Included here are *attention deficit hyperactivity disorder (ADHD), oppositional defiant disorder, and conduct disorder.* The symptoms of these disorders essentially constitute rule-breaking behaviour, i.e., violations of the informal norms of home or school and activities that are status or criminal offenses.

Attention deficit hyperactivity disorder is characterized by varying degrees of inattention, impulsiveness, and hyperactivity. The onset of ADHD is usually before age four, although one-third of those affected may continue to exhibit symptoms throughout adulthood. DSMIV indicates that ADHD may be anywhere from three to nine times more common in males than in females. Symptoms may disrupt social interaction at home, school, work, and among peers. Symptoms include fidgeting, distractibility, impatience, short attention span, difficulty in following instructions, and lack of recognition of danger. See Table 20.1.

The symptoms of conduct disorder are violations of formal rules, especially the criminal law. Juvenile status offenses are also included. In many respects, it also parallels the adult antisocial personality disorder. DSMIV notes that unchecked conduct disorders may develop into adult antisocial personality disorder. Further, children of adults with antisocial personalities are much more likely to be diagnosed with conduct disorders. Conduct disorder may also be linked with substance use disorders and ADHD. Again, diagnoses are nearly five times more common for males than for females. Conduct problems include stealing, lying, running away from home, truancy, arson, and cruelty. See Table 20.2.

Oppositional defiant disorder is characterized by a pattern of lesser rule-breaking behaviour. The symptoms here involve the violations of informal norms, particularly those related to social interaction with parents, other adults, and peers. Onset is usually in adolescence, with symptoms more evident in interactions with adults the child knows well. Substance use disorders and ADHD again might be associated. The symptoms are indicative of what many might term "typical" adolescent behaviour, and, interestingly enough, DSMIV notes that "children with the disorder are likely to show little or no signs of the disorder when examined critically." The symptoms include a short temper, argumentativeness, defiance, resentment, and a refusal to accept rules and to accept responsibility for their behaviour—some might say, the typical teenager. See Table 20.3.

Eating Disorders

The *eating disorders* involve disturbances in eating behaviour. Until DSMIV, DSM included anorexia nervosa and bulimia nervosa in this subclassification. Pica and rumination disorder of infancy are primarily disorders of very young children, and are equally prevalent among both sexes. Pica is usually a disorder of infants or very young children, and involves repeatedly "eating nonnutritive substances, such as paint, plaster, string." Similarly, rumination disorder of

Table 20.1 Diagnostic Criteria for Attention-Deficit Hyperactivity Disorder

A. Either (1) or (2):

(1) six (or more) of the following symptoms of inattention have persisted for at least 6 months to a degree that is maladaptive and inconsistent with developmental level:

Inattention:

(a) often fails to give close attention to details or makes careless mistakes in schoolwork, work, or other activities

(b) often has difficulty sustaining attention in tasks or play activities

(c) often does not seem to listen when spoken to directly

(d) often does not follow through on instructions and fails to finish schoolwork, chores, or duties in the workplace (not due to oppositional behaviour or failure to understand instructions)

(e) often has difficulty organizing tasks and activities

(f) often avoids, dislikes, or is reluctant to engage in tasks that require sustained mental effort (such as schoolwork or homework)

(g) often loses things necessary for tasks or activities (e.g., toys, school assignments, pencils, books, or tools)

(h) is often easily distracted by extraneous stimuli

(i) is often forgetful in daily activities

(2) six (or more) of the following symptoms of **hyperactivity-impulsivity** have persisted for at least 6 months to a degree that is maladaptive and inconsistent with developmental level:

Hyperactivity:

(a) often fidgets with hands or feet or squirms in seat

(b) often leaves seat in classroom or in other situations in which remaining seated is expected

(c) often runs about or climbs excessively in situations in which it is inappropriate (in adolescents or adults, may be limited to subjective feelings of restlessness)

(d) often has difficulty playing or engaging in leisure activities quietly

(e) is often "on the go" or often acts if "driven by a motor"

(f) often talks excessively

Impulsivity:

(g) often blurts out answers before questions have been completed

(h) often has difficulty awaiting turn

(i) often interrupts or intrudes on others (e.g., butts into conversations or games)

B. Some hyperactive-impulsive or inattentive symptoms that caused impairment were present before age 7 years.

C. Some impairment from the symptoms is present in two or more settings (e.g., at school [or work] and at home).

D. There must be clear evidence of clinically significant impairment in social, academic, or occupational functioning.

E. The symptoms do not occur exclusively during the course of a Pervasive Developmental Disorder, Schizophrenia, or other Psychotic Disorder and are not better accounted for by another mental disorder (e.g., Mood Disorder, Anxiety Disorder, Dissociative Disorder, or a Personality Disorder).

Code based on type:

314.01 Attention-Deficit/Hyperactivity Disorder, Combined Type: if both Criteria A1 and A2 are met for the past 6 months

314.00 Attention-Deficit/Hyperactivity Disorder, Predominantly Inattentive Type: if Criterion A1 is met but Criterion A2 is not met for the past 6 months

314.01 Attention-Deficit/Hyperactivity Disorder, Predominantly Hyperactive-Impulsive Type: if Criterion A2 is met but Criterion A1 is not met for the past 6 months

---

Coding Note: For individuals (especially adolescents and adults) who currently have symptoms that no longer meet full criteria. "In Partial Remission" should be specified.

Source: American Psychiatric Association, Diagnostic and Statistical Manual of Mental Disorders, 4th edition (Washington, DC: APA, 1994), pp. 83–85.

Table 20.2 Diagnostic Criteria for 312.8 Conduct Disorder

A   A repetitive and persistent pattern of behaviour in which the basic rights of others or major age-appropriate societal norms or rules are violated, as manifested by the presence of three (or more) of the following criteria in the past 12 months, with at least one criterion present in the past 6 months:

Aggression to people and animals

(1)   often bullies, threatens, or intimidates others

(2)   often initiates physical fights

(3)   has used a weapon that can cause serious physical harm to others (e.g., a bat, brick, broken bottle, knife, gun)

(4)   has been physically cruel to people

(5)   has been physically cruel to animals

(6)   has stolen while confronting a victim (e.g., mugging, purse snatching, extortion, armed robbery)

(7)   has forced someone into sexual activity

Destruction of property

(8)   has deliberately engaged in fire setting with the intention of causing serious damage

(9)   has deliberately destroyed others' property (other than by fire setting)

Deceitfulness or theft

(10) has broken into someone else's house, building, or car

(11) often lies to obtain goods or favors or to avoid obligations (i.e., "cons" others)

(12) has stolen items of nontrivial value without confronting a victim (e.g., shoplifting, but without breaking and entering: forgery)

Serious violations of rules

(13) often stays out at night despite parental prohibitions, beginning before age 13 years

(14) has run away from home overnight at least twice while living in parental or parental surrogate home (or once without returning for a lengthy period)

(15) is often truant from school, beginning before age 13 years

B. The disturbance in behaviour causes clinically significant impairment in social, academic, or occupational functioning.

C. If the individual is age 18 years or older, criteria are not met for Antisocial Personality Disorder.

Specify type based on age at onset:

Childhood-Onset Type: onset of at least one criterion characteristic of Conduct Disorder prior to age 10 years

Adolescent-Onset Type: absence of any criteria characteristic of Conduct Disorder prior to age 10 years

Specify severity:

Mild: few if any conduct problems in excess of those required to make the diagnosis and conduct problems cause only minor harm to others

Moderate: number of conduct problems and effect on others intermediate between "mild" and "severe"

Severe: many conduct problems in excess of those required to make the diagnosis **or** conduct problems cause considerable harm to others

---

Source: American Psychiatric Association, Diagnostic and Statistical Manual of Mental Disorders, 4th edition (Washington, DC: APA, 1994), pp. 90–91.

infancy involves disturbance in the very young, characterized by "repeated regurgitation, without nausea or associated gastrointestinal illness."

Tic Disorders
These disorders are characterized by tics, "involuntary, sudden, rapid, recurrent, nonrhythmic, stereotyped, motor movements or vocalizations." Tics feel as if they are irresistible, are made worse under stress, and may be simple or complex. Children who suffer from tics may have had head trauma or central nervous system abnormalities. Tics, whether chronic or transient, are three times more common in males than in females. Onset may be as early as age one, or as late as age twenty-one. They may be short-lived or lifelong.

Table 20.3 Diagnostic Criteria for Oppositional Defiant Disorder

A. A pattern of negativistic, hostile, and defiant behaviour lasting at least 6 months, during which four (or more) of the following are present:

(1) often loses temper

(2) often argues with adults

(3) often actively defies or refuses to comply with adults' requests or rules

(4) often deliberately annoys people

(5) often blames others for his or her mistakes or misbehaviour

(6) is often touchy or easily annoyed by others

(7) is often angry or resentful

(8) is often spiteful or vindictive

B. The disturbance in behaviour causes clinically significant impairments in social, academic, or occupational functioning.

C. The behaviours do not occur exclusively during the course of a Psychotic or Mood Disorder.

D. Criteria are not met for Conduct Disorder, and, if the individual is age 18 years or older, criteria are not met for Antisocial Personality Disorder.

Note: Consider a criterion met only if the behaviour occurs more frequently than is typically observed in individuals of comparable age and development level.

Source: American Psychiatric Association, Diagnostic and Statistical Manual of Mental Disorders, 4th edition (Washington, DC: APA, 1994), pp. 93–94.

Elimination Disorders

The two disorders cited here—functional encopresis and functional enuresis—are essentially toilet training issues. The elimination disorders are defined as involuntary and repeated defecation and urination into "places not appropriate for that purpose (e.g., clothing or floor)."

OTHER DISORDERS OF INFANCY, CHILDHOOD, OR ADOLESCENCE

As usual, DSMIV has a residual category for disorders not classified elsewhere. Identity disorder is one of the minor and typical childhood responses as mental illness. Reactive attachment disorder describes a condition that results from child abuse or neglect.

Identity disorder is characterized by "severe subjective distress regarding uncertainty about a variety of issues relating to identity, including three or more of the following: Long-term goals, career choice, friendship patterns, sexual orientation and behaviour, religious identification, moral value systems, or group "loyalties." Impairment in social or occupational (including academic) functioning is a result of the symptoms.

Reactive attachment disorder of infancy or early childhood describes a condition that results from abuse or neglect. Such a child would have a markedly disturbed ability to relate to others and would have received harsh or negligent childcare. As usual, DSMIV has a residual category for disorders not classified elsewhere. Included are separation anxiety disorder (i.e., excessive anxiety concerning separation from home); selective mutism (i.e., consistent failure to speak in specific social situations); stereotypic movement disorder (i.e., repetitive, nonfunctional motor behaviour); and reactive attachment disorder (i.e., disturbed and inappropriate social interaction as a result of abuse or neglect).

Almost any conceivable behaviour or condition of infancy, childhood, or adolescence might potentially result in a psychiatric diagnosis. DSMIV's definition of these disorders is broad enough to encompass everything from severe retardation to a mild stutter, from autism to occasional bedwetting, from anxiety to adolescent rebellion. If, indeed DSMIV's definitional scope is warranted, are there any youth who are *not* mentally ill? And, if all youth are ill, doesn't the medical distinction between ill and well lose all meaning? Are all these conditions really comparable, i.e., do we need to distinguish between issues related to physical development and those of a cognitive or social nature? Are all these conditions really "illnesses," i.e., do they really have an objective cause and a potential medical cure? And, are all these conditions really problems, i.e., might at least some be a reasonable response to an endless array of rules and adult-inflicted pressures to conform and comply?

Even the APA acknowledges that it may be "controversial" to refer to some of these conditions as "mental disorders." Being below one's reading level or refusing to clean one's room may be problematic, but it is difficult to imagine that psychiatric intervention is warranted. And, given labelling theories' concern over the impact of societal reaction on self-concept, one might wonder if psychiatric diagnoses for such commonplace and minimal difficulties might actually do more harm than good. Perhaps there are alternatives to the medicalization of childhood deviance that might be effective for dealing with conditions outlined by DICA.

The inherent difficulties with this diagnostic category is complicated by the medical model's lack of context. Under some conditions, the conditions and behaviour entailed in DICA might not be deviant at all. Consider, for example, the case of oppositional defiant disorder. If the youth in question lives in a situation where he/she is subject to abuse and/or neglect, might we not expect— even encourage—anger, annoyance, arguments, and defiance of adult requests or rules? A comparable illustration might be made with reference to the attention deficit hyperactivity disorder. Is this really a mental illness or a response to situational contingencies? Fidgeting, distractibility, talking or blurting out answers to questions, and interrupting might just as well be responses to a boring, overstructured, understimulating classroom setting. Implicit in DICA, and throughout much of the social control of youth, is the assumption that adults and their rules are always right, and that children/adolescents who question them are always wrong. This may not be the case.

The medical model's control and treatment of DICA also raises questions. First and foremost is the highly controlled age status of the clients. Unlike adults who often voluntarily seek psychiatric treatment, juveniles are almost universally referred by adults: parents, teachers, or juvenile justice personnel. Their entrance into the medical model is involuntary. The juvenile in American society has severely curtailed rights. Juveniles do not have the right to refuse psychiatric treatment. Here, as in the juvenile justice system, it is assumed that any adult's estimation of the problems and required course of social control is valid. To quote Supreme Court Justice William Rehnquist, "[Juveniles] unlike adults are always in a state of custody."[2] It matters little whether that custody is centered at home, at a psychiatric facility, or in a court-ordered juvenile detention center. Part of the social meaning of juvenile is that one is never fully free, but is always subject to the overarching adult control: informal, medical, or formal. Juveniles who are diagnosed and treated for DICA have no choice of or input into their treatment.

Those who receive a DICA diagnoses are primarily treated with somatic therapy, institutionalization (both public and private), and individual behaviour modification techniques. Often, these treatment options are used in combination.

The primary somatic treatment of DICA is the administration of psychotropic medications. Its most widespread use is the treatment of attention deficit hyperactivity disorder (ADHD). The use of drugs to treat this disorder actually predates the diagnostic category itself. (Prior to 1957, ADHD was more generally referred to as a "childhood behaviour disorder." Initially, it applied to impulsive, overactive children, but it has been broadened to include those who do not pay attention. Female teenagers and even adults are now more likely to receive this diagnosis. A support group for children and adults with attention-deficit disorder—CHADD—claims 28,000 members nationwide.[3] The disruptive behaviour and learning difficulties associated with ADHD were first treated with amphetamines in 1937.[4] Charles Bradley noted the "paradoxical" effect stimulants had on hyperactive children; rather than becoming more active, they were subdued. The development of Ritalin (a stimulant with amphetamine-like qualities, but few side effects) in the mid-1950s paved the way for the widespread treatment of ADHD with drugs. Since its FDA approval in 1961 for use with children, Ritalin has become the treatment of choice for ADHD diagnoses. ADHD is now the most common childhood psychiatric problem; anywhere from three percent to twenty percent of all elementary and secondary students have been labelled ADHD. The rate of treatment for this disorder has been doubling every four to seven years, and as many as 750,000 children are being treated with Ritalin; in the past four years, prescriptions for Ritalin have increased 390 percent.[5] Its use continues, despite psychiatry's inability to pinpoint any biological basis for ADHD, or even to fully understand exactly why Ritalin produces calming effects in hyperactive children.

The use of Ritalin is not without controversy. Many have argued that it is overused and serves as a mere social control mechanism, rather than an effective treatment. Indeed, school personnel have been shown to have a much looser definition of ADHD than have medical professionals.[6] It is possible that these recommendations for ADHD diagnosis and treatment are based on the self-serving motive of behaviour control. Others have expressed concern over Ritalin's sometimes negative side effects. Lawsuits totalling millions of dollars have been filed nationwide on behalf of parents who claim their children have been adversely affected. It has been charged that Ritalin numbed children's senses and produced insomnia, loss of appetite, and psychotic episodes. Still others suggest that ADHD is a set of symptoms, not a disease per se. Consequently, it is argued, ADHD should be treated holistically (i.e., through chiropractic and diet) to get to the root of the problem.[7]

Despite these objections, the APA still advocates the use of Ritalin as the treatment of choice for ADHD. Psychotropic medications also are used in the treatment of other DICA diagnoses. Antidepressants, antipsychotics, and sedatives are frequently prescribed for juveniles. These medications are used for the treatment of several DICA conditions, as well as for other DSMIV diagnoses that juveniles may additionally receive: schizophrenia, mood disorders, obsessive-compulsive disorders, anxiety disorders, and substance use disorders. The question of whether psychotropic medications are an effective treatment for mental illness or just a mechanism for behavioural control is always open; it is particularly relevant in regard to the treatment of adolescents. Evidence shows that prescriptions are used too readily, as a first rather than last resort, and inordinately used for such conditions as conduct disorders.[8] Further, these medications are most frequently used for juveniles in conjunction with institutionalization, a fact that lends credence to the argument that psychotropic drugs may be used to control rather than treat.

Institutionalization is another increasingly popular approach to the treatment of DICA. Throughout the 1970s and 1980s, juvenile admissions to psychiatric facilities doubled. Juvenile admissions to both public and private institutions totaled over 270,000. Much of this increase is accounted for by admissions to private hospitals. In 1971, 7,668 juveniles were admitted to such facilities; by 1988, that number had increased to over 99,000.[9] In 1992, an additional 135,000 youths were admitted to in-patient treatment facilities for alcohol and drug use.

While adults are usually institutionalized for serious psychotic episodes, substance use, or other obsessive-compulsive disorders, juveniles are often hospitalized for much lesser disorders. Conduct and oppositional defiant disorders are a common reason for institutionalization. Presently, symptoms may be as minimal as the "out-of-control behaviour" cited on an actual patient chart: "(1) Refusing to contribute to the family, (2) Dirty clothes left out, (3) Dirty room, (4) Consistent antagonism."[10] While such quintessential adolescent behaviour may warrant societal reaction, it is unlikely that institutionalization in a psychiatric facility is necessary.

The minor disorders for which juveniles are committed are only part of the problem. Failure of informal social control mechanisms at home or at school, in conjunction with the high-pressure, profit-motive approach of many private hospitals, may be the two largest contributors to the dramatic rise in juvenile admissions to psychiatric hospitals. Juveniles are most likely to be committed by their parents.[11] Because they are minors, this is viewed as voluntary commitment, regardless of the juvenile's wishes. It is subsequently exceedingly easy for parents to commit a "problem child"; the child has no legal standing to review their admission, or the freedom to leave.

Parents are often encouraged to commit children to private facilities via fear-inducing advertising and pressures to commit rather than seek outpatient options. Considering that such institutional treatment may cost as much as $27,000 per month, it is not surprising that referral often means automatic admittance. The number of clients admitted increases the amount of money paid to the institutions. The argument that all of this is really done only for the best interests of the child is further weakened by an analysis of insurance coverage on length of stay. Children and adolescents with private insurance remained in private hospitals an average of 32 to 38 days; those covered by HMOs stayed an average of approximately 16 days; those covered by Medicaid/ Medicare stayed an average of 13 days; while juveniles with no coverage remained only about 10 days on average.[12] In other words, a patient's length of stay seems determined *not* by need but by their insurance benefits. This would seem to indicate that profit, combined with parental inability to exert effective social control, lies at the root of increased juvenile psychiatric admissions. Psychiatric institutionalization may not be appropriate for dealing with the juvenile's problem; it is, however, a simple and lucrative solution for the attendant adults.

Juveniles are also treated with behaviour modification therapies. These may often be used in concert with psychotropic medications and/or institutionalization. This approach has been applied to the treatment of disruptive behaviours and elimination disorders, as well as juvenile cases of obsessive-compulsive behaviour and substance use.[13] Positive and negative reinforcement involving token economic tier systems and punishments have all been tried. Behaviour modification of juvenile psychiatric problems may be individually oriented; more often, however, a group approach involving family and/or peers is preferred. While behaviour modification may result in the reduction of original symptoms, it does not address the underlying causes for the juvenile's behaviour.

Finally, DSMIV's developmental disorders, especially learning disorders and communication disorders, are not technically treated by psychiatrists. These disorders are most often dealt with within the context of the school system. Special education sections and speech therapy are the major methods of addressing these developmental delays.

The Disorders Usually First Diagnosed in Infancy, Childhood, and Adolescence, then, encompass a monumental range of behaviours and conditions that are treated with a variety of therapies. Discretion is maximized here; almost any child potentially could be labelled with this diagnostic category. Juveniles are vulnerable to unchallenged medical model control.

NOTES

1. American Psychiatric Association, *Diagnostic and Statistical Manual of Mental Disorder*, 4ᵗʰ edition (Washington, DC: APA, 1994). All subsequent quotations or references to APA or DSMIV are to this edition.

2. Michael S. Serrell, "Reining in Juveniles and Aliens: The High Court Rules in Preventive Detention and Deportation," *Time*, 18 June 1984, p. 76; *Schall v. Martin*, 104 S. CT. 2403 (1984).

3. Peter Conrad and Joseph W. Schneider, *Deviance and Medicalization: From Badness to Sickness*, reprint of the 1980 edition (Philadelphia: Temple University Press, 1992), pp. 156–161; Claudia Wallis, "Life in Overdrive," *Time*, 8 July 1994, pp. 43–50.

4. Conrad and Schneider, *Deviance and Medicalization*, p. 156; C.A. Bradley, "The Behaviour of Children Receiving Benzedrine," *American Journal of Psychiatry*, 30 (November 1937): 577–588.

5. Conrad and Schneider, *Deviance and Medicalization*, pp. 156–157, 285; Doctors of Chiropractic International, "What Have They Done to Our Children?" *The Spinal Column* (January/February 1989), p. 2; D.J. Safer and Joe Krager, "A Survey of Medication Treatments for Hyperactive/Inattentive Students," *Journal of the American Medical Association*, 260(1988): 2256–2259; Wallis, "Life in Overdrive."

6. Conrad and Schneider, *Deviance and Medicalization*, p. 285.

7. DCI, "What Have They Done?" p. 2.

8. Conrad and Schneider, *Deviance and Medicalization*, p. 158; Katherine Barrett and Richard Green, "Mom, Get Me Out of Here!" *Ladies Home Journal*, May 1990, pp. 98–106.

9. Lisa A. Merkel-Holguin, *The Child Welfare Stat Book 1993* (Washington, DC: The Child Welfare League of America Inc., 1993); Barrett and Green, "Mom, Get Me Out of Here," p. 103.

10. Ibid., p. 104.

11. Ibid.

12. Ibid., p. 103.

13. Ibid., p. 104; Conrad and Schneider, *Deviance and Medicalization*, pp. 231–235.

Chapter 21

BEING SANE
IN INSANE PLACES

D.L. Rosenhan

IF SANITY AND INSANITY EXIST, HOW SHALL WE KNOW THEM?

The question is neither capricious nor itself insane. However much we may be personally convinced that we can tell the normal from the abnormal, the evidence is simply not compelling. It is commonplace, for example, to read about murder trials wherein eminent psychiatrists for the defense are contradicted by equally eminent psychiatrists for the prosecution on the matter of the defendant's sanity. More generally, there are a great deal of conflicting data on the reliability, utility, and meaning of such terms as "sanity," "insanity," "mental illness," and "schizophrenia."[1] Finally, as early as 1934, Benedict suggested that normality and abnormality are not universal.[2] What is viewed as normal in one culture may be seen as quite aberrant in another. Thus, notions of normality and abnormality may not be quite as accurate as people believe they are.

To raise questions regarding normality and abnormality is in no way to question the fact that some behaviours are deviant or odd. Murder is deviant. So, too, are hallucinations. Nor does raising such questions deny the existence of the personal anguish that is often associated with "mental illness." Anxiety and depression exist. Psychological suffering exists. But normality and abnormality, sanity and insanity, and the diagnoses that flow from them may be less substantive than many believe them to be.

At its heart, the question of whether the sane can be distinguished from the insane (and whether degrees of insanity can be distinguished from each other) is a simple matter: do the salient characteristics that lead to diagnoses reside in the patients themselves or in the environments and contexts in which observers find them? . . . [T]he belief has been strong that patients present symptoms, that those symptoms can be categorized, and, implicitly, that the sane are distinguishable from the insane. More recently, however, this belief has been questioned. . . . [T]he view has grown that psychological categorization of mental illness is useless at best and downright harmful, misleading, and pejorative at worst. Psychiatric diagnoses, in this view, are in the minds of the observers and are not valid summaries of characteristics displayed by the observed.[3-5]

Gains can be made in deciding which of these is more nearly accurate by getting normal people (that is, people who do not have, and have never suffered, symptoms of serious psychiatric disorders) admitted to psychiatric hospitals and then determining whether they were discovered to be sane and, if so, how. If the sanity of such pseudopatients were always detected, there would be prima facie evidence that a sane individual can be distinguished from the insane context in which he is found. . . . If, on the other hand, the sanity of the pseudopatients were never discovered, serious difficulties would arise for those who support traditional modes of psychiatric diagnosis. Given that the hospital staff was not incompetent, that the pseudopatient had been behaving as sanely as he had been outside of the hospital, and that it had never been previously suggested that he belonged in a psychiatric hospital, such an unlikely outcome would support the view that psychiatric diagnosis betrays little about the patient but much about the environment in which an observer finds him.

This chapter describes such an experiment. Eight sane people gained secret admission to 12 different hospitals.[6] Their diagnostic experiences constitute the data of the first part of this chapter; the remainder is devoted to a description of their experiences in psychiatric institutions. . . .

PSEUDOPATIENTS AND THEIR SETTINGS

The eight pseudopatients were a varied group. One was a psychology graduate student in his twenties. The remaining seven were older and "established." Among them were three psychologists, a pediatrician, a psychiatrist, a painter, and a housewife. Three pseudopatients were women, five were men. All of them employed pseudonyms, lest their alleged diagnoses embarrass them later. Those who were in mental health professions alleged another occupation in order to avoid the special attentions that might be accorded by staff, as a matter of courtesy or caution, to ailing colleagues.[7] With the exception of myself (I was the first pseudopatient and my presence was known to the hospital administrator and chief psychologist and, so far as I can tell, them alone), the presence of pseudopatients and the nature of the research program was not known to the hospital staffs.[8]

The settings were similarly varied. In order to generalize the findings, admission into a variety of hospitals were sought. The 12 hospitals in the sample were located in five different states on the East and West coasts. Some were old and shabby, some were quite new. Some were research-oriented, others not. Some had good staff-patient ratios, others were quite understaffed. Only one was a strictly private hospital. All of the others were supported by state or federal funds or, in one instance, by university funds.

After calling the hospital for an appointment, the pseudopatient arrived at the admissions office complaining that he had been hearing voices. Asked what the voices said, he replied that they were often unclear, but as far as he could tell they said "empty," "hollow," and "thud." The voices were unfamiliar and were of the same sex as the pseudopatient. . . .

Beyond alleging the symptoms and falsifying name, vocation, and employment, no further alterations of person, history, or circumstances were made. The significant events of the pseudopatient's life history were presented as they had actually occurred. Relationships with parents and siblings, with spouse and children, with people at work and at school, consistent with the aforementioned exceptions, were described as they were or had been. Frustrations and upsets were described along with joys and satisfactions. These facts are important to remember. If anything, they strongly biased the subsequent results in favor of detecting sanity, since none of their histories or current behaviours were seriously pathological in any way.

Immediately upon admission to the psychiatric ward, the pseudopatient ceased simulating *any* symptoms of abnormality. In some cases, there was a brief period of mild nervousness and anxiety, since none of the pseudopatients really believed that they would be admitted so easily. Indeed, their shared fear was that they would be immediately exposed as frauds and greatly embarrassed. Moreover, many of them had never visited a psychiatric ward; even those who had nevertheless had some genuine fears about what might happen to them. Their nervousness, then, was quite appropriate to the novelty of the hospital setting, and it abated rapidly.

Apart from that short-lived nervousness, the pseudopatient behaved on the ward as he "normally" behaved. The pseudopatient spoke to patients and staff as he might ordinarily. Because there is uncommonly little to do on a psychiatric ward, he attempted to engage others in conversation. When asked by staff how he was feeling, he indicated that he was fine, that he no longer experienced symptoms. He responded to instructions from attendants, to calls for medication (which was not swallowed), and to dining-hall instructions. Beyond such activities as were available to him on the admissions ward, he spent his time writing down his observations about the ward, its patients, and the staff. Initially these notes were written "secretly," but as it soon became clear that no one much cared, they were subsequently written on standard tablets of paper in such public places as the dayroom. No secret was made of these activities.

The pseudopatient, very much as a true psychiatric patient, entered a hospital with no foreknowledge of when he would be discharged. Each was told that he would have to get out by his own devices, essentially by convincing the staff that he was sane. The psychological stresses associated with hospitalization were considerable, and all but one of the pseudopatients desired to be discharged almost immediately after being admitted. They were, therefore, motivated not only to behave sanely, but to be paragons of cooperation. That their behaviour was in no way disruptive is confirmed by nursing reports, which have been obtained on most of the patients. These reports uniformly indicate that the patients were "friendly," "cooperative," and "exhibited no abnormal indications."

THE NORMAL ARE NOT DETECTABLY SANE

Despite their public "show" of sanity, the pseudopatients were never detected. Admitted, except in one case, with a diagnosis of schizophrenia,[9] each was discharged with a diagnosis of schizophrenia "in remission." The label "in remission" should in no way be dismissed as a formality, for at no time during any hospitalization had any question been raised about any pseudopatient's simulation. Nor are there any indications in the hospital records that the pseudopatient's status was suspect. Rather, the evidence is strong that, once labelled schizophrenic, the pseudopatient was stuck with that label. If the pseudopatient was to be discharged, he must naturally be "in remission"; but he was not sane, nor, in the institution's view, had he ever been sane.

The uniform failure to recognize sanity cannot be attributed to the quality of the hospitals. . . . Nor can it be alleged that there was simply not enough time to observe the pseudopatients. Length of hospitalization ranged from 7 to 52 days, with an average of 19 days. The pseudopatients were not, in fact, carefully observed, but this failure clearly speaks more to traditions within psychiatric hospitals than to lack of opportunity.

Finally, it cannot be said that the failure to recognize the pseudopatients' sanity was due to the fact that they were not behaving sanely. While there was clearly some tension present in all of them, their daily visitors could detect no serious behavioural consequences—nor, indeed, could other patients. It was quite common for the patients to "detect" the pseudopatients' sanity. . . . "You're not crazy. You're a journalist, or a professor [referring to the continual note-taking]. You're checking up on the hospital." While most of the patients were reassured by the pseudopatient's insistence that he had been sick before he came in but was fine now, some continued to believe that the pseudopatient was sane throughout his hospitalization.[10] The fact that the patients often recognized normality when staff did not raises important questions.

Failure to detect sanity during the course of hospitalization may be due to the fact that . . . physicians are more inclined to call a healthy person sick . . . than a sick person healthy. . . . The reasons for this are not hard to find: it is clearly more dangerous to misdiagnose illness than health. Better to err on the side of caution, to suspect illness even among the healthy.

But what holds for medicine does not hold equally well for psychiatry. Medical illnesses, while unfortunate, are not commonly pejorative. Psychiatric diagnoses, on the contrary, carry with them personal, legal, and social stigmas.[11] It was therefore important to see whether the tendency toward diagnosing the sane insane could be reversed. The following experiment was arranged at a research and teaching hospital whose staff had heard these findings but doubted that such an error could occur in their hospital. The staff was informed that at some time during the following three months, one or more pseudopatients would attempt to be admitted into the psychiatric hospital. Each staff member was asked to rate each patient who presented himself at admissions or on the ward according to the likelihood that the patient was a pseudopatient. . . .

Judgments were obtained on 193 patients who were admitted for psychiatric treatment. All staff who had had sustained contact with or primary responsibility for the patient—attendants, nurses, psychiatrists, physicians, and psychologists—were asked to make judgments. Forty-one patients were alleged, with high confidence, to be pseudopatients by at least one member of the staff. Twenty-three were considered suspect by at least one psychiatrist. Nineteen were suspected by one psychiatrist *and* one other staff member. Actually, no genuine pseudopatient (at least from my group) presented himself during this period.

The experiment is instructive. It indicates that the tendency to designate sane people as insane can be reversed when the stakes (in this case, prestige and diagnostic acumen) are high. But what can be said of the 19 people who were suspected of being "sane" by one psychiatrist and another staff member? Were these people truly "sane?" . . . There is no way of knowing. But one thing is certain: any diagnostic process that lends itself so readily to massive errors of this sort cannot be a very reliable one.

THE STICKINESS OF PSYCHODIAGNOSTIC LABELS

Beyond the tendency to call the healthy sick—a tendency that accounts better for diagnostic behaviour on admission than it does for such behaviour after a lengthy period of exposure—the data speak to the massive role of labelling in psychiatric assessment. Having once been labelled schizophrenic, there is nothing the pseudopatient can do to overcome the tag. The tag profoundly colours others' perceptions of him and his behaviour.

From one viewpoint, these data are hardly surprising, for it has long been known that elements are given meaning by the context in which they occur. . . . Once a person is designated abnormal, all of his other behaviours and characteristics are coloured by that label. Indeed, that label is so powerful that many of the pseudopatients' normal behaviours were overlooked entirely or profoundly misinterpreted. Some examples may clarify this issue.

Earlier I indicated that there were no changes in the pseudopatient's personal history and current status beyond those of name, employment, and, where necessary, vocation. Otherwise, a veridical description of personal history and circumstances was offered. Those circumstances were not psychotic. How were they made consonant with the diagnosis of psychosis? Or were those diagnoses modified in such a way as to bring them into accord with the circumstances of the pseudopatient's life, as described by him?

As far as I can determine, diagnoses were in no way affected by the relative health of the circumstances of a pseudopatient's life. Rather, the reverse occurred: the perception of his circumstances was shaped entirely by the diagnosis. A clear example of such translation is found in the case of a pseudopatient who had had a close relationship with his mother but was rather remote from his father during his early childhood. During adolescence and beyond, however, his father became a close friend, while his relationship with his mother cooled. His present relationship with his wife was characteristically close and warm. Apart from the occasional angry exchanges, friction was minimal. The children had rarely been spanked. Surely there is nothing especially pathological about such history. . . . Observe, however, how such a history was translated in the psychopathological context, this from the case summary prepared after the patient was discharged.

> This white 39-year-old male . . . manifests a long history of considerable ambivalence in close relationships, which began in early childhood. A warm relationship with his mother cools during his adolescence. A distant relationship to his father is described as becoming very intense. Affective stability is absent. His attempts to control emotionality with his wife and children are punctuated by angry outbursts

and, in the case of the children, spankings. And while he says that he has several good friends, one senses considerable ambivalence embedded in those relationships also. . . .

The facts of the case were unintentionally distorted by the staff to achieve consistency with a popular theory of the dynamics of a schizophrenic reaction.[12] Nothing of an ambivalent nature had been described in relations with parents, spouse, or friends. . . . Clearly, the meaning ascribed to his verbalizations (that is, ambivalence, affective instability) was determined by the diagnosis: schizophrenia. An entirely different meaning would have been ascribed if it were known that the man was "normal."

All pseudopatients took extensive notes publicly. Under ordinary circumstances, such behaviour would have raised questions in the minds of observers, as, in fact, it did among patients. Indeed, it seemed so certain that the notes would elicit suspicion that elaborate precautions were taken to remove them from the ward each day. But the precautions proved needless. The closest any staff member came to questioning these notes occurred when one pseudopatient asked his physician what kind of medication he was receiving and began to write down the response. "You needn't write it," he was told gently. "If you have trouble remembering, just ask me again."

If no questions were asked of the pseudopatients, how was their writing interpreted? Nursing records for three patients indicate that the writing was seen as an aspect of their pathological behaviour. . . . Given that the patient is in the hospital, he must be psychologically disturbed. And given that he is disturbed, continuous writing must be a behavioural manifestation of that disturbance, perhaps a subset of the compulsive behaviours that are sometimes correlated with schizophrenia.

One tacit characteristic of psychiatric diagnosis is that it locates the sources of aberration within the individual and only rarely within the complex of stimuli that surrounds him. Consequently, behaviours that are stimulated by the environment are commonly misattributed to the patient's disorder. For example, one kindly nurse found a pseudopatient pacing the long hospital corridors. "Nervous, Mr. X?" she asked. "No, bored," he said.

The notes kept by pseudopatients are full of patient behaviours that were misinterpreted by well-intentioned staff. Often enough, a patient would go "berserk" because he had, wittingly or unwittingly been mistreated by, say, an attendant. A nurse coming upon the scene would rarely inquire even cursorily into the environmental stimuli of the patient's behaviour. Rather, she assumed that his upset derived from his pathology, not from his present interactions with other staff members. . . . [N]ever were the staff found to assume that one of themselves or the structure of the hospital had anything to do with a patient's behaviour. One psychiatrist pointed to a group of patients who were sitting outside the cafeteria entrance half an hour before lunchtime. To a group of young residents he indicated that such behaviour was characteristic of the oral-acquisitive nature of the syndrome. It seemed not to occur to him that there were very few things to anticipate in a psychiatric hospital besides eating.

A psychiatric label has a life and an influence of its own. Once the impression has been formed that the patient is schizophrenic, the expectation is that he will continue to be schizophrenic. When a sufficient amount of time has passed, during which the patient has done nothing bizarre, he is considered to be in remission and available for discharge. But the label endures beyond discharge, with the unconfirmed expectation that he will behave as a schizophrenic again. Such labels, conferred by mental health professionals, are as influential on the patient as they are on his relatives and friends, and it should not surprise anyone that the diagnosis acts on all of them as a self-fulfilling prophecy. Eventually, the patient himself accepts the diagnosis, with all of its surplus meanings and expectations, and behaves accordingly (see note 5).

POWERLESSNESS AND DEPERSONALIZATION

Eye contact and verbal contact reflect concern and individualization; their absence, avoidance and depersonalization. The data I have presented do not do justice to the rich daily encounters that grew up around matters of depersonalization and avoidance. I have records of patients who were beaten by staff for the sin of having initiated verbal contact. During my own experience, for example, one patient was beaten in the presence of other patients for having approached an attendant and told him, "I like you." Occasionally, punishment meted out to patients for misdemeanours seemed so excessive that it could not be justified by the most radical interpretations of psychiatric canon. Nevertheless, they appeared to go unquestioned. Tempers were often short. A patient who had not heard a call for medication would be roundly excoriated, and the morning attendants would often wake patients with, "Come on, you m— f—s, out of bed!"

Neither anecdotal nor "hard" data can convey the overwhelming sense of powerlessness which invades the individual as he is continually exposed to the depersonalization of the psychiatric hospital. . . .

Powerlessness was evident everywhere. The patient is deprived of many of his legal rights by dint of his psychiatric commitment.[13] He is shorn of credibility by virtue of his psychiatric label. His freedom of movement is restricted. He cannot initiate contact with the staff, but may only respond to such overtures as they make. Personal privacy is minimal. Patient quarters and possessions can be entered and examined by any staff member, for whatever reason. His personal history and anguish is available to any staff member (often including the "gray lady" and "candy striper" volunteer) who chooses to read his folder, regardless of their therapeutic relationship to him. His personal hygiene and waste evacuation are often monitored. The [toilets] may have no doors.

At times, depersonalization reached such proportions that pseudopatients had the sense that they were invisible, or at least unworthy of account. Upon being admitted, I and other pseudopatients took the initial physical examinations in a semipublic room, where staff members went about their own business as if we were not there.

On the ward, attendants delivered verbal and occasionally serious physical abuse to patients in the presence of other observing patients, some of whom (the pseudopatients) were writing it all down. Abusive behaviour, on the other hand, terminated quite abruptly when other staff members were known to be coming. Staff are credible witnesses. Patients are not.

A nurse unbuttoned her uniform to adjust her brassiere in the presence of an entire ward of viewing men. One did not have the sense that she was being seductive. Rather, she didn't notice us. A group of staff persons might point to a patient in the dayroom and discuss him animatedly, as if he were not there.

One illuminating instance of depersonalization and invisibility occurred with regard to medications. All told, the pseudopatients were administered nearly 2,100 pills. . . . Only two were swallowed. The rest were either pocketed or deposited in the toilet. The pseudopatients were not alone in this. Although I have no precise records on how many patients rejected their medications, the pseudopatients frequently found the medications of other patients in the toilet before they deposited their own. As long as they were cooperative, their behaviour and the pseudopatients' own in this matter, as in other important matters, went unnoticed throughout.

Reactions to such depersonalization among pseudopatients were intense. Although they had come to the hospital as participant observers and were fully aware that they did not "belong," they nevertheless found themselves caught up in and fighting the process of depersonalization. . . .

THE CONSEQUENCES OF LABELLING AND DEPERSONALIZATION

Whenever the ratio of what is known to what needs to be known approaches zero, we tend to invent "knowledge" and assume that we understand more than we actually do. We seem unable to acknowledge that we simply don't know. The need for diagnosis and remediation of behavioural and emotional problems are enormous. But rather than acknowledge that we are just embarking on understanding, we continue to label patients "schizophrenic," "manic-depressive," and "insane," as if in those words we had captured the essence of understanding. The facts of the matter are that we have known for a long time that diagnoses are often not useful or reliable, but we have nevertheless continued to use them. We now know that we cannot distinguish insanity from sanity. It is depressing to consider how that information will be used.

Not merely depressing, but frightening. How many people, one wonders, are sane but not recognized as such in our psychiatric institutions? How many have been needlessly stripped of their privileges of citizenship, from the right to vote and drive to that of handling their own accounts? How many have feigned insanity in order to avoid the criminal consequences of their behaviour, and, conversely, how many would rather stand trial than live interminably in a psychiatric hospital—but are wrongly thought to be mentally ill? How many have been stigmatized by well-intentioned, but nevertheless erroneous, diagnoses? . . . [P]sychiatric diagnoses are rarely found to be in error. The label sticks, a mark of inadequacy forever.

Finally, how many patients might be "sane" outside the psychiatric hospital but seem insane in it—not because craziness resides in them, as it were, but because they are responding to a bizarre setting, one that may be unique to institutions which harbour neither people? Goffman (see note 4) calls the process of socialization to such institutions "mortification"—an apt metaphor that includes the processes of depersonalization that have been described here. And while it is impossible to know whether the pseudopatients' responses to these processes are characteristic of all inmates—they were, after all, not real patients—it is difficult to believe that these processes of socialization to a psychiatric hospital provide useful attitudes or habits of response for living in the "real world."

NOTES

1.   P. Ash, *J. Abnorm. Soc. Psychol.* 44, 272 (1949); A.T. Beck, *Amer. J. Psychiat.* 119, 210 (1962); A.T. Boisen, *Psychiatry* 2, 233 (1938); N. Kreitman, *J. Ment. Sci.* 107, 876

(1961); N. Kreitman, P. Sainsbury, J. Morrisey, J. Towers, J. Scrivener, *ibid.*, p. 887; H.O. Schmitt and C.P. Fonda, *J. Abnorm. Soc. Psychol.* 52, 262 (1956); W. Seeman, *J. Nerv. Ment. Dis.* 118, 541 (1953). For an analysis of these artifacts and summaries of the disputes, see J. Zubin, *Annu. Rev. Psychol.* 18, 373 (1967); L. Phillips and J.G. Draguns, *ibid.*, 22, 447 (1971).

2. R. Benedict, *J. Gen. Psychol.* 10, 59 (1934).

3. See in this regard H. Becker, *Outsiders: Studies in the Sociology of Deviance* (Free Press, New York, 1963); B.M. Braginsky, D.D. Braginsky, K. Ring, *Methods of Madness: The Mental Hospital as a Last Resort* (Holt, Rinehart & Winston, New York, 1969); G.M. Crocetti and P.V. Lemkau, *Amer. Sociol. Rev.* 30, 577 (1965); E. Goffman, *Behaviour in Public Places* (Free Press, New York, 1964); R.D. Laing, *The Divided Self: A Study of Sanity and Madness* (Quadrangle, Chicago, 1960); D.L. Phillips, *Amer. Sociol. Rev.* 28, 963 (1963); T.R. Sarbin, *Psychol. Today* 6, 18 (1972); E. Schur, *Amer. J. Sociol.* 75, 309 (1969); T. Szasz, *Law, Liberty and Psychiatry* (Macmillan, New York, 1963); *The Myth of Mental Illness: Foundations of a Theory of Mental Illness* (Hoeber Harper, New York, 1963). For a critique of some of these views, see W.R. Gove, *Amer. Sociol. Rev.* 35, 873 (1970).

4. E. Goffman, *Asylums* (Doubleday, Garden City, N.Y., 1961).

5. T.J. Scheff, *Being Mentally Ill: A Sociological Theory* (Aldine, Chicago, 1966).

6. Data from a ninth pseudopatient are not incorporated in this report because, although his sanity went undetected, he falsified aspects of his personal history, including his marital status and parental relationships. His experimental behaviours therefore were not identical to those of the other pseudopatients.

7. Beyond the personal difficulties that the pseudopatient is likely to experience in the hospital, there are legal and social ones that, combined, require considerable attention before entry. For example, once admitted to a psychiatric institution, it is difficult, if not impossible, to be discharged on short notice, state law to the contrary notwithstanding. I was not sensitive to these difficulties at the outset of the project, nor to the personal and situational emergencies that can arise, but later a writ of habeas corpus was prepared for each of the entering pseudopatients and an attorney was kept "on call" during every hospitalization. I am grateful to John Kaplan and Robert Bartels for legal advice and assistance in these matters.

8. However distasteful such concealment is, it was a necessary first step to examining these questions. Without concealment, there would have been no way to know how valid these experiences were; nor was there any way of knowing whether whatever detections occurred were a tribute to the diagnostic acumen of the staff or to the hospital's rumour network. Obviously, since my concerns are general ones that cut across individual hospitals and staffs, I have respected their anonymity and have eliminated clues that might lead to their identification.

9. Interestingly, of the 12 admissions, 11 were diagnosed as schizophrenic and one, with the identical symptomatology, as manic-depressive psychosis. This diagnosis has a more favourable prognosis, and it was given by the only private hospital in our sample. On the relations between social class and psychiatric diagnosis, see A.B. Hollingstead and F.C. Redlich, *Social Class and Mental Illness: A Community Study* (Wiley, New York, 1958).

10. It is possible, of course, that patients have quite broad latitudes in diagnosis and therefore are inclined to call many people sane, even those whose behaviour is patently aberrant. However, although we have no hard data on this matter, it was our distinct impression that this was not the case. In many instances, patients not only singled us out for attention, but came to imitate our behaviours and styles.

11. J. Cumming and E. Cumming, *Community Ment. Health* 1, 135 (1965); A. Farina and K. Ring, *J. Abnorm. Psychol.* 70, 47 (1965); H.E. Freeman and O.G. Simmons, *The Mental Patient Comes Home* (Wiley, New York, 1963): W.J. Johannsen, *Ment. Hygiene* 53, 218 (1969); A.S. Linsky, *Soc. Psychiat.* 5, 166 (1970).

12. For an example of a similar self-fulfilling prophecy, in this instance dealing with the "central" trait of intelligence, see R. Rosenthal and L. Jacobson, *Pygmalion in the Classroom* (Holt, Rinehart & Winston, New York, 1968).

13. D.B. Wexler and S.E. Scoville, *Ariz. Law Rev.* 13, 1 (1971).

Chapter 22

RETHINKING THE BRAIN

Tanya Talaga

Nearly 150 years ago, Vermont railway worker Phineas Gage unexpectedly became a towering figure in the field of neuroscience.

Gage miraculously survived a railroad blasting accident that drove a metal bar through the frontal lobe of his brain. The trauma, however, dramatically altered his personality. Gage changed from a kind-hearted, hard-working, courteous man to an unreliable, unfaithful, and cold person.

At the time, the accident cast an enigma upon the functions of the frontal lobes, says Dr. Marsel Mesulam, of the Cognitive Neurology and Alzheimer's Disease Centre at Northwestern University.

Doctors scratched their heads with wonder and began to ask, "How could this be?"

This week, 800 of the world's top neuroscientists were in town as the Rotman Research Institute hosted the 10th annual brain conference on the frontal lobes. New research was shared on everything from how the brain hard-wires itself, to severe childhood head injuries, the many faces of dementia, and the criminal mind.

Today, *The Star* attempts to unravel some of the mystery surrounding the human brain as we take a look back at the conference highlights.

The science of the frontal lobes is really the science of ourselves.

The lobes control the higher functions of the human mind, such as memory, mood, cognition, and consciousness.

In the last decade, neuroscientists have made leaps forward in their understanding of the frontal lobes. This is critical for advances in treating Alzheimer's disease, dementia, development problems, and for figuring out why it is that some people behave so differently from the rest.

Think of the frontal lobes as the leader of an orchestra and the rest of the brain as the instruments. Without the conductor, the instruments sound jumbled and disorganized.

"Evolution has given the human species a piece of brain that is not necessary for anything that is absolutely essential—like feeding, breathing, populating, or running away from danger," Mesulam told *The Star* during a break at the conference.

"This is a piece of luxury cortex that allows one to do things that are especially human and not essential for survival."

These kinds of "luxury aspects of cognition" are really what separates us from the rest of the evolutionary chain.

And scientists now know that the frontal lobes keep developing in humans past age 22 and maybe even to age 35, says Dr. Robert Knight, a professor in the department of psychology at the University of California.

For years, researchers have thought you are born with your brain, that your genetic load and your environment shape who you are, he says.

But, in fact, you are born with more cells than you need as an adult, he says. What happens, at least up to age 22, is called "neuronal pruning."

"It's like if you have a tree with branches all over the place. The tree is healthier if you decrease the number of branches and have stronger individual branches. That is what happens in normal (brain) development," he says.

The pruning and shaping turns us into the adults we are.

New research is starting to show that if something happens to interrupt that process, such as a serious accident or injury to the frontal lobes, the results can be devastating.

Australian neuropsychologist Vicki Anderson, from the University of Melbourne, told the conference that infants and young children who experience serious trauma to the frontal lobes can change their lives forever.

While a brain-injured child may seem to make a remarkable physical recovery, once he or she hits adolescence, the cognitive and behavioural problems start to show.

"They tend to grow into their injuries," she says. "Think of a 5-year-old. They don't have to work particularly independently. Everyone points them in directions—where their school bag is, what they need to take with them, etc."

"But as the child gets older, hits adolescence and has to behave independently, that is when these problems really start becoming evident."

"A number of kids in our study with these injuries have gone out and done impulsive, risk-taking things such as getting in trouble with the police."

This is a really big issue in a medical-legal context, she adds. "Families and lawyers want to settle (accident-related lawsuits) as soon as possible. But if you settle too early, with these kids, you don't get to see the extent of the problem."

Several behavioural changes, like those noted by Gage's doctors in the 19th century, can also happen in adults as a result of trauma to the frontal cortex, which is the area right above the eyes.

Infections, trauma, brain tumours, and strokes can cause these changes, which affect only a few hundred North Americans, says Daniel Tranel, a professor in the division of cognitive neuroscience at the University of Iowa.

He gave conference-goers an insight into new advances in understanding sociopathic behaviour and the criminal mind.

Sociopaths are people with a deviant behavioural streak—they can rape, murder, steal, and lie seemingly without remorse. It's generally recognized that sociopathy is something people are both born with and conditioned into becoming because of their upbringing.

But an emerging body of evidence shows sociopathic behaviour can be acquired as a result of trauma or injury to the ventromedial prefrontal region of the brain, another area just above the eyes.

In a series of studies designed to examine the role emotions play on decision-making, Tranel and a team from Iowa have shown that damage to this area of the brain can produce a profound change in personality. This seems to cause a severe impairment in judgment and the ability to make sound decisions.

Tranel's team is studying several dozen people with this condition.

"We call it acquired sociopathy because they are normal until they had their brain injury," says Tranel, who lectures on this provocative area of research.

"A patient can go along, entirely fine, they have evolved well, are normal, have a good job. Then something can happen to the bottom front part of the brain, the ventromedial prefrontal region, and after that develop a radical change in their personality and social conduct."

They never return to a normal life, Tranel says, and are challenging to rehabilitate and cope with.

His work is attracting attention among those who work in the field of criminology and law. He's often sought after to work on high-profile crime cases. One took place in New York in the late 1980s.

"A man strangled his wife and threw her out the window of their 13th-floor apartment in an attempt to disguise the murder as a suicide," he says, "That didn't work."

The man was brought to the University of Iowa for evaluation and was found to have a cyst that created dysfunction in the ventromedial part of the brain. The information influenced the man's sentencing, Tranel says.

The conference also heard of new insights into the understanding of dementia and Alzheimer's disease.

Dr. Bruce Miller, from the University of California at San Francisco, says that up to 10 per cent of people currently diagnosed as Alzheimer's patients or schizophrenics may be misdiagnosed.

What they may have is actually frontotemporal dementia, he says.

This disease is virtually unknown by most clinicians and it strikes adults in their 30s, 40s and 50s. Aggressive or antisocial behaviours are symptoms of this degenerative and fatal disease, Miller says.

And, as in the beginning of life, the frontal cortex plays a big role when we start to age.

"In normal aging, the structure that experiences the most changes is the frontal cortex," says Knight.

But Cheryl Grady, a University of Toronto psychology professor, says there is much to learn about how the brain handles the aging process.

For instance, new research suggests the aging brain has the ability to bypass damaged areas in search of new cognitive pathways, she says.

The more science is able to unravel the mystery of the frontal lobes, the greater our quality of life will be, says Donald Stuss, director of the Rotman Institute and co-chair of the conference.

Now that life expectancy is pushing 80 years and more, he says, "we want to have our minds as well as our bodies intact."

Part VI

YOUTH AND DEVIANCE

Chapter 23

TEEN GANGS:
FEAR IN OUR SCHOOLS

Michelle Shephard

STAR REPORTER MICHELLE SHEPHARD SURVEYED 1,019 STUDENTS IN 29 HIGH schools across Greater Toronto as part of a six-month investigation into school violence.

More than 180 youth gangs are carving out territories across Greater Toronto. Their weapon is intimidation. Their shield—students' frightened silence.

They call themselves Looney Toons, Boys in Blue, Punjab X-Ecution, Nubian Sisters, Trife Kids, Vice Lords, The Tuxedo Boys, Mother Nature's Mistakes, and the 18 Buddhas.

They are teen gangs.

And they are an increasingly violent part of life in our communities and high schools.

More than 180 of them are carving out territories across Greater Toronto.

Not all are dangerous. Some youths just band together, think up a name, and try to act tough.

But they are learning the art and power of intimidation. And they are using it daily in our schools.

At least 30 gangs are known by police to carry firearms.

"Anybody who thinks the kind of violent incidents that kids face today is the same as 20, 10, or even 5 years ago is so out of touch, they're not even worth talking to," says Toronto police Detective John Muise, who has watched gang violence grow over the past nine years.

"You rarely see one-on-one fights," Muise adds. "It's gangs, it's weapons, and it's definitely more sophisticated in a brutal way."

Students know exactly what they face.

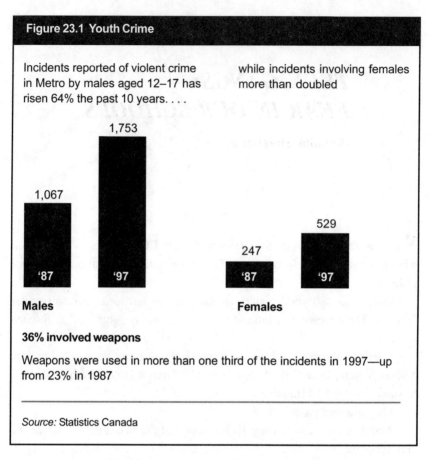

Figure 23.1 Youth Crime

Incidents reported of violent crime in Metro by males aged 12–17 has risen 64% the past 10 years. . . . while incidents involving females more than doubled

Males

Females

36% involved weapons

Weapons were used in more than one third of the incidents in 1997—up from 23% in 1987

Source: Statistics Canada

The Star surveyed 1,019 students in 29 of 275 public and Catholic high schools across Toronto, Durham, Peel, Halton, and York during May, June, and July.

The survey focused on teenagers in Grade 10, mainly 15 or 16 years old—a vulnerable age where peer pressure, teenage insecurities, or troubles at home can make the gang culture particularly alluring.

It revealed a frightening reality:

Gangs and their activities have become an unavoidable part of high school life for many students throughout Greater Toronto.

The majority—767 of the 1,019 students surveyed—said they still feel safe at school. But more than one in five—22 per cent—say they have gone to school filled with fear and anxiety about their safety.

More than half of the students surveyed—53 per cent—said there were gangs in their schools. One in 10 said they belonged to a gang.

Figure 23.2 Reported Violence in Schools

Police say most violent incidents in schools are not reported. Below are the incidents reported for 1996–1997 by the Ministry of Education for all elementary and high schools in Greater Toronto.

Physical assault, bodily harm

617

Possession of a weapon

228

Sexual Assault

42

Threats of serious physical harm

277

Robbery and extortion

139

Hate-motivated violence

40

Vandalism with extensive damage

62

Source: Ontario Ministry of Education

And just one in 10—only 10 per cent of respondents—said they would report a violent incident in their school to a teacher, vice-principal, principal, or any staff member.

The Star survey clearly illustrates one of the biggest problems police and school authorities face every day. Silence.

Most gang-related crimes—extortion, intimidation, assaults—are never reported. Fear breeds silence.

The public rarely sees gang-related violence and usually only finds out about flare-ups that can't be hidden. Consider these incidents in the past year:

Yesterday: Police brace for trouble outside Scarborough's Albert Campbell Collegiate, where they expected a retaliatory attack by the Ghetto Boys for an earlier stabbing of an 18 Buddhas gang member. Nothing happened, but police fear it's just a matter of time.

The Oct. 13 stabbing was itself a payback for a previous mall brawl between the two gangs.

Sept. 21, Scarborough: Two Sir Wilfred Laurier students are stabbed in the head, neck, and chest during a lunch-hour fight. Five Woburn students—police say they are members of the Tuxedo Boys, a Sri Lankan gang—are charged with aggravated assault. Police say the victims required "hundreds of stitches," and are under police protection.

June 9, East York: A 15-year-old girl is knifed in the chest and stomach at a 7-Eleven store across from Marc Garneau Secondary School at Don Mills and Gateway Blvd. The fight, involving about 40 students from nearby high schools, many armed, has been brewing for months between two female gangs.

Jan. 20, Toronto: The Spadina Girls—five 15-year-olds from Jarvis and Harbord collegiates—are arrested after a "reign of terror" inflicted on other students. Charges include assault, extortion, and uttering a death threat. The two ringleaders served eight, and six months, in protective custody.

School boards, administrators, and provincial education authorities—and until recently, the police themselves—have downplayed the presence of gangs in the city's classrooms and communities.

But with youth violence escalating, that's starting to change.

"To say (youth gangs) don't exist is a mistake because they do exist," Police Chief David Boothby said in an interview.

"A bigger mistake is to say they don't exist and to not do anything about it."

The new wave of organized youth gangs in Toronto appeared in the late 1980s, against a backdrop of "Gangsta" rap and the growing notoriety of drive-by shootings in south-central Los Angeles.

In 1989, the Untouchables—initially a group of suburban, white, middle-class boys—formed an alliance police consider one of the first organized gangs.

They cruised downtown on weekends, swarming victims for their jackets and shoes, and marking out their turf.

Slowly other gangs—the downtown B-Boys, the suburban Bayview Milliken Posse—began forming alliances to fight back and get in on the game.

Today, the downtown core boasts more than 50 groups—with names ranging from the Silver Boys to Young Guns, Pentagon, Lynch Mob, and Gators—that police identify as gangs.

Membership can be fluid. Two years ago, Latino-based La Familia was considered one of the city's largest gangs. Today, according to police, La Familia is smaller and more dispersed.

And today's Untouchables—a downtown multi-racial gang—bear little resemblance to their notorious predecessors. They simply adopted the name.

Defining and following youth gangs is difficult.

Police and the courts use the definition of "criminal organization" as outlined in Bill C-95, which says a gang must include five or more people involved in criminal activity.

Psychologist Fred Mathews, a leading Canadian expert on youth violence, defines gangs as a group of three or more whose members impulsively, or intentionally, plan and commit anti-social, delinquent, or illegal acts.

The consensus among high school students interviewed by *The Star* was four or five people who carry weapons have some loose sort of organization, are involved in criminal acts, and have a name.

If you're in a gang, the definition is less formal.

"They're my boys," says one 15-year-old male member of a west-end gang affiliated with The Untouchables.

A Latin Nation (NLs) gang member defined his group as "insurance" or "back up," and says he sometimes felt he had no other option but to join a gang—or to prove his loyalty by fighting.

"Sometimes you hafta do it (get in a brawl). If you don't do it, you can't show your face. It's like if you've lost your shit, you're gonna get picked on for the rest of your life."

Girls fight too—often more fiercely than their male counterparts. At least five of the 180 city gangs identified by police are strictly female, including the Ghetto Girls, Lady Crew, and the Rucus Girls. Many have both male and female members.

Figure 23.3 Toronto youth gang territories

Police have identified more than 180 youth gangs across Greater Toronto. Here are the major ones. Some territories are fluid, and membership varies.

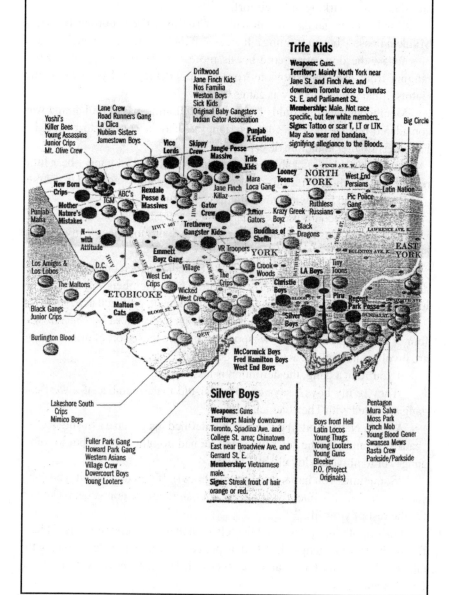

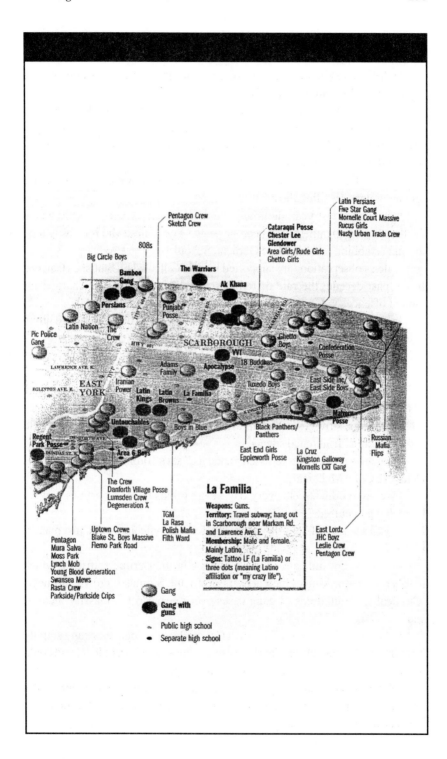

Latin Persians
Five Star Gang
Mornelle Court Massive
Rucus Girls
Nasty Urban Trash Crew

Pentagon Crew
Sketch Crew

Cataraqui Posse
Chester Lee
Glendower
Area Girls/Rude Girls
Ghetto Girls

808s

Big Circle Boys

Bamboo Gang

The Warriors

Ak Khana

Persians

Punjabi Posse

Latin Nation

The Crew

Pic Police Gang

SCARBOROUGH
WI

Ghetto Boys

Confederation Posse

HWY 401

LAWRENCE AVE. E.

Adams Family

Apocalypse

18 Buddhas

EAST YORK

EGLINTON AVE. E.

Iranian Power

Latin Kings

Latin Browns

La Familia

Tuxedo Boys

East Side Inc/East Side Boys

Untouchables

Boys in Blue

Black Panthers/Panthers

Maham Posse

Regent Park Posse

DANFORTH AVE.

DUNDAS ST. E.

Area 6 Boys

East End Girls
Eppleworth Posse

La Cruz
Kingston Galloway
Mornells CRT Gang

Russian Mafia
Flips

The Crew
Danforth Village Posse
Lumsden Crew
Degeneration X

La Familia

Weapons: Guns.
Territory: Travel subway; hang out in Scarborough near Markam Rd. and Lawrence Ave. E.
Membership: Male and female. Mainly Latino.
Signs: Tattoo LF (La Familia) or three dots (meaning Latino affiliation or "my crazy life").

TGM
La Rasa
Polish Mafia
Fifth Ward

Uptown Crewe
Blake St. Boys Massive
Flemo Park Road

Pentagon
Mura Salva
Moss Park
Lynch Mob
Young Blood Generation
Swansea Mews
Rasta Crew
Parkside/Parkside Crips

East Lordz
JHC Boyz
Leslie Crew
Pentagon Crew

Gang

Gang with guns

Public high school

Separate high school

One North York student talked about exclusive girl gangs in his Catholic school.

"Oh, they're killers. They're worse than us. I wouldn't go near them," he says, waving his hands as he talks.

"Girl gangs are . . . crazy. I don't go near those ones, they'd kill me. They grab rocks and put them (in their) purses and when someone comes they'll crack 'em with it. They also carry those bandanas with locks on the bottom of them. I don't go near them."

Toronto Constable Wendy Gales, of 54 Division in former East York, says female violence is often the most severe.

"During the last year, definitely the most violent-type crimes are where the female gang members have been suspects," says Gales, who is investigating the June stabbing outside Marc Garneau School.

Gales's observations are supported by data collected by Statistics Canada. In the past decade, the rate of females aged 12–17 who were charged for violent offences in Canada has increased by 179 per cent.

In Toronto, total violent crimes reported by police in that female age group rose 198 per cent—from 242 reported crimes in 1987 to 529 last year.

But StatsCan figures also show an overall 7 per cent drop in youth crime, continuing a six-year trend.

Police say those figures are misleading. Today's violence is not reported. It's no longer one-on-one. Teenagers are afraid to speak up.

The gangs' strongest weapons are fear and intimidation. And their shield is their victims' frightened silence.

"Statistics only reflect reported incidents," says Toronto 52 Division street Detective Colin McDonald.

"We are on the streets every day begging kids to report crimes that we know have occurred."

Says a 15-year-old North York boy: "Telling someone would just make it worse."

Police do not indicate gang affiliations in their crime statistics, which makes outside tracking of their activities difficult. Similarly, crown attorneys, who deal with hundreds of gang cases every year, do not classify them as gang-related.

In fact, says Toronto senior crown Calvin Barry, evidence of gang activity is rarely mentioned during trials because it is considered prejudicial and could cause a mistrial or draw criticism from the judge.

"The problem is that if you start alleging an accused is a member of a gang, that is a prejudicial assertion . . . because you are making allegations that are very difficult to prove," he says.

The dangerous nature of the city's gangs varies. Police say many have members with some sort of criminal record—offences ranging from shoplifting to assault to murder.

A criminal record or brief trip through the justice system—most are young offenders—is considered a badge of honour.

But police say many fringe members, sometimes known as "wannabes" or "foot soldiers," eventually will be involved in some of the worst activities— brutal assaults, armed robberies, swarmings—in attempts to earn respect from the leaders.

Some of the more dangerous gangs have adopted an American-gang-style initiation ritual called "jumping in" or "beat down." Other gang members, en masse, gather around kicking and punching the newcomer for at least a minute.

Many gangs are based on racial alliances.

Some of the Asian gangs, north of the city, define their membership by Vietnamese heritage; Scarborough's Tuxedo Boys generally will only admit Sri Lankans.

But others initially bound by race—Latino-based La Familia, Chinese-based 18 Buddhas—are now inter-racial.

In their cramped street crime office in Scarborough's 42 Division, Detectives John MacDonald and Steve Linn sit at their desks with the eyes of threatening young faces staring down on them.

Mugs of La Familia gang members fill one wall. The faces of the Confederation Posse gangs are tacked beside the Sketch Crew and the Black Panthers along another wall. The 18 Buddhas have their place beside the door.

White racist or neo-Nazi gangs—often grouped as skinheads, although not all members shave their heads—have a wall of their own.

The detectives' office is typical of most Greater Toronto police divisions, which all keep a close eye on gang activity. What is unique about this division is a new graffiti tracking database, the first of its kind in Canada.

The computer program will show gang members' names, pictures, their symbols, graffiti, affiliations, tattoos, rivals, and crimes.

The letters L and F on a cross signify a La Familia "tag"—their graffiti signature.

A tattoo of three dots between the thumb and forefinger signifies a Latino gang connection. A "T" etched into a youth's bare shoulder represents affiliation with the black North York gang Trife Kids.

The computer program is part of a pilot project, but the detectives hope it can one day be used at every division, and eventually other regions, to get a clear understanding of the growing gang problem.

"This system will only be as good as what we put in," says Linn. "We hope eventually we'll be able to just put in a name, come up with their gang affiliation, other members, turfs . . . it will be a great tool in investigating the gang incidents."

The initiative is a new step for Toronto police, who are often reluctant to discuss gang problems.

"There are two schools of thought," explains 52 Division Detective McDonald. "Either you don't want to talk about (gangs) for fear of glorifying them or you acknowledge that they exist."

McDonald believes open discussion is a better strategy so police and legislators can attack the problem.

School boards have traditionally averted any discussion about gangs until forced to deal with the issue.

"No school wants to get tarred with a (bad) reputation," admits Colleen French, superintendent of program services at the Toronto Catholic school board.

"Every school wants to create a safe, open learning environment." Neither the Catholic board nor the newly amalgamated Toronto District School Board have any formal plans to combat rising gang violence.

However, the Toronto district board is reviewing gang research conducted by the former North York board, spurred by a 1996 stabbing at William Lyon Mackenzie School involving two gangs.

Psychologist Mathews tried to promote that kind of research by school boards at the beginning of the decade.

He approached seven Ontario boards, offering his services for a study on school violence.

"We offered to give them all the results for free, in any form they wanted. We agreed there would be total anonymity, no children identified, no schools identified, no boards identified. All seven school boards all said not interested," Mathews says.

Eventually, two individual schools agreed to participate and Mathews published the Student Perceptions of Violence Survey from 850 responses of grades 6, 7, 8, and 9 students in 1993.

He found that students were frightened, gangs were becoming more popular, and weapons more prevalent.

"Gangs are not popular to talk about," says Mathews. "It's a frightening idea. So what happens is nobody talks about them, giving the perception there's no problem and then nothing is done to prevent gangs from forming."

Eric Roher, a lawyer who specializes in educational law, has seen a "dramatic change" in the types of crimes committed in schools.

"I've seen in recent years the intensity has increased and the kids are more organized and sophisticated," says Roher, who wrote an *Educators Guide to Violence in Schools*.

"Psychological terrorism . . . has students terrified into not saying anything to anybody.

"Generally, students are too reluctant to talk to police because they don't trust them and to school officials because they don't think they can do any good."

Chief Boothby says he has watched with frustration the growing reluctance of students reporting crimes.

"If the average student is being tapped for some money and five dollars a week isn't a big deal for them, I guess they start weighing the options—am I going to refuse to pay or am I going to go to the police or school administration or am I just going to pay it?

"It's sad that they consider paying it but it happens and that bothers me, it really does."

Crown Attorney Barry says gang members rely on the fact most victims won't speak out.

"You have a situation then where the youthful gangs know that there's a very slim chance of them being convicted," Barry says.

"And, therefore, they are very cavalier and they go and do these crime in front of other people knowing that people are scared to come forward, because they don't want to rat or fink on the gang member because of retribution."

The Toronto District School Board has hall monitors—call them "security guards"—placed in some school hallways.

The monitors, walkie-talkies in hand to contact school officials and police if needed, roam school halls and properties daily, keeping a wary eye out for trouble.

"Five or six years ago, forget it, there wasn't the gang problem like there is now," says one monitor. He asked *The Star* not to reveal his name or the school where he works.

"When I went to high school, there maybe were a few gangs but fights were still usually settled one-on-one. If two guys are fighting they deal with it and then it's usually over, no big deal. But now it's huge groups or lots of students on one kid.

"And weapons change the rules. It used to just be the big guy everyone was afraid of whereas now it can be the little guy with the big gun.

"That's the equalizer. Weapons and the numbers of friends who'll back you up in a fight."

Chapter 24

DEVIANT YOUTH: THE SOCIAL CONSTRUCTION OF YOUTH PROBLEMS

Julian Tanner

INTRODUCTION

The citizens of Canada, like those of other nations, are deeply concerned about law and order. Social surveys consistently indicate that crime, particularly violent interpersonal crime, ranks prominently among the features of modern life that people find least attractive. A disproportionately large amount of this anxiety focuses upon the behaviour of adolescents. No other social group receives as much negative attention as the young; they are viewed variously as troubling and troubled, a constant source of fear and worry. Newspaper and television reports fuel these fears with stories of youth riots, violence in schools, "swarming" teenagers, crack use, and so on. While the particular deviant motif varies—bike gangs yesterday, punks today—what remains constant is the tarnished view of youth that is portrayed.

The story that the unrelenting media coverage tells is of high and increasing incidents of juvenile crime, the explanation (and blame) for which is sought in a wide range of factors: too much leisure, broken homes, working mothers, the erosion of "family values," the lack of discipline in schools, the recession, and a reluctance to adequately punish young offenders. What also runs through these accounts is the assumption that the behaviour of modern youth is much worse than it ever has been in the past and that Canada in the late twentieth century has suddenly been confronted with a unique set of youth problems. In this regard, a Toronto *Globe and Mail* headline proclaiming "Another outbreak of street gang fighting has reawakened citizens to the extent of the problems these young people present" is instructive.

What incident do you imagine is being described here? A clash between rioters and police on Yonge Street in Toronto in the aftermath of the original trial verdict in the Rodney King case in Los Angeles? An outbreak of swarming at a suburban shopping mall? Both are reasonable guesses, but both are wrong. The headline is from an editorial in *The Globe and Mail* from January 1949— over forty-five years ago. The street-fighting men in question were, in fact, boys—the "Junction Boys," a then-prominent gang based in Toronto's West End. Their delinquent activities included car theft, breaking and entering, liquor offences, street brawls, and inciting riots (with baseball bats) in communities others than their own. Politicians and newspapers explained and deplored their behaviour in terms of broken homes, declining moral standards, and—this was in the days before television, don't forget!—violent gangster movies.

The 1949 *Globe and Mail* editorial was resurrected by journalist Colin Vaughan to introduce his own more recent commentary on youth gangs in Toronto (*The Globe and Mail*, June 8, 1992). The title of his article, "Everything old seems new again, to Teens" sums up his thesis: for all its apparent novelty, contemporary teenage behaviour is not really very different from that of the past.

Vaughan points out that the idea that Canada's largest city has until recently been immune to crime ("Toronto the Good") is a myth; from the beginning Toronto has had its fair share of gang conflicts. In support of his argument he describes the "Jubilee Riots" of 1875, when Protestant Orangemen attacked Irish Catholic immigrants on city streets, and recalls the notorious Christie Pit riots of 1933 when, toward the end of a long hot summer, young Jews were set upon by juvenile Fascists (members of the "Swastika Club"). Fighting fanned out along Bloor Street as both sides called in reinforcements. A sequel of sorts took place in 1965, when a neo-Nazi rally at a downtown park was protested.

Gang fights in Toronto have not been restricted to ethnic conflicts. For instance, the Hallowe'en riots of 1945 began when the police arrested a few trouble-makers and ended after a crowd of 7,000 besieged a West End police station. The outbreaks of trouble between youths and police that occur fairly regularly on the last day of the Canadian National Exhibition (CNE) should also be remembered. And, lest you gain the impression that Toronto alone experiences youth riots, cast your mind back to the disturbances that have occurred in recent years in Montreal and Vancouver after, respectively, Stanley Cup victories and defeats.

But back to Colin Vaughan: he is not alone in seeing basic similarities between contemporary teenagers and their predecessors. The British criminologist Geoffrey Pearson reached a similar conclusion and made it the starting point for his own investigation of the nature of the "youth problem" in the United Kingdom. His book, entitled *Hooligan* (1983), begins with an examination of contemporary (mid-1970s) press coverage of youth (mis)behaviour and finds a now familiar concern with a juvenile crime problem that seemingly has no precedent, the prescribed solution for which is sought in stiffer punishments for young offenders. Furthermore, the troubled present is compared with an apparently more tranquil past. Contemporary media commentators and politicians were able to recall a time—roughly twenty years earlier—when young people were not out of control, schools were still able to exert authority over the young, family values were intact, parents were more willing and able to supervise their children, police were not handcuffed by petty bureaucratic rules, and when the courts were able to administer appropriately severe punishments.

Intrigued by this rosy view of the 1950s, Pearson then examines newspaper coverage of youth behaviour from that time. And what do you imagine he finds? Virtually the same concerns and arguments expressed in roughly the same language! In the 1950s juvenile crime was seen as a new and disturbing problem; the youth of the nation was being corrupted by post-war affluence, and so forth. Again, there was a harking back to a time, twenty years earlier, when young people had not been a problem. Proceeding in this manner, Pearson delves further and further back into British history, trying to find a time when youthful deviance was not a source of anxiety. Always the crime-free "golden age" is reckoned to be twenty years prior to the present, and therefore remains a perpetually elusive utopia.

What are the sociological implications of Pearson's observations? First, and most obviously, societal anxieties about the delinquent activity of youth have a long pedigree: there is very little that is new about our current concerns with swarming, youth gangs, or violence in schools. As we shall see, our Victorian forebears were scarcely less concerned about unsupervised and uncontrolled youth on the streets than we are today. Second, the myth of the "good old days" influences our thinking about and prescriptions for contemporary juvenile offenders: if delinquency was once less of a problem than it is now, then today's problems can be solved by doing what they did yesterday. The usual assumption is that juveniles were punished more harshly in the past—and that is the reason why delinquency was less of a problem (Bernard, 1992:13). Third, and relatedly, studying reactions to delinquent behaviour is as important a task for students of crime as studying the behaviour itself.

This is partially a matter of acknowledging that how we respond to youth—what we celebrate, tolerate, or condemn—tells us much about society's moral boundaries. But more importantly, studying our reactions to delinquency alerts us to the fact that objective social conditions alone do not give rise to social problems such as crime and deviance.

Over the past several decades sociologists have pondered the nature of social problems and the reality of the threat that they pose to society. The traditional argument is that delinquency is a problem because the anti-social behaviour of adolescents is dangerous and damaging to persons and property within the community. This might be called an objectivist approach to social problems. In the case of deviance, its focus is upon norm-violating behaviour, particularly behaviour that is evaluated negatively because of the harm and injury that it causes.

From a second, more recent perspective, delinquency is a problem because it has been defined or labelled as such by some people. This is referred to as a constructionalist approach to social problems, and its proponents believe "that our sense of what is or is not a social problem is a product, something that has been produced or construed through social activities. When activists hold a demonstration to attract attention to some social condition, when investigative reports publish stories that expose new aspects of the condition, or when legislators introduce bills to do something about the conditions, they are constructing a social problem (Best, 1989:xviii).

MEDIA PORTRAYALS OF YOUTH DEVIANCE

The way in which the mass media present news stories about youth is an obvious example of the process described above. As Pearson's study suggests, media reports on youth invariably focus upon disreputable behaviour, a preoccupation confirmed by another British study. A content analysis of a sample of national and local newspapers revealed that the vast bulk of youth stories had a negative orientation in that they concentrated disproportionately on deviant activities (Porteous and Colston, 1980, cited in Muncie, 1984).

While no equivalent Canadian study has been conducted, two researchers have reported on a brief review of the *Toronto Star* during the first week of December 1990. They found that on each day of the week, at least one story managed to link youth with crime. And as you would probably have guessed, the incidents that these stories dealt with did not include the pilferage of Mars bars from "7-Eleven" stores or other trivial offences; they focused instead upon spectacular but atypical crimes of violence, such as "drive-by shootings" . . .

The media are also keenly interested in youth gang activity, and the way in which the Canadian print media cover gang stories has been the subject of a recent study carried out under the auspices of the Ministry of the Solicitor General (Fasiolo and Leckie, 1993). The authors analyzed daily news stories about gangs over a four-month period from July 1992 to October 1992, focusing on how gangs were characterized in the Canadian print media. They found that 77 percent of stories emanate from five cities: Vancouver, Montreal, Calgary, Ottawa, and Toronto. Rather than being precipitated by any specific event, gang stories in all regions of the country began life as part of a generally growing sense of concern about the gang problem in Canada.

Content analysis included the type of gang mentioned in news stories. Here there were regional variations: for everywhere except Quebec, the most frequently cited type was the Asian gang. In Quebec, the concern about gangs was not related to any specific racial group. The researchers also looked at details of gang activity as identified in news stories. They found that while gangs were associated with a broad sweep of criminal activity, their most common ventures were related to drugs, homicide, and extortion.

The origins or causes of gangs were not mentioned in the majority of stories. However, if and when explanations of rising gang activity were discussed or alluded to, the two most commonly occurring precursive factors were, tellingly, immigration and the condition of the economy. It seems likely, therefore, that, at least in English-speaking Canada, concern about Asian gangs is ultimately linked to race and immigration.

Supplementing the quantitative analysis with a qualitative reading of the news stories, the researchers identified a number of recurring themes and patterns. While this is seldom made explicit, the news stories imply that gangs are new and unique. Their depiction as a modern phenomenon emerges in a number of ways. First, they are seen as a consequence of profound social changes and economic uncertainties in modern society. Second, and relatedly, they are viewed as product of changing social values that are held responsible for increasing youth violence. Occasionally, the claim that gangs are a new phenomenon is given a statistical reference; for example, the *Ottawa Citizen* claimed on October 17, 1992, that while as recently as two years previously there were no youth gangs in the nation's capital, there are now thirteen.

According to the newspaper sources, gangs are not only new, they are also widespread. This assertion does not, however, relate well to actual patterns of youthful behaviour. Further, police action may actually contribute to the incidence of gangs. One newspaper article describes how a police department set up a telephone hotline to abort the emergence of youth gangs which existed in the community at that time. As Fasiolo and Leckie point out, such preventative action is more likely to stimulate gang activity than to deter it, a theme that I will be returning to in a moment. The qualitative analysis also reveals that gangs are depicted as a threat to society, a belief manifested in the headlines used to introduce the accompanying stories.

The final ingredient found in the vitriolic coverage of gangs in Canada is the focus on race. Most gangs are distinguished in media reports according to their racial or ethnic composition. Particularly when blanket terms are used— such as the constant reference to Asian gangs—this tendency results in polarized images of "us" (the law-abiding majority) and "them" (a minority of racially distinctive youthful gangsters). The authors quote a vivid example from an editorial in the *Calgary Sun*:

> For only when *they* [Asian gangs] live in fear that *our* investigators will almost
> certainly uncover *their* nefarious deeds, *our* courts will certainly find *them* guilty,
> and *our* prisons await *them*, will *they* stay away from *our* shores. *We* must let the
> purveyors of these obscenities know that *their* filth is not welcome in *our* city or
> in *our* province. (Fasiolo and Leckie, 1993:25, emphasis in original)

What makes this practice of identifying Asian gang activity so insidious is that there is no corresponding tendency to link the criminal activities of Caucasian youth to their racial or ethnic origins.

The common sense view about the relationship between the mass media and youth crime is that the journalists who write the stories that attract our attention in the newspaper or on the nightly newscasts are simply recording events as they unfold. According to this argument, media accounts about youth crime provide a more or less faithful reflection of an objectively existing social problem (Muncie, 1984; Surette, 1992). However, media organizations do much more than just report the facts. Whether they realize it or not, journalists shape how their readers, viewers, listeners feel and think about the behaviour of youth. Research on media institutions indicates that the news that we consume is the result of a selection process. Items for inclusion in news reports compete for time and space; stories about deviant youth have an advantage in this competitive process because they are deemed highly "newsworthy" (Muncie, 1984).

In his study of "law and order" news, the British sociologist Steve Chibnall (1977) identified a number of informal criteria (or rules) that are regularly used by journalists as the basis for story selection. These include visible and spectacular incidents, and possible political and sexual connotations. Chibnall's study also suggests that similar decisions are made about how crime stories are to be presented: how many photographs are going to accompany a story, and which ones; what headlines are going to be used, and so forth.

One common strategy is to introduce a story with a dramatic example. Here is an illustration used by Joel Best; it comes from the *Los Angeles Times* and concerns a gang intervention program in that city:

> Everything about him said it was no big deal: How he kicked back in his chair. How he tossed his blue gang-rag on the table in the interrogation room. Threatening to kill a woman—so what?
>
> The woman was a sixth-grade teacher. The suspect, the case-hardened veteran sitting across from Detective Jeffrey Greer, was 11 years old.
>
> "I thought that was, like, the worst," Greer remembered thinking. (Morrison, 1988:I–1; quoted by Best (1989:1)

This is what journalists refer to as a "grabber." As Best says, it captures the reader's attention by connecting, in this example, the broader problem of "gang warfare" to the specific image of a remorseless pre-adolescent. As he also points out, the message being relayed to the reader is not that this case is typical; rather, it is literally a worst-case scenario. Readers are given a sense of the growing magnitude of the youth gang problem.

These comments are not meant to suggest that the media invent or fabricate news stories about youth deviance, or that the problems of delinquency and crime would suddenly stop if journalists stopped writing about them (Muncie, 1984:20). Rather, the main point to be made about the reporting and presentation of youth stories is that they exaggerate and sensationalize events and situations, often presenting atypical cases as representative, and in so doing, they construct a problematic image of youth that does not always correspond to actual behaviour.

If media reports had no effect upon how their audiences view deviance, this discussion would be interesting but of no real consequence. But research suggests that media presentations of crime issues affect public perceptions of the criminal justice system. For instance, surveys conducted for the Canadian Sentencing Commission found that members of the public overestimated the amount of crime in Canada; believed that rates of recidivism are higher, and that maximum sentencing penalties are lower than they really are; and underestimated the severity of penalties routinely administered. . . .

Tellingly, the majority (95 percent) of respondents also revealed that they derived their knowledge about crime in Canada predominately from the mass media. The Commission also found—as have several American studies—that violent crime is overrepresented in news stories about crime. In fact, stories reporting that by the time a young person graduates from high school, he or she will have been witness to "x" number of both real and fictional stabbings, shootings, murders, and so forth, have become something of a cliché. *Time* magazine, in a cover story on "Our Violent Kids" (June 12, 1989), has put that figure in the United States at 200,000 (Acland, 1995:14, 147). Violent crime is actually more likely to appear in print and broadcast items than in real life! This has a predictable effect: the Canadian public believes that crimes of violence form a much higher proportion of the total volume of crime than they really do (Roberts and Doob, 1990). Reliance on the news media for information about crime therefore intensifies fear of crime, promotes negative evaluations of the criminal justice system, and encourages support for more punitive crime-control policies (Surette, 1992).

YOUTH AND MORAL PANICS

The mass media have also been held responsible for creating particularly exaggerated fears about youth problems, fears which have been referred to as "moral panics" (Cohen, 1973). Cohen coined this term after witnessing clashes between rival groups of "mods" and "rockers" on the beaches of England in the mid-1960s and analyzing media interpretations of those events. Media coverage was, in fact, intense, driven by a combination of fear, anxiety, and moral outrage about what this episode said about the condition of the British nation.

Cohen concluded—like Pearson before him—that many of the claims made about delinquent youth had been made before and were, in fact, part of a repetitive cycle in which the mass media were heavily involved:

> Societies appear to be subject, every now and then, to periods of moral panic. A condition, episode, person or group of persons emerges to become defined as a threat to societal values and interests; its nature is presented in stylized and stereotypical fashion by the mass media; the moral barricades are manned by editors, bishops, politicians and other right-thinking people; socially accredited experts pronounce their diagnoses and solutions; ways of coping are evolved or (more often) resorted to; the condition then disappears, submerges or deteriorates and becomes more invisible. Sometimes the object of the panic is quite novel and at other times it is something which has been in existence long enough, but suddenly appears in the limelight. Sometimes the panic passes over and is forgotten, except in folklore and collective memory; at other times it has more serious and long-lasting repercussions and might produce such changes as those in legal and social policy or even in the way the society conceives of itself. (Cohen, 1973:9)

According to Cohen, societies suffer from moral panic attacks at times of profound, but scarcely understood, social change, when established values and beliefs are believed to be threatened. "Folk devils"—witches in seventeenth-century New England, mods and rockers in mid-twentieth-century (Old) England—are identified as external threats to established values and institutions against whom "normal society" can unite and rally.

Moral panics frequently involve youth because their successful socialization into conformist behaviour is made problematic by a susceptibility to antisocial influences. They tend to occur when the major agencies of socialization (the family, the school system) appear to be breaking down: when young people are seemingly out of control. In Cohen's analysis, for instance, the fights between the mods and the rockers were seen by media commentators as a consequence of too much affluence, too much leisure, and the end of compulsory military training (national service). Post-war changes had weakened the influence of traditional authority (as vested in family, school, and religion), and gang fights at seaside resorts were one highly visible result.

As the case of the mods and rockers shows, in Britain the deviant and delinquent behaviour of working-class youth is most likely to inspire moral panics, particularly if their activities include violence and aggression. Often the disreputable activities of youth are traced back to the corrupting influences of popular entertainment and culture—an argument that has a long pedigree (Sacco and Kennedy, 1994:215).

In Victorian times, it was believed that crime melodramas available in cheap theatres would induce imitative behaviour among their young working-class audiences. In the course of the twentieth century, rising rates of youthful crime have been linked at different times to the spread of horror and crime comics, dimestore novels, gangster movies, rock and roll, and, more recently, video nasties. However, the most common focus is television. Our current concern with Ninja Turtles and Mighty Morphin Power Rangers reflects a prevailing belief that the mass media exerts a powerful and negative effect upon a young and impressionable audience, resulting in high rates of youthful crime particularly violent crime (Barrat, 1986; Murdock, 1982).

THE INVENTION OF ADOLESCENCE AND DELINQUENCY

If, as I am suggesting, there is a gap between the perception and reality of adolescent deviance, then what factors have encouraged the view that youth is a particularly troubling and problematic stage in the life cycle? Why do images of trouble and deviance colour so many people's understandings of adolescence?

The answer to these questions can be found in changes in the economic and social organization of society that have occurred over the past 200 or so years and that have had the cumulative effect of removing the young from adult society. The problematic image of modern youth is a consequence of their emergence as a separate and distinctive age-based social category.

Given the contemporary preoccupation with the transgressions, both real and imagined, of juveniles, it is hard to conceive of a time when the young were not so collectively burdened with the stigma of deviance. Yet the fact is that before the middle of the nineteenth century they were rarely a subject of public concern. For instance, the word "adolescence"—so much a part of contemporary discourse about the young—was rarely used outside of scientific writings before the turn of the century (Kett, 1971:97). Modern assumptions about youth—particularly the idea that young people are naturally inclined toward rebellion and nonconformity—are of relatively recent vintage; their origins can be traced back to the modern world created by the industrial revolution of the eighteenth and nineteenth centuries. Prior to that time no clearly defined intermediate stage between childhood and adulthood existed.

Medieval French children, for instance, often worked alongside adults from the age of 7 onwards; this egalitarian participation in economic activity extended into nonwork time as well. Children were present at, and participated in, all the great ceremonies and rituals of the life cycle—including death—to a degree that would be unheard of today. Children were treated, in effect, as little adults—as indicated by their dress, games, and legal status. Similarly, when they broke the law, and were caught by the authorities, the chronologically young were responded to in the same (or similar) punitive manner as adult offenders. They were neither treated more leniently nor were they placed in separate "juvenile" prisons. The law recognized no meaningful distinction among violators on the basis of age, hence there were no legal designation of delinquency.

What changed all of this? The short answer is that human societies became increasingly age-differentiated as a result of the industrial revolution. The connection between the two events is sometimes made quite explicit, as in Frank Musgrove's observation that "the adolescent was invented at the same time as the steam engine" (Musgrove, 1964:33).

When Musgrove talks about adolescence being invented, or when sociologists discuss the social construction of youth, what they mean is that those intermediary age-based categories that we now take for granted, and use more or less interchangeably, did not exist on any grand scale prior to the transformations ushered in by the industrial era.

At the risk of oversimplifying what was a very complex process, two key transitions associated with industrialization have relevance for arguments about the social construction of adolescence and delinquency: the transition from an agriculturally based economy and society to an industrial one; and the transition from home-based work (the cottage system) to the factory system.

Early versions of the factory system depended upon the relatively simple labour power provided by men, women, and children. However, the development of increasingly sophisticated machine technology, cheaper and more productive than human muscle power, eventually led to the displacement of large number of workers; the subsequent labour surplus resulted in plunging wage rates. In the face of competition for scarce jobs from cheap child labour, male factory workers, through their trade unions, campaigned to restrict the employment of children in the mines and factories. A similar goal was simultaneously sought by other individuals and groups. Albeit for very different reasons. Humanitarian reformers opposed the hiring of children on the grounds that the conditions and terms of employment in the factory system were sufficiently harsh and exploitative that the young should not be subjected to them. This alliance of male industrial workers and humanitarian reformers secured the passage of legislation that checked the use of child labour. As the nineteenth century progressed, the streets of major Canadian, American, and European cities were, therefore, filled with the unemployed young, now displaced from the production system.

In order to survive, they needed to steal. The urban milieu facilitated this objective by bringing the impoverished young into contact both with their potential victims and with other youth with whom they could forge predatory networks. What subsequently became recognized as juvenile delinquency was originally property crime committed on city streets by young working-class males directed against upper-class adults. For the first time in history, thanks to industrialization and urbanization, property crime had become the main form of criminal activity in society; and most of it was committed by young people (Bernard, 1992). This is not to suggest that all of the activities of nineteenth-century "street youth" were criminal. Working (selling newspapers and matches, and so on) and playing were more important.

Nonetheless, their work and leisure activities disturbed middle-class observers—reformers, clergymen, journalists—who deplored the morally corrupting lifestyle in which they were engaged. The introduction of compulsory education was one means of controlling street urchins and providing the sort of moral training and direction that was lacking in their home lives.

These concerns were particularly acute in Canada because Great Britain had utilized this country as a dumping ground for the orphans and destitute of its own cities. Between the 1860s and 1920s, Britain exported 90,000 children to Canada (Bean and Melville, 1989). Their presence was something of a mixed blessing. On the one hand, they solved a perennial problem facing Canadian farmers—the shortage of cheap labour. While it is doubtless the case that some children's lives were improved immeasurably by their involuntary migration to the New World, many others were ruthlessly exploited. They often worked a 16-hour day on isolated homesteads, were badly abused, and never saw their families or native country again. As one contemporary participant put it: "Adoption, sir, is when folks get a girl to work without wages" (Sutherland, 1976:10).

Nonetheless, the presence of these children in Canada was not an alloyed blessing. The economic advantages of cheap labour were offset by law and order considerations. Their origins as members of an impoverished underclass made them particularly vulnerable to the lure of criminal life. Likewise, their early experiences rendered them a source of contamination, spreading criminal values throughout Canada's major cities.

THE JUVENILE DELINQUENTS ACT OF 1908

The official history of juvenile delinquency in Canada begins in 1908. Following similar legislative initiatives in the United States and Great Britain, the first piece of legislation pertaining specifically to juveniles was passed in that year. The *Juvenile Delinquents Act* had the deliberate effect of legislating the distinction, which we now take for granted, between adult and young offenders. A separate juvenile court and a probation service were two of its most enduring features.

The legislative intent of the reformers was two-fold. First, they felt that treating old and young criminals alike was inhumane: the indiscriminate use of harsh punishment violated, to use the modern parlance, the civil rights of the young. Second, reacting to juvenile offenders as hardened criminals and placing them in adult prisons extinguished any possibility of reform. Unlike adult criminals—who were largely beyond redemption—there was still hope that inner-city street youth could be saved. On the one hand, therefore, the young were seen as being particularly prone to crime and deviance, but on the other hand, they were viewed as being most conducive to reform.

Applying these ideas resulted in legislation that not only targeted a diverse set of conditions—law-breaking, pauperism, and dependency—but also a wide range of prohibited acts. The *Juvenile Delinquents Act* in Canada, and its counterpart in other parts of the English-speaking world, ensured that young people got in trouble with the law for a much larger number of offences than did adult offenders. While some youth crime was the same as adult crime (robbery, assault, theft), there were other offences for which young people, and young people alone, were liable to arrest, punishment, and treatment (Frith, 1985). These latter violations are known collectively as status offences. They included the consumption of alcohol, truancy, running away from home, refusal to obey parents, having delinquent friends, and the use of profanity activities which were illegal solely because the individuals who engaged in them were underage.[1] The broad scope of what counted as delinquency is evident in revisions to the original Act, passed in 1924. According to the law, a delinquent was:

> any child who violates any provision of the *Criminal Code* or of any Dominion or provincial statute, or of any by-law or ordinance of any municipality, or who is guilty of sexual immorality or any similar form of vice, or who is liable by reason of any other act to be committed to an industrial school or juvenile reformatory under the provisions of any Dominion or provincial statute. (quoted in West, 1984:33)

The age of minimal legal responsibility was kept at 7, while the upper age limit (i.e., the age at which a young offender became an adult offender) varied according to province: 16 in Ontario, Alberta, New Brunswick, Nova Scotia, P.E.I., the Yukon, Saskatchewan, and the North West Territories; 17 in British Columbia and Newfoundland; and 18 in Manitoba and Quebec.

The most severe sentence the juvenile court could impose was institutionalization in a training school, where the emphasis was upon discipline and character training. It is also worth noting that, along with a broad definition of delinquency, judges were granted considerable discretion regarding the punishment that wrong-doers should receive, the severity of which was determined, not by the seriousness of the offence, but the "needs" of the offender—as decided by judges and probation officers (West, 1984).

ADOLESCENTS, DELINQUENCY, AND YOUTH CULTURE

While the history of delinquency begins with nineteenth-century street youth, the concerns aroused by their public behaviour quickly spread to include all adolescent activity. In the view of prominent Victorian opinion-makers, the nature of adolescence made all young people susceptible, or vulnerable, to the lures of delinquency.

From the beginning, adolescence has never been merely a transitional stage between childhood and adulthood. It has invariably been seen as a time of turmoil and conflict. Academics writing at the turn of the century are primarily responsible for this viewpoint. These experts—mainly psychologists and psychiatrists—were of the opinion that every young person skirted with delinquency because rebellion was a natural and universal characteristic of this intermediary stage in the life cycle.

The person most closely identified with this interpretation of adolescence was a prominent pioneer psychologist, G. Stanley Hall, a man much influenced by the work of Charles Darwin and his thesis regarding the biological evolution of the species. Hall argued that just as the human species as a whole passed through a series of stages in its development, so too did each individual human being. The human species and its individual units thus evolved through conditions of early animal primitivism into refined, civilized, mature entities. Paralleling Darwin's designation of an intermediate stage in the evolution of the species, Hall identified a similar phase in individual development: adolescence, a time of "sturm and drang" (storm and stress) that Hall felt corresponded to an equally unstable and tumultuous phase in the development of human civilization. Hall similarly allowed the biological doctrine of recapitulation to mould his views on the origins of juvenile delinquency, which he saw as the outcome of a clash between the "savage" inclinations of youth and the civilizing influences of society (Kett, 1977:255).

His prognostications unleashed a series of books on the adolescent years and inspired a coterie of experts prepared to counsel on the problem of youth. His assertions about the "natural" sources of adolescent rebellion were quickly and eagerly embraced by the educators and welfare workers of the day and had a significant effect upon the development of a justice system that caters specifically for the needs of those who are no longer children but not yet adults. Moreover, and not coincidentally, Hall's storm and stress model of adolescence informed other unfolding debates about rising juvenile crime, the effects of popular entertainment, and the relationship between the two (Murdock, 1982:64).

Hall and the psychologists who followed him operated with a view of adolescence that concentrated on the inborn inclination of young people toward problematic behaviour. Although they focused upon structural and cultural factors rather than individualistic ones—adolescence was a social as well as a personal experience—the early sociologists shared the same problem-centred view of their subject matter.

In the 1940s, sociologists began to draw attention to the growing importance of a separate, subsociety of adolescence; the premier American sociologist of the day, Talcott Parsons, referred to this "society within a society" as a "youth culture" (1942). Parsons was the leading light of the then dominant sociological paradigm of functionalism. However, it was left to other sociologists working within the same functionalist paradigm to enlarge upon the origins and nature of youth culture. The fullest flowering of the functionalist view was provided by S.M. Eisenstadt (1956). For Eisenstadt, youth culture was an outcome of disruptions in the transition from childhood to adulthood, characteristic of industrial society, and manifested as generational differences and conflicts. Let us elaborate.

Functionalists view social institutions as a set of interrelated parts that contribute to the smooth functioning of the whole. Hence, the function of the family is to equip children with an understanding of the basic norms of society, and the function of the educational system is to prepare the young for their future occupational roles. Successful fulfillment of the tasks allocated to society's various component institutions leads to strong social integration; weak integration leads to conflict. Intergenerational conflict is seen as a consequence of a poor fit—weak integration—between age-groups and society; weak integration, and hence generational conflict, is seen as being particularly pronounced in advanced industrial societies because of the problematic nature of the transition from childhood to adulthood.

Industrialization has ruptured the transitional process because an increasingly complex and constantly evolving division of labour has meant that appropriate job skills cannot be taught informally in the bosom of the immediate family. As a result, the preparation for future adult work roles has been transferred from the nuclear family setting to specialized educational institutions.

The elongated training period required for occupational roles and the absence of a ritual that publicly acknowledges the arrival of adulthood are seen as creating ambiguities and uncertainties for the young regarding their role and status in society. Their exclusion from adult work roles and subsequent confinement in a separate educational institution has cultivated a collective sense of marginality and distinctiveness.

It is the gap between what the family is no longer capable of delivering (occupational skills and training) and what an increasingly complex economy requires (specialized and extended periods of occupational training in educational institutions) that gives rise to autonomous youth groups. As one interpreter of Eisenstadt's functionalist argument has expressed it: "Peer groups are the bridge between childhood and adulthood when society is complex enough that attainment of full adult status cannot be insured in the family unit" . . .

Other factors have only served to make youth groups and youth culture even more important in the years following the Second World War. First, the massive increase in the birth rate after 1945—the "baby boom"—meant that the young made up an increasingly large proportion of the total population. Second, and as one would expect, the baby boom had a huge impact upon the schools, colleges, and universities of most Western nations. More and more young people were spending increasingly protracted periods of time in the educational system, where they interacted more or less exclusively with their age peers. The commonality and age-specific character of their experiences engendered a collective self-consciousness among them regarding their distinctive location in society.

These feelings were, in turn, reinforced by a second factor: the machinations of the growing teenage leisure industry, which was not slow to realize that the young constituted a new and largely untapped market. For the first time ever, goods, services, and entertainment—popular music in particular—were pitched specifically at the expanding youth population. Appealing to what were felt to be universal age-specific needs, emotions, and experiences, the youth-oriented leisure industries helped nurture a view of the young as a unique, distinctive, and homogeneous social category.

For many adults, the preoccupations of youth—new music, new fashions, new dances, fast cars, fast food—spell trouble: more and more "ordinary" adolescents "looked and behaved like Juvenile Delinquents" (Gilbert, 1986:17). High school was where ordinary adolescents ("teenagers") were increasingly forced to rub shoulders with the more obviously delinquent. As clear-cut distinctions between deviancy and conformity started to break down, the term "teenager" (invented at about the same time as "youth culture," in the 1940s) became increasingly interchangeable with, and indistinguishable from, delinquency. This development is nicely illustrated by an (apparently) popular joke of the time in which one suburban housewife tells another: "My husband was two hours getting home the other night. Oh, my God, I thought, the teenagers have got him" (Murdock and McCron, 1976:18).

Parallels between Gilbert's work and Pearson's discussion of the hooligan problem in British history have been noted by Brannigan (1987). He argues that moral panics about youth and delinquency grew out of post-war changes that saw adult society losing confidence in their ability to control the cultural activities of their teenage offspring. In the United States, in particular, it was felt that the developing financial independence of teenagers was creating a ready market for "Youth Culture," the content and behavioural directions of which parents were ill-equipped to manage. A major source of discretionary income for teenagers noted by Gilbert were part-time jobs.

Gilbert was not, however, the first person to notice similarities between delinquency and youth culture. David Matza had earlier (1961) made a similar observation, but with an important twist: rather than encouraging or facilitating delinquent activity, the growth and spread of youth culture had moderated the severity of adolescent deviance.

His starting point is the by now familiar one that the aforementioned conditions of modern life make young people prone to rebelliousness of various sorts. While delinquency is its most recognizable and most enduringly threatening form, it is not the only one; student radicalism and Bohemianism are other types that have occasionally proven attractive to largely middle-class youth.

However, Matza's thesis is that only a small number of adolescents engage in serious deviancy. The majority of young people are either not deviant at all, or engage in what he calls conventional versions of deviant youth traditions. Matza holds that delinquency (along with radicalism and Bohemianism) are subterranean traditions in American life, and that youth culture is little more than a cleaned-up, less serious form of the delinquent tradition. What delinquency and youth culture share is a similar spirit: a commitment to a leisure ethic rather than a work ethic; a disdain for the regularities and routine of school and work; and a general striving for excitement, thrills, and kicks. Where they differ is that youth culture stops short of serious illegality in pursuit of these goals. In practical terms, this means that the consumption of alcohol, sexual experimentation, and "partying" is OK, but that stealing, robbery, and physical assault are not—which brings us to the hub of Matza's argument. He concedes that for some adolescents involvement in youth culture serves as a preparation for more serious delinquent careers; but for most, it has a preventative and restorative function.

NOTE

1. Status offences have been formally eliminated from the new *Young Offenders Act*. However, it still appears that young offenders, particularly female ones, are subject to judicial intervention for a much broader range of wrongdoings that are adults (Bell, 1994).

Chapter 25

STYLE AND RESISTANCE IN THE PUNK SUBCULTURE

Stephen W. Baron

THERE IS NO KNOWN SOCIETY WITHOUT CRIME AND DEVIANCE, NOR ANY KNOWN society without rules and control. To Emile Durkheim, this fact suggested the normality—even the necessity—of crime and deviance. By provoking a punitive response, crime and deviance strengthen conformity to the existing rules. They also pull everyone together behind the police and other agents of control.

The same fact also suggests the sheer "everydayness" of deviance. A deviant act that seems, at first glance, to be odd or even bizarre soon turns out to be much like the most ordinary of events. No wonder, then, that with the discovery of deviant subcultures, criminology turned from an interest in social and personal pathologies to the study of competing images of the world.

This excerpt on West Coast punks provides a case in point. As in any other small group with its own culture, the members of this one dress, act, and talk in ways that foster group cohesion. They are rejecting dominant society and simultaneously provoking reactions by the dominant society, which strengthen the group's own boundaries. The group offers its members social support, activities to pass the time, and social status that is otherwise unavailable.

Neo-Marxists suggest that adolescent subcultures demonstrate their resistance to the dominant order through style or physical appearance. Accordingly, style allows members to "display" their opposition in "visual" terms for the general public to witness (Brake, 1980, 1985; Hall et al., 1976; Hebdige, 1979; Muncie, 1981). My respondents felt that their style was an individual creation, a representation of their feelings and attitudes. There was no admission of imitation.

These punks were very serious about the lifestyle they adopted. Style was not something to be embraced and discarded at certain times of the day, but represented an extension of the member. It became clear from the observation of members discussing new objects of style they would like to obtain and the excitement members displayed as they showed off new objects that considerable thought was put into the constructing of style. For example:

> It's the only fucking thing that I can identify with. I fucking hate people. I don't like people so I segregate myself as much as I can. The only way I feel comfortable about myself is the way that I dress. If I dressed like a preppie I'd feel like a goof because I wouldn't be dressing the way that I believe.
>
> The most creative and intellectual people I've found, and artsy people, are the people that dress differently. Like it reflects their personality. . . . I've found there's more expression in the friends I've chosen around here.

These responses reflect [a] libertarian "do your own thing" outlook. This sense of individuality discourages any group action. However, by refusing to dress in a certain manner, members criticized the dominant order. Punk style is the antithesis of "dressing for success." In fact, their style disqualifies them from even the low-wage, menial labour for which most are qualified. They refuse to fulfill the requirements of conventional society. In doing so they resist the dominant order, but in a way that does not depend upon collective solidarity.

The homologous nature of the subculture discussed by neo-Marxists also reflects resistance. "Homology" refers to the adoption of objects that correspond, reflect, or "possess" the values of the members (Brake, 1980, 1985; Hall et al., 1976; Muncie, 1981). The members were very conscious of style as a kind of self-representation, particularly as expression of attitudes and feelings regarding school, the family, and politics. Clear evidence of this is found in the slogans that the members decorated their clothes with, the rips and tears that depicted the poverty that many members were experiencing, the dark colours and work shirts that displayed their despair. "Bricolage" was also seen to be taking place. Bricolage refers to the transference of meaning that must occur before an object can be assimilated into the style (Brake, 1980, 1985; Hall et al., 1976; Muncie, 1981). Members took objects available in mainstream culture and altered their definitions to suit subcultural style. For example, male members took jean jackets and tore and decorated them with slogans. This process altered the definition of the jacket as a mere clothing item sold for profit to a personal expression of attitudes that at the same time represented the poverty and violence of the subculture. However, the style could only offer symbolic resistance to the dominant order and further offered no solutions to the problems which members encountered outside the subculture. Like the subcultural participation itself, the solution was, as British theorists argue, "magical." That is, punk style allowed members to escape their structural locations for a period, but offered no real solution to structural problems.

The importance of style to members was revealed through their descriptions of subcultural change. Members characterized the subculture as becoming "trendy" through the fashion industry. However, when questioned if they were "trendy," the response was always negative. There was so much criticism from members about "outsiders," referred to as "poseurs," who had adopted the punk style. Poseurs were criticized for adopting the punk style without adopting the accompanying attitudes and lifestyle. The poseurs were seen as adopting the style for reasons of social status rather than commitment to being a "real" punk:

> The poseurs and stuff like that kind of bother me. They go, yeah, like I'm a punk rocker, go home to mommy and daddy and have dinner, come downtown, change my clothes and be a punk rocker until 8:30 until I have to catch my bus right. I don't know, they miss the whole point of what it's supposed to be.
>
> Then there's the people out here on the street who sit around today, with a haircare. They're there for attention. Oh that's real cool man. They cause shit for everyone else . . . I mean nobody knows them . . . on the whole they don't have any idea what they're doing.

Poseurs embody the sanitization and attempted neutralization of the subculture through popular culture (see Gottdiener, 1985; Muncie, 1981; Ramirez, 1986). The products enable youth to adopt the style without actually participating in the subcultural lifestyle. The sanitized style leads them to be labelled poseurs, to be denied membership, and to be made targets for abuse. Thus, the potential dilution of punk by popular culture industries is resisted by subculture members.

A central aspect of the punk style is punk music. Lyrically, punk rock or "hard core" describes the problems and expresses the anger of youth while at the same time offering a critique of the dominant order. The music itself appears to represent the anger and frustration of its listeners. Neo-Marxists point to punk music as an important element in raising the political consciousness of youth (Frith, 1978a, 1978b, 1983; Laing, 1985; Levine and Stumpf, 1983; Marsh, 1977). Members of the local subculture also listen to speed metal (sometimes referred to as thrash or speed core) and death rock. The former can be described as a hybrid between punk and heavy metal. Like punk it is loud and fast, although it dwells on satanic themes as well as social issues. These themes, as with those in punk, can be seen as an attempt to offend, shock, and attack the mainstream. Death rock, sometimes called funeral music, is slower and dwells on more melancholy themes. Every member of the subculture responded that they had a great interest in music. They also felt that music was a central aspect of the subculture. The following are examples of members' responses:

> Well it's really powerful and straightforward. It's got something to say, most of it. I mean if it doesn't have something to say, then it's humourous or stupid. I'm pissed off; everyone listens to hardcore now. They don't know what it's about.
>
> I like hardcore a lot . . . I don't like idiotic stuff, though, like Venom and stuff. I like lyrics that actually say something and music that makes you want to beat up somebody.

The responses indicate that the music was homologous with members' attitudes. However, . . . the channeling of dissent through music may be able to raise or reflect political consciousness, but cannot precipitate political action.

Also part of subcultural style is a creative element. Most members were involved in some sort of creative activity, such as music, art, poetry, and short stories. Members developed individuality and expressed feelings through this nonalienating creativity. Creative expression was also another form of resistance, allowing members to display their displeasure with the dominant order. Again this mode of resistance is individualized and libertarian, each member tackles his/her experience his/her own way, and thus does not encourage collective politics. This results in a muted resistance expressed almost exclusively to other members:

> I think a lot of it comes out more. I figure a lot of the people that hang out here have problems in their life or, you know. Or they feel they have problems and it's a way of getting rid of them or explaining them by drawing or writing music or whatever.
>
> They have an outlet I can relate to. I may not be able to do it, like art, but I can relate to it because it's an outlet of what someone is trying to say and that's why people are so tight. We do have a family because everyone is showing what they're feeling inside by their artwork or their music or whatever, right.

On the face of it, these "creative" aspects would seem to support the notion that the punk phenomenon is partly "bohemian" in nature as has been suggested by some British researchers. Frith (1978a, 1978b, 1983) argues that punk is the first post-WWII working-class bohemianism. Brake (1985) and Muncie (1981) argue that part of the punk subculture is made up of middle-class art students. These students' leisure is lower class (the leisure of the streets), not their class location. For Brake this artist membership explains the presence of a libertarian resistance. He argues that a cultural rebellion by artists cannot be seen as political because artists have always been considered rebellious. Furthermore, artists are seldom organized and are libertarian rather than socialist or communist (Brake, 1985; Dancis, 1978; Frith, 1978a, 1978b, 1983).

Certainly the members of the local subculture display a libertarian resistance. However, the delinquent behaviours of some members (including theft, scams, violent crimes, and violence against other subcultures) make the bohemian label inappropriate. The fact that for many of the members, the street is, or has been, their home again suggests that the bohemian interpretation is flawed.

Since punk appears to contain both delinquent and bohemian elements, it seems more accurate to interpret it as a hybrid of "bohemian youth culture" and "delinquent youth culture." Scholars have tended to make clear distinctions between these two types of culture. "Delinquent youth culture" focuses on leisure because the members are marginal to the labour market (Young, 1971: 1944). "Bohemian youth culture" is focused on leisure because its members reject the labour market (Young, 1971: 147). Certainly the members of the punk subculture refuse the opportunities available, but many have restricted opportunities. Further, those members whose opportunities do not appear restricted in real terms have adopted delinquent patterns in their resistance that go well beyond "artistic" rebellion. In sum, although members resort to a libertarian resistance, and display this resistance through creative means, the delinquent aspects point to a cross between delinquent and bohemian cultures.

ALTERNATIVE STATUS

I have demonstrated that the members' problems, objectively rooted at a macro level, can not be solved because of [the] subculture's individual, often idiosyncratic, methods of resistance. The problems are addressed only at the "magical" level. That is, members do not attempt to address their problems in a manner in which change could be fostered but rather through symbolic resistance. However, the importance of status through membership, and the support for resistance within the subculture cannot be underestimated.

Both the functionalist and neo-Marxist theorists believe that the counter-norm developed in subcultures, and the criteria for status that emerge from these, enable members to gain a positive self-image (Brake, 1980, 1985; Cloward et al., 1960; A. Cohen, 1955; Hall et al., 1976; Hebdige, 1979; Muncie, 1981). My findings show that the achievement of status and support for resistance occurs in a variety of ways. Members' attitudes towards other subcultural groups displayed their feelings of superiority, reflecting a positive collective sense of identity. Similarly, the selective initiation that the subculture used to control membership implied that membership was something to be achieved. Not everyone could be a punk. The members also believed that participation was personally beneficial because other members understood their problems. This support allowed members to develop and test identities without fear of rejection, in the process providing them with status via membership. It allowed members to reject the dominant ideology and formulate their own counter-ideology at a personal level.

This is further reinforced by discussions among members about daily survival. The problems that tend to be dealt with inside of the subculture are those concerned with school, relationships with parents and others, housing, and financing. Members could count on others for shelter and money. They realized that it was easier to live in groups than to survive alone. It was not uncommon for those members who received money to use it to feed others. When members moved into residences of their own, this usually meant a number of guests (members) sleeping on their floor when other places to sleep could not be found. The members also provided physical protection for each other.

Participation in violence (and the threat of it) was also a source of status, strengthening members' allegiance for the subculture. It made being a punk even more prestigious and added another requirement for membership. Further, fighting may be seen as a display of masculinity in the male-dominated subculture. Violence may confer status on members that they cannot get through occupational success (Brake, 1980, 1985; Cloward et al., 1960; A. Cohen, 1955; Hall et al., 1976; Muncie, 1981).

These youths are reacting to their structural location based on age and generation. Their attitudes reflect "levels of resistance" to the dominant order. Some members are totally committed to a lifestyle of resistance. They are alienated from dominant goals, rebel at home and school, and live on the streets engaging in illegal activities to survive. At the other end of the spectrum are those who display resistance in only one of these areas (e.g., school), or whose resistance is muted (e.g., live at home).

While the members share common problems that emanate from their location in the labour market, the manner in which they carry out resistance provides few prospects for change. The style of the subculture only displays members' dissatisfaction with their position. The "libertarian consciousness" that fuels resistance is self-muting. Furthermore, the members do not participate in political institutions where change can be fostered. What the subculture does offer is an environment where youths experiencing similar problems can interact. The subculture offers them status where school and employment [do] not. It allows them to escape their low status location for a period of time in what neo-Marxist theorists have termed a "magical" manner.

Subcultural resistance is not without consequences. For many members it means the adoption of marginal socioeconomic locations. Members were forced into squatting, scamming, rolling (i.e., mugging), panhandling, and violence. The harshness of these consequences demonstrate[s] the depth of commitment to the subculture. It also brings to light problems associated with high levels of youth unemployment.

Males tend to adopt the more severe forms of resistance. They have little work experiences and few skills, and face a labour market where there is a declining demand for manual labour. At the same time, they do not desire the employment that is available since the pay is poor, provides little status, and is alienating. For the male, the subculture is an alternative source of status. The others share his problems and by dismissing the dominant ideology he can attain status via subcultural criteria.

Female participation was less severe perhaps because the service sector areas where they are most likely to be employed are still in need of cheap labour. Furthermore, they are still likely to be subject to parental supervision and view the subculture as a social vehicle.

This chapter shows that historical conditions have produced significant delinquent subcultures in Canada. However, the membership in these subcultures is still relatively small in comparison to the number of youths who are exposed to the same problems. If the trend in youth unemployment continues, one would expect that the number of youths participating in delinquent subcultures would increase. Not only should there be more youths who exhibit the severe forms of resistance but an even greater number who exhibit the less extreme forms. However, it is likely that even when conditions worsen, the majority of youth will not enter a delinquent subculture. What may begin to happen is that the young might start to reinterpret their situation. As Frith (1985) notes, one effect of unemployment is that more people than ever are returning to school. This "student" experience allows for the possibility of organization. The alternative to the delinquent subculture may be groups of youths organizing themselves in political interest groups. It may be in this manner that youth realize the political potential that the new subcultural theorists had predicted for delinquent youth subcultures.

Chapter 26

YOUTH COURT STATISTICS 2000/01

Paul deSouza

INTRODUCTION

Providing effective treatment and rehabilitation of young offenders, and ensuring community safety are primary objectives of the youth justice system. The *Young Offenders Act* (YOA), proclaimed in 1984, introduced rights for adolescents previously guaranteed to adults only. It recognized the special needs that youths have as a result of their varying levels of maturity, the necessity for youths to accept responsibility for unlawful action and the right of society to protection from illegal behaviour. In February 2001, the Minister of Justice tabled in Parliament Bill C-7, the *Youth Criminal Justice Act* (YCJA). The proposed legislation is intended to replace the *Young Offenders Act*. Key objectives of the YCJA include: (a) reducing the use of the court by dealing with less serious cases effectively outside the court process; (b) fairness in sentencing; (c) reducing the high rate of youth incarceration; and (d) clearly distinguishing between serious violent offences and less serious offences.

This *Juristat* presents case-based[1] data from the Youth Court Survey (YCS), which is conducted by the Canadian Centre for Justice Statistics (CCJS) in collaboration with provincial and territorial government departments responsible for youth courts. The YCS collects data from youth courts on persons aged 12 to 17, at the time of the offence, appearing on federal statute offences. In this report, federal statute offences include *Criminal Code* offences, *Drug* offences, offences against the *Young Offenders Act* (YOA), and all *Other federal statute* offences. All youth courts in Canada have reported to the YCS since 1991/92.

The YCS, through the collection and dissemination of youth court information, continues to assist administrators, research, policy-makers, and program managers as they redefine the nature of Canada's youth justice system.

As not all youth crime is reported to police and not all youths in conflict with the law proceed to court, the YCS focuses on the court process and the response to youth crime rather the prevalence of youth criminal activity.[2] These data should therefore not be used as an indicator of total youth criminal activity.

FIVE-YEAR TRENDS

Decline in Cases before Youth Courts
In the last five years, the number of cases heard in youth courts has generally followed a downward trend; the 99,590 cases processed in 2000/01 represent a drop of 10% from 1996/97 (Figure 26.1).

Marked Drop in the Number of *Property Crime* Cases
A decrease of 23% in the number of *Property crime* cases from 1996/97 to 2000/01 is primarily responsible for the overall decline in the youth court cases

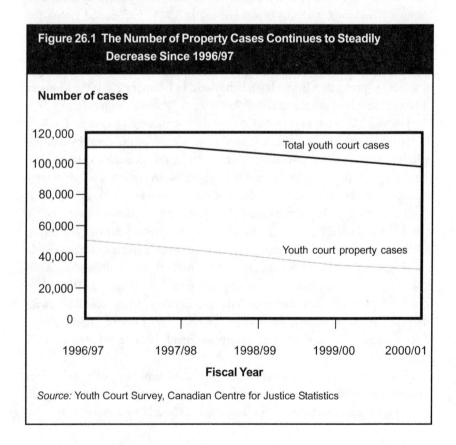

Figure 26.1 The Number of Property Cases Continues to Steadily Decrease Since 1996/97

Source: Youth Court Survey, Canadian Centre for Justice Statistics

during that period (Figure 26.1). The number of *Property crime* cases decreased markedly for several major offence groups: breaking and entering (-35%), possession of stolen property (-31%), and theft (-22%).

Overall, youth *Violent* crime cases have decreased by 6% from 1996/97 to 2000/01. However, large increases over the five years were noted for assaulting a peace officer (23%) and assault with a weapon (7%). Minor assault cases (which accounted for 46% of the *Violent crime* caseload) have decreased 11% since 1996/97. Notable decreases occurred with regard to sexual assault (-9%) and robbery (-8%).

While most offences under the *Other Criminal Code* offence category experienced declines, increases occurred in some administrative offence cases. For example, the number of youth "failure to appear" cases has increased by 7% since 1996/97, while cases heard under the *Young Offenders Act* increased

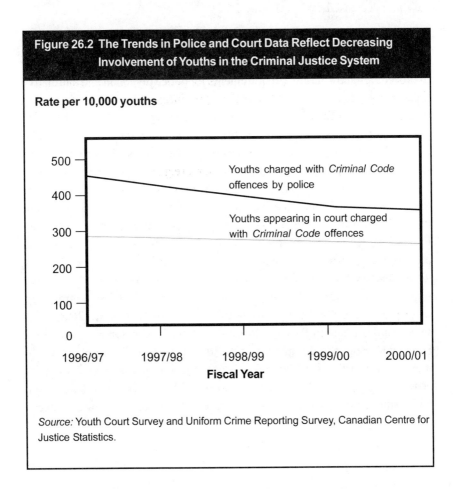

Figure 26.2 The Trends in Police and Court Data Reflect Decreasing Involvement of Youths in the Criminal Justice System

Rate per 10,000 youths

Youths charged with *Criminal Code* offences by police

Youths appearing in court charged with *Criminal Code* offences

Fiscal Year

Source: Youth Court Survey and Uniform Crime Reporting Survey, Canadian Centre for Justice Statistics.

by 10%. The number of *Drug-related offence* cases increased 30% since 1996/97. Narcotic possession and trafficking, which make up 72% and 28% respectively of total *Drug-related* offence cases, have increased 54% and 30% respectively since 1996/97.

Rate of Youths Charged by Police Increases Slightly

Youth court caseloads reflect police charging. That is, the composition and distribution of offences are largely determined by the incidents that come to the attention of the police and result in formal charges. However, due to post-charge alternative measures programs, some young offenders are diverted away from the criminal justice system into informal ways of dealing with the offence. For example, in 2000, the rate of youths per 10,000 aged 12 to 17 charged with criminal offences increased slightly (1%)[3], while the youth court case rate decreased by 3% (Figure 26.2).

Inter-jurisdictional Comparisons

Differences across the country in the reporting of criminal incidents to police, in procedures and eligibility requirements for police diversion and alternative measures programs, and differences in provincial policy directing Crown discretion may influence the volume and characteristics of cases heard in youth courts. For example, Alternative Measures programs, intended to be alternatives to formal judicial proceedings for youths, differ among the jurisdictions with regard to eligibility criteria (e.g., they may be restricted to first-time offenders), timing (i.e., pre-charge or post-charge) and coverage (e.g., they commonly involve less serious crimes only). Pre-charge screening by the Crown is mandatory in New Brunswick, Quebec, and British Columbia. Processes such as these serve to keep less serious cases out of the court process and, therefore, reduce court workload. These are examples of factors to be considered when making inter-jurisdictional comparisons.

    The national rate of youth court cases shows a gradual decline from 455 cases per 10,000 youths in 1996/97 to 403 in 2000/01 (Figure 26.2). This same trend is found in Prince Edward Island, the Yukon, Ontario, and Nova Scotia where the rate dropped by 55%, 30%, 21%, and 13% respectively. In most other jurisdictions, however, the rate tended to fluctuate annually with no discernible pattern. With the exception of a 7% increase in Saskatchewan, all jurisdictions showed an overall decrease in youth court case rates between 1996/97 and 2000/01.

Box 26.1 Youth and Youth Crime in Context

Population – 2000[1]	· total Canadian population was 31.1 million with 2.47 million youths aged 12 to 17 years (8% of total) · over the next decade, using an assumption of medium growth, the youth population aged 14 to 17 is expected to increase slightly until 2006, and then decline
Persons charged by Police in 2000[2]	· 481,818 adults and youths were charged with federal offences, excluding traffic crimes · 100,861 (21%) of these were youths
Cases processed in youth court, 2000/01	· 99,590 cases were heard in youth courts in 2000/01 · this represents a drop of 10% from 1996/97
Convictions in court, 2000/01	· 60,041 cases resulted in a conviction in 2000/01 · this represents a 7% drop from 1999/00

---

[1] Postcensal estimates as of July 1st, 2001, Demography Division, Census and Demographic Statistics Branch, Statistics Canada

[2] Uniform Crime Reporting Survey, 2000. Canadian Centre for Justice Statistics Canada.

CASE CHARACTERISTICS

Composition of Cases

In 2000/01 the types of cases processed in youth courts most often involved *Property crimes* (40%), *Violent crimes* (22%) and *Other Criminal Code* offences (18%), which include offences such as failure to appear in court and escaping custody. Less frequent were cases involving offences under the *Young Offenders Act* (12%), *Drug-related* offences (7%), and *Other federal statute* offences (<1%). (See Box 26.2.)

A Few Offences Account for a Large Proportion of the Total Caseload

While cases involving *Property crimes* accounted for the largest proportion of the caseload, only two of the five most frequent offences belonged to that category; "theft $5,000 and under" accounted for 15% of the total caseload

Box 26.2 Cases by Principal Offence Category, 2000/01		
	Number of Cases	% of Total Cases
Property crimes	40,023	40
Violent crimes	21,760	22
Other *Criminal Code* offences	18,264	18
YOA offences	12,447	12
Drug-related offences	6,967	7
Other federal statute offences	129	<1
Total	99,590	100

Source: Youth Court Survey, 2000/01, CCJS

and "breaking and entering" accounted for 9%. The other three most frequent types of cases before youth courts involved failure to comply with a court disposition under YOA offences (12%), failure to appear in court under *Other Criminal Code* offences (11%), and minor assaults under violent offences, which accounted for 10% of the total number of cases.

As can be seen in Figure 26.3, a very small number of offences accounted for a large proportion of the caseload. Together, the five types of offences mentioned above represented 57% of the caseload. In terms of frequency, these few offences far outranked all others.

Minor Assaults Accounted for Almost One-Half of *Violent Offence* Cases
While minor assaults[4] accounted for 10% of the total caseload, they made up 46% of all *Violent crimes*. Murder, manslaughter, and attempted murder cases together accounted for less than one-half of 1% of *Violent crime* cases heard in youth courts. There were 29 cases of murder, 16 cases of manslaughter, and 39 cases of attempted murder in 2000/01.

Half of Youth Court Cases Involve 16- and 17-Year Olds
Sixteen and 17-year olds appear more often in youth court than other age groups. In 2000/01, 16-year olds accounted for 25% of cases and 17-year

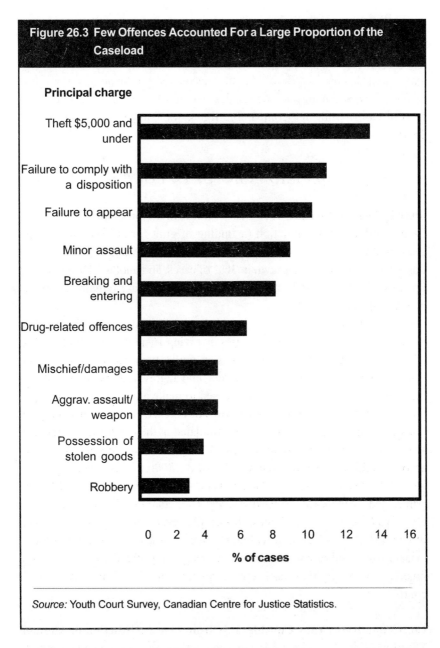

Figure 26.3 Few Offences Accounted For a Large Proportion of the Caseload

Principal charge

Theft $5,000 and under
Failure to comply with a disposition
Failure to appear
Minor assault
Breaking and entering
Drug-related offences
Mischief/damages
Aggrav. assault/ weapon
Possession of stolen goods
Robbery

0   2   4   6   8   10   12   14   16

% of cases

Source: Youth Court Survey, Canadian Centre for Justice Statistics.

olds made up 26%. Fifteen-year old young offenders represented the next most frequent age group, appearing in 22% of cases, while young offenders aged 12, 13, and 14 showed proportionately less involvement, accounting for 3%, 7%, and 15% of cases, respectively (Figure 26.4).

Males Account for Eight in Ten Youth Court Cases

Males accounted for eight in ten youth court cases and they predominated in all age groups. The proportion of cases against males increased with age, while cases against 15-year old females accounted for the largest proportion of cases against females. Among males, 16- and 17-year olds accounted for 54% of cases, while the comparable figure for females was 42% (Figure 26.4).

DECISIONS IN YOUTH COURT

Sixty Percent of Youth Court Cases Result in a Conviction

Cases resulting in a conviction (a finding of guilt for at least one charge) accounted for 60% of cases disposed in youth court in 2000/01 (Box 26.3). Cases were stayed or withdrawn in 36% of cases, and another 4% resulted in findings of not guilty or dismissal. These proportions have remained virtually unchanged since 1996/97.

Revisions to the YOA in 1995 made transfers to adult court the standard response for serious violent crime cases involving 16- and 17-year olds, unless otherwise ruled by the court. This provision applies to murder (first- or second-degree), manslaughter, attempted murder, and aggravated sexual assault. For these offences, the onus is on the accused to make an application to stay in youth court. For other crimes, the Crown or defence counsel must apply for transfer to adult court. The condition stipulated in the Act for these transfers specify a minimum age requirement of 14 years. Transfers to adult court accounted for less than one-tenth of 1% of the 2000/01 caseload.

Of the 86 cases transferred to adult court in 2000/01, 48 involved *Violent* crimes and 17 were for *Property crimes*. The remaining 21 cases fell under *Other Criminal Code* offences, *Young Offenders Act*, and *Drug-related* offences. Of the 48 cases involving *Violent* crimes, 18 were for murder, manslaughter and attempted murder. While young offenders aged 17 were involved in 26% of total cases, they accounted for 57% of transfers to adult court.

Conviction Rates Vary Considerably from One Jurisdiction to Another

The proportion of cases resulting in a conviction ranged from approximately 44% in the Yukon to 87% in New Brunswick. The proportions of charges withdrawn or stayed tend to vary considerably across the country. These variations can be explained in part by differences in charging practices. High

Figure 26.4 While Male Court Activity Continues to Increase, For Females, Court Activity Peaks at Age 15

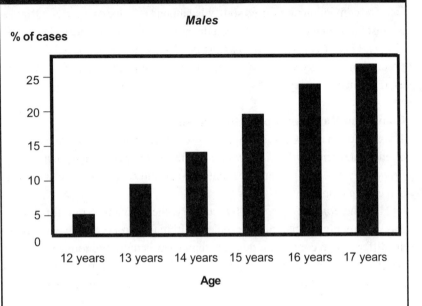

Males

% of cases

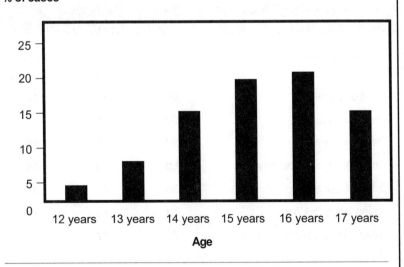

Females

% of cases

Note: Excludes 1,946 cases (2.0%), where the offender was older than 17 or the age was unknown, or in rare cases where the young offender was <12 years old.
Source: Youth Court Survey, Canadian Centre for Justice Statistics.

proportions of cases stayed or withdrawn are often indicative of charges set aside pending completion of alternative measures programs, or the systematic use of these decisions for administrative purposes.

The conviction rate varied somewhat among offence categories. Offences against the *Young Offenders Act* had the highest conviction rate (73%), while *Violent, Other Criminal Code and Drug-related* offences recorded the lowest proportion of guilty verdicts (58%). There was considerable variation within each offence category.

Conviction Rates Are Lower for Females

The conviction rate was substantially lower for females than for males in three offence categories: *Other federal statute* offences (35 percentage points lower), *Property crimes* (16 percentage points lower), and *Drug-related* offences (14 percentage points lower).

For the *Young Offenders Act* category, the conviction rate for females was slightly higher than that for males. Within the *Property crimes* category, the difference in conviction rates for females was more pronounced for theft (19 percentage points lower), possession of stolen property (12 percentage points lower), and breaking and entering (10 percentage points lower).

Box 26.3 Conviction Rates by Sex, 2000/01			
Most significant charge	% Total	% Male	% Female
Total offences	**60**	**62**	**54**
Violent crimes	58	58	57
Property crimes	59	62	46
Other *Criminal Code* offences	58	59	55
Drug-related offences	58	60	46
Young Offenders Act	73	73	75
Other federal statute offences	70	77	42

Source: Youth Court Survey, 2000/01, CCJS

Sentencing in Youth Court

Some factors considered by judges in sentencing include the type of offence committed, the circumstances in which the offence was committed, and the criminal history of the offender. In the case of a custody sentence under section 24(1) of the YOA, "the protection of society" and "the needs and circumstances of the young person" are also considered.

Most Youth Court Sentences Are Served in the Community

In 2000/01, probation was the most significant sentence in almost one-half (48%) of cases with convictions. Custody (34%) was the next most frequent sentence, comprising secure custody (17%), and open custody (17%). These sentences were followed by community service (7%), fines (6%), absolute discharge (2%), and other sentences (3%). The distribution of most significant sentence types has varied little since 1996/97.

Because sentencing information is generally presented by most serious or significant sentence, the use of some sentence types appears low relative to others when multiple sentences are imposed by the courts. In 2000/01, 52% of all cases with a conviction gave rise to one sentence, 35% resulted in two sentences, and 13% resulted in three or more sentences.

Offences against the *Young Offenders Act* Are More Likely to Result in a Term of Custody

Figure 26.5 shows that within offence categories, cases involving offences against the *Young Offenders Act* (49%) and *Other Criminal Code* offences (41%) have the highest proportion of cases with custody as the most significant sentence. Within the *Young Offenders Act* offence category, the great majority of cases involved failure to comply with a disposition, and in the *Other Criminal Code* offences category, it is administrative offences which were responsible for the higher proportion of custody sentences. These included escape from custody/being unlawfully at large (89%) and failure to appear/comply with a disposition/breach of recognizance (42%).

Although cases involving *Violent crimes* and *Property crimes* were less likely to result in a custody sentence, certain offences within these categories were more likely to receive such a sentence, particularly murder/manslaughter (94%) and attempted murder (62%).

Probation More Likely for Violent Crimes

Probation was most often ordered in *Violent crime* cases (59%), specifically those involving sexual assault/other sexual offences (66%), minor assault (63%),

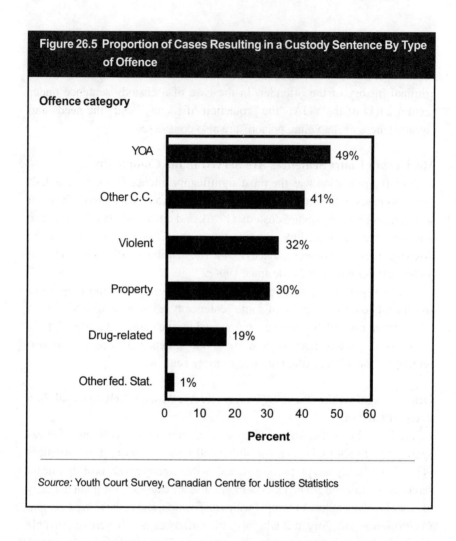

Figure 26.5 Proportion of Cases Resulting in a Custody Sentence By Type of Offence

Source: Youth Court Survey, Canadian Centre for Justice Statistics

and aggravated assault/assault with a weapon (59%). As well, *Drug offence* cases and *Property* cases more often resulted in probation (56% and 55% respectively). Within the *Property crimes* category, cases involving mischief/damage (61%) and fraud/forgery (57%) were the most likely to result in a probation sentence. Impaired operation offences had the highest proportion of fines imposed (58%). Of all types of offences, theft $5,000 and under, and failure to comply with a disposition cases had the highest proportion with a community service order (10%).

Females More Likely Than Males to Receive Probation

While one-half of convictions ended in a term of probation overall, females were more likely than males to receive probation as the most significant sentence in 2000/01 (54% versus 47%). The differences between male and female young offenders were also apparent in custody sentences. Thirty-six percent of cases involving males ended in a term of custody compared to 28% for females. Differences in other types of sentences were slight.

The Use of Custody Varies Widely across Canada

The use of secure custody ranged from 1% of cases with convictions in Nova Scotia to 30% in the Northwest Territories. The proportion of cases with convictions resulting in open custody was highest in Prince Edward Island and Nova Scotia (both 35%) and lowest in Alberta (10%) and Quebec (12%). The combined use of open and secure custody ranged from just over one-quarter of cases in Alberta (26%) to well over one-half of convictions in the Northwest Territories (57%). Indeed, in the Northwest Territories, the proportion of total custody orders was higher than the percentage of probation orders imposed (32%). The same was true of the Yukon (52% of cases receiving custody, 36% receiving probation) and PEI (50% receiving custody, 39% receiving probation). The availability and capacity of custodial facilities may have an impact on the use of custody orders across the country.

Sentence Lengths

Under the YOA, the maximum length for secure or open custody sentences is generally two years. However, this sentence can be three years if the crime would normally carry a maximum penalty of life imprisonment in adult court. In addition, the most serious crimes (first- or second-degree murder) carry higher sentences. First-degree murder carries a maximum custodial sentence of six years, followed by four years of conditional supervision. Second-degree murder carries a maximum four-year custodial term followed by three years of conditional supervision. However, not all murder cases first heard in youth court are sentenced in youth court as the YOA transfer provisions to adult court would apply.

The Majority of Custodial Sentences Are for Three Months or Less

Of the 20,809 cases resulting in a custodial sentence (open and secure) in 2000/01, 34% were for terms of less than one month, 44% were from one to three months, 15% from four to six months, and 6% were for more than six months.[5] The proportion of cases with short custodial sentences (three months

---

Box 26.4 Sentence Review

The length of sentence ordered by the court may be subject to revision under conditions stipulated in the *Young Offenders Act*. The court must review all custodial sentences after one year and may reduce the term or type of disposition at that time. Otherwise, the initial sentence ordered is to be served. There is no parole or statutory release in the *Young Offenders Act*. Sentences are subject to review upon request by the parent or young offender, although permission must be granted by the court if less than six months have been served. The principal correctional service administrator (Provincial Director) may ask the court for a review hearing if a revision to the sentence would be in the youth's best interest.

---

or less) increased from 75% of cases with convictions in 1996/97 to 79% in 2000/01.

Of the cases resulting in open custody in 1996/97, 27% were for terms of less than one month, compared to 30% in 2000/01. For secure custody cases, the proportion with orders of less than one month increased from 32% to 38% during the same period (Figure 26.6).

In 2000/01, the median sentence length for cases resulting in secure custody was 30 days, while for open custody, it was slightly longer, at 34 days.

Most Probation Terms Are 12 Months or Less

Under the YOA, youth courts may sentence a young offender to probation for a maximum of two years. In 2000/01, the median sentence length for a probation sentence was one year. Of the 29,053 cases resulting in a term or probation as the most significant sentence, 22% were for a period of six months or less, 56% ranged from seven to 12 months, and 22% were for more than 12 months.

One-half of Fines Are $100 or Less

Under the YOA, a young offender may be ordered to pay a fine not exceeding $1,000. In 2000/01, 3,502 cases or 6% of convictions ended in a fine as the most significant sentence. Fines in the $100 to $500 range were most often ordered (45%), followed by fines in the $50 to $100 range (39%), less than $50 (10%), and over $500 (6%). The median dollar amount of fines was $125.

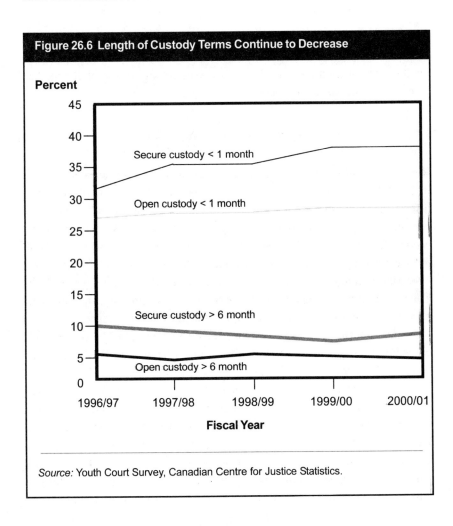

Figure 26.6 Length of Custody Terms Continue to Decrease

Source: Youth Court Survey, Canadian Centre for Justice Statistics.

CASE PROCESSING

One-Half of All Cases Are Processed in Two Months or Less

The successful rehabilitation of a young offender is often reliant on a prompt court process. In 2000/01, one-half of all cases were processed in two months or less (from the time of the youth's first court appearance to the date of decision or sentencing), with only 17% of cases taking longer than six months. In fact, 17% of cases were completed at the first court appearance. The median elapsed time for all cases was 60 days. Manitoba had the longest median elapsed time at 91 days, followed by Alberta (84 days), Saskatchewan (82 days), and Nova Scotia (78 days).

In 2000/01, 58% of cases involved only one charge, 23% had two charges, 9% three charges, and 10% had more than three charges. The number of charges did not seem to have a significant impact on the median amount of time taken to process a case in court.

REPEAT OFFENDERS

Repeat Offenders Are Involved in One-Third of Convictions

In 2000/01, approximately 21% of cases with convictions involved repeat offenders.[6] In comparison to first-time offenders, repeat offenders tended to be brought to court more often for *Property crimes* and less often for *Violent crimes*. In 2000/01, of the cases in which repeat offenders were involved, 53% were *Property* offences cases and 24% were *Violent* offence cases. Comparable figures for first-time offenders were 47% and 29% respectively. The use of police diversion and alternative measures programs for first-time property crime offenders may have contributed to this difference.

Males tend to re-offend at a higher rate than females. In 22% of convicted cases involving males in 2000/01, the young offender had been previously convicted; the corresponding figure for female offenders was 17%.

Unlike repeat offenders, first-time offenders were more likely to be given a term of probation (Figure 26.7). In 2000/01, 62% of convictions for first-time young offenders ended in probation compared to 35% for repeat offenders. Repeat offenders were over two times more likely to be ordered to serve a term of custody (51%) than were first-time offenders (20%). This wide gap was apparent for both *Violent crime* cases (59% of convictions resulting in custody for repeat offenders versus 24% for first-time offenders) and *Property crime* cases (50% versus 18%).

METHODOLOGY

The Youth Court Survey (YCS) is a census of *Criminal Code* and *Other federal statute* offences heard in youth court for persons aged 12 to 17 (up to the 18th birthday) at the time of the offence. Though every effort is made by respondents and the Canadian Centre for Justice Statistics (CCJS) to ensure complete survey coverage, slight under-coverage may occur in some jurisdictions.

The unit of analysis is the case, defined by the YCS as one or more charges laid against a young person first presented in a youth court on the same day. Case counts are categorized by the most significant charge, most significant

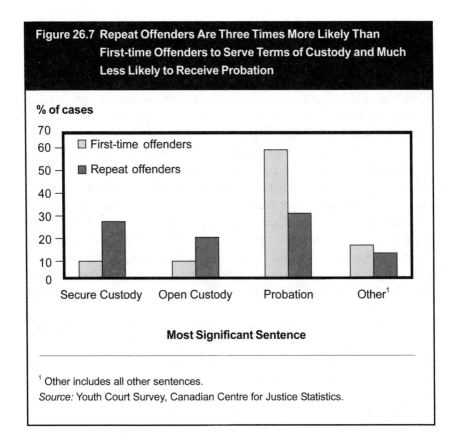

Figure 26.7 Repeat Offenders Are Three Times More Likely Than First-time Offenders to Serve Terms of Custody and Much Less Likely to Receive Probation

% of cases

☐ First-time offenders
■ Repeat offenders

Secure Custody   Open Custody   Probation   Other[1]

Most Significant Sentence

[1] Other includes all other sentences.
Source: Youth Court Survey, Canadian Centre for Justice Statistics.

decision, and the most significant sentence. Consequently, less serious charges, decisions, and sentences are under-represented.

The determination of the most significant charge at the beginning of court proceedings is by the ordering of charges from most to least serious. *Violent* charges are given first priority in the ordering process, followed by *Drug and narcotic* offences, *Property* offences, other *Criminal Code* offences, offences under the *Young Offenders Act* (YOA), and *Other federal statute* offences. Offences are further ranked within these offence categories.

Since a case with more than one charge may have more than one type of decision, the "most significant decision" has been selected for analysis on the basis of the following order from most to least serious: transfer to adult court; guilty; other decision (e.g., not fit to stand trial); stay of proceedings; charge withdrawn; or transfer to other jurisdiction; and not guilty or charge dismissed. The case is described by the most serious or "significant" charge in the case, which is associated with the court decision.

The most significant sentence is determined by the effect that the sentence has on the young person. Sentences are ordered from most to least significant as follows: secure custody, open custody, probation, fine, compensation, pay purchaser (a dollar amount paid back to the innocent purchaser of stolen goods), compensation in kind, community service order, restitution, prohibition/seizure/forfeiture, other sentences, conditional discharge, and absolute discharge.

The reader is advised that the use of the decisions "stay" and "withdrawn" for administrative purposes (e.g., to reduce charges or to correct details on an information) vary by jurisdiction. To terminate and recommence a case for administrative purposes has been found to inflate the total number of cases reported to the Youth Court Survey. As much as 30% of the national caseload is stayed or withdrawn and a proportion of these are the result of administrative procedures. Ontario, Manitoba, Alberta, British Columbia, and Yukon are most affected by this practice. Consequently the reader is encouraged, where possible, to analyze cases with guilty findings (convictions) to increase comparability among the jurisdictions.

Differences in data over time and across jurisdictions result from a number of factors that reflect how the YOA has been implemented. Pre-court screening procedures may affect the number of youth appearing in court. The Crown Attorney, for example, may decide not to proceed with a charge, or the initial charge may be changed. Pre-charge screening by the Crown is mandatory in New Brunswick, Quebec, and British Columbia. A youth may also be diverted from the court process into a program such as Alternative Measures (either before or after police lay charges) or a police diversion program.

Alternative Measures (AM) programs are generally reserved for first-time offenders and are often limited to specific types of less serious offences, although young offenders committing more serious offences can be considered for acceptance in the program in most jurisdictions. Except for New Brunswick, Ontario, and Yukon, all AM programs are combined pre- and post-charge programs where the preferences, and the general practices, are to refer youths at the pre-charge stage (i.e., before charges are laid). In New Brunswick, the AM program operates at the pre-charge stage only. In Ontario, youths are only referred to AM programs at the post-charge stage (i.e., after charges are laid). In Yukon, the general practice is to refer youths to the AM program at the post-charge stage, although, on occasion, they may be referred at the pre-charge stage. Alternative measures cases are excluded from the Youth Court Survey data either in the jurisdiction or at the CCJS, if they are identified. Nevertheless, differences in procedures and eligibility requirements of these programs influence the volume and characteristics of cases heard in youth courts.

NOTES

1. See the methodology section for the definition of a case and other key concepts related to the YCS and this *Juristat*.
2. Refer to *Juristat* Vol. 21, no. 8, "Crime Statistics in Canada, 2000," for counts of youths charged by police.
3. Refer to *Juristat* Vol. 21, no. 8, "Crime Statistics in Canada, 2000," for rates of youths charged by police.
4. Refer to the least serious form of assault that includes pushing, slapping, punching, and face-to-face verbal threats.
5. The YCS cannot distinguish between consecutive and concurrent sentences and does not include sentencing revisions made under review by the court. In multiple sentence cases, for example, the sentence length may be underestimated because of the assumption of concurrent sentences for all charges and may not reflect actual time ordered.
6. The information on repeat offenders, within jurisdictions, was obtained by selecting young offenders convicted in 2000/01 from the case file by date of sentencing and tracking any previous convictions for them from 1991/92 to 1999/00. The repeat offender analysis excludes Nova Scotia for all years, all offences under the YOA, and post-disposition offences under the *Criminal Code* (e.g., failure to comply, unlawfully at large and escape). Because of this, the number of cases presented in this section does

not correspond to the number of cases reported elsewhere in the *Juristat*.

JUSTICE PROCESS FOR YOUTHS

Dianne Hendrick

Presented below is a model of the criminal justice process for youths under the *Young Offenders Act*. The process is mapped by a flowchart and labelled

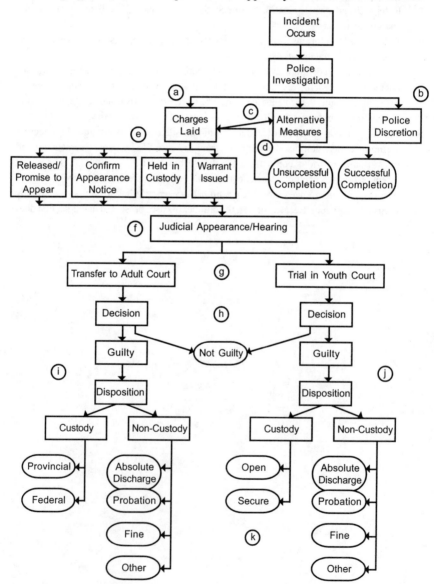

(a to k) to identify the corresponding description which is presented below the chart.

WHAT IS THE YOUTH JUSTICE PROCESS?

In order for youths to become involved in the justice system, the police must detect or be notified that a crime may have been committed. If the police are satisfied that an offence has occurred, they may use one of three options:

(a) The police may charge the youth with a crime.

(b) If it is a minor offence, the police may use discretion to divert the youth out of the formal justice system. This may involve speaking to the youth's parents about the incident and/or requiring the youth to apologize to the victim.

(c) The youth may be diverted into an Alternative Measures program. The youth will be required to fulfill an alternative measures agreement either before or after charges have been laid. Some alternative measures programs currently in use include apologizing to the victim, counselling, and restitution.

(d) Should the youth fail to meet any of the conditions of the agreement, the charges may be reinstated and the case referred back to the formal court process.

(e) Once charges are laid, a decision will be made about detention. Youths arrested by police on suspicion of a serious crime may be held in custody to await a hearing. A youth accused of a minor crime is likely to be served with an appearance notice at the scene of the crime instructing the youth when to appear in court or released into his or her parents' custody with a promise to appear at a hearing. An arrest warrant can be issued if the accused is known by police but has not been apprehended. Several factors, including the seriousness of the offence, the criminal history of the accused, and the province or territory within which the offence has occurred will affect what happens at this stage. Although the YOA applies equally across Canada, provinces and territories have different policies and programs.

(f) Most youths are dealt with in youth courts; these are provincial/ territorial courts that have special expertise and facilities. However, depending on the age of the youth, his or her background, and the type of crime, a hearing may be conducted to determine if the youth should be transferred to adult court. Any youth aged 14 or over who has been charged with a serious (indictable) can be transferred. In such cases, the Crown must apply to have the case moved. All 16- and 17-year olds charged with a serious violent offence (first-degree and second-degree murder, attempted murder, manslaughter, and aggravated sexual assault) are transferred automatically. However, the individual's lawyer or the Crown can apply to have the case stay in youth court.

(g) In youth court, all trials are conducted by a youth court judge. The only exception is the offence of murder, where the accused has the option of a judge and jury trial. In adult court, the youth is treated as an adult. For most serious offences, adults can select trial by judge or trial by judge and jury.

(h) If the court decides that the youth is guilty, the judge will determine an appropriate disposition or sentence.

(i) If found guilty in adult court, youths face the same sentences as adults, except that youths sentenced to life in prison are eligible for parole earlier. At most, youths serve 10 years before becoming eligible for parole, whereas adults may have to serve up to 25 years.

(j) Youths found guilty in youth court can be sentenced to secure custody, meaning that they serve time in a youth detention/correctional facility. This is the most severe kind of sentence and is generally reserved for violent, repeat, and older offenders. A less severe form of incarceration is open custody; these sentences are usually served in community group homes. Non-custodial sentences include absolute discharge, conditional discharge, probation, a fine, compensation for the victim, or community service.

Two years in custody is the maximum penalty for offences not punishable by life under the *Criminal Code*. (Youths found guilty of more than one of these offences can be sentenced to a maximum of three years in custody.) For offences punishable by life, such as robbery, the maximum penalty is three years in custody. The maximum penalty for second-degree murder is seven years (four years custody and three years supervision) and 10 years (six years custody and four years supervision) for first-degree murder.

(k) Sentences expire when the youth has fulfilled all of the requirements set out by the judge or when the judge changes the sentence at a review hearing. Otherwise, the youth may be sent back to court for failing to complete the sentence.

Depending on the seriousness and frequency of the offences, young offenders who do not become re-involved in the justice system for three to five years after successfully completing their sentence will have their criminal records destroyed. For young offenders who become re-involved in the justice system before their three- to five-year period ends, their records will be considered during sentencing for all subsequent offences, including those committed as an adult.

YOUTH AT RISK: A REVIEW OF ONTARIO YOUNG OFFENDERS, PROGRAMS, AND LITERATURE THAT SUPPORTS EFFECTIVE INTERVENTION

Alan W. Leschied, D.A. Andrews, and Robert D. Hoge

BACKGROUND

The Ministry of Community and Social Services initially expressed its interest in the study of the concept of risk with young offenders through the Ministry's Risk/Needs Study. This study began in 1990 and focused interest in young offenders at risk by providing:

- A review of the prediction and treatment literature with young offenders.
- An evaluation of the predictive validity of the Ministry's Risk Indicator Form as a predictor of program adjustment and short-term reoffending.
- An evaluation of the Toronto Case Management System, a risk-based, objective case planning approach for probation service.

The initial three evaluations were completed between April 1990 and March 1991. These evaluations provide an appreciation of the current status of knowledge in regard to the prediction and treatment of young offenders, an evaluation of the predictive validity of the Ministry's Interim Risk Indicator Form, and an evaluation of a risk-based, objective case management project for Toronto probation.

REVIEW OF THE PROFILE, CLASSIFICATION, AND TREATMENT LITERATURE WITH YOUNG OFFENDERS: A SOCIAL-PSYCHOLOGICAL APPROACH

The single largest body of literature in criminology is that which examines the characteristics of youth who become offenders. The full report reviews the general theories of youth criminal conduct, cross-sectional and longitudinal studies examining descriptors of youth at risk for offending and chronically reoffending, classification systems developed to differentiate "kinds" of offenders, mental health issues related to youth criminal conduct, assaultive and substance-abusing youth. The treatment section reviews the overall findings of what constitutes effective delivery of service to young offenders, the components of effective programs and concludes with examples of three ineffective and seven effective programs.

Young Offender Characteristics

Even taking into account the literature of other cultures (U.S.A. and Great Britain), there is a surprising convergence of findings in describing characteristics of youth at risk for becoming offenders. Twelve key characteristics include:

- Behavioural history
- Early and current family conditions (low levels of affection/ cohesiveness/monitoring)
- Interpersonal relationships (generalized indifference, weak affective ties)
- Lower-class origins (a consistent but modest predictor variable)
- Peer influence (association with antisocial/drug using other; isolation from non-criminal other)
- Personal attitudes/values/beliefs/feelings (high tolerance for deviance in general)
- Personal educational/vocational/socio-economic achievement
- Personal temperament, aptitude, and early behavioural history
- Problems in the family of origin
- Psychopathology
- School-based risk factors
- Other factors (being male, young, variety of neuro-psychologic indicators)

While the concept of criminogenic risk examines characteristics present in a young offender sample (as compared to a non-offender sample), criminogenic need reflects the changes in status which influence the probability of an antisocial outcome. That is, individuals with critical (risk) factors interact with their environment in a manner that increases the probability that an antisocial event will occur. Cross-sectional and longitudinal studies convincingly support a social-psychological approach to understanding youth crime.

Studies on risk also demonstrate decisively that the probability of illegal conduct increases dramatically as the number and variety of predisposing factors increase.

Predictors of Chronicity

The major factors of chronicity, both from cross-sectional and longitudinal studies include:

- Early and generalized problematic behaviours
- Weak attachment to ties of convention (family, teachers, peers)
- Low levels of involvement in conventional pursuits
- Delinquent associates
- Antisocial attitudes, feelings, and cognitions

Developmental Factors

The most consistent findings from the literature suggest that factors in early life such as nurturance, attachment, discipline, and monitoring interact to form a response pattern that can be criminogenic. In other words, youthful offending begins for many early in life when parental inconsistency, modelling of inappropriate behaviour, and antisocial thinking and reinforcement of coercive behaviour within a family set the stage for later antisocial thinking and behaviour.

Mental Health Disorders

While many professionals in the young offender system speak frequently of "emotional" or "mental health" problems, findings from the literature are much more equivocal. Overlap of diagnosis of mental health (i.e., psychiatric, depressive) disorders and antisocial behaviour ranges from 8% to 50% in epidemiological studies. Major affective disorders (i.e., depression) are most common among violent youth and less predominant among property offenders. Overall, the presence of some form of mental health disorder may ultimately further impair existing deficits in problem-solving ability which lead to antisocial behaviour.

Violent Offenders

For some time there has been a belief that, due to many methodological concerns, the prediction of violent behaviour is not a very fruitful pursuit. In part, this reflects the fact that violent behaviour is a low frequency event and comparisons between violent and non-violent offenders frequently reveal no differences. However, the literature also suggests a social-psychological approach to understanding violent behaviour can lead to more promising approaches in prediction. There are two specific examples from the violence literature. The family violence literature strongly supports the fact that young persons exposed to violent models have an overwhelmingly increased probability of becoming violent toward family members and a generalized increase in violence potential (Jaffe, Wolfe, and Wilson, 1990). The second area supportive of the prediction for violent behaviour comes from the victimization literature, which notes that persons victimized from a violent event (i.e., sexually abused victims) have increased potential of becoming sexual perpetrators themselves (Finkelhor, 1984). The conclusion from the present review suggests prediction for violence potential should include not only characteristics of the individual, but also of the milieux of origin and interaction.

The major findings from this review suggest a combination of predisposing characteristics and precipitating environmental factors interact in a manner that affects the probability of delinquent acts occurring, thus a social-psychological approach. A shift in personal and/or situational factors affects the probability of offending.

Characteristics identified in the literature review representing youth at risk suggest the need for broad-based classification systems to reflect the relevant predisposing and precipitating factors for youth criminality. Some of the promising approaches include the use of:

- The Youth Level of Service Inventory
- Wisconsin Juvenile Probation and Aftercare Risk Involvement Instrument
- Toronto Case Management System

These examples of risk classification systems reflect the empirically derived factors most frequently cited in the literature. Inventories in the developmental (I-Level; Conceptual Level), behavioural (Behaviour Problem Checklist; Achenbach Behaviour Checklist), and personality areas (MMPI; BPI), while presenting important information for the differential understanding of the needs of young offenders, only offer a limited description of youth, and are too limited in scope to be a sole basis for case management decision-making.

Effective Correctional Treatment

In the past five years, numerous thorough reviews of the youth rehabilitation literature, including both subjective and meta-analytic reviews, have appeared. Meta-analytic reviews of the treatment literature allow for more critical conclusions in regard to the kinds of interventions that appear to be most promising in reducing reoffending. The meta-analytic approach capitalizes on subjective reviews of intervention in subjecting reported studies to a statistical review of the nature and target of intervention, and expected outcome (i.e., lowered reoffending). Our review firmly concludes that there is a great deal known about what constitutes effective intervention. Specifically, interventions reflecting appropriately targeted treatment with awareness of criminogenic risk and need, (factors directly related to youth antisocial behaviour), and programs reporting high levels of program integrity, represent the most sound basis of intervention.

> "What works, in our view, is the delivery of appropriate correctional service, and appropriate service reflects these psychological principles: (1) delivery of service to higher risk cases; (2) targeting of criminogenic needs; and (3) use of styles and modes of treatment (cognitive, behavioural), that are matched with client need and learning styles."
>
> D.A. Andrews et al. (1990)

Effective intervention that follows these lines can take place both within residence and community. Further, the literature firmly establishes the fact that it is the nature and content of programming and not the legal sanction that constitute components of effective intervention. Moreover, while the components of effective service follow along the lines of what we now refer to as the *risk principle*, there are specific kinds of intervention that show themselves superior to other forms of intervention. For example, cognitive-behavioural intervention is superior to psychoanalytic or client-centred therapy; short-term behaviourally oriented systems-intervention with families is superior to more process-oriented family interventions.

Reviews of the literature also identify approaches to antisocial youth which are not rewarded with lower rates of reoffending. From this literature, deterrence-based interventions which promote the importance of punishment appear ineffective. A recent review for the Canadian Sentencing Commission emphatically stated there is no evidence from the literature that harsher sentences or sentences considered equitable with the crime will reduce reoffending (Cousineau, 1988).

"Drawing upon some nine bodies of research addressing the deterrence question, we contend that there is little or no evidence to sustain an empirically justified belief in the deterrent efficacy of legal sanctions."

Douglas Cousineau for the Canadian Sentencing Commission (1988)

There is some suggestion from the deterrence/punishment literature that sanctions without program can actually promote antisocial behaviour with some youth (Schneider & Ervin, 1988).

Several high-profile programs were reviewed that have been recently cited both in the professional literature and public media. A review was made of boot camp/militaristic style programs and intensive supervision/probation programs as responses to antisocial youth. The review of boot camp suggests that punishment or harsh discipline seems not to carry over in reductions in antisocial behaviour. Intensive supervision/probation programs seem to be effective only when the content of the interaction is focused in a rehabilitative way. In other words, it appears not to be the *amount* of contact that is made between persons in authority and antisocial youth but rather the *nature* of the interaction which reflects itself in lowered reoffending.

The "nothing works" debate, which has plagued much of the discussion as to the place of rehabilitation in juvenile justice, is now over. The recent meta-analytic reviews of the literature have consistently and convincingly established the fact that programs that are appropriate to the nature of risk show meaningful reductions in reoffending from 25% to 40% (Lipsey, 1990). American researchers have also translated these reductions in reoffending not only to the lessening of crime, but in economic savings to the community at large, as well as to the correctional community (Greenwood & Turner, 1987).

"A chronic juvenile offender with a projected 80 percent recidivism rate and an expected arrest rate of 1.5 per year can be expected to continue committing crimes for 13.3 years. Clearly, then, it is in society's best interests to pay somewhat more for juvenile corrections programs that significantly reduce recidivism rates."

Peter W. Greenwood and Susan Turner, The Rand Corporation (1987)

These statements are encouraging. However, there is no cure for crime even in those areas where the literature reflects a firm understanding of the nature of the factors that constitute risk with young offenders and programs that can be tailored to the individual risk and need of youth and their families. Meaningful reductions in reoffending, however, can be achieved in humane, sensitive, and caring ways which can lessen human misery both for the offender and for the community.

RISK INDICATOR STUDY

In the spring of 1989, MCSS developed a form to be completed on young offenders entering residence that would assist in the identification of potential risk to self and the community. The items included:

- Previous suicide attempts
- Previously physically/sexually assaultive
- Previous use of a weapon
- Previous conviction of a violent offense
- Assault on authority figure
- Previous incidents of fire setting
- Previous escape from custody
- Previously diagnosed psychotic
- Threat by third party who meets abuse criteria
- Other

This study identified the presence/extent of these risk factors in a residential sample of Ontario young offenders and assessed the predictive validity of each factor, and their aggregate, to program adjustment and reoffending.

The data suggest that 85% of the 480 youth in the review reported at least one of the indicators, 25% had four or more areas of risk noted, and the average number of risk indicators per case was 2.33. In descending order of frequency (high to low) the four most frequently cited indicators were:

- Sexually, physically assaultive
- Escape from custody
- Assault on authority figure
- Conviction for violent offense

A large number of "other" risk indicators were noted by the case manager, including substance abuse, sexual problems, social problems, and behaviour/conduct problems. Clearly, the youth in residence represent a high-risk population.

Two areas of prediction included: in-program adjustment, and reoffending during the follow-up period. Overall, youth under study continued to demonstrate adjustment difficulties both while in program and following discharge. Half of the youth demonstrated poor adjustment based on case summaries within the program. Almost half (48%) reoffended during the follow-up (data collected over a six-month period), while three-quarters of the group incurred a new charge or were breached on a term of probation. This reoffending rate reflects the time both within the program and where appropriate, after discharge.

The total interim risk score was predictive of adjustment. Individual items relating to adjustment included previous conviction for a violent offence and escape from custody, while assault on authority figures and escape from custody were the major predictors of non-compliance with disposition. Case manager estimates of risk made at the initial assessment period were predictive of reoffending. Generally, the individual risk items were not predictive of reoffending.

Conclusions from the risk/needs indicators underscore the extremely disturbing characteristics of youth in residence. Characteristics reflective of this conclusion include:

- 75% show some evidence of reoffending, which may include a new conviction or breach/willful failure to comply.
- 48% show at least one new conviction (finding of guilt under the Criminal Code of Canada includes escape from custody, where applicable).
- only 20% of the group received "good" overall adjustment ratings.
- average number of new convictions was 1.9; 37% of this group were found in breach or willful failure to comply.

As a predictive instrument, the Ministry's Risk Indicator Form demonstrated competence in the following areas:

- previous suicide attempt predicts later self-destructive behaviour
- assault on authority figure and escape from custody predict later aggressive behaviour

The individual items were not as successful in predicting longer-term adjustment.

There was also a differential use of facilities, with youth judged highest risk evenly split between open and secure custody, and more represented in facilities dedicated to young offenders.

Case manager estimates of risk were more highly predictive of reoffending than the individual factors or total risk score.

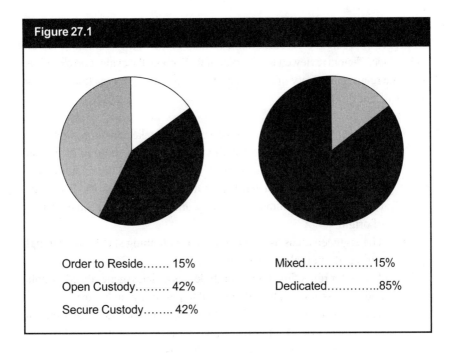

Figure 27.1

Order to Reside....... 15%

Open Custody......... 42%

Secure Custody........ 42%

Mixed..................15%

Dedicated..............85%

THE TORONTO CASE MANAGEMENT SYSTEM: EVALUATING THE EFFECTIVENESS OF AN OBJECTIVES-BASED CASE PLANNING PROBATION PROGRAM

Professor Todd Clear of Rutgers University was consulted in the development of a progressive delivery system for probation services in Toronto. The Toronto Case Management System (TO-CMS) incorporates a broad-based classification system reflecting many of the factors referred to in the literature review. It encourages the use of differing levels of intensity of service (minimum-medium-maximum) targeting specific aspects of a youth's criminogenic risk and need. Clear (1989) writes:

> "(Objectives-based case planning) requires the officer to specify the objectives he/she intends to achieve during supervision in terms of changes in the client's behaviour."

> Todd Clear (1989)

The evaluation involved two stages. First, there was interest in establishing the degree of prediction of reoffending validity of the twenty-six intake factors and eighteen factors reviewed in case planning. Second, the evaluation examined outcome relating intensity of service and problem/strength area targeted. The results of this study suggest:

- The twenty-six characteristics assessed at intake constitute six factors related to the general personality and social psychology of deviant behaviour. They include: a family factor, problematic relations with the community (school, work, recreation, peers), emotional instability, criminal history, health and sexuality, and history of crime in the family of origin.
- The eighteen areas assessed at the case planning stage reflect a high degree of internal consistency.
- The factor reflecting deviant attitudes, associates, generalized trouble, and aggressivity is strongly related to past criminal history.
- The five strongest areas related to reoffending include, in descending order: response to authority, employment, use of non-work/school time, family dynamics, and peer relations.
- Level of contact (minimum, medium, maximum) by the case manager increased with increased level of need on the intake ratings.
- The most frequent targets based on identified need were: response/ attitude toward the current offense (17%), education (15%), and family dynamics (12%).
- There was a discrepancy between frequency of identified need and the number of plans appropriately focused.
- Consistent with the risk principle of case classification, achievement of appropriate objectives was associated with reduced reoffending, particularly with higher-risk cases.

Part VII

STREET CRIME

Chapter 28

THE JUSTICE
DATA FACTFINDER

Richard Du Wors

THIS CHAPTER PROVIDES A SUMMARY OF THE MOST RECENT DATA FROM THE SURVEYS of the Canadian Centre for Justice Statistics, a division of Statistics Canada. The format is organized to address some of the most frequently asked questions about crime and justice in Canada:

- Are police-reported crime rates increasing?
- Are reported crime rates higher in big cities?
- Are firearms frequently used to commit violent crimes?
- What are the most common offences brought to criminal court?
- How long does it take for cases to go through the court system?
- What proportion of adult criminal cases result in conviction?
- What proportion of adult convictions result in a prison sentence?
- How many adults are in custody or under some form of supervision?
- With what offences are youth most likely to be charged?
- What type of sentences do young offenders receive?

The chapter begins with an overview of the criminal justice system from the reporting of a crime to the serving of a sentence. However, there are many challenges to tracking the flow of persons or events from one justice sector to another. For example, the data for the different sectors do not always operate on the same time frames, such as calendar or fiscal years. Also, some justice surveys are still being implemented and have not yet achieved complete or representative coverage across Canada. There are also problems such as identifying repeat offenders in the same year, or linking police-reported offences with court cases, due to reporting variations. However, despite these limitations, a useful high-level picture of the criminal justice system can be presented.

According to victimization surveys, about four in ten criminal acts are reported to police (Gartner and Doob, 1994). Figure 28.1 shows that of those incidents reported to the police, 34% are cleared, 22% result in the laying of a charge, 15% result in conviction, and 4% result in a prison sentence.

Notable in Figure 28.1 is the sharp decline in the percentage points from "offences cleared by charge" by the police (22%) to "convictions" by the courts (15%). Discrepancies between the police-reported and court surveys do not appear to account for this difference since there are almost identical numbers of offences cleared by charge as there are total court cases. The decrease also cannot be explained by the dropping of secondary charges or plea-bargaining since both police and court surveys report one offence or case no matter how many charges are associated with it. The decrease in the percentages in Figure 28.1 from "offences cleared by charge" to "convictions" appears to be largely due to the proportion of stays and withdrawals in court. (Please see the section "What proportion of adult criminal cases result in conviction?") A lesser factor is the absence of conviction data for Superior Court, although little more than 2% of all criminal cases are dealt with in Superior Court.

ARE POLICE-REPORTED CRIME RATES INCREASING?

In Canada, in 1996, over 2.6 million incidents were reported to the police and were confirmed as actual *Criminal Code* incidents, excluding traffic.[1] Although there was a long-term increase in the police-reported crime rate from 1962 to 1991, the rate has dropped over the past five years. In 1996, the national rate was similar to that of ten years ago (Kong, 1997). This trend is similar to decreases in the crime rate reported in the United States, England, and Wales.

Victimization survey data also suggest that levels of criminal activity have not been increasing. In both 1988 and 1993, approximately one-quarter of Canadians reported being a victim of a crime (Gartner and Doob, 1994). Of the crimes measured by Statistics Canada's General Social Survey, rates of robbery, theft, break and enter, motor vehicle theft, and vandalism declined.

From 1992 to 1996, the police-reported crime rate decreased each year for a total reduction of 15%. For the fourth year in a row, the violent crime rate decreased in 1996 (2%), while the property crime rate fell 1%. As well, the rate of other *Criminal Code* offences such as mischief (vandalism), prostitution, breach of probation, and arson fell 3% (Figure 28.2). Although rates have declined in general, in 1996, rate increases were reported for some offences, including homicide (6%), robbery (2%), motor vehicle thefts (9%), and cannabis offences (6%).

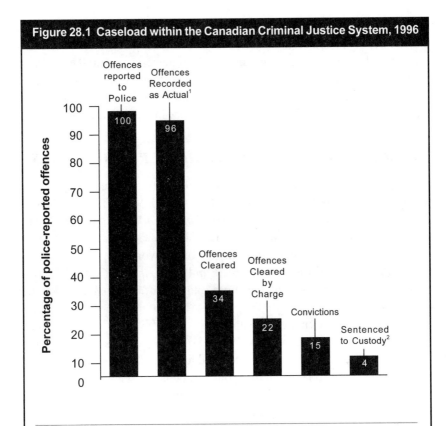

Figure 28.1 Caseload within the Canadian Criminal Justice System, 1996

1. An offence is considered to be "actual" when, following an initial investigation, the police have confirmed that a criminal offence has occurred. An offence is "cleared" when the police are satisfied they have identified an offender. However, it may not be possible to lay a charge against the offender because he/she is dead, under age 12, has diplomatic immunity, is already in prison, etc. If, in the view of the police, it is possible to lay a charge against an offender, the offence is cleared by charge.
2. Includes secure custody only for young offenders and any custodial sentence for adults.

Source: Statistics Canada, Canadian Centre for Justice Statistics, Uniform Crime Reporting Survey, Adult Court Survey, and Youth Court Survey

Police-reported data are based on the Uniform Crime Reporting Survey (UCR), which gathers information on offences that come to the attention of the police. The reporting of offences to the police is affected by a number of factors, including amendments to the law (e.g., sexual assault), changes to police charging practices (e.g., in the area of domestic violence), and citizens' changing tolerance for particular crimes and willingness to report these crimes to police (e.g., with respect to schoolyard violence). Such changes can influence long-term trends in police-reported data and are mirrored in data from victimization surveys, which enhance confidence in the information.

ARE REPORTED CRIME RATES HIGHER IN BIG CITIES?

According to a detailed analysis (Leonard, 1997) of police-reported data for the nation's 25 Census Metropolitan Areas (CMAs) in 1995 (excluding Oshawa), these urban areas had an overall rate of *Criminal Code* violations similar to smaller cities, towns, and rural areas.[2] The analysis of CMA data for 1996 that follows is a previously unpublished update for this work.

In 1996, 61% of Canada's over 2.6 million *Criminal Code* violations occurred within these metropolitan areas, and 61% of Canadians lived in the 24 CMAs.

Violent crime does not occur with greater frequency in major metropolitan areas than in non-CMA areas. In 1996, 58% of violent crimes occurred in the 24 biggest cities, and these cities accounted for 61% of the population.

The analysis also revealed that youth crime is not specifically an urban phenomenon. The proportion of youth crime occurring within CMA boundaries is less than the proportion of Canada's youth population living in these areas. In 1996, 51% of young offenders were charged within a CMA boundary, and 57% of Canada's youth population lived in a CMA.

The picture is somewhat different when examining specific offences. Specific offences show rates that vary considerably between CMAs and non-CMA areas. In 1996, CMA rates were notably higher for attempted murder, robbery, break and enter, motor vehicle theft, and prostitution. Non-CMA rates were higher for such offences as sexual assault, common assault, weapons and explosive offences, and impaired driving.

Similarly, the nine largest CMAs with 500,000 or more population may be compared to the smaller CMAs with populations between 100,000 and 499,999. Of the 18 million Canadians living within a CMA, 80% live in the nine largest CMAs. In 1996, these larger CMAs also accounted for nearly 80% of all crime in CMAs, so it may be concluded that crime occurred in larger and smaller CMAs in relative proportions. Larger CMAs had higher rates for homicide, attempted murder, robbery, motor vehicle theft, and prostitution, while smaller CMAs had higher rates for sexual assault, common assault, weapons and explosive offences, and impaired driving.

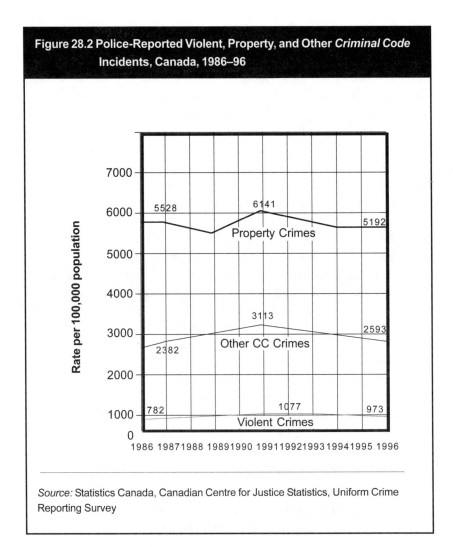

Figure 28.2 Police-Reported Violent, Property, and Other *Criminal Code* Incidents, Canada, 1986–96

Source: Statistics Canada, Canadian Centre for Justice Statistics, Uniform Crime Reporting Survey

There is also considerable variation from one CMA to another. Vancouver had the highest crime rate among the nine largest metropolitan areas in 1996, ranking highest for robbery, arson, weapons offences, break and enter, and motor vehicle theft. By contrast, Toronto's rates for offences were generally below both the larger CMA average and the national average. In summary, the biggest cities do not necessarily have the highest crime rates.

ARE FIREARMS FREQUENTLY USED TO COMMIT VIOLENT CRIMES?

In 1996, there were 633 homicides in Canada, an increase of 6% in the homicide rate over the previous year. Firearms were the most common weapons used to commit a homicide (33%). Of these incidents, half involved handguns, and a further 38% involved rifles or shotguns. The remaining 12% of firearm homicides involved either a sawed-off rifle or shotgun or a fully automatic firearm. Between 1995 and 1996, all types of firearm homicides increased by 20%, and those using rifles or shotguns increased by 33%. However, the levels are still significantly lower than they were in 1991 and 1992.

An interesting picture emerges when looking at the use of firearms in homicides for areas of different populations size within Canada. In 1996, the three largest Consensus Metropolitan Areas—Toronto, Montreal, and Vancouver—accounted for one-third of the national population, while non-CMAs accounted for 39% of the population. In both of these areas, firearms were the weapons most frequently involved in homicides. What differs, however, are the types of firearms used to commit homicides in these areas. While the use of handguns dominated firearm homicides in the larger areas (76%) in non-CMAs, the majority of firearm homicides involved either shotguns or rifles (56%) (Figure 28.3).

In 1996, robberies accounted for 11% of all violent crimes, and weapons were involved in 54% of all robberies. While the rate of robberies involving weapons other than firearms has remained relatively stable since 1991 (an average of 34 per 100,000 population), the rate of firearm robberies decreased by 31% from 32 per 100,000 population in 1991 to 22 in 1996.

WHAT ARE THE MOST COMMON OFFENCES BROUGHT TO CRIMINAL COURT?

In fiscal year 1995–96, half of all cases heard by adult criminal courts involved either crimes against property (26%) or other *Criminal Code* violations (25%) (Figure 28.4) (Grimes, 1997).

The single most frequent type of case heard was impaired driving. Almost 15% of the 436,000 cases reported by participating jurisdictions in the Adult Criminal Court Survey involved impaired driving.[3] The next most frequent type of case was the violent crime of common assault (12%), followed by the property crime of theft (11%). Apart from assault, most violent crimes accounted for a small number of cases. Homicide, attempted murder, robbery, kidnapping, sexual abuse, and abduction each represented less than 1% of cases.

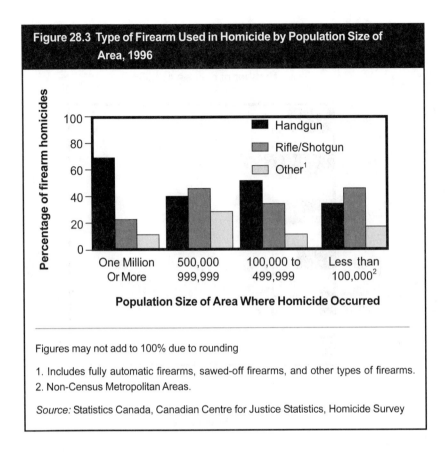

Figure 28.3 Type of Firearm Used in Homicide by Population Size of Area, 1996

Percentage of firearm homicides

Population Size of Area Where Homicide Occurred

- Handgun
- Rifle/Shotgun
- Other[1]

One Million Or More / 500,000 999,999 / 100,000 to 499,999 / Less than 100,000[2]

Figures may not add to 100% due to rounding

1. Includes fully automatic firearms, sawed-off firearms, and other types of firearms.
2. Non-Census Metropolitan Areas.

Source: Statistics Canada, Canadian Centre for Justice Statistics, Homicide Survey

All adult criminal proceedings begin in provincial/territorial courts, although some may end up in Superior Court, depending on the nature of the offence, decisions made by the Crown, and elections made by the accused. In 1995–96, just over 2% of the 436,000 cases first heard in provincial court were transferred to Superior Court. Three types of cases—sexual assault, drug trafficking, and major assault—made up almost half of those cases that were transferred.

The majority of accused persons (65%) were under the age of 35, and approximately 85% were males. The type and prevalence of cases varied with the age of the accused. For the 18–24 year age group, the most common offence type was theft. For individuals over 24 years of age, impaired driving was the most common type of case, and the frequency of these cases increased with age so that the highest proportion occurred in the 55+ age group (26% of all cases for this group).

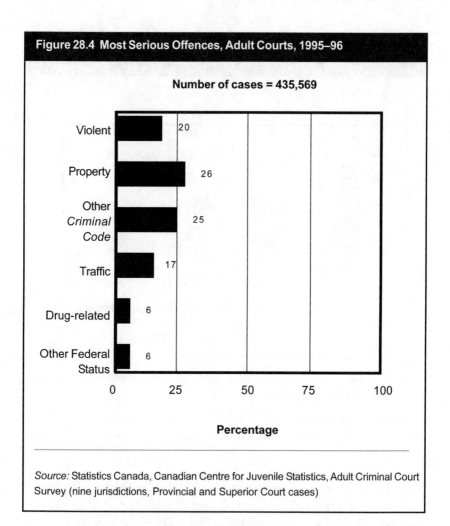

Figure 28.4 Most Serious Offences, Adult Courts, 1995–96

Number of cases = 435,569

Source: Statistics Canada, Canadian Centre for Juvenile Statistics, Adult Criminal Court Survey (nine jurisdictions, Provincial and Superior Court cases)

The distribution of youth court cases differed from that for adults (Figure 28.5). In 1995–96, about half of the cases were property offences, such as theft under $5,000 (18%), break and enter (12%), and possession of stolen goods (6%). There were 10% of cases that involved violations of the *Young Offenders Act*, such as failure to comply with a disposition. The only other type of offence that represented 5% or more of youth court cases were common assault (10%), failure to appear or comply (10%), and mischief (5%).

Young offenders are rarely transferred to adult court. Seventy-four out of 111,000 cases were transferred in 1995–96. Of these, a majority (54%) involved violent offences.

HOW LONG DOES IT TAKE FOR CASES TO GO THROUGH THE SYSTEM?

The courts have a responsibility to deliver justice services fairly and efficiently. In 1995–96, the median time for completion of cases in adult provincial court was 77 days.[4] On average, four court appearances were required to complete a case. However, 60% of cases were completed in four months or less. The court process is complex, often involving a judicial interim release or bail hearing, resolution of questions concerning trial court jurisdiction, a preliminary inquiry, entering of a plea, a trial, a decision of guilty or not guilty, and a sentencing disposition. A particular case, however, may not involve all these steps.

In youth court, cases were processed more quickly. In 1995–96, the median time was 68 days for youth courts. Sixty-nine percent of all youth cases were dealt with in four months or less.

The median elapsed time of court cases was related to the number of appearances and the type of offence. For example, in 1995–96, the median number of days in adult court varied from 28 for cases with only two appearances to 109 for cases with four appearances. Sexual assault cases had the longest elapsed time (188 days); offences against the administration of justice, such as failure to appear in court, had the shortest (27 days). Court cases involving homicide and related offences were relatively long (161 days). Theft cases were very brief by comparison (43 days). Impaired driving cases exceeded the median at 97 days.

WHAT PROPORTION OF ADULT CRIMINAL CASES RESULT IN CONVICTION?

Two-thirds (64%) of adult provincial court cases, excluding those dealt with in Superior Court, resulted in a conviction in 1995–96, either by plea or by trial. Nearly one-third (30%) of cases resulted in a stay or withdrawal of charges.[5] Only 3% of cases resulted in an acquittal, while 4% were resolved through other means, including not criminally responsible on account of mental disorder, and waived to another jurisdiction.[6]

The highest rates of conviction were for other federal statute offences[7] and traffic cases (both 78%). Traffic cases, for the most part, involve impaired driving-related offences. Violent crime offences had the lowest rates of conviction at 49% (Figure 28.6). Of the remaining 51% of violent crime cases not resulting in conviction, 5% were referred to Superior Court, 38% received

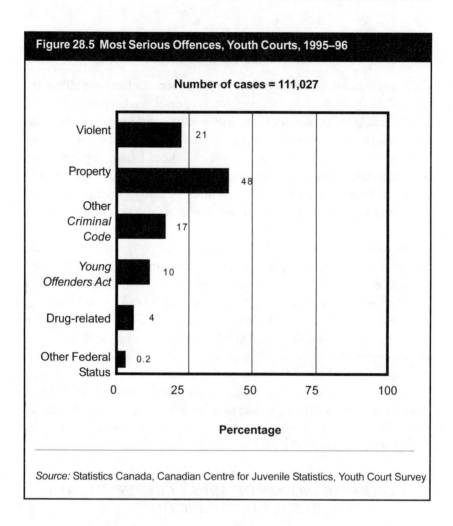

Figure 28.5 Most Serious Offences, Youth Courts, 1995–96

Number of cases = 111,027

Percentage

Source: Statistics Canada, Canadian Centre for Juvenile Statistics, Youth Court Survey

a stay or withdrawal of charges, 4% were acquitted, while 4% received an "other" disposition. Among violent offences leading to a finding of guilt in provincial court, the highest rates of conviction were for robbery (60%) and sexual offences (60%), followed by common assault (53%).

Offences with high rates of referral to Superior Court, such as homicide offences (58% referred) and attempted murder (26% referred), had relatively low rates of conviction in provincial court (42% and 17% respectively). These homicide offences represent infanticide and manslaughter only, as first- and second-degree murder are under the absolute jurisdiction of Superior Court. Data on conviction rates for Superior Court are not currently available.

WHAT PROPORTION OF ADULT CONVICTIONS RESULTS IN A PRISON SENTENCE?

In 1995–96, one-third of convictions received a prison sentence. This was second only to fines, which were the most serious sanction in 36% of convictions.[8] As would be expected, the frequency of prison sentences varied by offence type, ranging from 1% for morals/gaming cases (e.g., book-making) to 84% for robbery cases.

The median prison term was 46 days. Half of all prison terms were one month or less, and only 3% of terms were two years or longer (Figure 28.7), which implies federal penitentiary time. Again, the length of prison term varied

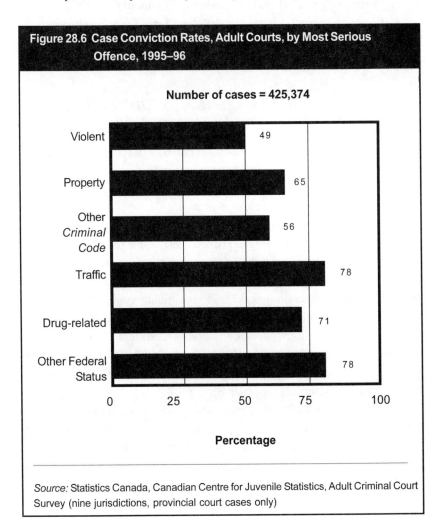

Figure 28.6 Case Conviction Rates, Adult Courts, by Most Serious Offence, 1995–96

Number of cases = 425,374

Offence	Percentage
Violent	49
Property	65
Other Criminal Code	56
Traffic	78
Drug-related	71
Other Federal Status	78

Source: Statistics Canada, Canadian Centre for Juvenile Statistics, Adult Criminal Court Survey (nine jurisdictions, provincial court cases only)

by offence type, with more serious offences receiving longer sentences. Robbery offences, for example, had a median sentence of two years.

Probation was the most serious sanction in 26% of cases resulting in conviction. Offences such as property damage/mischief and common assault tended to receive probation sentences. The median probation term was one year.

Fines were the most frequently used sanction. The types of offences receiving fines as the most serious sanction included Other federal statute offences (89% of cases), impaired driving (66% of cases), and morals/gaming (50% of cases). Other federal statues are mostly regulatory and, for that reason, normally receive a fine. There is a mandatory minimum fine of $300 on first conviction for impaired driving. On the other hand, cases involving crimes against the person had a fine as the most serious sanction in only 10% of cases. Overall, the median fine amount was $300.

HOW MANY ADULTS ARE IN CUSTODY OR UNDER SOME FORM OF CORRECTIONAL SUPERVISION?

There are three distinct groups in the adult correctional population: (1) those sentenced to a custodial term; (2) those in custody on remand/temporary detention; and (3) those serving all or part of their sentence under supervision in the community (such as parole or probation).

On an average day in 1995–96, 154,000 persons were under the supervision of correctional agencies (Morrison and Reed, 1997). Nine percent were inmates in federal penitentiaries (serving sentences of two years or more), 13% were in provincial/territorial facilities (serving sentences of under two years or on remand/temporary detention), and 78% were offenders on probation or some form of conditional release in the community. After a decade of rapid growth, Canada's adult correctional population has stabilized since 1993–94.

The increase from 1986–87 to 1993–94 was largely among those serving sentences in the community (a 53% increase), rather than among those in custody (a 22% increase) (Figure 28.8).

A similar number of adults were incarcerated in Canada in 1995–96 as in the previous year (33,800 on an average day). Over the last five years, the percentage increase in the custodial population has been larger in federal institutions, where inmates serve a sentence of two years or longer than in provincial institutions, where sentences are of less than two years' duration (19% compared to 4%).

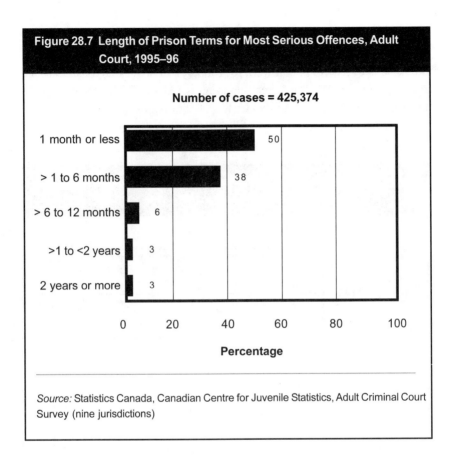

Figure 28.7 Length of Prison Terms for Most Serious Offences, Adult Court, 1995–96

Number of cases = 425,374

Source: Statistics Canada, Canadian Centre for Juvenile Statistics, Adult Criminal Court Survey (nine jurisdictions)

Men make up 91% of those admitted to provincial/territorial correctional institutions. In 1995–96, the median age of sentenced offenders on admission was 31. While women are under-represented among admissions, aborigninal peoples are over-represented. Overall, the proportion of aboriginal peoples in the inmate population (16%) is more than five times their representation in the Canadian population (3%). Aboriginal peoples made up less than 9% of provincial sentenced admissions to custody in all provinces east of Manitoba, but accounted for 72% in Saskatchewan, 55% in Manitoba, 36% in Alberta, and 17% in British Columbia.

Almost one-third of sentenced admissions in the nine provinces reporting adult corrections data on the most serious offence or disposition were offenders convicted of property offences (31%). The next largest group of offenders were sentenced for crimes of violence (19%), followed by impaired driving offences (13%).

Offenders sentenced to federal facilities are admitted with convictions for more serious crimes than offenders in the provincial sector. The most frequent admissions to federal prison were for robbery (24%), sexual assault (14%), major assaults (12%), and break and enters (12%). Other offenders were incarcerated federally for homicide (8% of admissions) and drug trafficking (4% of admissions).

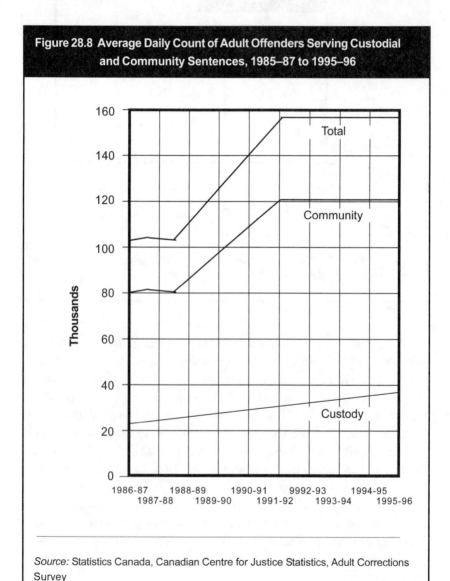

Figure 28.8 Average Daily Count of Adult Offenders Serving Custodial and Community Sentences, 1985–87 to 1995–96

Source: Statistics Canada, Canadian Centre for Justice Statistics, Adult Corrections Survey

WITH WHAT OFFENCES ARE YOUTH MOST LIKELY TO BE CHARGED?

Continuing the decline between 1991 and 1995, the overall rate of youth charged with *Criminal Code* offences, per 100,000 youth, decreased by 4% in 1996, with the result that a total of 117,773 youth aged 12 to 17 years were charged. Of these youth, over half (56%) were charged with property offences, approximately one-fifth were charged with violent crimes,[9] and the remainder were charged for other *Criminal Code* violations such as mischief and offences against the administration of justice (e.g., breach of probation). The most frequent property crime charges were for theft (49% of youth property offenders). Just over one-half (51%) of violent offence charges consisted of level 1 assaults (common assaults).[10]

The distribution of youth charged has changed since 1986, when seven in ten youth (72%) were charged with property offences and 9% with violent offences. This long-term increase in the proportion of young offenders charged with violent crime is largely due to the increasing proportion of common assaults, the least violent or serious form of assault (Figure 28.9). However, youth are still less likely to be charged with violent crime than adults. For example, in 1996, 28% of adult offenders were charged with violent crimes, compared to 19% of youth.

While the past decade has witnessed an increase in the proportion of youth charged with violent crimes, in 1996, the rate of youth charged decreased for most crime categories. This resulted in the first notable annual reduction (4%) in the total rate of violent youth crime since 1986, the first year following the implementation of the *Young Offenders Act*, which standardized the age of youth to include 12 to 17 year olds. Charge rates for property crimes decreased for the fifth consecutive year (5%), and all property crime categories experienced reductions. Although an overall decrease between 1995 and 1996 in the youth charge rate for violent crime is noted, the 1996 rate is still more than two time higher than in 1986 (an increase of 121%) (Kong, 1997).

WHAT TYPE OF SENTENCES DO YOUNG OFFENDERS RECEIVE?

About one-third of young offenders found guilty of an offence in 1995–96 were sentenced to either secure custody (15%) or open custody (19%) (Hendrick, 1997). This is similar to the 33% of adult offenders who received a prison sentence in 1995–96.

Three-quarters of custodial sentences for youth were for a period of three months or less. Murder/manslaughter cases had the highest median sentence length of 25 months. The two most common types of custodial cases, break and enter and theft under $5000, resulted in median sentence lengths of 90 days and 30 days, respectively.

A major difference from sentencing patterns for adults was the proportion of cases for which a fine was the most serious disposition handed out.[11] For young offenders, only 6% received a fine as the most serious disposition, compared to 36% of adults. This perhaps reflects the recognition by the courts of the relative abilities of adults and youth to pay. As well, among the reasons for the difference could be the nature of the offences youth commit; for example, they commit fewer impaired driving and Other federal statute offences, which

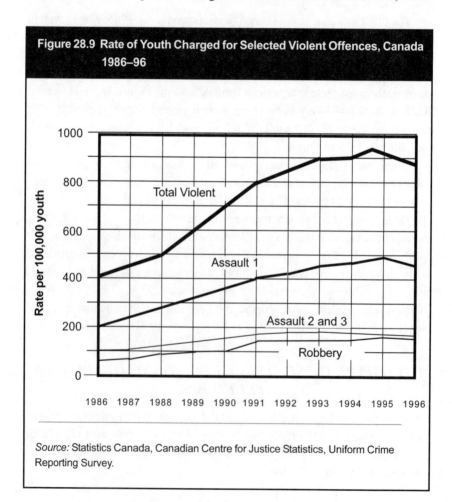

Figure 28.9 Rate of Youth Charged for Selected Violent Offences, Canada 1986–96

Source: Statistics Canada, Canadian Centre for Justice Statistics, Uniform Crime Reporting Survey.

more frequently result in fines. As well, there is no mandatory fine in youth court for impaired driving.

According to the *Young Offenders Act*, youth that are given custodial dispositions by the courts are kept in either *secure* or *open* custody facilities. Open custody refers specifically to the following: community residential centre, group home, childcare facility, forest or wilderness camp, or any other similar facility, all of which must be designated by the province. Secure custody implies custody in a facility designated for the secure containment or restraint of young persons. Secure custody is used only in the most serious cases or when all else fails. The young offender is obliged to serve the full length of the imposed disposition, unlike adults, who may be released early under parole or mandatory supervision. All of these factors must be taken into consideration when making comparisons in sentencing patterns between adults and young offenders.

The most frequent disposition given to young offenders was probation, the most serious disposition in 49% of cases. This far exceeded the adult figure of 26%.

Stand-alone Community Service Orders (CSOs) were the most serious disposition in only 7% of cases. The percentage of CSOs appears low because in most cases, they are used as a condition of probation or in conjunction with a more significant disposition. Overall, 29% of all cases resulting in a conviction included a CSO.

Data also reveal that the pattern of dispositions for young offenders varies from one type of offence to another. For example, probation was the most serious disposition for 65% of minor assaults, but a fine was the most serious disposition in 53% of impaired driving cases.

NOTES

1. Crime rates based on police-reported data are calculated exclusively on "actual" incidents. See Figure 28.1, footnote 1.
2. A CMA represents an urbanized core of at least 100,000 population and includes adjacent urban and rural areas that have a high degree of economic and social integration. The 25 identified CMAs in Canada in 1996 were: Toronto, Montreal, Vancouver, Ottawa-Hull, Edmonton, Calgary, Québec, Winnipeg, Hamilton, Kitchener, St. Catharines-Niagara, London, Halifax, Victoria, Windsor, Saskatoon, Regina, St. John's, Chicoutimini-Jonquière, Sudbury, Sherbrooke, Trois-Rivières, Thunder Bay, Saint John,

and Oshawa. There are 25 CMAs in Canada, but due to mapping difficulties between police jurisdictions and the geographical boundaries of the CMA, Oshawa was not included in the analysis.

3. Provincial criminal courts in nine jurisdictions (Newfoundland, Prince Edward Island, Nova Scotia, Québec, Ontario, Saskatchewan, Alberta, Yukon, and the Northwest Territories) report to the survey. This represents about 80% of national coverage.

4. The "median" is the value or score that exactly divides an ordered frequency distribution into equal halves.

5. A "stay" is a temporary or permanent halt in proceedings; a "withdrawal" refers to a withdrawal of charges by the Crown, Québec is the only jurisdiction included in the survey in which the decision to lay charges is made by Crown prosecutors. Québec has a relatively low percentage (10%) of stays/withdrawals. This suggests that this procedure may affect the outcome of cases. It is possible that the national rate of stays/withdrawals could be somewhat lower if the other two provinces with Crown charging, British Columbia and New Brunswick, were included in the survey.

6. Percentages do not add to 100% due to rounding.

7. Other federal statute offences include all federal statutes other than the *Criminal Code* and drug-related statutes, e.g., the *Income Tax Act* and the *Unemployment Insurance Act*. Other *Criminal Code* offences include those other than violent or property crimes, such as mischief, prostitution, and arson.

8. Sanction types are ordered from most to least serious as follows: prison, probation, fine, restitution/compensation, and other. For example, a case resulting in both prison and fine would be recorded as having a most serious sanction of prison.

9. Violent youth (and adult) crime includes homicide and related, attempted murder, sexual assault, assault, robbery, weapons offences, kidnapping, extortion, other sexual offences, and criminal negligence.

10. An example of a common assault would be a minor fight at a party that leads to the police being called to break it up. A threatened assault, or an actual assault that did not produce a serious physical injury, would be categorized as a common assault.

11. Dispositions are ordered in severity, from highest to lowest, as follows: secure custody, open custody, probation, fine, community service, absolute discharge, other.

Figure 28.10 Federal Statute Incidents Reported to Police, by Most Serious Offence, Canada, 1997–2001[1]

	1997 Number	1997 Rate	1998 Number	1998 Rate	1999 Number	1999 Rate	2000r Number	2000r Rate	2001 Number	2001 Rate	% change in rate* 2000-2001	% change in rate* 1991-2001
Population	**29,987,214**		**30,248,210**		**30,499,219**		**30,769,669**		**31,081,887**			
Homicides	586	2.0	558	1.8	538	1.8	546	1.8	554	1.8	0.4	-33.7
Attempted murder	865	2.9	745	2.5	687	2.3	767	2.5	721	2.3	-6.9	-37.7
Assaults – Total (levels 1, 2, 3)	**222,397**	**741.6**	**223,926**	**740.3**	**221,348**	**725.7**	**233,719**	**759.6**	**239,163**	**769.5**	**1.3**	**3.2**
Level 1	183,087	610.6	183,999	608.3	181,330	594.5	190,467	619.0	193,495	622.5	0.6	4.4
Level 2-Weapon	36,665	122.3	37,302	123.3	37,501	123.0	40,686	132.2	42,959	138.2	4.5	2.5
Level 3-Aggravated	2,645	8.8	2,625	8.7	2,517	8.3	2,566	8.3	2,709	8.7	4.5	-37.1
Other assaults	11,807	39.4	12,147	40.2	12,126	39.8	12,164	39.5	13,091	42.1	6.5	-33.1
Sexual assaults – Total	**27,013**	**90.1**	**25,553**	**84.5**	**23,859**	**78.2**	**24,001**	**78.0**	**24,419**	**78.6**	**0.7**	**-27.4**
Level 1	26,142	87.2	24,805	82.0	23,185	76.0	23,428	76.1	23,923	77.0	1.1	-25.4
Level 2-Weapon	602	2.0	529	1.7	461	1.5	391	1.3	329	1.1	-16.7	-69.4
Level 3-Aggravated	269	0.9	219	0.7	213	0.7	182	0.6	167.	0.5	-9.2	-67.5
Other sexual offences	3,650	12.2	3,445	11.4	3,300	10.8	3,114	10.1	3,026	9.7	-3.8	-30.6
Abduction	985	3.3	829	2.7	729	2.4	750	2.4	713	2.3	-5.9	-41.3
Robbery – Total	**29,587**	**98.7**	**28,963**	**95.8**	**28,740**	**94.2**	**27,037**	**87.9**	**27,414**	**88.2**	**0.4**	**-25.6**
Firearms	5,486	18.3	5,324	17.6	5,122	16.8	4,323	14.0	3,833	12.3	-12.2	-53.0
Other Weapons	9,945	33.2	10,326	34.1	10,500	34.4	9,901	32.2	10,362	33.3	3.6	-0.4
No Weapons	14,156	47.2	13,313	44.0	13,118	43.0	12,813	41.6	13,219	42.5	2.1	-2.8
Violent crime – Total	**296,890**	**990.1**	**296,166**	**979.1**	**291,327**	**955.2**	**302,098**	**981.8**	**309,101**	**994.5**	**1.3**	**-6.1**
Break&enter – Total	373,316	1,244.9	350,774	1,159.7	318,054	1,042.8	293,357	953.4	282,512	908.9	-4.7	-41.4
Business	100,696	335.8	92,590	306.1	83,971	275.3	82,074	266.7	80,421	258.7	-3.0	-46.0
Residential	233,724	779.4	221,366	731.8	197,022	646.0	175,804	571.4	167,322	538.3	-5.8	-38.8
Other	38,896	129.7	36,818	121.7	37,061	121.5	35,479	115.3	34,769	111.9	-3.0	-41.3
Motor vehicle theft	177,130	590.7	165,920	548.5	161,388	529.2	160,315	521.0	170,213	547.6	5.1	10.2
Theft over $5,000	24,035	80.2	23,600	78.0	22,493	73.7	21,354	69.4	21,146	68.0	-2.0	-83.8
Theft $5,000 and under	758,292	2,528.7	713,632	2,359.3	678,367	2,224.2	663,040	2,154.8	665,961	2,142.6	-0.6	-30.5
Possession of stolen goods	29,799	99.4	29,156	96.4	29,308	96.1	28,530	92.7	29,565	95.1	2.6	-21.7
Fraud	96,964	323.4	94,819	313.5	90,371	296.3	85,791	278.8	88,332	284.2	1.9	-41.8
Property crime – Total	**1,459,536**	**4,867.2**	**1,377,901**	**4,555.3**	**1,299,981**	**4,262.3**	**1,252,387**	**4,070.2**	**1,257,729**	**4,046.5**	**-0.6**	**-34.3**

	1997 Number	1997 Rate	1998 Number	1998 Rate	1999 Number	1999 Rate	2000r Number	2000r Rate	2001 Number	2001 Rate	% change in rate* 2000-2001	% change in rate* 1991-2001
Mischief	341,854	1,140.0	326,918	1,080.8	312,266	1,023.8	326,374	1,060.7	338,425	1,088.8	2.7	-34.4
Counterfeiting currency	33,272	111.0	39,830	131.7	36,265	118.9	35,937	116.8	37,771	121.5	4.0	489.4
Bail violation	70,367	234.7	73,034	241.4	72,192	236.7	78,105	253.8	91,249	293.6	15.7	38.1
Disturbing the peace[2]	57,704	192.4	65,513	216.6	69,570	228.1	80,085	260.3	88,729	285.5	9.7	39.4
Offensive weapons	16,103	53.7	16,766	55.4	16,007	52.5	15,324	49.8	17,456	56.2	12.8	-20.0
Prostitution	5,828	19.4	5,969	19.7	5,255	17.2	5,051	16.4	5,103	16.4	0.0	-56.4
Arson	12,693	42.3	12,947	42.8	12,756	41.8	13,733	44.6	14,513	46.7	4.6	5.6
Other	240,519	802.1	246,112	813.6	241,212	790.9	243,674	791.9	247,945	797.7	0.7	-8.6
Other Criminal Code – Total	778,340	2,595.6	787,089	2,602.1	765,523	2,510.0	798,283	2,594.4	841,191	2,706.4	4.3	-13.3
CRIMINAL CODE WITHOUT TRAFFIC – TOTAL	2,534,766	8,452.8	2,461,156	8,136.5	2,356,831	7,727.5	2,352,768	7,646.4	2,408,021	7,747.3	1.3	-25.1
Impaired driving[3]	90,145	300.6	87,660	289.8	85,997	282.0	84,044	273.1	90,454	291.0	6.5	-42.0
Fail to stop/remain[4]	49,781	166.0	39,087	129.2	17,972	58.9	19,522	63.4	20,294	65.3	2.9	-72.3
Other-Criminal Code Traffic	15,302	51.0	14,406	47.6	13,681	44.9	13,698	44.5	15,550	50.0	12.4	-27.6
Criminal Code Traffic – Total	155,228	517.6	141,153	466.6	117,650	385.7	117,264	381.1	126,298	406.3	6.6	-49.6
CRIMINAL CODE – TOTAL	2,689,994	8,970.5	2,602,309	8,603.2	2,474,481	8,113.3	2,470,032	8,027.5	2,534,319	8,153.7	1.6	-26.9
DRUGS	66,593	222.1	70,922	234.5	80,142	262.8	88,091	286.3	91,920	295.7	3.3	45.2
Cannabis	47,933	159.8	50,917	168.3	60,011	196.8	66,274	215.4	70,624	227.2	5.5	91.5
Cocaine	11,468	38.2	12,183	40.3	11,963	39.2	12,829	41.7	12,233	39.4	-5.6	-31.5
Heroin	1,235	4.1	1,323	4.4	1,323	4.3	1,226	4.0	965	3.1	-22.1	-36.1
Other drugs	5,957	19.9	6,509	21.5	6,845	22.4	7,762	25.2	8,098	26.1	3.3	15.0
OTHER FEDERAL STATUTES	35,204	117.4	35,816	118.4	38,942	127.7	34,632	112.6	38,257	123.1	9.4	-5.8
TOTAL FEDERAL STATUTES	2,791,791	9,309.9	2,709,047	8,956.1	2,593,565	8,503.7	2,592,755	8,426.3	2,664,496	8,572.5	1.7	-26.6

* Percent change based on unrounded rates.
r Revised figures.
1 Rates are calculated on the basis of 100,000 population. The population estimates come from the Annual Demographic Statistics, 2001 report, produced by Statistics Canada, Demography Division. Populations as of July 1st: final postcensal estimates 1997, updated postcensal estimates for 1998, 1999, and 2000, and preliminary postcensal estimates for 2001.
2 The increase in "disturbing the peace" may be, in part, attributable to a national data quality initiative undertaken by the RCMP to properly account for the types of offences that are aggregated under this offence.
3 Includes impaired operation of a vehicle causing death, causing bodily harm, alcohol rate over 80 mg, failure/refusal to provide a breath/blood sample.
4 Beginning in 1999, "fail to stop or remain" incidents for Toronto are now included under "provincial statutes" instead of the Criminal Code.
Source: Uniform Crime Reporting Survey, CCJS

Chapter 29

GO BOY AND SURVEILLANCE SQUAD

Frederick J. Desroches

THE POLICE REFER TO ROBBERY AS A "DUMB" CRIME BECAUSE THE RISKS ARE great and the payoffs are small. The chance of getting caught on a single robbery may be low, but serial robberies increase the risks substantially. Because the amounts of money obtainable are modest, anyone who wishes to support himself or herself this way has to rob one bank after another. Given the fact that police and banks respond immediately to a bank robbery, the odds against anyone surviving in this career for long are great. This is evident by the fact that the Hold-Up Squad typically clears over 70 percent of all bank robberies. . . .

Roger Caron is one of Canada's most famous bank robbers. His fame comes not from bank robbery nor from his many escapes from federal penitentiaries, rather it comes from his literary successes. Beginning with *Go Boy*, his award-winning autobiography, followed by *Bingo*, an account of the violent 1971 Kingston Penitentiary riot, and now with *Jojo*, a crime fiction novel, Roger has established himself as the most successful practitioner of "Con-lit" in Canada. From the age of 16 he had never been free longer than a few weeks or months at a time. For 24 years Roger spent every birthday and every Christmas incarcerated in federal penitentiaries. Then for 12 years he enjoyed his freedom and made a living as a writer. Recently, however, at age 55, Roger Caron was convicted of a number of armed robberies in Ottawa and sent to prison once more. He blames his downfall on the fact that he developed a cocaine habit in his attempt to deal with Parkinson's disease.

The interview with Roger is followed by an interview with the head of a special O.P.P. task force surveillance squad that arrested Roger and his partner in the act of robbing a bank.

"We used to rob banks gangster style. You go into the bank, jump the counter, and give an Apache yell, 'Everybody freeze! Back away from the tills. Back away from the phones. Lay down on the floor.' People go numb in a bank. Some tellers are really dumb and you have to shout at them. The first few seconds there is a lot of shouting. You want them to freeze so they can't think. If they can't think, they can't function so they follow orders. The idea is to terrorize them so they don't push the alarms and then when they're on the floor to pacify them, 'Don't worry, we're not going to hurt you. We just want the bank's money. Just do what you're told and everything will be all right.' Even today I will look at a bank the way a guy looks at a girl, 'Boy, that's an attractive bank. Boy, in the old days I would have gone crazy over that bank.'

"The most dangerous elements in bank robbery are the unknowns—the flukes that you can't control. For instance, a cruiser drives by as you're running out with the loot. Bank robbers jumping into a car look like bank robbers jumping into a car. Everybody is piling into the car in a big hurry. There is an atmosphere about it. If you're robbing a lot of banks, you are almost inevitably heading for a downfall. Mathematically the odds are against you. The odds are great that some fluke will sink you. It's like parachuting, the more jumps you do, the more likely you are to get injured. Sooner or later something will malfunction.

"I never liked robbing banks. As a kid I did, but even then I didn't. There was a lot of dread and a lot of danger and a lot of fear. As you get older you start realizing the danger even more and it's the last thing in the world you want to think about. So you subconsciously put it off until your funds are so low that you have to do it. And the more you do it, the better you become. You experience fear, but that fear becomes cold, controlled fear. I'd be uptight and sweating until the moment of truth. My moment of truth was when I was about to pull into the driveway of the bank. I'd drive by and look to see if there were any strange cars or strange people parked nearby. What invariably happens is that you're ready to go but you can't for one reason or another. You're cruising by the bank to see if someone is parked in your spot or if there's a policeman cashing a cheque. I'm not going to rob a bank while someone is sitting in his car with nothing better to do than watch people go into and out of the bank. I'm not going to go into the bank and let him see me pull my hood down.

"When it looked right we'd go in. I never drove—the guy who is the muscle never drives. I'd tap the driver on the shoulder and say, 'We go.' That was my by-word. The moment I'd say, 'We go,' a whole transformation would come over me. I would be fearful and jumpy until then, but now I knew that fear could destroy me, doubt could destroy me. It was no longer a time for pessimism, it was a time to think positive. You can't let doubt enter your mind. And no fear. You say to your partner, 'We go,' and the transformation comes over you and you're a light beam. You focus on that bank. You've got a one-track mind and you go right to the bank. From now on every second counts. There's no backing out now. It's go all the way. If anyone gets in your way, if a policeman comes between you and the money, then look out. It's me or him and one of us is going down. It's survival. It's the final moment of truth.

"And for God's sake, let no one try to be a hero or they'll get what they have coming to them. It's cut and dried. Don't be a hero. We're not after your money, we don't want to hurt you, just give us space, give us room, we've got enough problems without you guys interfering. So please, no heroes. If you're going to be a hero, we're in an awful big hurry, our life is at stake here, and you're going to get wiped. Bank robbers get indignant, 'Who is this son-of-a-bitch who suddenly deputized himself? If he wants to be a headline grabbing hero, then he's going to get what he deserves.'

"You balance the risk against the gain. It's a gamble. If you're caught, you're caught. If you're not, you're not. And if you're shot, you're shot. For any one score the odds are in your favour. When you're planning to rob a bank you know that there's the possibility that you are going to die brutally or that you are going to be wounded, captured, and sent away for life. It's not a game. You say to yourself, 'Please, I hope everything goes well. I know I'm dumb, I should go out and get a job, but I'm not. I'm robbing banks. I've made up my mind and I'm willing to gamble my life that I can get away. I just hope there are no police in there.' In your heart you know that you can't bat 1000. Every time you do a job you are that much closer to a fall. It just takes one bad day and you'll regret it for the rest of your life. It's not baseball—three strikes and you're out.

"I never really thought of myself as a thief. Bank robbery was glamorous to me and I wasn't stealing from a person. I saw myself as an outlaw. An outlaw has his own ethics on what is right and wrong. A thief is just a thief. I would look down on petty thieves. Old-time bank robbers are basically honest guys, you can trust them. They steal from institutions, but they wouldn't rob a guy on the street. You could invite a bank robber to your home and not have to worry about him stealing from you. I can rob a bank, but I couldn't keep the extra change that some store clerk might give me by accident. I'd think about keeping it, but I couldn't. My conscience would bother me. Today it's mostly drugs. I'm discouraged about bank robbery today.

"Back in 1972, Rollie and I were planning a score. We would check out banks three, four, six times over several weeks. After you've robbed a bank and you rush out you never know what's going to be there. We didn't know it, but we were under surveillance by an O.P.P. squad formed just to nab us. We were looking at this bank and it was a Friday night and only three banks in the city were open. The police have a tailor-made situation and they only have to sit and wait. I'm a real suspicious guy. I would say to myself, "If I was a policeman, where would I set an ambush on this bank?' My partner was ready to go in, but I wouldn't go. I would drive a wider and wider and wider circle. I kept expanding my arch until I spotted them. They were parked behind a nursing home. I spotted one and once I spotted one, I spotted the others right after. They admitted to me later that they were waiting with high-powered rifles on the rooftops and they had me in their sights. This was the city police force. Meantime, this O.P.P. special squad was also following us around in six unmarked police cars.

"The city police were on a stakeout and this special task force was on our tail. I hadn't made up my mind which bank I was going to do and I scouted them all. They saw me checking out many banks and they didn't know which bank would be the one I was going to knock off. They knew I was very alert. We were looking everywhere, but we couldn't spot them. When we finally decided on a score and came out of the bank, they hit us from three different directions. They smashed one car into us and I opened the car door on the passenger side and was about to put my foot on the pavement. As I levelled my gun over the window, a second car hit us on the side. I was aiming at the car that had hit us from the front. I looked into his eyes and I had an automatic pistol and I had him. I tried to shoot, but as I held the gun up, the second car hit us on the side and knocked me down onto the seat and the gun went flying. I wasn't expecting it. I was lucky I didn't lose a foot. If a second car had hit a second later, I would have had my foot on the ground. He would have slammed the car into the door and it would have cut my foot off. That saved the cop. If I had had a shotgun or a machine-gun, I would have fired through the window.

"I could never understand why they didn't shoot. I think it's because I didn't have a gun in my hand and my partner didn't have a gun in his hand. They made a mistake; they should have shot. One guy jumped onto the hood and was laying across it with a shotgun pointed at the windshield. I was reaching for the gun that went flying when a third car hit and knocked me off balance again. By that time I was looking into the barrel of a shotgun—I finally got the message. He should have shot me by all rights. I think he didn't quite have it in him. He was very verbal. The guy who was on the hood was very verbal and usually guys who talk the most do the least. I don't think that anybody, just anybody can kill. They should have killed me."

SURVEILLANCE SQUAD

"This was the first time our force had formed a surveillance squad and it was meant for the higher echelon of criminals. This is back in 1972. We trained for awhile and then we went out on the road. It was believed that Rollie had done one prior to March, but we couldn't prove it. Both he and Roger were known bank robbers. We found out where Rollie lived and we decided to do a project on them. We had six men on our surveillance team and two technical guys who looked after the wires. We had their phones tapped, but they didn't say much on the phone. We tailed them from March 5th until we busted them on the 21st and they had no idea we had ever tailed them. It's hard to do. Rollie lived in an apartment and Roger lived in a townhouse. We decided to key on Rollie because his residence was easier to observe. They would meet for breakfast anytime after 10:00 a.m. and then case banks. They'd drive around, have lunch, work out in the afternoon at a health club, then drive around and case some more banks.

"Initially we lost them a lot until we got used to them. We didn't know the city that well at first so it was better to lose them than to be spotted. After that we didn't lose them very often. Roger was very surveillance conscious. We began by watching Roger's townhouse, but we saw him with binoculars a couple of times! Oh yes, he used to case the area looking for anybody sitting around. We would have been spotted after awhile so we laid back. That's why he was so surprised when we nabbed him. He said to us, 'I should have seen you guys. I don't believe it.'

"They went through subdivisions looking for tails and they were always recording licence plate numbers at the police station. They were cautious about what they said when they talked to each other on the phone. They knew what they were doing. Since we were from out of town, we stayed in the same hotel and we'd be up a little after 7:00 a.m., and have breakfast as a group. We stayed together and lived together. The odd weekend we went home because there were no banks open. They cased some on Friday nights so we stayed a few Friday nights. We'd watch Rollie's place from around 8:00 a.m. and if his rental vehicle was in the driveway, we assumed that he was at the apartment. He'd come out and get in the car and we'd follow him wherever he went.

"The only way to get these guys is to get them right in the act. We watched them do it; you can't get them any better than that. If we had grabbed them, we would have had them for nothing. The way they were going we never knew when they were going to do it. This happened so fast. Bang, they did it. They would have shot us if they had the chance. Our strategy was to smash them when they emerged from the bank. My boss didn't like that idea initially, but I said, 'Would you sooner have a high-speed chase or a hostage situation?' I told him that we had one thing going for us and that was surprise. They didn't know we were on to them. They were going to be flabbergasted and they were.

"Before that, they were looking at doing another bank on a Friday night. It was loaded with money and we knew that Roger loved it. He wanted to do that one and we were ready. They were around that bank 20 times a day for three days. Rollie was in four or five times just changing money and having a look. Then they got spooked. We let the city police know we were there and that we had everything under control. We told them to keep their men back and if we got them, we'd turn everything over to them. But Roger checked the perimeter and he saw two guys in a detective car drinking coffee and went close enough to hear their police radio. That blew the whole thing.

"They were all set to do it. In fact that night we watched them steal a truck. They planned the escape route and had left their cool car, the rental car, sitting a half minute away. They were there to do it, but before Roger would do it he'd go through the whole thing again. Then he spotted the detectives. Roger called them 'skunks.' We thought initially he had spotted one of our guys, but then they talked on the phone about the 'two skunks in the D-car.' We were on a real high because we know they were about to strike. Then it was a downer because they didn't do it. We had put in days following them and got up to that high where we thought they were going to go. We were with them and we knew they had that stolen truck. And then they cancel out! It's hard coming down. We were on a low. Christ, all that work gone.

"Then we almost missed them. After the weekend, we'd drive back Sunday night or Monday morning because they didn't leave until after 10:00 a.m. As long as we were there before 10:00, we could pick them up. We got a call that something was up and we drove like madmen to get down there at 9:15 a.m. We got to Rollie's apartment and his car was gone! He had never left at that time before. He never left the house before ten and here it is 9:15 and he's not there! Everybody fanned out to the places they usually went to and I found them in a restaurant not too far from the house. They were having breakfast. We knew something was up because they had a car from a guy who had reported it stolen. He must have known what was going on and reported it stolen after they went to do the bank.

"Surprise was our biggest advantage. We knew these guys were professionals and wouldn't be spending much time in the bank. From my observations from a snowbank with binoculars I saw them pull the car up and leave it running. It was cold enough that you could see the exhaust. They got out of the car and they had on toques—balaclavas. As soon as they got to the front steps they pulled the balaclavas down over their heads. Roger had never gone into a bank before. It had to be. They had two cars. They left the cool car a short distance away and had done a lot of spinning looking for tails. They went through a subdivision and we stayed off them.

"As soon as they walked into the bank I picked up the radio and said, 'They're in the bank. Count to ten and start closing in.' I jumped into my Mustang and pulled out in front of an air force officer. I was driving very slowly and I stopped at the green light. He was blowing his horn probably wondering what is wrong with this guy. Then we saw them run out of the bank. Roger had a gun. He ran around the passenger side and his partner opened the driver's door. He threw the satchel with the money inside the car. They were both wearing balaclavas. They got in the car and pulled their balaclavas up. They just started to move when I pulled across the curb and hit them broadside. Roger's eyes were that big [indicating with his hands]. They were both laughing because they thought it was a successful bank job. When I hit them I was going about 15, 20, 25 miles an hour—enough to bounce them back. I gave it a good shot as I went over the curb. Roger had the gun on the dash and I had a shotgun in the car and my sidearm. When I hit their car, his gun fell to the floor. My door jammed and I couldn't get the shotgun out and I couldn't get my sidearm. We were looking each other in the eyes, just the hood of the car separating us, and he was reaching for the gun. I knew what for, but I couldn't get mine.

"Just then J.C. hit them the other way and they were done. Roger would have shot me if he had got to that gun. There's no doubt he was going to do that. By the time I got the door open it was over. There was a car behind, another one of our guys with a shotgun, another one with a rifle. It happened in seconds, it was so fast. I came out of the car and we put them up against the bank and Roger said, 'You bastards are real cool. I knew we shouldn't have done this. You're something else.' And then he said, 'We have only one gun, it's in the car.' All Rollie would say is, 'Take this stupid thing off my head,' referring to the balaclava. Roger asked me afterwards, 'Who are you guys?'

"Meanwhile the air force officer saw everything. He went into a restaurant to phone the police and said, 'I can't believe what's happening. There's a

Mustang. He's drunk. He pulled out and passed me and then he slowed down. He's gone off and hit a car broadside and they're out of the car with guns and now they're going to kill each other.' There was one cruiser in the area when the bank alarm did go off and he came over with his gun out and he was shaking like a leaf.

"Roger still can't get over that we didn't waste him. He told me that several times. I told him that we didn't have any reason. We had them. It would have been like shooting fish in a barrel. If they had fired a shot, it might have been different. We knew they were runners so we put the cuffs on their feet so they couldn't run. Their records included 'Escape,' 'Escape,' 'Escape.' They were put in two separate jails because they were escape artists, but they both escaped! I couldn't believe it when I heard that Roger had escaped. We were working on another case and we heard it on the news. 'Jesus Christ!' And then Rollie escapes too! Jesus, they both do it! They were recaptured and each got 12 years. Roger and I kept in touch, I even dropped in and saw him in prison. He was not like the others you deal with. He was looked at by other criminals as top dog because he never squealed on anybody. He kept telling me that he was going to make something of himself and his book. I didn't believe him. He wrote me a long, long letter asking me to go to bat for him on parole— no way. There's no way I'd take the chance because I figured that Roger, sure he had changed, but if he ended up with a crisis and something didn't go right, there would be no doubt in my mind that he'd be right back into it. I feel he's done well and he deserves a lot of credit, but if that book had failed, he would have either killed himself or gone right back to robbing banks. We treated Roger fairly and he recognizes that."

Chapter 30

ONE ON ONE
WITH A KILLER

Erin Anderson

WHEN I FIRST MEET THE MAN CLAIMING THE SLAUGHTER OF 16 PEOPLE AND THE title as Canada's most horrifying serial killer, he is asking after his mom like any good son.

She has been receiving crank calls, it seems, and her health is frail, and Michael Wayne McGray pleads with a prison official for time tonight to phone her, to make sure she's okay. When he is promised the call, he relaxes back into his chair. We're left alone, with a wall of glass between us.

And Mr. McGray begins, ever so nonchalantly, to talk about the killings. How it made him feel good to stab those prostitutes in the dark. How eagerly the gay men took him home, never suspecting. How the death and pain and blood of it all fuelled his fantasies for months.

He never flinches once in the telling. His soft voice sounds the same tallying victims as it did speaking of his mother. To anyone watching, we might be chatting about the Oscars.

The guards at the maximum-security prison where Mr. McGray has begun his life sentence, after pleading guilty to first-degree murder in Moncton on Monday, are not taking any chances. They joke about "his urges," but they know that he has threatened to kill a guard if he has the chance, and he is not allowed around other prisoners.

I put in the request on Tuesday for an interview, and for two days, prison officials had told me that Mr. McGray wasn't feeling up for visitors of any kind—he was fighting his homicidal "urges," what he calls his "hunger."

On Wednesday, he apparently smashed the television in his room. But by Thursday, he was prepared to talk, and I headed to Renous, about 150 kilometres by bumpy highway north of Moncton.

Before my trip, police warned me to be extra careful with him—one officer helpfully described how it would only take a second for such a hulking man to slip his shackled wrists over my head and snap my neck, if he felt so inclined.

There was never a chance of that happening. The glass divider penned him in, and the guards watched us from a window overlooking the room.

But every so often, Mr. McGray would casually drag his fingers across the glass surface while making some point, and though I knew I couldn't be in any danger, I had to fight the instinct to jump away.

He is still the man who strangled a Moncton woman named Joan Hicks with his bare hands, beat her head against her bathroom wall, and then slashed her throat just to make certain she was dead.

And I have seen the sickening crime-scene photo of what happened next to her 11-year-old daughter Nena, who so loved the Maple Leafs and was learning French.

Even if Mr. McGray's story is true and another man killed the girl, he was still there in her bedroom when she was strung up—just for show—in her polka-dotted underwear, among the clothes in her closet. (A second murder charge against Mr. McGray for Nena's death was stayed this week, after his guilty plea.)

We sit across from each other in the prison interview room for about 90 minutes, speaking by phone. I ask my questions and try not to linger too long on the answers, and he recounts the killing of all those people—a string of lonely gay men and prostitutes and homeless drug addicts—with careful civility, but not even a play at remorse.

He doesn't have anything "against" homosexual men, he informs me; they're just easy to kill.

He is also uncertain of specific dates—he says he crisscrossed the country so often he can't remember when he was where—which will make it harder for police to prove that he is telling the truth.

"I remember places by the victims," he says.

He claims to have killed at least once a year since 1985, in such cities as Ottawa, Calgary, Vancouver, and Toronto—and even two people across the border in Seattle.

On request, he starts matter-of-factly listing them off; the two prostitutes he stabbed in Vancouver, a gay man in Montreal, an acquaintance named "Fluff" in Saint John's south end, two women in Nova Scotia.

He says he could lead the way to the body he buried in Toronto's High Park, in, he believes, the summer of 1997—a claim the city's police said yesterday that they consider dubious.

It's possible Mr. McGray killed people in Toronto "and we are looking into it," Det. Sgt. Doug Grady said.

But the homicide detective suggested that the man is "playing games" and is getting his kicks by trying to get the country's police "running all over hell's half-acre."

"We just want to get his blood," Det. Sgt. Grady said, suggesting that DNA testing will tell more about Mr. McGray's activities than his boasts ever will.

When I ask Mr. McGray for names, he shrugs. He did not take the time to learn their names, he says.

Police have already charged him, in the wake of his own statements, with the stabbing deaths of two gay men in Montreal in 1991, and the 1987 killing of an acquaintance after a failed taxi robbery in Saint John.

Mr. McGray suggests that he wants to bring closure to the families, but he says he won't talk to police until three conditions are met: He doesn't want to be charged with any more killings, as he is already serving the maximum sentence; he wants treatment, and he doesn't want any accessories charged in relation to the killings.

But the RCMP has said it cannot negotiate with him, certainly not before learning details of his claims. "It's like putting a gun to our head," said Sergeant Wayne Noonan, a Halifax RCMP spokesman. Too many jurisdictions and too many families are involved, and any deal could taint the statement for use in court later.

Mr. McGray does not want to spend the rest of his life in segregation, but he accepts there is little chance that he will ever be freed. "I know that I'm going to spend the rest of my life in prison, and I think I belong here."

***

A few times during the interview, he loses his temper—because I suggest to him that he might not be telling the truth.

When this happens, he spits out an obscenity and his voice starts to rise. Then, he switches back to his soft tone, as if reining in his anger.

He is a large man, and has a potbelly and black beard, both acquired since his arrest for the killings of Joan and Nena Hicks in March, 1998. His hair is puffy, and his eyes brown, and if you didn't know whom you were talking to, you might consider them soulful.

In any event, I look him in the eyes as little as possible—how do you meet the gaze of someone telling you that he stays sober when he kills so that the memories are sharper? Whenever our eyes meet, he is never the first to look away.

***

Mr. McGray was born in Collingwood, Ont., and grew up in Yarmouth, N.S., a struggling fishing village a few hours southwest of my hometown. While he was mulling over his biographies of serial killers, and feeding his urges, I would have probably been playing basketball there with my junior high school.

He claims to have found his first victim, not far away, on the road to Digby. Her name was Elizabeth Gail Tucker, and she was 17, hitchhiking to a fish plant job, when Mr. McGray says he and a friend picked her up.

He is not sure where his "urge" comes from, he says, or how it started. He knows only he can't control it.

Maybe it grew out of an unhappy childhood as the second youngest of six siblings, with a father who worked as a welder and was an abusive alcoholic in between.

He says it was there even before he suffered sexual and physical abuse at a group home in near Shelbourne, where he was sent for being "unmanageable" at home.

Whatever the cause, he says he quickly discovered that he liked killing, he "liked it a lot."

***

At 3:40 p.m., prison official Rick Matthews knocks on the glass and gives me two minutes to wrap up the interview.

Once more, we go over the list of cities where he says he has left bodies, and his tally remains the same.

He doesn't slip up—but he doesn't get specific either. He tells me that he hopes his story gets out there, so that perhaps the police will make him a deal.

He's not seeking notoriety, he insists, but just wants help so that the killing stops and, maybe, his nightmares will go away.

When the time's up and Mr. Matthews returns, Mr. McGray says, "Call me any time." Then he hangs up his phone and stands at the door waiting for the guards.

I don't see him look back. And that is a good thing.

REFERENCES

GENERAL INTRODUCTION

Durkheim, Emile. [1938] 1966. *The Rules of Sociological Method*. New York: The Free Press.

PART I: DEVIANCE AND SOCIETY

Chapter 2: Prescientific Approaches to Deviance

Ben-Yahuda, Nachman. 1985. *Deviance and Moral Boundaries: Witchcraft, the Occult, Science Fiction, Deviant Sciences and Scientists*. Chicago: University of Chicago Press.

Best, Joel. 1985. "The Razor Blade in the Apple: The Social Construction of Urban Legends." *Social Problems* 32 (5), 488–499.

Blumenfeld, Laura. 1991. "Procter and Gamble's Devil of a Problem." *Toronto Star* (July 18).

Boyle, Thomas. 1989. *Black Swine in the Sewers of Hampstead: Beneath the Surface of Victorian Sensationalism*. Harmondsworth: Penguin.

Briggs, Katherine M. 1978. *The Vanishing People*. London: B.T. Batsford.

Brunvand, Jan Harold. 1981. *The Vanishing Hitchhiker*. New York: W.W. Norton.

_____. 1989. *Curses! Broiled Again!: The Hottest Urban Legends Going*. New York: W.W. Norton.

Bulthuis, Jack. 1989. "The Teen Satanism Workshops—Ingersoll, Ontario." Unpublished report.

Canadian Broadcasting Corporation. 1991. "Dungeons and Dragons." *Ideas*. Toronto: CBC. Transcript of program aired May 29.

Cassar, Carmel. 1993. "Witchcraft Beliefs and Social Control in Seventeeth-Century Malta." *Mediterranean Studies* 3 (2), 316–334.

Cave, Alfred A. 1995. "The Failure of the Shawnee Prophet's Witch Hunt." *Ethnohistory* 42 (3), 445–475.

Christie-Murray, David. 1989. *A History of Heresy*. New York: Oxford University Press.

Chruscinski, Theresa, and Peter Gabor. 1990. "Meeting the Needs of Troubled Teens." *The Globe and Mail* (March 28).

Claridge, Thomas. 1988. "You Ooze Evil, Demeter Told, as Judge Adds Two Life Terms." *The Globe and Mail* (July 29), A1.

Cohn, Norman. 1976. *Europe's Inner Demons*. St. Albans: Dutton.

_____. 1981. *Warrant for Genocide: The Myth of the Jewish World Conspiracy and the Protocols of the Elders of Zion*. Toronto: Canadian Scholars' Press.

Cornwell, John. 1991. *Powers of Darkness, Powers of Light: Travels in Search of the Miraculous and the Demonic*. London: Penguin.

Coudert, Allison P. 1992. "The Myth of the Improved Status of Protestant Women: The Case of the Witchcraze." In Brian P. Levak (ed.), *Witchcraft, Women and Society: Articles on Witchcraft, Magic and Demonology*, vol. 10. New York: Garland.

Daly, Mary. 1978. *Gyn/Ecology: The Metaethics of Radical Feminism*. Toronto: Fitzhenry and Whiteside.

Dominick, Joseph R. 1978. "Crime and Law Enforcement in the Mass Media." In Charles Winick (ed.), *Deviance and Mass Media*. Beverly Hills: Sage.

Dunning, John. 1989. *Mystical Murders: True Murders of the Occult*. London: Arrow.

Eastlea, Brian. 1980. *Witch-hunting, Magic and the New Philosophy*. Brighton: Harvester.

Erikson, Kai T. 1966. *Wayward Puritans: A Study in the Sociology of Deviance*. New York: John Wiley.

Fukurai, Hiroshi, Edgar W. Butler, and Richard Krooth. 1994. "Sociologists in Action: The McMartin Sexual Abuse Case, Litigation, Justice, and Mass Hysteria." *The American Sociologist* 25 (4), 44–71.

Garrett, Clarke. 1977. "Women and Witches: Patterns of Analysis." *Signs: Journal of Women in Culture and Society* 3 (2), 461–470.

Goode, Erich. 1992. *Collective Behavior*. Fort Worth: Harcourt Brace Jovanovich.

Groh, Dieter. 1987. "The Temptation of Conspiracy Theory, Part II." In C.F. Grauman and S. Moscovici (eds.), *Changing Conceptions of Conspiracy*. Berlin: Springer-Verlag.

Guiley, Rosemary Ellen. 1991. *Harper's Encyclopedia of Mystical and Paranormal Experience*. San Francisco: HarperCollins.

Gutin, Jo Ann C. 1996. "That Fine Madness." *Discover* 17 (10), 75–82.

Harris, Marvin. 1978. *Cows, Pigs, Wars, and Witches: The Riddles of Culture*. New York: Random House.

Hester, Marianne. 1990. "The Dynamics of Male Domination: Using the Witch Craze in 16th and 17th Century England as a Case Study." *Women's Studies Institute Forum* 13 (1/2), 9–19.

Hicks, Robert D. 1991. *In Pursuit of Satan: The Police and the Occult*. Buffalo: Prometheus.

Hoffman, Sr., Heinrich. n.d. *Der Struwwelpeter*. Germany: Pestalozzi Verlag.

Hume, Lynne. 1995. "Witchcraft and the Law in Australia." *Journal of Church and State* 37 (1), 135–144.

Inverarity, James M., Pat Lauderdale, and Barry C. Field. 1983. *Law and Society: Sociological Perspectives on Criminal Law*. Boston: Little, Brown.

Jenkins, Philip, and Daniel Maier-Katkin. 1992. "Satanism Myth and Reality in a Contemporary Moral Panic." *Crime, Law and Social Change* 17 (1), 53–75.

Karlsen, Carol F. 1989. *The Devil in the Shape of a Woman: Witchcraft in Colonial New England*. New York: Random House.

Kelly, Francis. 1988. "Judge Convicts Lab Technician of Witchcraft." *Toronto Star* (December 8).

Kent, Stephen A. 1993a. "Deviant Scripturalism and Ritual Satanic Abuse Part One: Possible Judeo-Christian Influences." *Religion* 23, 229–241.

_____. 1993b. "Deviant Scripturalism and Ritual Satanic Abuse Part Two: Possible Masonic, Mormon, Magick and Pagan Influences." *Religion* 23, 355–367.

Korem, Dan. 1994. *Suburban Gangs: The Affluent Rebels*. Richardson: International Focus Press.

Kramer, Heinrich, and James Sprenger. 1971. *The Malleus Maleficarum of Heinrich Kramer and James Sprenger*. New York: Dover.

Larner, Christina. 1980. "Criminum Exceptum? The Crime of Witchcraft in Europe." In V.A.C. Gatrell, Bruce Lenman, and Geoffrey Parker (eds.), *Crime and the Law: The Social History of Crime in Western Europe Since 1500*. London: Europa, 49–75.

Levack, Brian P. 1987. *The Witch-Hunt in Early Modern Europe*. New York: Longman.

_____, ed. 1992a. *Possession and Exorcism. Articles on Witchcraft, Magic and Demonology*, vol. 9. New York: Garland.

_____, ed. 1992b. *Witchcraft, Women and Society. Articles on Witchcraft, Magic and Demonology*, vol. 10. New York: Garland.

Lowney, Kathleen S. 1995. "Teenage Satansim as Oppositional Youth Subculture." *Journal of Contemporary Ethnography* 23 (4), 453–484.

Macfarlane, Alan. 1970. *Witchcraft in Tudor and Stuart England*. London: Routledge and Kegan Paul.

Marron, Kevin. 1989. *Witches, Pagans, and Magic in the New Age*. Toronto: McClelland-Bantam Seal Books.

Marty, Martin E. 1990. "Satan and the American Spiritual Underground." In *Britannica Book of the Year*, 308–309.

Medved, Michael. 1991. "Popular Culture and the War Against Standards." *New Dimensions: The Psychology Behind the News* (June), 38–42.

Morgan, Ted. 1988. *Literary Outlaw: The Life and Times of William S. Burroughs*. New York: Avon Books.

Morison, Samuel Eliot. 1955. *The Parkman Reader: From the Works of Francis Parkman*. Boston: Little, Brown.

Murray, Margaret. 1921. *The Witch Cult in Western Europe*. London: Oxford.

Oake, George. 1990. "Tales of Devil Worship Chill Albertans." *Toronto Star* (November 12).

Oppenheimer, Judy. 1988. *Private Demons: The Life of Shirley Jackson*. New York: Putman's Sons.

Owomoyela, Oyckan. 1990. "No Problem Can Fail to Crash on His Head: The Trickster in Contemporary African Folklore." *The World and I* (April), 625–632.

Pearson, Ian. 1984. "The Cat in the Bag and Other Absolutely Untrue Tales from Our Urban Mythology." *Quest Magazine* (November).

Peck, M. Scott. 1983. *People of the Lie: The Hope for Healing Human Evil*. New York: Simon and Schuster.

Pelka, Fred. 1992. "The Women's Holocaust." *The Humanist* 52 (5), 5–9.

Pollock, Jack. 1989. *Dear M.: Letters from a Gentleman of Excess*. Toronto: McClelland & Stewart.

Radin, Paul. [1956] 1972. *The Trickster: A Study in American Indian Mythology*. New York: Schocken.

Redondi, Pietro. 1987. *Galileo: Heretic*. Princeton: Princeton University Press.

Reed, Christopher. 1989. "Diabolical Debauchery or Mere Stories from the Mouths of Babes?" *The Globe and Mail* (May 20).

Richards, Jeffrey. 1990. *Sex, Dissidence and Damnation: Minority Groups in the Middle Ages*. New York: Barnes and Noble.

Roberts, David. 1996. "Study Ordered of Criminal Prosecutions." *The Globe and Mail* (March 26), A6.

Russell, Jeffrey Burton. 1984. *Lucifer: The Devil in the Middle Ages*. Ithaca: Cornell University Press.

_____. 1988. *The Prince of Darkness: Radical Evil and the Power of Good in History*. Ithaca: Cornell University Press.

Sagan, Carl. 1995. *The Demon-Haunted World: Science as a Candle in the Dark*. New York: Random House.

Santino, Jack. 1990. "Fitting the Bill: The Trickster in American Popular Culture." *The World and I* (April), 661–668.

Scher, Len. 1992. *The Un-Canadians: True Stories of the Blacklist Era*. Toronto: Lester.

Sherman, Josepha. 1990. "Child of Chaos, Coyote: A Folkloric Triad." *The World and I* (April), 645–650.

Simpson, Jacqueline. [1973] 1996. "Olaf Tryggvason versus the Powers of Darkness." In Venetia Newall (ed.), *The Witch in History*. New York: Barnes and Noble.

Thomas, Keith. 1971. *Religion and the Decline of Magic*. New York: Charles Scribner's Sons.

Toronto Star. 1990a. "Albertan Denies Suicide Link: Satanist Cult Cited in Trio of Teen Deaths" (March 15).

_____. 1990b. "Police Seize Satanic Objects" (October 31).

Trevor-Roper, H.R. 1969. *The European Witchcraze of the Sixteenth and Seventeenth Centuries*. Harmondsworth: Penguin.

Victor, Jeffrey S. 1993. *Satanic Panic: The Creation of a Contemporary Legend*. Chicago: Open Court.

Watters, Ethan. 1991. "The Devil in Mr. Ingram." *Mother Jones* (July-August).

Watts, Sheldon. 1984. *A Social History of Western Europe, 1450–1720*. London: Hutchinson University Library and Hutchinson University Library for Africa.

Webster, Charles. [1982] 1996. *From Paracelsus to Newton: Magic and the Making of Modern Science*. New York: Barnes and Noble.

Wilkins, Charles. 1994. "The Bird and Haida Call the Trickster." *Canadian Geographic* (March/April), 71–79.

Wilmer, Harry A. 1988. "Introduction." In Paul Woodruff and Harry A. Wilmer (eds.), *Facing Evil: Light at the Core of Darkness*. LaSalle: Open Court.

Wilson, Colin. 1987. *Aleister Crowley: The Nature of the Beast*. Northhamptonshire: Aquarian Press.

Worobec, Christine. 1995. "Witchcraft Beliefs and Practices in Pre-Revolutionary Russian and Ukrainian Villages." *The Russian Review* 54, 165–187.

Wright, Lawrence. 1993. "A Reporter At Large: Remembering Satan" (Parts 1 and 2). *The New Yorker* (May 17 and 24). Copyright 1993 by Lawrence Wright. Appeared originally in *The New Yorker*. Reprinted by permission.

Zeidenberg, Jerry. 1990. "Persecuted Professor: Celebrated Scientist Was Driven into Exile by Cold War Witch-Hunt in Canada." *The Globe and Mail* (March 16).

Chapter 3: Lay Definitions of Crime

Backhouse, C. 1991. *Petticoats and Prejudice: Women and Law in Nineteenth-Century Canada.* Toronto: Butterworths.

Bala, N. 1997. *Young Offenders Law.* Concord: Irwin.

Burtch, B. 1992. *The Sociology of Law: Critical Approaches to Social Control.* Toronto: Harcourt Brace Jovanovich.

Carrington, P., and S. Moyer. 1994. "Trends in Youth Crime and Police Response, Pre- and Post-YOA. *Canadian Journal of Criminology* 36, 1–28.

Clark, B., and T. Fleming. 1993. "Implementing the *Young Offenders Act* in Ontario: Issues of Principles, Programmes and Power." *Howard Journal of Criminal Justice* 32, 114–126.

Comack-Antony, A.E. 1980. "Radical Criminology." In R.A. Silverman and J. Teevan (eds.), *Crime in Canadian society*, 2nd ed. Toronto: Butterworths.

Corrado, R., N. Bala, R. Linden, and M. LeBlanc, eds. 1992. *Juvenile Justice in Canada.* Toronto: Butterworths.

Doob, A., and J. Meen. 1993. "An Exploration of Changes in Dispositions for Young Offenders in Toronto." *Canadian Journal of Criminology* 35, 19–29.

Durkheim, E. 1964. *The Rules of Sociological Method.* New York: Free Press.

Edgerton, R.B. 1985. *Rules, Expectations, and Social Order.* Berkeley: University of California Press.

Evans, J., and A. Himmelfarb. 1996. "Counting Crimes." In R. Linden (ed.), *Criminology: A Canadian perspective*, 3rd ed. Toronto: Harcourt Brace Jovanovich.

Gillin, J. 1945. *Criminology and Penology*, 3rd ed. New York: Appleton-Century-Crofts.

Hagan, J. 1992. "Class Fortification against Crime in Canada." *Canadian Review of Sociology and Anthropology* 29, 126–139.

Kennedy, L.W. 1990. *On the Borders of Crime.* New York: Longman.

Kent, S. 1990. "Deviance, Labelling, and Normative Strategies in 'The Canadian New Religion/ Counter-Cult' Debate." *Canadian Journal of Sociology* 15, 393–416.

Law Reform Commission of Canada. 1974. *The Meaning of Guilt: Strict Liability.* Ottawa: Information Canada.

McGarrell, E., and T. Castellano. 1991. "An Integrative Conflict Model of the Criminal Law Formation Process." *Journal of Research in Crime and Delinquency* 28, 174–196.

Rodrigues, G.P. 1998. *Pocket Criminal Code 1999.* Toronto: Carswell.

Sacco, V. 1992. *Deviance: Conformity and Control in Canadian Society.* Scarborough: Prentice-Hall.

Sacco, V., and H. Johnson. 1990. *Patterns of Criminal Victimization in Canada.* Ottawa: Minister of Supply and Services Canada.

Turk, A.T. 1993. "A Proposed Resolution of Key Issues in the Political Sociology of Law." In F. Adler and W. Laufer (eds.), *New Directions in Criminological Theory*, vol. 4. New Brunswick: Transaction.

Young, J., and R. Matthews. 1992. *Rethinking Criminology: The Realist Debate.* London: Sage.

Chapter 4: Media Constructions of Crime

Baker, M.H., et al. 1983. "The Impact of a Crime Wave: Perceptions, Fear, and Confidence in the Police." *Law and Society Review* 17, 317–334.

Best, J., ed. 1989a. *Images of Issues: Typifying Social Problems*. Hawthorne: Aldine de Gruyter.

_____, ed. 1989b. "Secondary Claims-making: Claims about Threats to Children on the Network News." *Perspectives on Social Problems* 1, 277.

_____, ed. 1991. "Road Warriors on Hair-trigger Highways. Cultural Resources and the Media's Construction of the 1987 Freeway Shootings Problem." *Sociological Inquiry* 61, 327–345.

Bortner, M.A. 1984. "Media Images and Public Attitudes toward Crime and Justice." In R. Surette (ed.), *Justice and the Media*, 15–30. Springfield: Charles C. Thomas.

Brownstein, H.H. 1991. "The Media and the Construction of Random Drug Violence." *Social Justice* 18, 85–103.

Carlson, J.M. 1985. *Prime Time Law Enforcement: Crime Show Viewing and Attitudes toward the Criminal Justice System*. New York: Praeger.

Cook, F.L., and W.G. Skogan. 1990. "Agenda Setting and the Rise and Fall of Policy Issues: The Case of Criminal Victimization of the Elderly." *Government and Policy* 8, 395–415.

Crouch, B.M., and K.R. Damphousse. 1992. "Newspapers and the Anti-satanism Movement: A Content Analysis." *Sociological Spectrum* 12, 1–20.

Doob, A.N. 1982. "The Role of Mass Media in Creating Exaggerated Levels of Fear of Being the Victim of a Violent Crime." In Peter Stringer (ed.), *Confronting Social Issues: Applications of Social Psychology*, 145–159. Toronto: Academic Press.

Ericson, R.V. 1989. "Patrolling the Facts: Secrecy and Publicity in Police Work." *British Journal of Sociology* 40, 205–226.

_____. 1991. "Mass Media, Crime, Law and Justice." *British Journal of Sociology* 31, 219–249.

Fishman, M. 1981. "Police News: Constructing an Image of Crime." *Urban Life* 9, 371–394.

Garofalo, J. 1981. "Crime and the Mass Media: A Selective Review of Research." *Journal of Research in Crime and Delinquency* 18, 319–350.

Gilbert, N. 1994. "Miscounting Social Ills." *Society* 31, 24–25.

Gordon, M.T., and S. Riger. 1989. *The Female Fear*. New York: Free Press.

Gorelick, S.M. 1989. "Join Our War: The Construction of Ideology in a Newspaper Crimefighting Campaign." *Crime and Delinquency* 35, 421–436.

Gusfield, J.R. 1989. "Constructing the Ownership of Social Problems: Fun and Profit in the Welfare State." *Social Problems* 36, 431–441.

Heath, L. 1984. "Impact of Newspaper Crime Reports on Fear of Crime: Multi-methodological Investigation." *Journal of Personality and Social Psychology* 47, 263–276.

Hilgartner, S., and C.I. Bosk. 1988. "The Rise and Fall of Social Problems: A Public Arenas Model." *American Journal of Sociology* 94, 57.

Howitt, D. 1982. *The Mass Media and Social Problems*. Oxford: Pergamon.

Humphries, D. 1981. "Serious Crime, News Coverage and Ideology: A Content Analysis of Crime Coverage in a Metropolitan Newspaper." *Crime and Delinquency* 27, 191–205.

Jenkins, P. 1994. *Using Murder: The Social Construction of Serial Homicide*. Hawthorne: Aldine de Gruyter.

Jenkins, P., and D. Maier-Katkin. 1992. "Satanism: Myth and Reality in a Contemporary Moral Panic." *Journal of Crime, Law and Social Change* 17, 53–76.

Katz, J. 1987. "What Makes Crime News." *Media, Culture and Society* 9, 60.

Liska, A.E., and W. Baccaglini. 1990. "Feeling Safe by Comparison: Crime in the Newspapers." *Social Problems* 37, 360–374.

Lotz, R.E. 1991. *Crime and the American Press*. New York: Praeger.

Marsh, H.L. 1991. "A Comparative Analysis of Crime Coverage in Newspapers in the United States and Other Countries from 1960 to 1989: A Review of the Literature." *Journal of Criminal Justice* 19, 67–80.

Newman, G.R. 1990. "Popular Culture and Criminal Justice: A Preliminary Analysis." *Journal of Criminal Justice* 18, 261–274.

O'Keefe, G.J. 1984. "Public Views on Crime: Television Exposure and Media Credibility." In R. Bostrom (ed.), *Communication Yearbook 8*, 514–535. Beverly Hills: Sage.

Orcutt, J.D., and J.B. Turner. 1993. "Shocking Numbers and Graphic Accounts: Quantified Images of Drug Problems in the Print Media." *Social Problems* 40, 190–206.

Palmgreen, P., and P. Clarke. 1977. "Agenda-Setting with Local and National Issues." *Communication Research* 4, 435–452.

Protess, D.L., et al. 1985. "Uncovering Rape: The Watchdog Press and the Limits of Agenda Setting." *Public Opinion Quarterly* 49, 19–37.

Sacco, V.F. 1982. "The Effects of Mass Media on Perceptions of Crime: A Reanalysis of the Issues." *Pacific Sociological Review* 25, 475–493.

Schlesinger, P., H. Tumber, and G. Murdock. 1991. "The Media of Politics, Crime and Criminal Justice." *British Journal of Sociology* 42, 397–420.

Schlesinger, P., et al. 1992. *Women Viewing Violence*. London: BFI.

Schneider, J.W. 1985. "Social Problems Theory: The Constructionist View." *Annual Review of Sociology* 11, 209–229.

Sherizen, S. 1978. "Social Creation of Crime News: All the News Fitted to Print." In Charles Winick (ed.), *Deviance and Mass Media*, 213–224. Beverly Hills: Sage.

Skogan, W.G., and M.G. Maxfield. 1981. *Coping with Crime: Individual and Neighborhood Reactions*. Beverly Hills: Sage.

Soothill, K., and S. Walby. 1991. *Sex Crime in the News*. London: Routledge.

Sparks, G.G., and R.M. Ogles. 1990. "The Difference between Fear of Victimization and the Probability of Being Victimized: Implications for Cultivation." *Journal of Broadcasting and Electronic Media* 34, 351–358.

Sparks, R. 1992. *Television and the Drama of Crime*. Buckingham: Open University Press.

Surette, R. 1992. *Media, Crime and Criminal Justice*. Pacific Grove: Brooks/Cole.

Tyler, T.R. 1984. "Assessing the Risk of Crime Victimization: The Integration of Personal Victimization Experience and Socially Transmitted Information." *Journal of Social Issues* 40, 27–38.

Voumvakis, S.E., and R.V. Ericson. 1984. *News Accounts of Attacks on Women: A Comparison of Three Toronto Newspapers*. Toronto: University of Toronto, Centre of Criminology.

Williams, P., and J. Dickinson. 1993. "Fear of Crime: Read All about It: The Relationship between Newspaper Reporting and Fear of Crime." *British Journal of Sociology* 33, 34.

Zillman, D., and J. Wakshlag. 1987. "Fear of Victimization and the Appeal of Crime Drama." In D. Zillman and J. Bryant (eds.), *Selective Exposure to Communication*, 141–156. Hillsdale: Lawrence Erlbaum.

PART II: SOCIAL CONTROL

Chapter 6: The Body of the Condemned

Faucher, L. 1838. *De la reforme des prisons*.
de Mably, D. 1789. *De la législation, Oeuvres complètes*, IX.
Pièces originales et procédures du procès fait à Robert-François Damiens, III, 1757.

PART III: SOCIOLOGICAL CONCEPTS AND APPROACHES

Chapter 9: Foundations of Sociological Theory

Brym, Robert J. 1986. "Anglo-Canadian Sociology." *Current Sociology* 34 (1), 1–152.

Douglas, John D. 1967. *The Social Meaning of Suicide*. Princeton: Princeton University Press.

Durkheim, Emile. [1897] 1951. *Suicide: A Study of Sociology*. New York: The Free Press.

_____. [1966] 1985. *The Rules of the Sociological Method*, 8th ed., C. Catlin (ed.), S. Solovay and J. Mueller (trans). New York: The Free Press.

Fox, Bonnie J., and John Fox. 1986. "Women in the Labour Market, 1931–81: Exclusion and Competition." *Canadian Review of Sociology and Anthropology* 23, 1–21.

Gerth, H.H., and C. Wright Mills. 1946. "The Man and His Work." In H. Gerth and C. Mills (eds. and trans.), *From Max Weber: Essays in Sociology*, 174. New York: Oxford University Press.

Goffman, Erving. 1959. *The Presentation of Self in Everyday Life*. Garden City: Anchor.

Goyder, John C. 1981. "Income Differences between the Sexes: Findings from a National Canadian Survey." *Canadian Review of Sociology and Anthropology* 18, 321–342.

Hartmann, Heidi I. [1978] 1984. "The Unhappy Marriage of Marxism and Feminism: Towards a More Progressive Union." In A. Jaggar and P. Rothenberg (eds.), *Feminist Frameworks: Alternative Theoretical Accounts of the Relations between Women and Men*, 2nd ed., 172–189. New York: McGraw-Hill.

Marx, Karl. [1859] 1904. *A Contribution to the Critique of Political Economy*, N. Stone (trans.). Chicago: Charles H. Kerr.

_____. [1932] 1972. "The German Ideology: Part I." In R. Tucker (ed.), *The Marx-Engels Reader*, 110–164. New York: Praeger.

Marx, Karl, and Friedrich Engels. [1848] 1972. "Manifesto of the Communist Party." In R. Tucker (ed.), *The Marx-Engels Reader*, 331–362. New York: Praeger.

Meissner, Martin, et al. 1975. "No Exit for Wives: Sexual Division of Labour and the Culmination of Household Demands." *Canadian Review of Sociology and Anthropology* 12, 424–439.

Ornstein, Michael D. 1983. "Class, Gender and Job Income in Canada." *Research in Social Stratification and Mobility* 2, 41–75.

Parkin, Frank. [1971] 1972. *Class Inequality and Political Order: Social Stratification in Capitalist and Communist Societies*. London: Paladin.

Samuelsson, Kurt. [1957] 1961. *Religion and Economic Action*, E. French (trans.). Stockholm: Scandinavian University Books.

Weber, Max. [1922] 1946. "Class, Status, Party." In H. Gerth and C. Mills (eds. and trans.), *From Max Weber: Essays in Sociology*, 180–195. New York: Oxford University Press.

_____. [1922] 1947. *The Theory of Social and Economic Organization*, T. Parsons (ed.). New York: The Free Press.

_____. [1904–1905] 1958. *The Protestant Ethic and the Spirit of Capitalism*, T. Parsons (trans.). New York: Charles Scribner's Sons.

Zeitlin, Irving. 1968. *Ideology and the Development of Sociological Theory*, 2nd ed. Englewood Cliffs: Prentice-Hall.

Chapter 12: The Influence of Situational Ethics on Cheating Among College Students

Baird, John S. 1980. "Current Trends in College Cheating." *Psychology in Schools* 17, 512–522.

Davis, Stephen F., Cathy A. Grover, Angela H. Becker, and Loretta N. McGregor. 1992. "Academic Dishonesty: Prevalence, Determinants, Techniques, and Punishments." *Teaching of Psychology*.

Edwards, Paul. 1967. *The Encyclopedia of Philosophy*, no. 3, Paul Edwards (ed.). New York: Macmillan Company and Free Press.

Eisenberger, Robert, and Dolores M. Shank. 1985. "Personal Work Ethic and Effort Training Affect Cheating." *Journal of Personality and Social Psychology* 49, 520–528.

Haines, Valerie J., George Dickhoff, Emily LaBeff, and Robert Clark. 1986. "College Cheating: Immaturity, Lack of Commitment, and the Neutralizing Attitude." *Research in Higher Education* 25, 342–354.

LaBeff, Emily E., Robert E. Clark, Valerie J. Haines, and George M. Diekhoff. 1990. "Situational Ethics and College Student Cheating." *Sociological Inquiry* 60, 190–198.

Michaels, James W., and Terance Miethe. 1989. "Applying Theories of Deviance to Academic Cheating." *Social Science Quarterly* 70, 870–885.

Norris, Terry D., and Richard A. Dodder. 1979. "A Behavioural Continuum Synthesizing Neutralization Theory, Situational Ethics and Juvenile Delinquency." *Adolescence* 55, 545–555.

Perry, Anthony R., Kevin M. Kane, Kevin J. Bernesser, and Paul T. Spicker. 1990. "Type A Behaviour, Competitive Achievement-Striving, and Cheating among College Students." *Psychological Reports* 66, 459–465.

Sykes, Gresham M., and David Matza. 1957. "Techniques of Neutralization: A Theory of Delinquency." *American Sociological Review* 22, 664–670.

Tittle, Charles, and Alan Rowe. 1973. "Moral Appeal, Sanction Threat, and Deviance: An Experimental Test." *Social Problems* 20, 488–498.

Ward, David. 1986. "Self-Esteem and Dishonest Behaviour Revisited." *Journal of Social Psychology* 123, 709–713.

Ward, David, and Wendy L. Beck. 1990. "Gender and Dishonesty." *Journal of Social Psychology* 130, 333–339.

Chapter 13: Freud's Psychoanalytic Theory of Personality

Abbreviations:
G.S. = Freud, *Gesammelte Schriften* (12 vols.), Vienna, 1924–1934
G.W. = Freud, *Gesammelte Werke* (18 vols.) London, from 1940
C.P. = Freud, *Collected Papers* (5 vols.), London, 1924–1950
Standard Ed. = Freud, *Standard Edition* (24 vols.), London, from 1953

Freud, S. 1905. *Drei Abhandlungen zur Sexualtheorie.* Vienna. G.S., 5, 3; G.W., 5, 29 (6, 7–9, 30, 54)
[Trans.: *Three Essays on the Theory of Sexuality*, London, 1949; Standard Ed., 7, 3.]
_____. 1908. "Die 'kulturelle' Sexualmoral und die moderne Nervosität." G.S., 5, 143; G.W., 7, 143 (7, 56, 73)
[Trans.: "'Civilized' Sexual Morality and Modern Nervous Illness." C.P., 2, 76; Standard Ed., 9, 179.]
_____. 1926. *Hemmung, Symptom und Angst.* Vienna. G.S. 11, 307; G.W. 14, 113 (75, 82)
[Trans.: *Inhibitions, Symptoms and Anxiety*, London, 1960; *The Problem of Anxiety*, New York:, 1960; Standard Ed., 20, 77.]
_____. 1930 *Das Unbehagen in der Kultur.* Vienna. G.S., 12, 29; G.W., 14, 421.
[Trans.: *Civilization and Its Discontents*, London, 1930, New York, 1962; Standard Ed., 21, 59.]

Chapter 14: Why Is It So Difficult for People to Be Happy?

G.S. = Freud, *Gesammelte Schriften* (12 vols.), Vienna, 1924–1934
G.W. = Freud, *Gesammelte Werke* (18 vols.) London, from 1940
C.P. = Freud, *Collected Papers* (5 vols.), London, 1924–1950
Standard Ed. = Freud, *Standard Edition* (24 vols.), London, from 1953

Freud, S. 1908 "Die 'kulturelle' Sexualmoral und die moderne Nervosität." G.S., 5, 143; G.W., 7, 143 (7, 56, 73)
[Trans.: "'Civilized'" Sexual Morality and Modern Nervous Illness." C.P., 2, 76; Standard Ed., 9, 179.]
_____. 1915. "Triebe und Triebschicksale." G.S., 5, 443; G.W., 10, 210 (8, 14, 64)
[Trans.: "Instincts and Their Vicissitudes," C.P., 4, 60; Standard Ed., 14, 143.]
_____. 1920. *Jenseits des Lustprinzips.* Vienna, G.S., 6, 191; G.W., 13, 3 (8, 66, 69)
[Trans.: *Beyond the Pleasure Principle*, London, 1961; Standard Ed., 18, 3.]
_____. 1927. *Die Zukunft einer Illusion.* Vienna. G.S., 11, 411; G.W., 14, 325 (5, 7, 11, 12, 21, 34, 36, 41, 58, 83, 91)
[Trans.: *The Future of an Illusion*, London and New York, 1928; Standard Ed., 21, 3.]
_____. 1933. *Warum Krieg?* G.S., 12, 349; G.W., 16, 13 (7, 45)
[Trans.: *Why War?* C.P., 5, 273; Standard Ed., 22.]

PART IV: SEXUAL, DOMESTIC, AND COMMERCIAL DEVIANCE

Chapter 15: Prostitution

Badgley Report. 1984. *Sexual Offences against Children in Canada.* Ottawa: Canadian Government Publishing Centre.

Benjamin, H., and L. Masters. 1964. *Prostitution and Morality*. New York: Julian.

Boritch, H. 1997. *Fallen Women: Female Crime and Justice in Canada*. Toronto: Nelson.

Bryan, J.H. 1965. "Apprenticeships in Prostitution." *Social Problems* 12, 287–297.

Canadian Press Newswire. 1997. "Morin to Get $1.25 M in Compensation" (January 24).

Carman A., and H. Moody. 1985. *Working Women: The Subterranean World of Street Prostitution*. New York: Harper and Row.

Clinard, M.B., and R.F. Meier. 1989. *Sociology of Deviant Behaviour*. Chicago: Holt, Rinehart and Winston.

Crook, N. 1984. *Report on Prostitution in the Atlantic Provinces. Working Papers on Pornography and Prostitution Report No. 12*. Ottawa: Department of Justice.

Committee on Sexual Offences against Children and Youth (CSOACY). 1984. *Sexual Offences against Children*. Ottawa: Ministry of Supply and Services.

Davis, Kingsley. 1937. "The Sociology of Prostitution." *American Sociological Review* 2, 744–755.

Davis, N. 1978. "Prostitution: Identity, Career and Legal-Economic Enterprise." In J.M. Henslin (eds.), *The Sociology of Sex*. New York: Schocken.

Duchesne, D. 1997. "Street Prostitution in Canada." *Juristat Service Bulletin* 17 (2). Ottawa: Canadian Centre for Justice Statistics, Statistics Canada.

Enables, G. 1978. *Juvenile Prostitution in Minnesota: The Report of a Research Project*. St. Paul's: The Enablers.

Fleishman, J. 1984. *A Report on Prostitution in Ontario. Working Papers on Pornography and Prostitution Report No. 10*. Ottawa: Department of Justice.

Fraser Committee. See Special Committee on Pornography and Prostitution.

Gadd, J. 2000. "Law against Marijuana Struck Down in Ontario." *The Globe and Mail* (August 1), A1, A7.

Gemme, R., A. Murphy, M. Bourque, M.A. Nemeh, and N. Payment. 1984. *A Report on Prostitution in Quebec. Working Papers on Pornography and Prostitution Report No. 11*. Ottawa: Department of Justice.

Greenspan, Edward. 1994. *Annotated Criminal Code of Canada*. Toronto: Carswell.

Heyl, B.S. 1979. "Prostitution: An Extreme Case of Sexual Stratification." In F. Adler and R.J. Simon (eds.), *The Criminality of Deviant Women*. Boston: Houghton Mifflin.

Lautt, M. 1984. *A Report on Prostitution in the Prairie Provinces. Working Papers on Pornography and Prostitution Report No. 9*. Ottawa: Department of Justice.

Lowman, J. 1984. *Vancouver Field Study of Prostitution. Working Papers on Pornography and Prostitution Report No. 8*. Ottawa: Department of Justice.

_____. 1990. "Notions of Formal Equality before the Law: The Experience of Street Prostitutes and Their Customers." *Journal of Human Justice* 1, 55–76.

_____. 1991 "Prostitution in Canada." In M.A. Jackson and C.T. Griffith (eds.), *Canadian Criminology*. Toronto: Harcourt, Brace and Jovanovich.

_____. 1995. "Prostitution in Canada." In M.A. Jackson and C.T. Griffiths (eds.), *Canadian Criminology: Perspectives on Crime and Criminality*. Toronto: Harcourt Brace.

Mitchell, Sharon, and Laura Smith. 1984. *Juveniles in Prostitution: Fact vs. Fiction*. California: R + E.

Moyer, S., and P. Carrington. 1989. *Street Prostitution* Ottawa: Ministry of Supply and Services.

Prus, R., and S. Irini. 1988. *Hookers, Rounders and Desk Clerks: The Social Organization of the Hotel Community*. Salem: Sheffield.

Roberts, D., and R. Ubha. 2000. "Wrongfully Convicted Sophonow Ready to Forgive." *Toronto Star* (June 9), A3.

Sansfacon, D. 1985. *Prostitution in Canada: A Research Review Report*. Ottawa: Department of Justice.

Schultz, David. 1978. *Pimp*. New York: New York Press.

Schwendinger, H., and J. Schwendinger. 1983. *Rape and Inequality*. Beverly Hills: Sage.

Shaver, H. 1988. "A Critique of Feminist Charges against Prostitution." *Atlantis* 14, 82–89.

Shaver, H. 1993. "Prostitution: A Female Crime." In E. Adelberg and C. Currie (eds.), *In Conflict with the Law: Women and the Canadian Justice System*. Vancouver: Press Gang.

Special Committee on Pornography and Prostitution (SCPP). 1985. *Pornography and Prostitution: Report of the Special Committee on Pornography and Prostitution*. Ottawa: Department of Justice.

Toronto Street Youth Project. 1986. Toronto: Ministry of Community and Social Services.

Visano, L.A. 1987. *This Idle Trade*. Toronto: VitaSanta Books.

Weisberg, Kelly. 1985. *Children of the Night: A Study of Adolescent Prostitution*. Massachusetts: D.C. Heath and Co.

Chapter 19: The Canadian Criminal Justice System: Inequalities of Class

Aboriginal Justice Inquiry of Manitoba. 1991. *The Justice System and Aboriginal People*, Vol. I. Winnipeg: Queen's Printer.

Adler, F. 1975. *Sisters in Crime*. New York: McGraw-Hill.

Alberta. 1991. *Justice on Trial*. Edmonton: Task Force on the Criminal Justice System and Its Impact on the Indian and Métis People of Alberta.

Allison, M. 1991. "Judicious Judgements? Examining the Impact of Sexual Assault Legislation on Judicial Definitions of Sexual Violence." In L. Samuelson and B. Schissel (eds.), *Criminal Justice: Sentencing Issues and Reforms*, 279–297. Toronto: Garamond Press.

Berzins, L., and S. Cooper. 1982. "The Political Economy of Correctional Planning for Women: The Case of the Bankrupt Bureaucracy." *Canadian Journal of Criminology* 24, 399–417.

Berzins, L., and B. Hayes. 1987. "The Diaries of Two Change Agents." In E. Adelberg and C. Currie (eds.), *Too Few to Count: Canadian Women in Conflict with the Law*, 163–179. Vancouver: Press Gang.

Boyle, C. 1984. *Sexual Assault*. Toronto: Carswell.

Brannigan, A. 1984. *Crimes, Courts, and Corrections*. Toronto: Holt, Rinehart and Winston.

Brodeur, J.P., C. LaPrairie, and R. McDonnell. 1991. *Justice for the Cree: Final Report*. Cree Regional Authority, Grand Council of Crees (of Quebec).

Burris, C., and P. Jaffe. 1983. "Wife Abuse as a Crime: The Impact of Police Laying Charges." *Canadian Journal of Criminology* 25, 309–318.

Calgary Herald. 1992. "Tough Laws Catch Up with Corporate Polluters" (September 10).

Canada. 1991. *Aboriginal Peoples and Criminal Justice*. Ottawa: Law Reform Commission of Canada.

_____. 1996. *Commission of Inquiry into Certain Events at the Prison for Women in Kingston*. Ottawa: Public Works and Government Services.

Canada, Department of Justice. 1990. *Sexual Assault Legislation in Canada: An Evaluation-Overview*. Ottawa: Supply and Services Canada.

Canadian Committee on Corrections. 1969. *Toward Unity: Criminal Justice and Corrections*. Ottawa: Queen's Printer.

Carey, Carolyn. 1996. "Punishment and Control of Women in Prison: The Punishment of Privation." In B. Schissel and L. Mahood (eds.), *Social Control in Canada: A Reader in the Social Construction of Deviance*. Toronto: Oxford University Press.

Chambliss, W., and R. Seidman. 1971. *Law, Order, and Power*. Reading: Addison-Wesley.

Chesney-Lind, M., and B. Bloom. 1997. "Feminist Criminology: Thinking about Women and Crime." In B. MacLean and D. Milovanovic (eds.), *Thinking Critically about Crime*. Vancouver: Collective Press.

Chunn, D., and S. Gavigan. 1995. "Women, Crime and Criminal Justice in Canada." In M. Jackson and C. Griffiths (eds.), *Canadian Criminology*. Toronto: Harcourt Brace.

Clinard, M., and P. Yeager. 1980. *Corporate Crime*. New York: The Free Press.

Comack, E. 1992. "Women and Crime." In R. Linden (ed.), *Criminology: A Canadian Perspective*, 2ⁿᵈ ed., 127–162. Toronto: Harcourt Brace Jovanovich.

_____. 1996a. "Women and Crime." In R. Linden (ed.), *Criminology: A Canadian Perspective*, 3ʳᵈ ed. Toronto: Harcourt Brace.

_____. 1996b. *Women in Trouble*. Halifax: Fernwood Publishing.

Cooper, S. 1987. "The Evolution of the Federal Women's Prison." In E. Adelberg and C. Currie (eds.), *Too Few to Count: Canadian Women in Conflict with the Law*, 127–144. Vancouver: Press Gang.

_____. 1993. "The Evolution of the Federal Women's Prison." In E. Adelberg and C. Currie (eds.), *In Conflict with the Law: Women and the Canadian Justice System*. Vancouver: Press Gang.

Currie, D. 1986. "Female Criminality: A Crisis in Feminist Theory." In B. MacLean (ed.), *The Political Economy of Crime*. Scarborough: Prentice Hall.

_____. 1990. "Battered Women and the State: From a Failure Theory to a Theory of Failure." *Journal of Human Justice* 1, 77–96.

Currie, D., and B. MacLean, eds. 1992. *Rethinking the Administration of Justice*. Halifax: Fernwood Publishing.

Currie, D., B. MacLean, and D. Milovanovic. 1992. "Three Traditions of Critical Justice Inquiry: Class, Gender, and Discourse." In D. Currie and B. MacLean (eds.), *Rethinking the Administration of Justice*. Halifax: Fernwood Publishing.

Daubney, D. 1988. *Taking Responsibility: Report of the Standing Committee on Justice and Solicitor General on Aspects of Corrections*. Ottawa: Supply and Services Canada.

DeKeseredy, W., and M. Schwartz. 1996. *Contemporary Criminology*. Toronto: Wadsworth.

Dobash, R.E., R.P. Dobash, and L. Noaks, eds. 1995. *Gender and Crime*. Cardiff: University of Wales Press.

Ekstedt, J., and C. Griffiths. 1988. *Corrections in Canada*. Toronto: Butterworths.

Ellis, D. 1986. *The Wrong Stuff*. Toronto: Collier McMillan.

Engels, F. 1892. *The Condition of the Working Class in England in 1844*. London: George Allen and Unwin.

Faith, K. 1993. *Unruly Women: The Politics of Confinement and Resistance.* Vancouver: Press Gang.

Forcese, D. 1992. *Policing Canadian Society.* Scarborough: Prentice-Hall.

Geller, G. 1987. "Young Women in Conflict with the Law." In E. Adelberg and C. Currie (eds.), *Too Few to Count: Canadian Women in Conflict with the Law*, 113–126. Vancouver: Press Gang.

Gimenez, M.E. 1991. "The Feminisation of Poverty: Myth or Reality?" *Social Justice* 17 (3), 43–67.

The Globe and Mail. 1995. "Penitentiaries Close to Overcrowding Crisis" (February 6).

Goff, C., and C. Reasons. 1978. *Corporate Crime in Canada.* Scarborough: Prentice-Hall.

Gordon, R., and I. Coneybeer. 1995. "Corporate Crime." In M. Jackson and C. Griffiths (eds.), *Canadian Criminology.* Toronto: Harcourt Brace.

Greenberg, D. 1977. "Delinquency and the Age-Structure of Society." *Contemporary Crises* 1, 189–223.

Gregory, J. 1986. "Sex, Class, and Crime: Towards a Non-sexist Criminology." In B. MacLean (ed.), *The Political Economy of Crime.* Scarborough: Prentice-Hall.

Griffiths, C., and S. Verdun-Jones. 1994. *Canadian Criminal Justice*, 2nd ed. Toronto: Harcourt Brace.

Hagan, J. 1985. *Modern Criminology.* Toronto: McGraw-Hill Ryerson.

_____. 1992. "White Collar and Corporate Crime." In R. Linden (ed.), *Criminology: A Canadian Perspective*, 2nd ed., 451–473. Toronto: Harcourt Brace Jovanovich.

Hartnagel, T. 1992. "Correlates of Criminal Behaviour." In R. Linden (ed.), *Criminology: A Canadian Perspective*, 2nd ed. Toronto: Harcourt Brace Jovanovich.

_____. 1996. "Correlates of Criminal Behaviour." In R. Linden (ed.), *Criminology: A Canadian Perspective*, 3rd ed. Toronto: Harcourt Brace.

Hawkins, D. 1987. "Beyond Anomalies: Rethinking the Conflict Perspective on Race and Criminal Punishment." *Social Forces* 65 (3), 719–745.

Heald, S. 1985. "Social Change and Legal Ideology: A Critique of the New Sexual Assault Legislation." *Canadian Criminology Forum* 7.

Hinch, R. 1985. "Canada's New Sexual Assault Law: A Step Forward for Women? *Contemporary Crises* 9 (1).

Hylton, J. 1982. "The Native Offender in Saskatchewan: Some Implications for Crime Prevention Programming." *Canadian Journal of Criminology* 24, 121–131.

Jackson, M., and C. Griffiths. 1995. *Canadian Criminology.* Toronto: Harcourt Brace.

Jaffe, P., and C. Burris. 1981. *An Integrated Response to Wife Assault: A Community Model.* Ottawa: Solicitor General of Canada.

Johnson, H., and K. Rodgers. 1993. "A Statistical Overview of Women and Crime in Canada." In E. Adelberg and C. Currie (eds.), *In Conflict with the Law: Women and the Canadian Justice System.* Vancouver: Press Gang.

Kendall, K. 1993. "Creating Safe Places: Reclaiming Sacred Spaces." Paper prepared for the 7th National Roundtable for Women in Prison Family Violence Programming in Jail and Prisons Workshop, Washington.

LaPrairie, C. 1994. "Native Women and Crime in Canada: A Theoretical Model." In E. Adelberg and C. Currie (eds.), *Too Few to Count: Canadian Women in Conflict with the Law.* Vancouver: Press Gang.

_____. 1996. *Examining Aboriginal Corrections in Canada*. Ottawa: Supply and Services Canada.

Linden, R., ed. 1996. *Criminology: A Canadian Perspective*, 3rd ed. Toronto: Harcourt Brace.

MacLean, B., and D. Milovanovic. 1997. *Thinking Critically about Crime*. Vancouver: Collective Press.

MacLeod, L. 1980. *Wife Battering in Canada: The Vicious Circle*. Ottawa: Canadian Advisory Council on the Status of Women, Minister of Supply and Services.

_____. 1987. *Battered But Not Beaten . . . Preventing Battering in Canada*. Ottawa: Canadian Advisory Council on the Status of Women.

Mandel, M. 1983. "Imprisonment, Class, and Democracy in Contemporary Canadian Capitalism." Mimeograph. Toronto: Osgoode Hall Law School.

Markwart, A. 1992. "Custodial Sanctions under the Young Offenders Act." In R. Corrado, N. Bala, R. Linden, and M. Leblanc (eds.), *Juvenile Justice in Canada*. Toronto: Butterworths.

McMullan, J. 1992. Beyond the Limits of the Law: Corporate Crime and Law and Order. Halifax: Fernwood Publishing.

McMullan, J., D. Perrier, S. Smith, and P. Swan. 1997. *Crimes, Laws and Communities*. Halifax: Fernwood Publishing.

McMullan, J., and S. Smith. 1997. "Toxic Steel: State-Corporate Crime and the Contamination of the Environment." In J. McMullan, D. Perrier, S. Smith, and P. Swan (eds.), *Crimes, Laws and Communities*. Halifax: Fernwood Publishing.

Mikel, D. 1979–1980. "Native Society in Crisis." *Crime and Justice* 617, 32–41.

Pappajohn v. The Queen. 1980. 52 Canadian Criminal Cases, 2nd ed. 481–515.

Prairie Research Associates, Inc. 1994. *Manitoba Spouse Abuse Tracking Project Final Report*, vol. 1. Winnipeg: Manitoba Research and Statistics Directorate.

Quinney, R. 1970. *The Social Reality of Crime*. Boston: Little, Brown and Company.

Ratner, R., and J. McMullan. 1987. *State Control: Criminal Justice Politics in Canada*. Vancouver: University of British Columbia Press.

Reasons, C., L. Ross, and C. Patterson. 1991. "Your Money and Your Life: Workers Health in Canada." In S. Brickey and E. Comack (eds.), *The Social Basis of Law*, 2nd ed., 131–141. Toronto: Garamond Press.

Reiman, J. 1994. The Rich Get Richer and the Poor Get Prison: Ideology, Crime and Criminal Justice, 4th ed. Toronto: Allyn and Bacon.

Rock, P. 1986. *A View from the Shadows*. Oxford: Clarendon Press.

Royal Commission on Aboriginal Peoples (RCAP). 1993. Aboriginal Peoples and the Justice System: Report of the National Roundtable on Aboriginal Justice Issues. Ottawa: Minister of Supply and Services Canada.

_____. 1996. *Bridging the Cultural Divide*. Ottawa: Minister of Supply and Services Canada.

Ruebsaat, G. 1985. *The New Sexual Assault Offences: Emerging Legal Issues*. Ottawa: Supply and Services Canada.

Samuelson, L. 1995. "Canadian Aboriginal Justice Commissions and Australia's 'Anunga Rules: Barking Up the Wrong Tree.'" *Canadian Public Policy* 21 (2), 187–211.

Satzewich, V., and T. Wotherspoon. 1993. *First Nations: Race, Class, and Gender Relations*. Toronto: Nelson.

Schissel, B. 1996. "Law Reform and Social Change: A Time-Series Analysis of Sexual Assault in Canada." *Journal of Criminal Justice* 24 (2), 123–138.

_____. 1997. Blaming Children: Youth Crime, Moral Panics and the Politics of Hate. Halifax: Fernwood Publishing.

Sherrill, R. 1987. "Murder Inc.: What Happens to Corporate Criminals?" *Utne Reader* (March/April). As cited in *Beyond the Limits of the Law*, R. McMullan. Halifax: Fernwood Publishing.

Smith, D., and C. Visher. 1980. "Sex and Involvement in Deviance/Crime." *American Sociological Review* 45, 691–701.

Snider, L. 1985. "Legal Reform and the Law: The Dangers of Abolishing Rape." *International Journal of the Sociology of Law* 4.

_____. 1988. "Commercial Crime." In V. Sacco (ed.), *Deviance: Conformity and Control in Canadian Society*, 231–283. Scarborough: Prentice-Hall.

_____. 1991. "The Potential of the Criminal Justice System to Promote Feminist Concerns." In E. Comack and S. Brickey (eds.), *The Social Basis of Law*, 2nd ed. Toronto: Garamond Press.

_____. 1993. Bad Business: Corporate Crime in Canada. Toronto: Nelson.

_____. 1994. "The Regulatory Dance: Understanding Reform Processes in Corporate Crime." In R. Hinch (ed.), *Readings in Critical Criminology*. Scarborough: Prentice-Hall.

Solicitor General of Canada. 1985. "Female Victims of Crimes." *Canadian Urban Victimization Survey*. Ottawa: Supply and Services Canada.

Star-Phoenix [Saskatoon]. 1991a. "21 Female Prisoners Charged After Riot" (February 13), A15.

_____. 1991b. "Dying to Get Out of P4W" (March 23), D1.

_____. 1997. "Half of Canadians Polled Believe Natives Well Off" (June 21).

Statistics Canada. 1988. *Canadian Crime Statistics*. Ottawa: Supply and Services Canada.

_____. 1996. *Canadian Crime Statistics*. Ottawa: Supply and Services Canada.

Sugar, F., and L. Fox. 1989–1990. "Nistum peyako sht'wawin iskwewak: Breakin Chains." *Canadian Journal of Women's Law* 3, 465–482.

Sutherland, E.H. 1977. "Crimes of Corporations." In G. Geis and R. Meier (eds.), *White-Collar Crime: Offences in Business, Politics, and the Professions*, 71–84. New York: Free Press.

Task Force on Federally Sentenced Women. 1990. *Creating Choices*. Ottawa: Correctional Service of Canada.

Task Force on the Status of Women. 1985. *A Feminist Review of Criminal Law*. Ottawa: Supply and Services Canada.

Taylor, I., P. Walton, and J. Young. 1973. *The New Criminology: For a Social Theory of Deviance*. London: Routledge and Kegan Paul.

Turpel, M. (Aki-Kwe). 1992. "Further Travails of Canada's Human Rights Record: The Marshall Case." In J. Mannette (ed.), *Elusive Justice: Beyond the Marshal Inquiry*. Halifax: Fernwood Publishing.

Ursel, J. 1991. "Considering the Impact of the Battered Women's Movement on the State: The Example of Manitoba." In E. Comack and S. Brickey (eds.), *The Social Basis of Law*, 2nd ed., 261–288. Toronto: Garamond Press.

_____. 1998. "Eliminating Violence against Women: Reform or Cooptation in State Institutions." In L. Samuelson and W. Anthony (eds.), *Power and Resistance*. Halifax: Fernwood Publishing.

Waldram, J. 1994. "Canada's 'Indian Problem' and the Indian's Canada Problem." In L. Samuelson (ed.), *Power and Resistance*. Halifax: Fernwood Publishing.

West, G. 1984. *Young Offenders and the State*. Toronto: Butterworths.

York, G. 1990. The Disposed: Life and Death in Native Canada. Toronto: Little, Brown.

PART VI: YOUTH AND DEVIANCE

Chapter 24: Deviant Youth: The Social Construction of Youth Problems

Acland, C. 1995. *Youth, Murder, Spectacle*. Boulder: Westview Press.

Aries, P. 1962. *Centuries of Childhood*. New York: Random House.

Barrat, D. 1986. *Media Sociology*. London: Tavistock.

Bean, P., and Melville, J. 1989. *Lost Children of This Empire*. London: Unwin Hyman.

Bell, S. 1994. "An Empirical Approach to Theoretical Perspectives on Sentencing in a Young Offender Court." *Canadian Review of Sociology and Anthropology* 31 (1), 35–64.

Bernard, T. 1992. *The Cycle of Juvenile Justice*. New York: Oxford University Press.

Bernard, W. 1949. *Jailbait*. New York: Green.

Best, J. 1989. *Images of Issues: Typifying Contemporary Social Problems*. New York: Aldine de Gruyter.

Brannigan, A. 1986. "Mystification of the Innocents: Comics and Delinquency in Canada." *Criminal Justice History* 3, 111–144.

_____. 1987. "Moral Panics and Juvenile Delinquency in Britain and America." *Criminal Justice History* 8, 181–191.

Chibnall, S. 1977. *Law and Order News*. London: Tavistock.

Cohen, S. 1973. *Folk Devils and Moral Panics*. London: MacGibbons and Kee.

Corrado, R. 1994. "The Need to Reform the Y.O.A. in Response to Violent Young Offenders: Confusion, Reality or Myth?" *Canadian Journal of Sociology* 36 (3), 343–378.

Eisenstadt, S. 1956. *From Generation to Generation*. Glencoe: Free Press.

Fasiolo, R., and S. Leckie. 1993. *Canadian Media Coverage of Gangs: A Content Analysis*. Ottawa: Solicitor General of Canada.

Frith, S. 1985. "The Sociology of Youth." In M. Haralabos (ed.), *Sociology: New Directions*. Ormskirk: Causeway Press.

Gilbert, J. 1986. *A Cycle of Outrage*. New York: Oxford University Press.

Kett, J. 1971. "Adolescence and Youth in Nineteenth-Century America." In T. Rabb and R. Rothberg (eds.), *The Family in History*. New York: Harper and Row.

_____. 1977. *Rites of Passage*. New York: Basic Books.

Matzda, D., and G. Sykes. 1961. "Juvenile Delinquency and Subterranean Values." *American Sociological Review* 26, 712–719.

McRobbie, A. 1994. *Post-modernism and Popular Culture*. London: Routledge and Kegan Paul.

Morrison, P. 1988. "Ounce of Prevention vs. Weight of Gang Influence." *Los Angeles Times* (May 29), 25–26.

Muncie, J. 1984. *The Trouble with Kids Today: Youth and Crime in Post-war Britain*. London: Hutchinson.

Murdock, G. 1982. "Mass Communication and Social Violence." In P. Marsh and A. Campbell (eds.), *Aggression and Violence*. Oxford: Blackwell.

Murdock, G., and R. McCron. 1976. "Youth and Class: The Career of Confusion." In G. Mungham and G. Pearson (eds.), *Working-Class Youth Culture*. London: Routledge and Kegan Paul.

Musgrove, F. 1964. *Youth and the Social Order*. London: Routledge and Kegan Paul.

Parsons, T. 1942. "Age and Sex in the Social Structure of the United States." *American Sociological Review* 7, 604–616.

Pearson, G. 1983. *Hooligan*. London: Macmillan.

Roberts, J., and A. Doob. 1990. "News Media Influences on Public Views on Sentencing." *Law and Human Behaviour* 14, 451–468.

Sacco, V., and L. Kennedy. 1994. *The Criminal Event*. Toronto: Nelson.

Surette, R. 1992. *Media, Crime and Criminal Justice: Images and Realities*. Pacific Grove: Brooks/Cole.

Sutherland, N. 1976. *Children in English-Canadian Society: Framing the Twentieth-Century Consensus*. Toronto: University of Toronto Press.

West, W.G. 1984. *Young Offenders and the State*. Toronto: Butterworths.

Chapter 25: Style and Resistance in the Punk Subculture

Alford, Robert R. 1963. *Party Suicide: The Anglo-American Democracies*. Chicago: Rand McNally.

Babbie, Earl. 1979. *The Practice of Social Research*, 2nd ed. Belmont: Wadsworth Pub. Co. Inc.

Bailey, Kenneth. 1982. *Methods of Social Research*, 2nd ed. New York: The Free Press.

Becker, Howard. 1963. *Outsiders: Studies in the Sociology of Deviance*. New York: The Free Press.

Benston, Margaret. 1982. "Feminism and the Critique of the Scientific Method." In Geraldine Finn and Angela Miles (eds.), *Feminism in Canada: From Politics to Pressure*, 47–66. Montreal: Black Rose Books.

Berger, Bennett M. 1963. "On the Youthfulness of Youth Cultures." *Social Research* 30 (2), 319–342.

Bowles, Samuel, and Herbert Gintis. 1976. *Schooling in Capitalist America: Educational Reform and the Contradictions of Economic Life*. London: Routledge & Kegan Paul.

Brake, Mike. 1980. *The Sociology of Youth Culture and Youth Subcultures*. London: Routledge & Kegan Paul.

_____. 1985. *Comparative Youth Culture*. London: Routledge & Kegan Paul.

Cashmore, E. Ellis. 1984. *No Future*. Guildford: Biddles Ltd.

Clarke, Michael. 1974. "On the concept of subculture." *British Journal of Sociology* 25, 428–441.

Clinard, M.B., and R.E. Meier. 1985. *Sociology of Deviant Behaviour*, 6th ed. Toronto: Holt, Rinehart and Winston.

Cloward, Richard A., and Lloyd E. Ohlin. 1960. *Delinquency and Opportunity*. Glencoe: The Free Press of Glencoe.

Cohen, Albert K. 1955. *Delinquent Boys*. Glencoe: The Free Press of Glencoe.

Cohen, Stanley. 1980. *Folk Devils and Moral Panics*. London: Macgibbon and Kee.

Corrigan, Paul. 1979. *Schooling the Smash Street Kids*. London: The Macmillan Press.

Curtis, Jim, Ed Grabb, Neil Guppy, and Sid Gilbert. 1988. *Social Inequality in Canada: Patterns, Problems and Policies*. Scarborough: Prentice-Hall.

Dancis, Bruce. 1978. "Safety-pins and Class Struggle: Punk Rock and the Left." *Socialist Review* 8 (3), 58–83.

Downes, D. 1966. *The Delinquent Solution*. London: Routledge and Kegan Paul.

Downes, D., and P. Rock. 1982. *Understanding Deviance*. Oxford: Clarendon Press.

Everhart, R. 1982. *The In Between Years*. London: Routledge & Kegan Paul.

Festinger, L. 1954. "A Theory of Social Comparison Processes." *Human Relations* 7, 117–140.

Fine, Gary Alan, and Sherryl Kleinman. 1979. "Rethinking Subculture: An Interactionist Analysis." *American Journal of Sociology* 85 (1), 1–20.

_____. 1983. "Network and Meaning: An Interactionist Approach to Structure." *Symbolic Interaction* 6 (1), 97–110.

Forcese, Dennis. 1980. *The Canadian Class Structure*, 3rd ed. Toronto: McGraw-Hill Ryerson Ltd.

Frith, Simon. 1978a. *The Sociology of Rock*. London: Constable.

_____. 1978b. "The Punk Bohemians." *New Society* 43 (805), 535–536.

_____. 1983. *Sound Effects: Youth Leisure and the Politics of Rock*. London: Constable.

_____. 1985. "The Sociology of Youth." In Michael Haralabos (ed.), *Sociology: New Directions*, 301–368. Ornskirk: Causeway Press.

Gibbons, D.C. 1981. *Delinquent Behaviour*, 3rd ed. Englewood Cliffs: Prentice-Hall.

Glaser, Barney, and Anselm Strauss. 1967. *The Discovery of Grounded Theory: Strategies for Qualitative Research*. New York: Aldine Pub. Co.

Gordon, Milton M. 1947. "The Concept of Subculture and Its Applications." *Social Forces* 26, 40–42.

Gottdiener, M. 1985. "Hegemony and Mass Culture: A Semiotic Approach." *American Journal of Sociology* 90 (5), 979–1001.

Goyder, John C., and Peter C. Pineo. 1979. "Social Class Self-Identification." In J. Curtis and W. Scott (eds.), *Social Stratification: Canada*, 2nd ed., 431–447. Scarborough: Prentice-Hall.

Hagedorn, R., and S. Labovitz. 1973. *An Introduction into Sociological Orientations*. Toronto: Wiley and Sons.

Hall, Stuart. 1980. "Encoding/Decoding." In Stuart Hall, Dorothy Hobson, Andrew Lowe, and Paul Wells (eds.), *Culture, Media, Language*, 128–138. London: Hutchinson.

Hall, Stuart, and Tony Jefferson. 1976. *Resistance through Ritual: Youth Subcultures in Post-War Britain*. London: Hutchinson.

Hartmann, Donald, and David Wood. 1982. "Observational Methods." In A.S. Bellack, Michael Hersen, A.E. Kazdin (eds.), *The International Handbook of Behaviour Modification and Therapy*, 109–138. New York: Plenum Press.

Hebdige, Dick. 1979. *Subculture: The Meaning of Style*. London: Methuen and Co.

Hendry, Leo. 1982. *Growing Up and Going Out: Adolescents and Leisure*. Aberdeen: Aberdeen University Press.

Humphreys, L. 1975. *Tearoom Trade: Impersonal Sex in Public Places*, enlarged ed. Chicago: Aldine Pub.

Hunter, Alfred A. 1986. *Class Tells: On Social Inequality in Canada*, 2nd ed. Toronto: Butterworth.

Johnson, John M. 1975. *Doing Field Research*. New York: The Free Press.

Johoda, Maria, Morton Deutsch, and Stuart Wood. 1951. *Research Methods in Social Relations: Part Two, Selected Techniques*. New York: The Dryden Press.

Kane, Eileen. 1983. *Doing Your Own Research*. New York: Marian Bayars Co.

Kendal, Denis B. 1978. "On variations in adolescent subculture." *Youth and Society* 19 (4), 372–384.

Kilian, Crawford. 1985. *School Wars: The Assault on B.C. Education*. Vancouver: New Star Books.

Laing, Dave. 1985. *One Chord Wonders: Power and Meaning in Punk Rock*. Milton Keynes: Open University Press.

Lambert, R.D., S.D. Brown, J.E. Curtis, and B.J. Kay. 1986. "Canadians' Beliefs about Differences between Social Classes." *Canadian Journal of Sociology* 11 (4), 379–399.

Leonard, Peter. 1984. *Personality and Ideology*. London: MacMillan Education Ltd.

Levine, Harold, and Steven Stumpf. 1983. "Statements of Fear through Cultural Symbols: Punk Rock as a Reflective Subculture." *Youth and Society* 14 (4), 417–435.

Liebow, Elliot. 1967. *Tally's Corner: A Study of Negro Streetcorner Men*. Boston: Little, Brown and Co.

Liska, A.E. 1987. *Perspectives on Deviance*. Englewood Cliffs: Prentice-Hall Inc.

Lofland, John, and Lyn H. Lofland. 1984. *Analyzing Social Settings*. Belmont: Wadsworth Inc.

McLaren, P. 1980. *Cries from the Corridor: The New Suburban Ghetto*. Toronto: Methuen.

McRobbie, A., and J. Garber. 1976. "Girls and Subcultures—a feminist critique." In S. Hall et al. (eds.), *Resistance through Ritual: Youth Subcultures in Post-War Britain*, 209–222. London: Hutchinson.

Marchak, M. Patricia. 1975. *Ideological Perspectives on Canada*. Toronto: McGraw Hill Ryerson Ltd.

Marsh, Peter. 1977. "Dole que rock." *New Society* 39 (746), 112–115.

Matza, D., and G.M. Sykes. 1961. "Juvenile Delinquency and Subterranean Values." *American Sociological Review* 26, 712–719.

Mayntz, Renate, Kurt Holm, and Roger Huebner. 1969. *Introduction to Empirical Sociology*. Bungay: Clay (The Chaucer Press) Ltd.

Merton, Robert K. 1957. *Social Theory and Social Structure*. Glencoe: The Free Press of Glencoe.

_____. 1968. *Social Theory and Social Structure*. New York: The Free Press.

Miller, W.B. 1958. "Lower Class Culture as a Generating Milieu of Gang Delinquency." *Journal of Social Issues* 14, 5–19.

Monday Magazine. 1980. 6 (44), 8.

_____. 1982. 8 (8), 14–15.

_____. 1983. 9 (34), 6.

_____. 1984. 10 (5), 7.

_____. 1986a. 12 (7), 5.

_____. 1986b. 12 (43), 7.

_____. 1986c. 12 (44), 5.

_____. 1987a. 12 (49), 29.

_____. 1987b. 13 (19), 3.

_____. 1987c. 13 (21), 13–14.

Muncie, John. 1981. *Politics, Ideology and Popular Culture*. Walton Hall, Milton Keynes: The Open University Press.

Mungham, G., and G. Pearson. 1976. *Working Class Youth Cultures*. London: Routledge & Kegan Paul.

Murdock, Graham, and Robin McCron. 1973. "Scoobies, Skins and Contemporary Pop." *New Society* 26 (547), 690–692.

Myles, J., G. Picot, and T. Wannell. 1988. "The Changing Wage Distributions of Jobs 1981–1986." *The Labour Force Statistics Canada Catalogue* #71-001 Oct.: 85-138.

Philips, Bernard S. 1971. *Social Science, Strategy and Tactics*. New York: The Macmillan Co.

Philliber, S.G., Mary Schwab, and G. Sam Sloss. 1980. *Social Research: Guides to Decision Making Process*. Ithasca: F.E. Peacock Pub. Inc.

Porter, John. 1965. *The Vertical Mosaic: An Analysis of Social Class and Power in Canada*. Toronto: University of Toronto Press.

Ramirez, Daniel M. 1986. "Ideology and the Subject of History in Marxian Semiotics." *Insurgent Sociologist* 8 (3), 97–102.

Rock, Paul. 1980. "Has Deviance a Future?" In Hubert Blalock (ed.), *Sociological Theory and Research*, 290–303. New York: The Free Press.

Rothaus, L.G. 1984. "Punk Femininity: Style and Class Conflict." Paper presented at American Popular Culture Association, Toronto, Department of Education, University of Madison-Wisconsin, unpublished.

Sellitz, Claire, Marie Jahota, Morton Deutsch, and Stuart W. Cook. 1959. *Research Methods in Social Relations*. New York: Henry Holt and Co.

Shaffir, William B., Robert A. Stebbins, and Alan Turowitz. 1980. *Fieldwork Experience: Qualitative Approaches to Social Research*. New York: St. Martin's Press.

Sherif, Muzafer, and Carolyn Sherif. 1964. *Reference Groups*. New York: Harper and Row Pub.

Shibutani, Tamatsu. 1955. "Reference Groups as Perspectives." *American Journal of Sociology* 60 (6), 562–569.

Shragge, E. 1982. "The Left in the 80s." *Our Generation* 15 (2), 5–12.

Streeter, Thomas. 1984. "An Alternative Approach to Television Research, Developments in British Cultural Studies at Birmingham." In W.B. Rowland and B. Watkins (eds.), *Interpreting Television*, 74–97. London: Sage.

Tajfel, H. 1981. *Human Groups in Social Categories*. Cambridge: Cambridge University Press.

Tanner, Julian. 1978a. "New Directions for Subcultural Theory: An Analysis of British Working-Class Youth Culture." *Youth and Society* 19 (4), 343–373.

_____. 1978b. "Youth Culture and the Canadian High School: An Empirical Analysis." *Canadian Journal of Sociology* 3 (1), 89–102.

The Victoria Downtowner. 1985. (August), 8.

Times Colonist. 1986a. (January 30).

_____. 1986b. (September 24).

_____. 1986c. (October 1).

Vaz, E.W. 1969. "Delinquency and Youth Culture in Upper and Middle-Class Boys." *Journal of Criminal Law, Criminology and Police Science* 60 (1), 33–46.

Whyte, W.F. 1943. *Street Corner Society*. Chicago: The University of Chicago Press.

Willis, Paul. 1977. *Learning to Labour*. London: Saxon House.

Yinger, J. Milton. 1960. "Contraculture and Subculture." *American Sociological Review* 25, 625–635.

Young, Jock. 1971. *The Drugtakers*. London: Macgibbon and Kee Ltd.

yyyChapter 26: Youth Court Statistics, 2000/01

Statistics Canada, Canadian Centre for Justice Statistics. Logan, Ron. 2001. "Crime Statistics in Canada, 2000" *Juristat* (July). Catalogue no. 85-002-XIE, vol. 21, no. 8. Ottawa.

Youth Court Survey. 2000/01. Canadian Centre for Justice Statistics, Statistics Canada.

Chapter 27: Youth at Risk: A Review of Ontario Young Offenders, Programs, and Literature That Supports Effective Intervention

Andrews, D.A., I. Zinger, R.D. Hoge, J. Bonta, P. Gendreau, and F.T. Cullen. 1990. "Does Correctional Treatment Work? A Clinically Relevant and Psychologically Informed Meta-analysis." *Criminology* 28 (3), 309–404.

Clear, T.R. 1989. *Objectives-Based Case Planning*. Washington: National Institute of Corrections, Bureau of Prisons.

Cousineau, D. 1988. *Legal Sanctions and Deterrence*. Research report of the Canadian Sentencing Commission. Ottawa: Ministry of Justice and the Attorney General.

Finkelhor, D. 1984. *Child Sexual Abuse: New Theory and Research*. New York: The Free Press.

Greenwood, P., and S. Turner. 1987. *The Vision Quest Program: An Evaluation*. Washington: The Rand Corporation and the U.S. Department of Justice.

Jaffe, P.G., D.A. Wolfe, S.K. and Wilson. 1990. *Children of Battered Women*. Newbury Park: Sage Publishing.

Lipsey, M.W. 1990. "Juvenile Delinquency Treatment: A Meta-analytic Inquiry into the Variability of Effects." Paper prepared for the Research Synthesis Committee of the Russell Sage Foundation.

Schneider, A.L., and L. Ervin. 1988. "Deterrence and Juvenile Crime: Examining the Behavioural Assumptions of Public Policy." Presented at American Society of Criminology, Chicago.

PART VII: STREET CRIME

Chapter 28: The Justice Data Factfinder

Birkenmayer, A., and S. Besserer. 1997. "Sentencing in Adult Provincial Courts. A Study of Nine Canadian Jurisdictions: 1993 and 1994." *Juristat* 17 (1).

Gartner, Rosemary, and Anthony N. Doob. 1994. "Trends in Criminal Victimization: 1988– 1993. *Juristat* 14 (13).

Grainger, B. 1996. "Data and Methodology in the Area of Criminal Justice." In L.W. Kennedy and V. Sacco (eds.), *Crime Counts: An Event Analysis*. Toronto: ITP Nelson Canada.

Grimes, Craig. 1997. "Adult Criminal Court Statistics, 1995–96." *Juristat* 17 (6).

Hendrick, Diane. 1997. "Youth Court Statistics 1995–96 Highlights." *Juristat* 17 (10).

Kong, Rebecca. 1997. "Canadian Crime Statistics, 1996." *Juristat* 17 (8).

Leonard, Tim. 1997. "Crime in Major Metropolitan Areas, 1991–95." *Juristat* 17 (5).

Morrison, Peter, and Micheline Reed. 1997. "Adult Correctional Services in Canada, 1995–96." *Juristat* 17 (4).